Human
Socialization

CORE BOOKS IN PSYCHOLOGY, Edward L. Walker, Series Editor

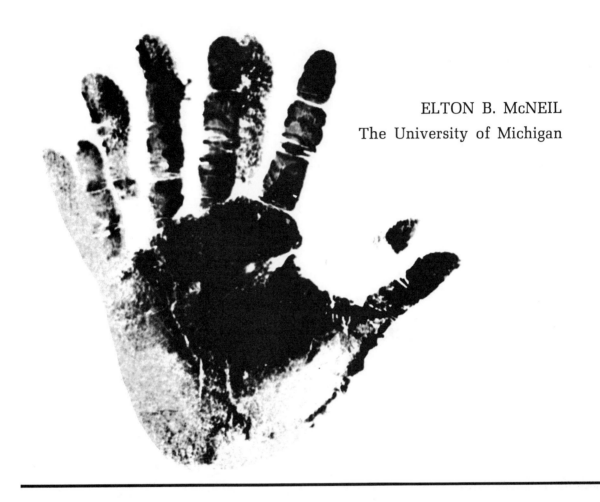

ELTON B. McNEIL
The University of Michigan

Human
Socialization

BROOKS/COLE PUBLISHING COMPANY

Belmont, California

A Division of Wadsworth Publishing Company, Inc.

19987

Second printing: July 1969

All photographs created especially for this volume
by John and Regina Hicks, Carmel-by-the-Sea, California

There are sins of omission and there are sins of commission, and, by all that's holy in the textbooks of child development and socialization in the last decade, I am culpable on both counts. Two forces prompted me to violate the sanctity of the educational directions of my time. First, college students have become, for a variety of reasons, more intellectually selective; that is, in the course of a decade, my students have demanded more congress with ideas and less exposure to undigested bits and pieces—relevant and irrelevant—of child growth, development, and socialization. Second, what is important and useful for the typical student of growth and development is not the details of childhood but the broad sweep of socialization imposed on these details. In other words, what are the problems posed by development, and what should the parent, teacher, psychologist, sociologist, or nurse consider and explore in order to be able to offer realistic assistance to the developing organism?

The needs of my students were paramount in my decision to write a text focused on the process of socializing the child. I have included those "facts" and research reports I thought useful in explicating the presentation of how to civilize a child, and that has meant jettisoning the mass of detail and data collected and packaged into a

Preface

typical text. Consequently, the instructor comfortable with the status quo may find this departure somewhat alien to his view of what students need most if they are to make use of their educational experience. It was a calculated risk, but I am confident that this approach will provide a more meaningful base for the interaction between teacher and student than would otherwise be possible. Facts and details are reputed to be forgotten within six to eight weeks after their memorization; ideas, firmly implanted, can survive at an incredible rate.

This is a book of suggestions, ideas, views, implications, and practical proposals for action. It resembles but does not duplicate the catalog from which students typically study. Being a text in socialization, it necessarily violates the boundaries of discipline because its aim is to emphasize directions, philosophies, ideas, and approaches touched on only briefly in other books. It is thus a work that is oriented toward the meaning of facts rather than a detailed consideration of the facts themselves and one that expresses confidence in the power of the curiosity and native intelligence in the student of the decade to come.

I would like to thank the following people, who contributed many useful comments and suggestions: Professors Edward L. Walker, of The University of Michigan and Series Editor of *Core Books in Psychology*; Urie Bronfenbrenner, of Cornell University; Dale L. Johnson, of the University of Houston; Gene R. Medinnus, of San Jose State College; and William C. Morse, of The University of Michigan.

Contents

PART TWO

THE AGENTS OF EARLY SOCIALIZATION

PART THREE

THE COMPONENTS OF SOCIALIZATION

PART FOUR

EDUCATION, THE SOCIALIZER

Part one

The nature of socialization

The developing child is time-bound. He has a limited life expectancy on this earth. If newborn children could be expected to reach the age of 150, we might worry less about achieving early the correct form of human response to social life, and some of our anxiety about the proper development and socialization of children might lose its urgency. As it is, the brief moment of childhood, during which human beings are most malleable, is the period when the whole process of *socialization* —the shaping the person into a socially acceptable form—must occur. The newborn organism is at once exposed to a complex set of related training practices designed to shape his behavior to conform to the conventions of the society into which he is born. The profound influence of socialization pervades every area of human experience and behavior because it determines much of how the child will understand his world, how he will react to it, and what goals, motives, tastes, appetites, attitudes, habits, and preferences he will acquire.

Socialization is an experience of such fundamental significance for human beings that it has become the intersection at which all the disciplines concerned with man meet. The psychologist studying socialization seeks to understand the internal psychological experience of the individual, while the cultural anthropologist is more con-

1

Socialization:
An overview

cerned with the product of socialization—the typical adult in a particular culture. In contrast, the social psychologist attempts to assess the influence of the group on the individual, while the sociologist studies the reflection of individual socialization in the institutions that society devises to regulate individual behavior.

Although in each of the social sciences is an acute awareness of the impact of socialization in making us uniquely human, civilized animals, no single discipline is devoted solely to its study. Social scientists do not view themselves as "socialization specialists" and, as a consequence, the observations, insights, and research efforts of the many subdivisions of social scientific interest remain scattered and disconnected.

THE MEANING OF SOCIALIZATION

The most direct and least jargon-laden definition of "socialization" is the one contained in the sprightly psychological dictionary compiled by English and English (1958). "Socialization: The processes whereby a person (esp., a child) acquires sensitivity to social stimuli (esp., the pressures and obligations of group life) and learns to get along with, and to behave like, others in his group or culture; the process of becoming a social being . . ."

In addition to this concern with social behavior, psychologists are interested in the uniqueness of the individual. Thus, for the psychologist, the word "socialization" also refers to "all the processes by which an individual acquires his personality characteristics, motives, values, opinions, standards, and beliefs. These include the child-rearing practices of parents, training in the schools, imitation of peers, religious indoctrination, and teaching by the mass media" (Mussen, 1967, p. 54).

It is possible to collect a number of additional definitions from a variety of theorists; each discipline stresses some aspects of socialization more than others. For example, sociologists and

" 'Socialization: The processes whereby a person (esp., a child) acquires sensitivity to social stimuli (esp., the pressures and obligations of group life) and learns to get along with, and to behave like, others in his group or culture; the process of becoming a social being . . .' "

anthropologists are concerned with why and how cultures are perpetuated. Thus, these theorists focus less on man's adjustment to society than on the means by which the "raw material of biological man [is transformed] into a person suitable to perform the operations of society" (Brim and Wheeler, 1966, p. 4). The sociological position is best described by Elkin (1960), who notes that "although it is true that no two individuals are alike, and that each person has a singular heredity, distinctive experiences, and a unique personality development, socialization focuses not on such individualizing patterns and processes but on similarities and those aspects of development which concern the learning of, and adaptation to, the culture and society" (p. 5).

Adding detail to these definitions will be the task of this book. Consequently, at this point, a diagram of the process of socialization and its components would be helpful as a frame of reference for what is to come (see Figure 1). The relationship between the process and the components of socialization suggests that human raw material (the newborn biological organism) becomes an end product whose character, personality, behavior, role preference, and goals are acceptable to his society.

The child must be socialized along emotional, social, cognitive, perceptual, intellectual, behavioral, and expressive dimensions. He will in the process acquire a self-image composed of skills, knowledge, attitudes, values, motives, habits, beliefs, needs, interests, and ideals. These tasks of socialization are accomplished by a great many agents, ranging from parents and peers to other adults, and are influenced by the cultural pressures of social class, school, community, race, and religion. The agents and influences of socialization work against a backdrop of individual differences in age, sex, rate and stage of development, intelligence, and physical constitution. In this process, the primary and secondary needs and impulse systems are patterned into systems of behavior that together establish what Professor Richard L. Cutler has designated as *life themes* (McNeil, 1966). Life themes contribute to the form of adult character and personality by organizing the various components of attitudes, values, motives, habits, beliefs, ideals, and interests.

LIFE THEMES AND SOCIALIZATION

The concept of life themes is one way of explaining why adults in our society differ from one another in personality and social adjustment. This concept is a distillation of many older theories. The stages of development envisioned by

Freud and the "life styles" delineated by Alfred Adler contributed in almost equal parts to the formulation of the life themes concept as a graphic means of describing an organizing psychological force in development. Learning theory and behavioristic psychology also assisted at the birth of the concept, and the Neo-Freudian views of the role of society have had an equal impact.

To understand the fundamental meaning of life themes, consider the example of religious difference between two perfectly normal adults—one a Moslem, the other a Roman Catholic. Each has a set of beliefs. Each has experienced *consensus* in his culture (that is, he was raised in a society that supported this particular set of beliefs), and each is convinced that truth is the spiritual code that he learned early in his childhood. When a confrontation between the two people and the two faiths occurs, each person discovers that he is incapable of viewing the other's religion dispassionately and that a common ground of communication about religion is almost nonexistent.

The Roman Catholic and the Moslem have a different view of the external world and perceive religious truth in a different way. *Perception* is the attribution of meaning to a set of stimuli from the environment. Attitudes, beliefs, motivation, perception, and behavior are all very closely related; indeed, what a person perceives a situation to be largely determines the response that he makes to it. In the example, the Moslem sees his religious beliefs as a fundamental truth in life and finds it difficult to understand that others could see a different truth. So, too, with the devout Roman Catholic. Each reacts to the other as though he were misinformed.

There is strong clinical evidence to suggest that everyone is unusually sensitive to certain classes of happenings in the world around him. Each person has his favorite way of looking at the world. Some stress such things as dependence, sex, achievement, or height and weight; still others see status or friendship or acceptance as most important—even though the individual is not always conscious of these elements in his environment. These major concerns are a person's life themes,

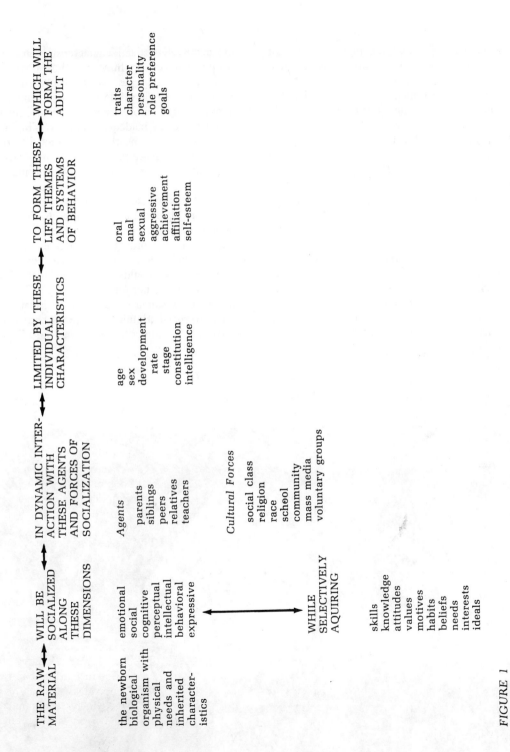

FIGURE 1

The Process and Components of Socialization

those selected aspects of the total environment that serve to organize other parts of his behavior.

A life theme is a shorthand system for describing the way in which the individual's identifiable, unique, and enduring features came into existence and persist through his life span. The notion that certain life themes develop in each individual is a way of describing personality that is perhaps less cumbersome than some of the *type*, *trait*, *developmental*, or *dynamic* theories. A brief recounting of these theories might help to delineate further the concept of life themes.

Theories of personality types reflect the fact that most people manifest a dominant pattern of emotion and behavior throughout their lives. Personality types can be based on physiological or bodily characteristics or can be formulated from observation of an individual's regular behavior pattern. However, these type theories often assert too much about the individual because they as-

cribe extremely general characteristics and patterns of behavior to him and thus invite the formation of stereotypes. No one is content to be described in a single word or by a type name (for example, tough, ambitious, stingy, cold). Such a description seems inadequate and oversimplified. The simplicity of type theories is probably their greatest weakness—although that simplicity is their greatest source of attraction to the man on the street.

Trait theory takes a different approach to the description of human personality. Rather than grouping people according to type, this theory classifies them according to a number of traits: *cardinal traits,* any one of which may completely dominate the personality of the individual; *central traits,* which together form the core of adult personality; or *secondary traits,* fairly isolated responses to social stimuli and perhaps better characterized as "attitudes" rather than "traits."

"Attitudes, beliefs, motivation, perception, and behavior are all very closely related; indeed, what a person perceives a situation to be largely determines the response that he makes to it."

Traits are not objects we possess, like cars, clothing, or houses; they are descriptions of the ways in which we usually act or feel and can be accurately interpreted only with full knowledge of the circumstances and social settings in which those traits are observed. Observers may find that two people possess identical traits; however, these two individuals may have quite different personalities because of the way in which these traits interact and because the kind of person one is depends in part on the environment he is in and the people he is with. A person shy in the company of his superiors may be the life of the party among his peers.

Still other theories can be broadly characterized as developmental. Some developmental theorists stress the importance of history in the formation of personality. For these theorists, the important issue is the continuity of growth and the way in which each prior event subtly alters the shape of subsequent events. In this respect, the idea of life themes has a developmental ring to it because the continuing perceptual, cognitive, and experiential life of the child acts to fashion his personality into a predictable pattern that will serve as a filter for all future experiences.

Finally, theories of personality dynamics emphasize the interaction—both cooperative and conflictual—between various elements of the personality. A classic example of dynamic theory is the work of Kurt Lewin (1935). Using the concept of a *force field*, in which the behavior of any one part is influenced by the total field in which it is at a particular moment, he attempted to assess the forces acting on a person at that moment. Lewin views the psychological structure of the individual as a series of regions. As the individual grows and learns, these regions of the self become increasingly complex and differentiated from one another. For example, the newborn infant would have comparatively simple and undifferentiated personality regions. The boundaries between regions would be so permeable that the infant would hardly distinguish between himself and the outside world, between the real world and his thoughts about the real world, or even between

such simple concepts (to adults) as up and down or before and after.

This brief overview of theories about the nature of mankind can serve as a background for consideration of the concept of life themes. This concept is a framework for understanding socialization in terms that do not require extensive exposure to type, trait, developmental, or dynamic theories. The notion of life themes is designed less as a radical departure from earlier theories than as a convenient means of organizing the great variety of events that make up human socialization.

The Shaping of Life Themes

In the course of growth from infancy to adulthood, the child is subjected to a bewildering host of experiences. He is fed, weaned, toilet trained, schooled, taught attitudes, values, beliefs, and ways of behaving. He is rewarded and punished, exposed to planned and accidental happenings, and introduced to a variety of peers and adults. Out of this welter of events, the child emerges as an adult, but he does not emerge unscathed by what has been his lot. Life themes delineate the kind of person distilled from this life experience.

Perhaps an example of the development of one dominant theme will clarify the concept. Let us use an oversimplified example for the dramatic emphasis that it provides. We can take materialism—the attachment to material things and possessions—because other societies with great regularity accuse Americans of being grossly materialistic and, as a consequence, decadent. If you set out deliberately to socialize a child whose primary life theme is to be extreme materialism, how would you go about it?

One way would be to take a newborn infant and treat him in such a way that he will develop a high degree of anxiety about life. Be frightened of life yourself, transmit that fear to the child by word and deed, keep him from exploring the world, overprotect him whenever possible, worry about him when there is no basis for worry, and, in a variety of ways, teach him that the world is a jungle in which one is constantly in danger of losing everything he possesses.

Then arrange for him to learn on both an intellectual and an emotional level that things can

"*We are taught from an early age to cooperate with others and to help them.*"

be trusted and people cannot. Teach him that security in an uncertain world can issue only from possessions. Teach him that money is a measure of a person's worth, that money is power, and that power alone keeps a hostile humanity at a safe distance. Finally, teach him to believe that all other people are the same as he is and share his anxieties. This is the recipe for materialism as a life theme, and, once assembled, it becomes the guiding principle for the individual.

Thus, the dominant themes of the adult are transmitted to the psychic life of the child and in large part determine his fate. Materialism fashioned in early life can have a tenacity and pervasiveness difficult to comprehend in the adult if the "unthinking" nature of the young child is not taken into consideration. Nonetheless, the child is not just a passive recipient of the life themes originally held by his socializers. Life themes operate in a complicated context of many minor themes unique to the individual and fluctuate in intensity according to his life situation. Not all materialistic people are materialistic all the time or in all circumstances.

Two other theoretical observations are important here. First, our culture produces contradictory life themes in all of us. We are taught from an early age to cooperate with others and to help them. Yet we are also instructed in the importance of competing with others and defeating them in life's contests. These opposite life themes exist side by side in our psychic lives and, as do many other contradictory life themes, subject us to conflict throughout our lives. Second, the early formation of dominant life themes tends to color all the subsequent experiences that we have. A fearful, anxious child sees life through eyes quite different from those of the adventurous, confident, successful child. Life themes force the individual to see the world in very selective terms, to interpret it in a biased way, and to react to it accordingly.

With this general exposition of the concept of life themes in mind, we are now ready to examine the stages of development and socialization.

The Passive-Dependent Period

At birth the infant is almost totally helpless. He has emerged from the uterus, where his needs were immediately and automatically provided for, into a world where he simply cannot survive without a long period of care. His resources are very limited—a few basic survival reflexes plus a degree of physiological tolerance for deprivation. He has no language or thoughts and perceives things only in a vague and disorganized way. How does this helpless child begin to establish an effective way of relating to the world around him, so that order emerges from chaos?

The early relationship between mother and child is a crucial element in this development. Nearly all the child's appreciation of and reaction to the world around him is in some fashion related to the way he is handled by his mother. Consider, first of all, the infant's need for food. He needs his supply often, but he has almost no resources for getting food on his own. Therefore, his food supply typically comes from his mother via the following sequence of events: (1) The child experiences deprivation, or a need for food. (2) His signal system, in the form of a cry, notifies the outside world of this need. (3) The

"Yet we are also instructed in the importance of competing with others and defeating them in life's contests."

mother takes steps to secure food and to present it to the child. (4) His reflex sucking and swallowing responses are activated; he eats, and the need is reduced. (5) Following the gratification of the need, the child relaxes and falls asleep. The salient features of these events occur in roughly the same sequence again and again.

Because the child feels one way when he is getting hungry and quite another way when he is getting his hunger reduced, he can tell the difference between the two situations. The "getting hungry" situation is unpleasant; the "being fed" situation is pleasant. Because his mother constantly provides the food, the child comes to associate her with pleasant experiences and to perceive her as an entity separate from himself. Thus, he has begun to discriminate between and to organize his perceptions.

When, on repeatedly experiencing this sequence, the child finds that his mother appears to meet his needs in predictable ways, he develops a sense of trust that she will appear. This sense of high anticipation that the mother (or, later, some other person) will be there to make things better is termed by Erikson (1950) *basic trust*. Erikson believes that closely related to this sense of basic trust are personality characteristics such as optimism and self-regard. If the child does not develop this basic trust, he may come to regard his environment with uncertainty and suspicion.

Another life theme that may develop during this period is related to the physical process of food intake, or *incorporation*. Just as the child learns to distinguish hunger from gratification and mother from self, he begins to discriminate between two general classes of objects: those that are to be incorporated and those that are not. If the conditions surrounding the feeding process are improperly managed, the activity of incorporation can become a major concern for the child. An anxious mother who hovers solicitously over her child in constant worry that his appetite is insufficient to maintain good health can easily convert the normally satisfying process of eating into a nightmare of force feeding and painful emotions. Similarly, a rejecting parent can make eating a source of extreme psychological and physiological upset by punishing the child for the inevitable food accidents or by feeding him erratically or in an inconsistent and painful fashion. A child deprived or overindulged may develop a life theme concerned with the process of "taking in" that is quite separate from his physiological need for food. He may become, in Freud's terminology, an oral character.

Freud's concept of the oral character suggests that, as a consequence of unusual deprivation or gratification in the infant feeding experience, the child will as an adult possess a particular constellation of personality characteristics. The adult oral character is oriented toward the world in a passive-dependent manner in that he may need to lean on other people and have them take care of him throughout his life. When he is emotionally disturbed, he may regress and seek solace in eating. Depending on the nature of his early feeding experience—deprivation or gratification—the adult may be pessimistic or optimistic about life. The difficulty is that the oral character tends to be excessively optimistic or pessimistic even though the facts of his experience do not warrant such extreme responses.

Another important aspect of the early relationship between mother and child is the opportunity it affords the child to develop *frustration tolerance*. Basically, frustration tolerance is the ability to delay the gratification of one's needs without becoming enraged, depressed, or otherwise psychologically upset. At first the infant's frustration tolerance is very low; he does not have the physiological or psychological equipment to allow him to go without gratification for very long. His stomach is small, his metabolic rate is very high, and he has not "learned" to get along without immediate supplies.

Gradually, as the cycle of the feeding process is repeated, he becomes a more efficient physiological being, but he also learns to wait for food. This learning is possible because, on repeated exposure to the fact that food will be provided (that gratification will come), he develops an expectation (closely related to basic trust) that it will be provided again. If this expectation continues to be confirmed (if he is not forced to wait too long), it grows in strength, and the child becomes able to wait longer and longer periods before exceeding the limits of his tolerance. Certain periods of deprivation, then, are necessary if the child is to develop frustration tolerance.

The Beginning of Active Mastery

In the first few weeks of his life, the infant develops skills and capacities that permit him to take a much more active role in his own affairs. Let us take a simple example to illustrate this point. At a very early age the child is capable of random activity—turning, twisting, thrashing about, moving his arms and legs. Later, he learns —probably quite by chance—that such activity can influence conditions in the outside world. While he is being fed, he may become restless (for some reason entirely unrelated to the feeding process—perhaps his diaper is wet or a pin is pricking him), and his movement may cause the bottle or the breast to slip from his mouth. His activity has produced a result in the world that has real consequences for him; he is no longer getting the food he wants.

Now suppose that on a later occasion the child finds this food unpleasant (because of its flavor, because he is too full, or because his attention is drawn to something else). In such circumstances, he may apply what he has learned about how to get the bottle or the breast out of his mouth. (There is no implication here that the child figures out how to bring about the desired result; the learning involved is much more like *conditioning*, in which the presentation of a stimulus is followed almost automatically by the learned response.)

Through his own actions, the child has found a means of resisting various offerings (food, drink, direct physical contact) that the culture makes to him. These actions, developing out of a period of total passivity and dependence, are sometimes viewed by the parents as undesirable expressions of stubbornness or resistance. They are in fact the earliest beginnings of the child's expression of the wish to decide and do things for himself. He now has certain options available to him and no longer has to be entirely the passive recipient of society's decisions. In a small way, he is able to assert himself and his own wishes.

This beginning of independence and self-assertion commonly occurs around the time that the first teeth erupt. The experience of teething is unpleasant for the infant, and he tries to allay the pain by biting, by spitting, by applying pressure to the source of discomfort. Thus, when the breast is presented to him, he may chew on it instead of sucking as he is supposed to. Apart from the fact that this development would soon discourage the mother from breast feeding, she may interpret the child's efforts to reject food or people as aggressive or deliberately destructive: "He feels mean," "He's just being stubborn," "He has to learn who's boss."

The child may find himself confronted with adults who have the power to deter him from using his slim (but growing) resources. If the use of his resources becomes an issue between him and his parents, an important life theme may be established around such behaviors as independence, self-assertion, adequacy, self-confidence, and initiative. He may become excessively self-assertive, or he may be afraid to assert himself at all. In either case, the area of self-assertion will have important meaning for him.

The establishment of a life theme determines an attitude and an area of sensitivity, but the specific expression of that life theme is determined by a great many other factors. Thus, the child's self-assertiveness or his lack of it will probably be expressed indirectly. For example, he may become ruthlessly argumentative as a way of asserting his independence from others and, as a consequence, quit or be fired from one job after another throughout his life. In our culture, where independence and self-assertiveness are felt to be desirable traits, it is paradoxical that we often greet their first expressions with less than full joy.

As a result of this reaction, we may intrude on the child's beginning expressions of self-assertion and thus create unhealthy areas of sensitivity or struggle.

An important stage in the development of active mastery and self-assertion is that of beginning to walk. In the typical middle class family, the child's first step is an occasion for celebration. Beginning to walk means that the child is growing and developing normally, and it relates in an important way to middle class attitudes about achievement and mobility. The mother and father are thrilled that the child has begun to walk and encourage him to continue. However, this initial joy is short-lived. Parents soon discover that the walking child causes more trouble than the crawling child; he is harder to keep track of, he is able to reach things that he could not before, he "gets into" more things. If walking is a problem for the parents, the next step in the process, running (accompanied by falling down), is a catastrophe. The running child becomes a kind of missile with legs—a mobile engine of destruction. He crashes into things, people, and open space; he bowls over toys, visitors, and objects of value.

With these developments, a shift occurs in the attitude of the middle class parent. Walking, which at first was a desirable sign of the child's normal growth and initiative, is now recognized as something to be "coped with"—to be limited and socialized. The child is expected to be vigorous and take initiative, but at the same time he must respect property and the physical integrity of others. Thus, when the child seeks to express his growing ability to move about in the world, he encounters some strong, well-defended, and conflicting value systems held by his parents. This conflict may be framed in many terms: freedom versus conformity, personal rights versus property rights, or self-control versus self-expression.

Against the child's growing ability and wish to move vigorously into and through the world are leveled strong prohibitions: "Look out, you'll fall and hurt yourself," "Don't bump into that coffee table again," "For heaven's sake, will you stop all that running—you're driving your mother crazy."

"Thus, when the child seeks to express his growing ability to move about in the world, he encounters some strong, well-defended, and conflicting value systems held by his parents."

As a result of this conflicting set of urges and prohibitions, the middle class child may become uncomfortable with his body and with free bodily expression. Feelings of awkwardness and of alienation from one's body parts are common. Perhaps you have had the experience of standing in front of a group of people and not knowing what to do with your hands and feet. If so, you have a great deal of company, for the cultural practices that produce such discomfort are widespread.

Nor is the effect of developing life themes of body use relevant only to free bodily expression. Once established, these themes may generalize into areas that are only symbolically related to the literal fact of free bodily expression. Warnings about "getting into things" can affect the basic curiosity that the child is expressing about his world. Once the child has learned to walk, he comes into contact with a variety of fascinating objects of different sizes, colors, shapes, and tastes that arouse his curiosity and offer new experiences. His means of satisfying that curiosity is via handling, crawling around and through, seeing things from different positions, dropping things, and recovering them. We all want our children to be curious, but at the very time that this drive reaches its natural peak, we restrict the opportu-

nity to be curious. Eventually, the curiosity itself may be reduced. Similarly, the middle class child's experience during this period will affect his general self-expression, initiative, and willingness to take risks.

In the lower class, on the other hand, there is less emphasis on the protection of property and upon "not getting oneself bumped." Thus, lower class children have not had to learn to be so uncomfortable with their bodies as have most middle class children. And, consequently, lower-class children are typically much less restrained in their use of their bodies. In fact, they often have a hard time controlling their impulses to run, jump, or wiggle around in school and frequently use their bodies in open expression of emotions such as anger, disappointment, or happiness. Because these children are much less awkward in the use of their bodies, they often excel in sports and in spontaneous dancing and musical expression.

The Development of Sexual Identity

The child's learning to walk is associated with the development of an intense and pervasive curiosity. The toddler gets into everything; he is

"We all want our children to be curious, but at the very time that this drive reaches its natural peak, we restrict the opportunity to be curious."

fascinated by the qualities and workings of the objects in the world. He wants to investigate and to understand. Although this level of understanding is not very sophisticated (mainly he tries to find out how things move and how they are stuck together), exploration of all parts of his world is necessary for further socialization. And, naturally, he wishes to explore and understand the vehicle that carries him into the world—his body.

From an early age, the child shows an interest in the workings of his body; he manipulates his fingers, makes faces in the mirror, and pinches and tickles himself to see what it feels like. When he learns to walk, this curiosity increases markedly. He wants to know more about his legs, his joints, his body openings, and his appendages. In the same spirit, we believe, he discovers his sexual parts.

After that discovery, the child's attention is first called to the fact that certain kinds of exploration have special significance. Second, taboos about sex become inadvertently attached to more general activities. Third, the culture reacts as though the child were aware of the sexual implications of his actions and undertakes the socialization of the child in those terms. It is as though the culture sees the child reacting in a sex-relevant way and then undertakes to treat the child generally as a sexual being. Boys are more strongly encouraged to take an active, aggressive role; girls are encouraged to be passive and "ladylike." Sex-relevant toys are provided—boys get action toys, suited to the occupational and interpersonal roles that they are expected to assume; girls get household toys and dolls for the same reason. Differential expectations about modesty and openness of sexual expression are imparted. Cultural attitudes about how one should treat members of the opposite sex are communicated with increasing intensity. In short, exhortations about the proper functions and attitudes of the two genders become increasingly evident.

None of this is to suggest that little boys and little girls are not always treated differentially because in fact they are. However, after the recognition of the child's "awareness" of his sexual apparatus, the urgings become increasingly strong and are paired with rewards and punishments of greater consequence.

Out of this interaction between parent, child, and culture grow several important life themes. The child punished for exploring his sexual parts may come to feel that exploration in general is wrong. Or he may interpret the disapproval as disapproval of the body parts involved— he becomes concerned with how decent or how proper they are. Later, as a result of a further generalization, he may become embarrassed about or ashamed of other parts of his body. It takes no imagination to see that basic attitudes toward the decency and propriety of sexual activity may be instilled at this time.

Moreover, life themes concerned with general masculinity and femininity often develop during this period. The male is supposed to be assertive in our culture and to take the initiative in sexual relationships. But suppose that the little boy who takes "sexual" initiative in exploring his own or a little girl's body is made to feel that his action is shameful and that he is evil because of his interest. Sexual inversions such as homosexuality or lesbianism may be established in this way. Assertiveness and self-determination may also be influenced, as may basic attitudes toward self-acceptance and self-confidence.

Biological sex characteristics initially set the stage for the development of sexual identity, but the form that the expression of biology will eventually take depends on secondary sex characteristics (manner, voice, dress, interests, and so forth), which are forged early in life. The establishment of sexual identity influences the manner in which the child experiences the world and will dictate how men and women will react to him socially. The growing child's discovery of sex becomes a monumental event in his life; American society is overconcerned (other cultures would call it obsessed) with every aspect of sex. Our society has managed to entrap itself in a circle of its own making; this society raises its children in a fashion that produces patterns of behavior that prove to be a chronic source of dissatisfaction in later life.

"The growing child's discovery of sex becomes a monumental event in his life; American society is overconcerned (other cultures would call it obsessed) with every aspect of sex."

The Development of Language

In many respects, man is his language. It is an immensely useful tool. Instead of consisting of vague, disorganized, and occasionally unrecognizable objects, the world takes on form and organization for man through language. With it he rises above the other species in the evolutionary chain and assures himself of a future limited only by the reach of his imagination.

In the infant's life the ability to name things appears very early and is evidence of his growing comprehension of what transpires around him. In addition to providing a basis for organizing and experiencing the world, language serves as a means for effective communication of socialization demands and pressures. What the parent wants the child to do and how the child feels about doing it are more efficiently communicated by language than by anything else.

Language, like other kinds of interaction, becomes the basis for the establishment of important life themes. To talk or not; to speak clearly or not; to use language for relating to parents and other significant adults in important ways; to joke, communicate feelings, dominate, or submit via speech—all of these are central and frequently appearing life themes of speech. At one extreme is the mute mental patient, who, fearing life, will not communicate with others. At the other extreme is the compulsive chatterer, who must issue a continuous stream of conversation if he is to ward off the onslaught of anxiety. The kind, quality, and manner of speech are important indicators of the course that socialization has taken for the individual. Think, for example, of what might happen to a child's willingness to talk if he were ridiculed at the time that he first started experimenting with language skills.

The acquisition of language makes possible the generalization of acquired life themes along a number of dimensions not previously available. Consider, for example, the child who is slapped on the hand for attempting to handle a valuable object that his parents are trying to protect. Before language, his grasp of this prohibition exists only in the form of a conditioned motor response, which has the effect of making him draw back in anticipation of another slap when he reaches for something else. But now suppose the words "don't reach" are attached to this same prohibition. "Reach" has many physical and psychological associations besides the literal ones attached to the situation described. This word can be confused with numerous other words that sound like it, and it will soon be associated with words like "aspire," "stretch," "grasp," "acquire." These meaning similarities add a vast number of opportunities for the generalizing of attitudes and prohibitions. In this way, life themes acquired during one period of the child's life can affect all the rest of it.

Language, then, is a double-edged sword in human development. A means for increasing knowledge and insight about the nature of life, language can also be a weapon that destroys the humanity of an individual. Language is the vessel of meaning for man, and, as he grows older, it becomes increasingly important to the conduct of his life. In the last half of the twentieth century, education has become the cornerstone of our survival as a society. And without language, only primitive education is possible.

"Language is the vessel of meaning for man, and, as he grows older, it becomes increasingly important to the conduct of his life."

School

School is both an important test of the adequacy of parental child-rearing techniques and the arena in which social acceptance or rejection are expressed. The child's teachers do not judge him in the same way that his parents do. At home he is judged as a child member of the family; he is pronounced good or bad and is loved or punished in terms of himself. To a degree, but only to a small degree, this remains true when he enters school. Generally, his teachers judge him on the basis of what he produces in comparison to what the other children produce. Our society is highly competitive, and, no matter how permissive or

understanding an individual teacher may be, the school forcefully communicates the goals of society to its children. The child is no longer simply a child; he is a child asked to produce in a competitive-comparative climate.

At home the child has a unique position; unless he happens to be an identical twin or triplet, no one else occupies exactly the same role position. He is an individual, and prerogatives accrue to him because of his individuality. In school he is surrounded by dozens of children who occupy a role position identical to his. He is cast among peers, where no role-defined prerogatives exist for any individual and where essentially similar demands are made upon everyone from the beginning.

The child is expected to develop a position within the group—as leader, follower, dominant or submissive member, and so on. To a very large extent, role behavior within the peer group follows the same lines that exist for adults; that is, the same roles that gain favor and reward in the larger society are prized in the school. Like the adult in society, the child in school needs to be an initiative taker, a competitor, a leader, a cooperative worker, and a producer of socially approved goods. (In this case, of course, the "goods" are only symbols of his later productivity and are likely to be more abstract and intellectual.)

The child is also expected to learn to put the group's welfare and interests ahead of his own. He must learn to share the significant adult, to control his own impulses (selfishness, greed, and egocentrism have little place even in the least structured of kindergartens), and to participate cooperatively in activities that are either group determined or adult determined in the interests of the entire group.

The physical setup of most classrooms lends itself to communal existence. There is little room for personal privacy; the child's free sphere of private operation has shrunk remarkably. At home the middle class child may have at least a private play area, if not a whole room, for his personal use. Personal property, although respected and defended by the teacher, is subject to use and intrusion by the group under the mandate of "share." Even the child's inner thoughts and family life are subject to group scrutiny during "show and tell" periods.

In his first contact with this miniature society, the child learns to use the basic adjustment patterns that will carry him through similar situations, not only as he progresses through school, but also as he slowly advances to full membership in the larger society. As stressed previously, these basic patterns are subject to constant modification. However, once the child is cast in the role of group leader or scapegoat, he will find it difficult to escape his designation. Success and self-confidence tend to perpetuate themselves in subtle ways, as do failure and self-derogation.

The role of the school as a major agent of socialization cannot be overemphasized. It is at the minimum a 10–12 year rehearsal in how the child is expected to behave when he grows up. For the typical middle class child, school is a means to the end of a "successful" life and is presented to the child as such. School is an opportunity to train oneself in the skills that bring rewards valued by the middle class—social status and material success and comfort. Children do not go to school primarily to exercise their minds or to have fun (although we attempt to make it "fun" so that they will not tire of it). They go to school with a purpose, and that purpose is consistent with the values of the middle class society, from which the public school concept rose.

In accepting school and in doing well by its standards, the child has already made a long stride toward the kind of life that the society desires him to have. Conversely, the child who fails in school has lowered the odds that he will be a success by the standards of the society. The child who encounters problems in school such that he rejects the values and expectations the school holds out to him is also a child who will find it necessary to reject the values and expectations of society. In this way, school problems become social problems.

On the other hand, social problems may generate school problems. Probably the clearest example of this is the lower class child, whose socialization has not stressed upward mobility and achievement as major ways of life. He may not have had firm lessons in impulse control or in the "proper" use of his body. Thus, the lower class child sometimes approaches school poorly fitted to meet its fundamentally middle class demands. He is, by middle class standards, poorly motivated (he has not incorporated the prevailing attitudes about the importance of doing well in school), poorly controlled (the importance of sitting still and keeping in tight control of his body was not part of his early training), and poorly endowed (his native intelligence has been channeled into activities that are not common in middle class homes). From such a situation arise the familiar problems of the school-resistant, hyperaggressive, acting out child.

Social Man

Man is a social being, and, as civilization has progressed, he has developed an increasing dependence upon his fellow human. When the economic structure was that of simple food gathering, the rules by which men lived together could be equally simple and still regulate behavior in a socially satisfactory way. However, as man's technology advanced—first to low-level agricultural pursuits, then to trade, then to crafts and manufacturing—the rules that men set for themselves developed with a parallel complexity.

This increasing interdependence, coupled with the increasing complexity of social regulations, has reached an apex in today's world. Evidence of greater social regulation can be seen in the development of more powerful centralized governments, the sacrifice of certain individual prerogatives for the sake of a smoother-running society, and the emergence of what we have come to think of as the conformist, organization-man character of our business world.

Our social and value system is rooted in the Judeo-Christian ethic. Basically, this ethic advises us to live together as brothers; to have compassion and kindness for others; to profess and demonstrate love for our associates; to preserve individual life; to restrict the use of brute force, self-seeking, and greed; and to hold in check the expression of many of our basic biological needs, primarily sex and aggression.

Nevertheless, man's biological needs sometimes become so pressing (either when he is a child or when the process of socialization fails) that he loses sight of the regulations that society seeks to impose on him. Examples of this "impulse breakthrough" are manifold. When a man is starving, or when his children are starving, he may steal. When his life is threatened, he may resort to very aggressive survival actions rather than turn the other cheek. When he is sexually deprived at a time of high sexual drive (as in the school years), he may engage in sexual activities specifically prohibited by the culture.

Moreover, not all of the values in our culture are congruent with the Judeo-Christian ethic. For example, we believe in competition. We believe that the man who works harder or is more clever, intelligent, or skillful should have greater rewards than his less energetic or skillful brother. We teach our children to work hard and to compete with others. It is very difficult to teach children to be kind and self-sacrificing at the same moment that we urge them on as competitors. There are other such contradictions in the culture—for instance, group conformity versus individual expression and status seeking versus humility.

Whether these attitudes are communicated deliberately or unconsciously, they determine in a very fundamental way not only how the child sees the world but even what he is able to see in it—that is, which of the sensations that come to him through his eyes, ears, nose, mouth, and skin will have meaning for him. What a child from a Pakistani village sees when he looks at a busy New York street is probably the same thing that a native New York child sees, but the meaning of it is quite different. It is the job of the family and the school to teach the child the meaning of what he sees; that is, it is their task to prepare him to experience the world in the terms that will be the most useful to him in the particular society in which he will live out his life.

PROSPECTUS

A complete account of socialization must survey theoretical observations and experiments conducted in psychology and a wide variety of related fields. We must examine the source of theories on the process of socialization and explore the relationship between that source and theoretical observations having to do with motivation, learning, and language acquisition. We need to account for the application of the scientific method to the study of socialization and compare this modern approach with the conceptualization of the problem in the past.

The primary agents of socialization in the beginning of the child's life are the parents, who teach values, attitudes, and patterns of behavior and instruct the child in the role performance expected by others in the society. However, no simple model of the socialization process can be constructed. The home and family are frequently disrupted by deviations and discontinuities, such as an absent father, divorce, or mental illness, so that the effect of these factors should be examined. For some children, deviation in the mother-child relationship radically alters the model of learning how to be civilized. The child may contribute an additional problem through the nature of his intellect. Thus, exploring the socialization of the gifted and the retarded is important. Race and socio-economic class also contribute variations to the model of socialization, just as physical differences and limitations make special demands on the agents of socialization.

If the child passes through the first stages of training successfully, he is exposed to new socializing forces in the form of peers and teachers. Here the issues of values, goals, and methods of socialization outside the family become important. We must examine the schools and look closely at the children who master these civilizing lessons of childhood and at those who do not. The adolescent and the youth group add another dimension to socialization; the task of continuing to socialize the young person presents special problems for our society.

Socialization continues through the adult years, when marriage, a job, or continued education become important influences on the emotional and psychological shape of the young adult. As delinquency may represent the failure of social-ization for the youth, drug taking may be the escape for the young adult incapable of managing the tasks of social existence.

As age takes its inevitable toll, the individual's role and status in society are altered, and relationships with others must be adjusted to a new set of requirements. Death ends the sequence, but even this event is surrounded by rituals calculated to teach the survivors the proper form of conduct in life.

The impact of the family on the infant occurs against a backdrop of human biology. The biological organism is motivated to seek out experience, and in his encounters with life, he learns certain things at the same time that he unlearns others; that is, he becomes able to respond selectively to his environment. As he progresses in these learnings, he acquires the complicated patterns of behavior called *roles*. *Biology, motivation*, and *learning*, then, constitute the basic elements of socialization.

BIOLOGY AND PSYCHOLOGY

Psychologists in general take a psychogenic rather than an organic approach to the study of man; that is, they insist that man's essential nature is explained primarily through his experiences with his fellow human beings—not by means of his chemistry or his nervous system or his glandular activity. However, almost all psychologists agree that knowledge about man's physical construction and functions can be helpful in assembling a total view of him; man is clearly a biological-physiological being even though he transcends any simple adding together of his parts described in purely electrochemical terms.

2

Psychological mechanisms in socialization

The connection between biological and psychological events is best illustrated by the work of Pasamanick and his colleagues (Kawi and Pasamanick, 1959; Pasamanick and Lilienfeld, 1955a; Pasamanick and Lilienfeld, 1955; Pasamanick, Knobloch, and Lilienfeld, 1956; Pasamanick and Kawi, 1956; Pasamanick, Constantiniou, and Lilienfeld, 1956; Pasamanick, Rogers, and Lilienfeld, 1956). Pasamanick and his co-workers suspected that brain damage during the prenatal or paranatal periods could account for later behavioral abnormalities. Using a sample of 363 white and 108 Negro children referred for special services because of behavioral disturbances such as hyperactivity, confusion, and disorganization, the research group studied the course of pregnancy and birth complications in both.

Their research confirmed the suspicion that the medical histories of these children would display a much greater incidence of prematurity and complications in pregnancy and birth than would the histories of a control group of children who were free of adjustmental difficulties. In particular, children described as "hyperactive, confused, and disorganized" more often had histories that suggested exposure, before or at about the time of birth, to conditions such as bleeding during pregnancy, anoxia (an undersupply of oxygen), or toxemia (the presence of harmful toxins in the mother's blood stream).

In contrast, Pasamanick and his co-workers found that speech disorders and tics (involuntary muscular movements) were less clearly related to abnormal conditions during pregnancy or at birth. This finding confirms common speculation that these are learned psychological disorders unlikely to have an organic base.

It is in this kind of systematic investigation of both the physiological and the psychological correlates of human behavior that biology is most relevant to the study of socialization. Like other handicaps, biological difficulty changes the socialization task for the parent. Pasamanick's view is that unsuspected brain damage in children may produce abnormalities in later behavior that pose distinct difficulties in child management for par-

ents. Otherwise imperceptible brain damage may appear, for example, only at stages in life that make critical demands on the child—that is, when he must attend school, learn to read, and organize his cognitive and perceptual life in order to succeed at academic tasks.

MOTIVATION

The search for the why of man's behavior has long occupied those devoted to the study of man, and there are almost as many approaches to motivation as there are theorists. However, the various approaches can be roughly classified as *hedonistic, instinctual, cognitive,* and *drive* theories. All of these theories, in spite of their differences, acknowledge that the motive force for humans—the force that keeps humanity from curling in the fetal position for ever and ever—is some internal factor, inferred from man's observable behavior, that "arouses, drives, and integrates a person's behavior [and] . . . is terminated by reaching a goal or obtaining a *reward*" (Murray, 1964, pp. 7–8).

The hedonistic (or hedonic) theory of motivation is an ancient idea that man's primary motivation is to seek pleasure and avoid pain. The early eighteenth and nineteenth century versions of this theory were, however, too simple to encompass something as complex as human behavior. These theories assumed, for example, that man's decisions are fully conscious ones in which he calculates a simple balance of pleasure and pain and acts accordingly; the unconscious parts of man's motives were not considered. The circularity of such a theory was another drawback to its acceptance; that is, theorists insisted that those who seem to seek pain or avoid pleasure (masochists, suicides, neurotic failures, Puritans, and so forth) are really "pleasured by their pain" and thus do not violate the basic principle of this theory.

Modern attempts to modify and update hedonistic theories have taken the form of creation of systems of experimental hedonism in which objective measures of actual approach and avoidance behavior are used instead of personal, subjective reports of what constitutes pleasure and pain. This experimental hedonism has become theoretically sophisticated by the addition of references to recent discoveries on the physiological bases of pleasure and pain. Man learns to anticipate what stimuli will arouse positive or negative reactions in him, but these may originally be based more than we suspect in his biological nature.

The human organism is born with some fixed, instinctual reactions to certain objects in his environment. Reactions to food, water, and stimulation of a sexual or a painful sort seem to produce immediate and intense responses that do not have to be learned from others. The newborn child has certain simple reflex responses (breathing, sucking) and some other complex patterns of reaction that occur as a consequence of physical maturation, not of learning or practice.

Instinct theory assumes that man is motivated as much by what he inherited physiologically as by what he learns as he grows up. This concept has recently become more important through European and American ethologists' discovery of the effect of *imprinting* in the very early life of animals. It seems that, during a critical period in the early life of most animals, patterns of behavior are "instinctively" formed by the kind of stimulation received from the environment. Perhaps, these theorists argue, our inheritance acts to fix our response to certain parts of our environment during particular phases of our lives. Man's motivation, then, would be partly fixed prior to the learnings he would experience in the years to come.

The notion of *social instincts*, a set of innate responses passed genetically through the species, was once used to account for social motivation. However, this notion collapsed of its own weight when the list of social instincts became too long and complicated. Moreover, social anthropological evidence accumulated to demonstrate that what seems native and instinctual for a human in one culture is totally irrelevant and not practiced in a different social setting. Because instinct has about it a fixed and inflexible quality, it has to be everywhere or nowhere at all. Thus, social instinct as an explanation for motives died. Nonetheless, how much of human behavior can be attributed to instinct (however flexibly defined) remains an important source of controversy in the study of motivation; instinct, like so many once abandoned theoretical concepts, keeps returning in one guise or another to plague the motivational theorist. What constitutes an instinct and how many exist in man are still subjects for dispute and may never see resolution.

Cognitive theories of motivation free man of dependence on simple hedonism and fixed instincts and endow him with a rational capacity to make choices. This ancient philosophy involves the concepts of *willing* and *desiring*, which give purpose to human behavior. Conceding to man the power of conscious decision and control provides a different view of the nature of the developing individual and of the steps necessary to socialize him in that it frees him from the limitations of his instinctual inheritance. The notion of free will is highly suspect among psychologists bent on pursuing a natural science model of behavior, although the issue of whether or not man has free will has reared its head in an almost cyclical fashion ever since man began thinking about his behavior.

The subjective experience of the man on the street—he decides to engage or not engage in certain behaviors, and he chooses the way in which he will respond to stimuli—convinces him that little of human behavior is predetermined or predestined. The issue of free will is of substantial concern to cognitive theorists because they begin with the assumption that man is essentially a rational being. Man, they say, is aware of his needs and desires and uses his skills and capacities to satisfy them. The cognitive theorists care less about what starts behavior than they do about how man decides between alternative ideas and values once he seeks some goal. Although attention to this aspect of man's behavior furnishes us with useful information about how choices and decisions are made, it does little to lay bare the basic urges, impulses, and drives that impel him onward in the first place.

Drive theories occupy a more respectable niche in modern theory even though their roots are ancient. In the older theories, the concept of drives was used to describe the energy source that drives man to behave (the fuel supply of human behavior). However, drives were attached theoretically to a variety of motive systems such as curiosity, sex, hunger, and thirst and so began to resemble the concepts of instinct that had been elaborated by earlier theorists. Thus, drives are often described as a euphemism for the hoary concept of instinct. Yet they seem to be a construct that still has some survival value.

Drives have most often been considered as facets of man's motivation that were originally based on the need for the body to maintain a biological balance (homeostasis) in order to function effectively. Theorists believed that the more powerful the drive, the more fixed and persistent would be the habits of behavior associated with it. Thus, a great deal of why man acts as he does and becomes the kind of person he does might be traced theoretically to the pattern of learned reactions that he accumulates in the process of satisfying the needs and drives that impelled him to action early in his life.

There is still another way to phrase the issue of motivation. Birch and Veroff (1966) maintain that the central issue of motivation is the question of why the organism selects one activity rather than another, why it is vigorously pursued, and why it persists over time. For these two theorists, "the basic unit of study for motivation theory is an activity" (p. 1). Assuming what they designate as a "principle of action," they stress that the aim of studying motivation is to be able to predict "when an organism will shift from one activity to another, what activity the organism will shift to, and also the intensity with which the organism will engage in the activity" (p. 2).

The action that the organism will take depends on the varying strengths of competing tendencies; the strongest one, of course, determines the action. Thus, the study of motivation must involve an assessment of the strength of such motive tendencies by means of the study of *incentives to action*. Birch and Veroff (1966) describe motivation in terms of seven incentive systems (sensory, curiosity, affiliative, aggressive, achievement, power, and independence). These systems propel the individual into active engagement with the environment and make him learn the physical and social lessons that constitute socialization: ". . . organisms typically confront developmental problems of regulating their bodily (sensory) experience; reacting to new stimuli (curiosity); depending on contact with others (affiliation); reacting to frustration by others (aggression); evaluating their own performance (achievement); withstanding influence by others (power); and operating on their own (independence)" (p. 42). Each incentive system is matched with a set of *consummatory behaviors* designed to gratify. In the operation of incentives and consummatory behaviors is the necessary motivation for learning.

LEARNING

The concept of the learned response is needed to explain how we manage, generation after generation, to civilize the newborn human beast. Learning basically amounts to arranging a connection between a stimulus and a response where no connection existed before. The simplest form of learning is the attachment of a reflex nervous system response to a particular stimulus —or simple conditioning à la Pavlov and his salivating dogs. This form of learning appears in the newborn child; for example, presenting him with a bottle activates his reflex sucking and swallowing. However, as he grows older, complex patterns of response begin to appear as well.

In order for either sort of response to appear, some form of motivation must be operative. Gratification, whether biological or psychological, is a great motive force for response. When the supply of possible gratifications for the child is controlled

by adults interested in transmitting some cultural lessons rather than others and when the demand for gratification is insistent (as it is with a young child), we have most of the necessary ingredients for the learning process. If reward and punishment are consistently administered by the same people, then we have an almost ideal circumstance for learning.

In the course of the learning process, the supply of possible gratifications expands because events associated with reward can acquire reward value in their own right. In two now classic experiments, tokens meaningless to animals (money) became valuable in their eyes once they learned that the tokens could be exchanged for prized food (Cowles, 1937; Wolfe, 1936). In the same way, the child learns to value money. After he has learned to derive gratification directly from tokens of reward, they can be used later as reinforcement to ensure a continuation of the behavior preferred by the socializer. Money, a gold star, a pat on the head, glowing admiration, respect, fame, and a host of similar symbols become prime motivators and thus facilitate teaching the child desirable patterns of behavior.

An additional observation should be made at this point. Not all that either the child or the adult learns becomes a permanent fixture in his psychological makeup. Even though he may have learned an undesirable pattern of behavior, that pattern can be extinguished. Furthermore, what is appropriate behavior only for a child can be unlearned; if it could not, we would all be adults saddled with childish ways of reacting to events. Finally, as comprehension and experience expand, imperfect learnings are modified and refined.

Patterns of behavior can be extinguished in a variety of ways. The most direct means of eliminating a response is to remove the reward that the response usually brings. Everyone stops going to the well when it runs dry. Punishment also works. Behavior that once brought pleasure and now produces nothing but pain is soon discarded as psychologically unprofitable. Thus, when reward and punishment are used in combination, both learning and unlearning take place with great speed and efficiency. However, even though the child simultaneously punished for the wrong move and rewarded for the right move may learn faster than his rewarded-only twin, punishment carries with it side effects that may prove undesirable for other purposes in socialization.

Socialization and Learning

These broad and fundamental observations about the nature of learning are easiest to verify when the subject of study is the simple learnings about the physical world that all of us must experience. A hot stove is a great teacher of avoidance of hot stoves even if it is not a perfect teacher (the child may also avoid the cold stove until he learns to detect the difference between the two). Learning that something is too heavy to lift, too steep to climb, or too hot to handle is grossly simple in contrast to the complexity of learning about other human beings. This learning is the hardest kind of all—some people never quite master it.

One school of behavioral science insists that learning ought to be as lawful and predictable as other aspects of nature. Ellen Reese (1966) suggests that parents use *operant techniques* (reinforcement, or reward, following the emission of a response in order to modify behavior by increasing the appearance of that response) to make children learn socialized forms of response. Her work and the work of an increasing number of researchers (Azrin, Hutchinson, and McLaughlin, 1965; Bandura, 1965; Findley and Brady, 1965; Geiss, Stebbins, and Lundin, 1965; Goldaimond, 1965; Hale and Azrin, 1965; Holland and Skinner, 1961; Krasner, 1965; Rheingold, Gewirtz, and Ross, 1959; Ullmann and Krasner, 1965; Verhave,

1966) have offered an updated model of how to socialize the child best.

For a model of operant conditioning of behavior, Reese (1966) outlines a series of steps. To begin with, it is important to specify what pattern of behavior the socializer wishes to establish in the child. Is it toilet training, good eating habits, non-aggressiveness, politeness, obedience, or the elimination of crying behavior? The question is this one: What *exactly* do you wish the child to do when you have successfully completed training, and what measure will you use to decide whether the learning has been accomplished? The difference between how the child acts now and how you wish him to perform in the future measures the size of the task at hand.

The next step is to set up a favorable situation for the behavioral modification to occur; that is, there should be minimal distraction, time available, and no other possible behaviors to contaminate the behavior that is the target. In this setting, some basic motivation—something that will reward or reinforce the behavior desired in the child—must be established. The reward may range from adult attention and approval to a piece of candy, a privilege, or an escape from unpleasantness. These rewards are then withheld from the child or granted him according to a schedule designed to extinguish unwanted behaviors and reinforce desired ones. Extraneous and unintended rewards are eliminated in order not to confuse the process of modifying the child's behavior (a favorite toy can absorb the child's attention while learning is supposed to be taking place).

The shaping of behavior can now take place until the final desired behavior is achieved. In great part, success in this venture depends on maintaining a planned and organized program of reinforcement of behavior in the beginning and a fading-out or intermittent reinforcement as the desired behavior begins to appear in a regular and predictable fashion. These methods are designed to produce learning and socialized behavior in children if properly applied. The program cannot demand more than the child is capable of delivering and so must be paced with an eye to the child's ability and emotional response to training.

Behavioral modification of the sort outlined here is a popular contender to displace other theories of socialization. The emotional objection that theorists and practitioners have had to behavioral theory is its suggestion of inhumanity—the child is an organism, an animal, an object to be manipulated. However, this method is not unkind or heartless; rather, it is systematic. The method works, but the arguments about applying it to human beings will rage hot for many years.

Identification

Learning can take place through insight and understanding, as a consequence of reinforcement, and as part of the process of *identification*. The concept of identification has long concerned theorists, and in recent years a resurgence of interest and experimentation in making this idea explicit and scientifically measurable has occurred (Mussen, 1967). Further exploration of this topic is warranted because it is assumed that learning proper social roles depends heavily on this way of acquiring new patterns of behavior.

The child learns to "be like" the parent in a variety of ways, and on this base he adds a series of other identifications with others that form a unique state of being for him as an individual. Somehow—without explicit training—each person acquires facets of the self that can be traced to contact with others in his environment. The concept of identification attempts to explain this phenomenon.

As early as 1917, Freud discussed this molding of the self after other people. The concept of acting like another goes beyond simple imitation. The molding amounts to "becoming like" another person in temperament and mannerisms, in meeting standards of conduct held by others, and in performing in social roles as valued others do (Sears, Rau, and Alpert, 1965). All of us imitate others for brief periods in our lives, but these imitations are transitory and have little impact on

the basic structure of the self. Identification clearly reaches beyond imitation in altering the kind of person one is.

Recently some theorists have insisted that this distinction between imitation and identification is an artificial one. Bandura and Walters (1963) insist that the same process may simply be labeled differently; that is, what is called identification by personality theorists is designated as imitation by experimental psychologists. In both cases, the theorists are referring to "the tendency for a person to reproduce the actions, attitudes, or emotional responses exhibited by real-life or symbolized models" (p. 89).

The experimental research of Bandura and his co-workers with young children seems to confirm this suggestion (Bandura, 1965; Bandura, 1966; Bandura and Huston, 1961; Bandura and Kupers, 1964; Bandura and McDonald, 1963; Bandura and Mischel, 1965; Bandura, Ross, and Ross, 1961; Bandura, Ross, and Ross, 1963; Bandura and Walters, 1963; Bandura and Whalen, 1966). The mass of recent research is convincing, but there may be many special cases of learning in which the process of identifying with another is the best theoretical explanation of events. Simple imitation may be too restrictive an explanation for learning that takes place without direct exposure to a model whose behavior can be mimicked.

Many modern theorists contend that identification is a necessary concept if we are to explain the complex learning process that children demonstrate as they develop (Bronfenbrener, 1960; Kagan, 1958; Whiting, 1960). For example, Whiting (1960) has broadened identification into a status-envy hypothesis. He states, "If a child perceives that another has more efficient control over resources than he has, if, for example, he sees other people enjoying and consuming resources of high value to him when he is deprived of them, he will envy such a person and attempt to emulate him" (p. 118). This definition suggests a much less mechanical and imitative process of bringing about change in a growing child and indicates that insight and covert practice may be involved in becoming like another.

In a similar fashion, Kagan (1958) treats identification as an acquired cognitive response in which the child selectively takes over some of the attributes, motives, and emotional states of the model. However, Kagan makes no explicit reference to envy as a motive force in identification. According to him, it is the child's need for love and affection and for power and mastery over the environment that leads him to emulate the life style of another; he wants to be like the other in order to gratify his needs and reduce his sense of helplessness. For both Kagan and Whiting, the child's reasoning is quite direct: "If he has what I want, perhaps I can have it, too, if I am like him."

Identification of the kind described here—*defensive identification*, or *identification with the aggressor*—most often occurs when the child is envious of the status of others or is afraid of hostile, punitive, or painful treatment at their hands. The kind of identification that emphasizes the close affectionate bond between mother and child has been defined as *anaclitic* or *developmental identification*. Theorists of this persuasion insist that such a concept is needed to explain the becoming like another through respect, love, and affection. Becoming like the loved or respected one can be a way of assuring the continuation of this needed relationship with another.

Because socialization is the means of learning proper role behavior, both the defensive and the developmental form of identification (and imitation, for that matter) are important tools in the learning process. As Mussen (1966) has indicated, "according to the principles of role theory, the boy identifies with his father, not *only* because he is threatening and potentially punitive, and not *only* because he is warm and nurturant, but because, in the child's eyes, he is extremely powerful in controlling the administration of both rewards and punishments" (p. 87). Identification and imitation, then, are two means by which the young are socialized in the family circle early in life and in the larger society later.

SOCIALIZATION AND COPING

Learning to cope with life under normal and abnormal circumstances is the caldron in which maturity is fashioned. Thus, vital to a consideration of socialization is some discussion of the learning process as a way of acquiring the capacity to cope with life's problems. *Coping* is the individual's ability to manage both the demands of his environment and the tensions aroused by stress. Two kinds of coping can be distinguished: *primary coping*, the attempt to deal with a problem in the first place, and *secondary coping*, the attempt to manage the consequences of having made an inadequate mastery of the problem in the first place (Murphy, 1957). Even though the individual may have failed to solve a problem the first time he encountered it, if he solves it the second time around, he is free to react in a natural manner when that problem occurs again. When the attempt to solve a problem fails for the second time, he may engage in frenzied attempts to adapt even though he is without the means to do so.

Coping Strategies

Every individual learns—with greater or lesser success—a series of basic coping strategies from the agents of his socialization. Because the lives of many children in Western society are similar in broad design, they learn the same general strategies. In most cases, these strategies are age-specific or developmental-stage-specific in that they must be modified or abandoned as the child grows older and faces new tasks. If he has not learned adequate coping strategies or if he employs a strategy inappropriate to a particular challenge, he will experience the very stress that he is seeking to avoid.

Although just a few studies of children's coping mechanisms have been made to date, one study by Lois Murphy (1957) describes the following eight strategies formulated after observing preschool children in a variety of social situations:

1. Children select from their environment what can reasonably be coped with in order to reduce stress to proportions that can be handled. Murphy recounts the simple act of bringing children into a testing situation and offering them large glasses of juice. For some children, this new situation was greeted without fear or concern about their capacity to cope; they gulped down the juice and started to play. Other children prolonged the juice drinking period by sipping the beverage slowly as they surveyed the nature of their surroundings and calculated how to manage it. This delay in entering the social and play situation was a way to select those aspects of the environment that these children would most likely be able to manage.

2. Children also use fantasy to deal with stressful situations. If a child can successfully insist that what is real is not real, he no longer needs to deal with it. By retreating into a fantasy world, the child can thus avoid the pain of stress for a short time.

3. Evading excessive or unwelcome demands is another way of fending off the environment. Pretending illness, sleep, apathy, or stupidity may release the child from the demands made on him. Another common evasion that a child may use is to hide behind his parents when strangers are present and thereby control the amount of stress to which he will be subjected. Withdrawal of this sort is criticized by parents and prompts apology to others, but it remains an effective means by which children cope with situations that produce anxiety.

4. Children may also accept—or at least tolerate —the anxiety provoking situation. They may not be very enthusiastic about meeting certain situations (the doctor, the dentist, the stranger), but, knowing that the confrontation is inevitable, chil-

dren may tolerate it reluctantly and try to comprehend the necessity for accepting it.

5. Practice, extra effort, and/or compulsive repetition may be used to face stress. The compulsive repetition of an act and the mobilization of extra energy are in the long run self-destructive because they occupy the child's time and energy to such an extent that he has little of either left for coping with new demands.

Coping as mobilizing extra energy resembles the idea that each of us possesses a reserve of *adaptation energy* (Selye, 1956), which is used to meet unusual circumstances. Although the notion of adaptation energy is vague and abstract, something akin to extra energy seems regularly available to both adults and children for meeting stressful situations. The stories of injured persons dragging themselves for miles to find help, surviving against incredible odds, and finding sudden strength in an emergency are excellent examples of the availability of adaptation energy in times of dire emergency.

6. Children also protect themselves from stress by "cushioning," or taking advantage of available gratifications. Children may seize upon ways out of the situation even if these are no more than temporary escapes from pressure. Reassurance in various forms can also sustain the child in stress. Cushioning pain with pleasure—the lollipop at the dentist's, for example—may help the child to cope successfully.

7. Under tension, a great many children and an uncounted number of adults regress and revert to patterns of action that were workable in the past but are ineffective in the present. Regression does not solve problems, but it does bring relief from what would otherwise be an unbearable situation.

8. Finally, restructuring the situation into a manageable one may be the last resort. The child unwilling or unable to deal with the situation as it

is may redefine the elements of the problem—much like the student who, when he cannot answer the question asked, converts it into one that he can answer. The answer may be irrelevant, but at least it can be managed. The child unable to attain what he wishes may also restructure the situation so that he can insist that he did not want it in the first place.

Not all theorists are content with defining coping in the way that Lois Murphy and her associates do. Lazarus (1966) elevates threat and psychological stress to a central position in the psychology of man and prefers to use the term "coping" primarily to refer to strategies for dealing with what the organism views as threatening. For Murphy (1962), coping covers not only the means by which children deal with crises but also the means by which they try to master any new situation or problem. There is an overlap, of course. Many of the life crises described by Murphy fit Lazarus's specifications for threat. However, coping for Murphy involves problem solving, which includes the aim of mastery over difficulty; for Lazarus, coping is focused on just those events that threaten some important motive or value. What kind of coping process comes into play is, naturally, a function of the nature of the threat and the nature and variety of alternative responses and resources available to the threatened person.

In some as yet unknown formula, the mixture of coping defined as mastery of life and of coping defined as response to threat constitutes the child's reaction. What complicates our understanding of the coping process is the existence of what Lazarus (1966) has described as *secondary appraisal*. Somehow, between a stimulus and the response to it, a cognitive activity occurs in which the threat is evaluated, alternative responses are quickly examined, and a behavioral outcome is fashioned. Coping becomes, then, a complex event subject to all the complications of human mental and emotional life. These emotional and cognitive intervening variables form a person's

idiosyncracies and thus make each of us unique yet the same as all others. The socialized child can cope with life's problems and threats, but how he does so remains an event as intricate as any recorded for man.

The coping strategies employed by children have counterparts in the ways adults view and respond to stress. Torrance (1965) studied adults' reactions to stress in a number of extreme conditions (cold, heat, fatigue, sleeplessness, deprivation of food and water, enemy danger, and so on) and concluded that adults exhibit several characteristic patterns of response, which are also part of the child's repertoire. Among these mechanisms is what Torrance calls "risking and avoiding." Some risks must be taken in life, and it is through taking risks that both the child and the adult establish the limits of their own abilities. Some of us are high-risk-taking personalities, while others are low-risk-taking personalities. Which one each of us is reflects how the process of socialization has given us each coping preferences. Some risks in life can be avoided successfully; others must be faced squarely. A person's position on the risk taking continuum is an indicator of how successfully he can cope.

Mastering and failing is another dimension of coping with stress. Training young people to meet stress with the expectation of succeeding is vital to their continuing their attempts to adapt to difficult times during their lives. One skill for meeting some stressful situations with success is the appropriate use of aggression. According to Torrance, aggression is appropriate when it is used in self-defense, when it is directed against the real and proper enemy, when it is justifiable, and when the offense provoking it is considerable.

Finally, built into the psychological apparatus of both adults and children is the means of handling stress by unloading an overloaded system. Regression is one way of dumping a stressful overload in that, when one regresses, he abandons responsibility for the circumstances in which he finds himself. These mechanisms for unloading the system are sometimes unconscious.

The Failure of Coping Strategies

Socialization produces both adults who seem "normal" and those who find themselves unable to adapt to the stresses of society. If socialization procedures can produce extreme forms of adult adjustment, it ought to be possible to seek out problem laden adults in our culture and, through a study of their life histories, discover those experiences and child rearing practices that caused the problems. Eliminating their causes would help to eliminate the entry of more disturbed adults into society.

It has long been felt that the socialization process in the early years is crucial in determining later socially acceptable and unacceptable adjustment. Three common theories attempt to account for social maladjustment. One theory is that at a critical time in the child's life, he is exposed to some traumatic incident—an event so incapable of being psychologically assimilated and coped with that further attempts to socialize the child produce either no result or more distortion. This theory is less in vogue today than it was because single causes are rarely found for any kind of disturbance. The second view of the failure of socialization is a modified traumatic theory. This one has been particularly popular with the lay public, which tends to believe that, if not a single trauma, then certainly a piling up of blows accounts for deviant adults. The third view is that, as the child grows and is trained by those about him, he learns patterns of maladaptive response.

In order to test this third view, Schofield and Balian (1959) explored the early life histories of schizophrenic and "normal" adults in an attempt to determine whether the life histories of the two groups were distinguishable. The researchers chose a sample of 150 normal subjects and a sample of 178 schizophrenics matched for age, sex, and marital status. Comparisons were made along a wide range of dimensions thought to be relevant to adult maladjustment.

The findings of this study are startling because they suggest we should use substantial cau-

tion in assuming that the early life of the schizophrenic will reveal a warped socialization process while the early life of a normal will not. For example, the relationship between the parents of *both* schizophrenics and normals was one of affection. In fact, slightly more parents of normals were ambivalent, indifferent, or hostile toward each other. Moreover, that the mothers and fathers of schizophrenics had had a clear-cut total lack of affection for them could not be demonstrated with the life history method. And less than one-quarter of the mothers of the schizophrenics in this study were the dominating, overprotective type thought to be characteristic of mothers of schizophrenics.

Schizophrenics did report much more academic difficulty than the normals did. Although 85 percent of the normals had satisfactory or superior records of academic achievement, nearly 25 percent of the schizophrenics experienced failure or difficulty with their schoolwork. However, academic difficulty is less cause than effect because the prepsychotic personality of the schizophrenic is notably passive and thus little capable of active participation in classwork or of mustering the concentration needed for good academic habits. This passivity can be seen in the school conduct records of the two groups. Of the schizophrenics, 90 percent had records of good deportment in school, while only 50 percent of the normals did.

Startling findings also appeared when occupational success, religious belief and church attendance, dating history and marital or sexual adjustment were considered. For all of these variables, there was a sizable overlap in the life histories of schizophrenics and normals. Schofield and Balian conclude:

The data of this study seem to cast serious doubt on the etiological significance of certain early life factors for which such import has been frequently claimed. These factors may in fact play a causal role in the development of personality disturbance, but not as solitary pathogenic elements. It would appear that it is the patterning

COPING STRATEGIES

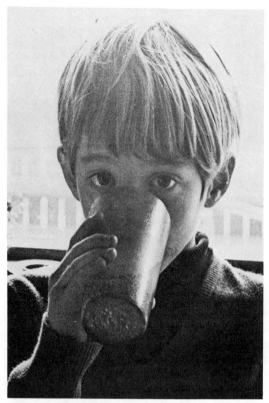

"*Other children prolonged the juice drinking period by sipping the beverage slowly as they surveyed the nature of their surroundings and calculated how to manage it.*"

"*Another common evasion that a child may use is to hide behind his parents when strangers are present and thereby control the amount of stress to which he will be subjected.*"

"*By retreating into a fantasy world, the child can thus avoid the pain of stress for a short time.*"

"*They may not be very enthusiastic about meeting certain situations (the doctor, the dentist, the stranger), but, knowing that the confrontation is inevitable, children may tolerate it reluctantly and try to comprehend the necessity for accepting it.*"

"*Practice, extra effort, and/or compulsive repetition may be used to face stress.*"

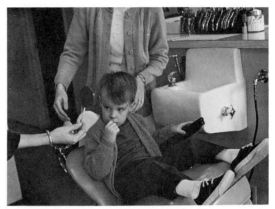

"*Cushioning pain with pleasure—the lollipop at the dentist's, for example—may help the child to cope successfully.*"

"*Under tension, a great many children and an un-counted number of adults regress and revert to patterns of action that were workable in the past but are in-effective in the present.*"

"*Finally, restructuring the situation into a manageable one may be the last resort.*"

or chaining of experience rather than occurrence or absence which must be examined.

These researchers also suggest that, if so many forms of pathogenic experience appear in the life histories of normals, more consideration should be given to the study of what keeps these events from warping the socialization of most of us.

THE GOALS OF SOCIALIZATION

Some Guidelines for Child Rearing

What should parents do in order to furnish society with more people who are acceptable to it than unacceptable? A cookbook of specific methods will probably never be accomplished; human beings are not inert substances that can be chemically altered in a predictable manner. However, some general prescriptions for child rearing have been advanced. According to the guidelines suggested by Goodenough and Tyler (1959), the first and most basic requirement is a feeling of security. The feeling of being wanted and loved should be given to every child from the beginning and should not be contingent on good behavior or performance.

A second basic factor is the opportunity for unhampered development. Goodenough and Tyler do not interpret "unhampered" as meaning total freedom from restraint; they mean that restrictions should be imposed with reason, consistency, and leeway to make mistakes and to learn from them. The freedom to explore, experiment, and discover for oneself is vital to the psychological growth of the child, as are initiative, independence, and encouragement to explore life.

Two other needs are also important. Every child must know success, and applying the general child rearing rule "Happiness first—all else follows" will help him experience success. It must not be a fantasy; the child's experience of success must have substance and produce in him a self-confidence that is realistically based. The other

"The feeling of being wanted and loved should be given to every child from the beginning and should not be contingent on good behavior or performance."

need is the freedom to shift emotional attachments from the family to members of the child's own generation. The emotional upheaval that often accompanies this natural alteration of relationships is always costly for the growing child and, in terms of the form that his personality and character will eventually take, is probably unnecessary. This stage of development should be made as natural and as painless as possible.

Even given these guidelines, the interpretation of general child rearing goals will always remain an individual affair that must be worked out day by day in the interaction of the sets of values held by the parents. Consequently, the child will be required to adjust—whether he likes it or not—to a welter of sometimes conflicting demands that other human beings will make on him. If he fails to conform, he will become an object of great distress to his parents and to other people important in his life.

Thompson (1962) reviewed the adjustments that most theorists feel are important and assembled a list of the psychological adjustments that the growing child must make. Among the adjustments required of the child is that he deny himself the privilege of immediately satisfying his needs. To be civilized, a child must learn to introduce delay between his experience of an impulse and his expression of that impulse in behavior. Another adjustment is learning how to tell the difference between socially acceptable and unacceptable goals. In at least the majority of the decisions that the child makes, society anticipates that he will choose socially acceptable goals. If he chooses too great a percentage of socially unacceptable ones, society considers him maladjusted.

Furthermore, the child must examine all the goals available to him as need satisfiers and from them choose those that are reasonably within his grasp. This does not mean that the child should never aspire to what is beyond his reach at the moment; rather, in aspiring, the child should make a realistic appraisal of his abilities, so that he does not devote the bulk of his life to attempting what he can never accomplish. A reasonable correlation between one's abilities and one's aspirations is one of the hallmarks of social adjustment. The decision to become a basketball star may be totally unrealistic for a child of small stature and poor co-ordination.

Children also need to learn to vary their behavior in response to the demands of the environment. To achieve some reasonable balance between flexibility and rigidity, every child must learn at one level or another to accept substitute goals. In turn, learning to tolerate a reasonable amount of frustration is important, for the child is bound to experience failure as well as success. Both must be put in proper perspective. Seeking to attain goals is also bound to involve a certain amount of anxiety, and part of acceptable adjustment is the ability to tolerate anxiety. Not being able to can be a crippling force in a person's life. If anxiety overwhelms a child and consequently renders him ineffective, he is apt to be immensely unhappy. Nonetheless, if he grows up without ever having experienced anxiety, there will be little to keep him producing socially acceptable behavior.

Finally, it is important that children learn how to establish warm personal relationships with a reasonable number of associates. No individual should develop such a heavy dependence on one other human being that he is incapable of functioning within a broader spectrum of his peers, seniors, and juniors. However, an individual's personality is equally distorted by a life oriented toward nothing more than a cocktail-party-conversation level of acquaintanceship with other human beings. Popularity at the expense of depth in relationship is probably as good a representative of failure as is total dependence on a single individual.

Maturity

The goal of development and socialization is the mature person. As Heath (1965) indicates, the words "mature" and "normal" should not be confused. "Normal" typifies the behavior of most people in any situation; that is, in the midst of panic, fear driven behavior may be normal if not ideal or mature. Moreover, the mature person is not always the one best adjusted psychologically to the particular society or time in which he finds himself. It may, on occasion, be more mature to disagree with the course of human affairs than to go along with it passively. For Heath, the terms "maturity" and "psychological health" are synonymous.

"Mature" and "immature" are, of course, relative terms—terms that speak of the developmental distance traveled rather than an end point reached. No one is perfectly certain what the totally mature person looks like or acts like because maturity is a process that begins but never really ends. Maturity, like the development of personality, is better described not as a structure but as "a river, for it continuously flows . . . to be a person is to be engaged in a perpetual process of becoming" (Fosdick, 1943).

Despite the complexity of the concept of maturity, which has yet to yield to the experimental and theoretical onslaughts launched to understand it (Allport, 1961; Barron, 1963; Bloom, 1964; Erikson, 1952; Heath, 1945; Jahoda, 1950; Maslow, 1950; Rogers, 1961; Saul, 1960; White, 1952), expert and nonexpert views on it seem to be in general agreement. The mature person is described as a realistic individual who has found an important underlying meaning in his life yet remains capable of absorbing new experiences and of continued growth. He may be subject to temporarily disruptive forces in his life, but his long-term adaptations to these situations are consistently more productive than the adaptations of an immature person. The mature person can manage the daily tensions of living, and, because he has a basic human warmth and compassion for his fellow man, he can adapt comfortably to others. He is self-reliant, creative, capable of tender and loving relationships, and he accepts rather than rejects himself as a person. Heath adds that the nonexperts who judge maturity flesh out this description by including that such a person has wide interests, is happily married, has close family ties, is generous, and is sensitive to others.

The degree of agreement among experts and nonexperts comes about because the descriptions of maturity are vague. Judges can agree, but we may have no idea of what they are agreeing about. If those who judge the maturity of another all share some stereotype of what the mature person ought to be, then they can easily agree about the definition of "maturity" while disagreeing violently about who is or is not mature. Perhaps, too,

"maturity" may be no more than a description of a person whose immaturities are either fewer in number, less visible to the observer, or less central to our view of what a mature person ought to be. Those of us who are members of Western culture share a set of values and ideals that corrupt our perceptions and thus make our judgments biased and parochial. Whom we find most mature may be the person we judge most worthy of our reward or acclaim. We may be incapable of making generalizations that reach very far beyond our own culture. And maturity today may not be what it was in the past or what it will be in the future.

Nonetheless, any view of maturity would claim that a growth in maturity always involves a continuous process of discarding past beliefs and

"It may, on occasion, be more mature to disagree with the course of human affairs than to go along with it passively."

substituting new ones as increased knowledge indicates that new orientations are necessary for the successful conduct of living. No one is called mature who retains the beliefs of early childhood or adolescence when he has reached middle adulthood. A kind and quality of psychological response is required for each stage of development, but truth must be faced at every age even if that truth is painful and contrary to the way one would like the world to be. The acceptance of what is real is the only path to maturity and the freedom that maturity eventually brings.

Every mature individual is finally able to accept some reasonable version of what most or many others believe to be real. Acceptance of this common reality is one measure of sanity that every society uses for evaluating its members. However, maturity does not dictate the blind acceptance of a view of reality based solely on consensus. Some of our most mature citizens have disagreed bitterly with the accepted view of things. Then the measure of maturity becomes how the individual manages the disparity between what he believes to be true and what everyone else accepts as true.

The tempering, channeling, and focusing of emotions also become hallmarks of maturity. The selection of which stimuli one responds to and which one ignores, the intensity of one's reaction, and the kind of behavior in which emotion is expressed all reflect maturity or the lack of it. These patterns of emotional response are in great part culturally determined; the capacity to understand and adapt to these cultural forms becomes a measure of maturity. Any individual who enters adulthood with an infantile pattern of emotional reactions cannot be successfully integrated into society. Maturity also calls for the capacity to

tolerate the inevitable frustrations in life and for the ability to function in the face of fear. In part, then, maturity is a form of knowing oneself—that is, of recognizing emotions and coping with them in a variety of circumstances.

Finally, learning to accept the necessity for work is evidence of maturation. Selecting goals and laboring to achieve them is a means of assessing maturity for our culture, which stresses the importance of continuous productivity. Although at each stage of life, accomplishment assumes a different guise, it always remains important to being a mature person.

SUMMARY

The basic elements of socialization are biology, motivation, and learning. The biological organism acquires its sophisticated psychological form in the interaction of the motive forces that drive the organism into active contact with the world and the learning and unlearning that he will inevitably experience. Socializing the child is a process of providing controlled learning experiences combined with identification as a mechanism for having the child become like the adult model in our society.

Our orientation toward the goals of socialization determines many of the techniques that we use for raising children. Maturity as our society defines it is a vital aspect of our efforts at socialization. However, maturity is a vague, much-sought-after end state that appears to be difficult to define even by people whom we believe possess the most of it.

Parents do not consciously raise their children for the sole purpose of promoting the future welfare of society. Nonetheless, if the child rearing practices of a society do not produce adults who fit its role systems, the society will either disintegrate or change into a different one. "The maintenance of a social system over a number of generations signifies *de facto* that the children are brought up to function in the system in much the same way as their parents did" (Baldwin, 1967, p. 550). Socialization requires the training of people to fit the roles that society needs to have filled, yet a host of individual and familial interpretations of social living must direct that training. As Baldwin (1967) observes, "By and large, people raise their children in their own fashion, with never a worry about whether there will be too big a supply of diplomats and not enough engineers" (pp. 551–552).

Socialization involves the transmission of vital information from one generation to another. The sum total of this information is the cultural accretion that lets society continue without any severe break with the immediate past. Part of this transmission is the development of values and motives in the individual that will cement the society together. Hopefully, this process is accomplished in a way so pleasurable to its victims that

Theories of
socialization

3

being what one must be and occupying a needed role fulfills the individual while it suits the demands of society. When the process is not accomplished that way, young people decide to "tune in, turn on, and drop out" and seek chemical escape from a social reality not to their taste. Nevertheless, most children somehow learn to find satisfaction in fulfilling social needs—although satisfaction was once derived only from fulfilling personal biological and psychological needs. This learning process is the core issue of socialization and is the basis from which theorists have endlessly spun their theories.

THE EARLY THEORIES

The concern with how man learns to become civilized is a relatively recent one. In the early days of that concern, the inquiry was pursued by social scientists who generally relied on armchair theorizing, self-contained insight, and limited observation. In the late nineteenth century, for example, the physiologist Preyer made unsystematic

but detailed observations of the first four years of his son's mental development. These baby diaries or biographies liberally mixed fact and inference —to the detriment of scientific reliability—but did manage to make secure the role of careful and detailed observation in any scientific study. This early beginning led to the work of G. Stanley Hall and the development of the questionnaire during the same period that Alfred Binet was fashioning the first intelligence test. Pavlov, meanwhile, experimented with conditioning techniques that provided a foundation for the behaviorism of Watson.

Although these techniques, mostly providing a descriptive analysis of childhood and of certain aspects of physical and intellectual growth, can be described as quaint when compared to more modern methodology, the crude conclusions of the early studies at least provided a procedural base for future study of the child's social and emotional development. It is important to keep in mind that the discipline we call "child psychology" is not much more than 50 years old and that few of the earlier insights remain intact today.

"Socialization involves the transmission of vital information from one generation to another."

Interestingly, these early studies evolved at the same moment that psychoanalysis was maturing. However, the interchange between their distinct trains of thought was, until about 25 years ago, minimal. Psychoanalytic theorists addressed themselves to facets of child socialization that were being totally ignored by early American theorists and used a distinct and unique technical language. Scientific communication between the two groups barely existed; indeed, each had little theoretical use for the concepts of the other. Nonetheless, as Sewell (1963) has observed, "Kurt Lewin, Henry A. Murray, John Dollard, Neal Miller, O. Hobart Mowrer, and Robert Sears . . . helped to give the psychoanalytic view academic respectability by conducting research in part guided by psychoanalytic theories and by integrating various psychoanalytic views with behavior" (p. 164).

One of the most important contributions of this restructuring to modern theory is the emphasis on the impact of both early life on later experience and early socialization on that to come later. To this base, developments in social psychology and social-learning theories added the wealth of discrete experimental findings that acted as limiting conditions on psychoanalytic as well as all other theoretical concepts.

FREUD

Freud's impact on psychology was enormous. He looked at man with uncommon sense and then constructed a theoretical framework that made sense of the seemingly incomprehensible jumble of psychological growth. Freudian theory includes an outline of the nature of personality, diagnostic tools, and a therapeutic method.

Freud's theoretical formulations have more in common with modern theories than most of us would suspect. Basically, all modern theories assume the Freudian idea that adult psychological states can be understood only if they are viewed as a pattern of personality traits that issue from the interaction of the individual's biological constitution with his environment. The debate among modern theorists is aimed at reaching a decision about just what is biologically, what psychologically, and what socially determined in the individual.

All modern theorists also agree with Freud that the whole of man is greater than the sum of his parts and that, as one aspect of man changes, the change produces alteration in other, related parts. Thus, psychological growth amounts to a restructuring process, or a reorganization of what exists into something more complex. All modern theories also include a basis for man's motivation. According to Freudian theory and most modern theories, some part of the prime mover of man is not available for conscious manipulation or inspection. Freud labeled that part of the self the *unconscious*, which is a concept important to the study of socialization.

The Unconscious

Consciousness is usually divided into three parts—the conscious, the preconscious, and the unconscious—and can be viewed as a continuum of memory, or of availability and recoverability of experience. The conscious consists of what the individual is thinking and feeling right now. The preconscious contains material that he is not focusing on at the moment but that he can dredge up when needed (home phone number, age, weight, middle name). The unconscious consists of thoughts and feelings that he cannot summon up at will, although he may be aware of them under special circumstances.

For most of us, dreams are the only regular form of contact that we have with the hidden world of our unconscious, and even they tend to be a distorted version of the real thing. Daydreaming, too, is only a pale imitation of the full intensity of the impulses that the normal person has. The nearest we come to experiencing that moment when the unconscious takes control of the conscious self is when we fall asleep. That we fall asleep without ever knowing exactly when is an excellent example of how we may be unaware when our unconscious takes over.

The existence of the human unconscious would be of little interest if it contained only innocuous material as a kind of overflow that the conscious processes simply could not manage; the unconscious might then be considered no more than a handy means of discarding unnecessary events in order to allow the efficient pursuit of daily tasks. However, even though material relegated to the unconscious is no longer accessible to conscious control and alteration, that material continues to influence the individual's total emotional and psychological life.

For Freud, the notion of *repression* explained how this material is shunted out of awareness. Repression allows thoughts, feelings, and events to be removed from awareness in order for one's view of oneself to remain neat, clean, and unblemished. If the society in which one lives and the parents who represent that society set standards and ideals for the kind of person he ought to be and have little toleration for deviation from the model, then failure to fit the model must be managed psychologically in some fashion.

A simple example might make this procedure clear. You are a young girl who hates her brother. Your brother picks on you and seems to be favored by your parents. Therefore, you consider your feelings toward him natural and justifiable. Your problem becomes acute when you are repeatedly notified in no uncertain terms that nice, decent, lovable girls do not have such horrid thoughts about others—much less express them in aggressive action. If you do not want to be an awful person and if you need the love and acceptance of grown-ups (as children regularly do), then you must rid yourself of such feelings. The feelings may not change, but they cease to be a conscious anxiety producer once they have disappeared from consciousness. The unconscious can thus become a handy receptacle for anything forbidden by the elders—on whom the child is dependent—or for anything that makes the child feel less than worthwhile as a person.

"Consciousness is usually divided into three parts—the conscious, the preconscious, and the unconscious—and can be viewed as a continuum of memory, or of availability and recoverability of experience."

The unconscious is not like a simple trap door through which all forbidden material drops into oblivion. The unconscious operates by altering the process of attention and awareness. Thus, an ancient means of escaping from painful anxiety is to engage in a ceaseless round of social activities or in total immersion in work. Looking away from unpleasant issues makes them invisible. Or the unacceptable facts can be kept in full consciousness, but the meaningful relationship between them can be obscured. Suppose, for example, that you were constantly reminded during your childhood that industriousness and hard work are prime virtues and that, as an adult, you discover that you are highly anxious when you are not engaged in productive work. Your early training and the domination of your adult life by work might both be available to consciousness, but you can dismiss the importance of the former in determining the latter and insist that you work incessantly for good and rational reasons.

It is impossible to estimate how early in life

the process of repression begins (though it probably comes with the acquisition of functional language) or the degree to which it is the handmaiden of daily life for most of us. Nonetheless, repression seems to be an important aspect of successful socialization. Theoretically, it should be possible to raise a child with total honesty and without sham, guilt, or anxiety, but whether such a child could survive in society today is also only speculation. If neurosis is the cost of civilization, then repression should be considered a necessary tool in socialization. Conflict and compromise are the lot of most of us.

Psychosexual Development

Freud views psychosexual development as a series of stages. According to Freud, the child progresses through *oral, anal,* and *phallic stages* of development. These stages blend invisibly into one another even though each of them is characterized by particular biological, social, and psychological events. Each psychosexual stage leaves its unmistakable mark on the psychological organization of the individual and affects his readiness to move comfortably through the stage to follow.

In Freudian theory, the first psychosexual stage following birth, the oral stage, is one in which socialization is begun on an organism whose primary source of gratification and pleasure is only the oral regions of the body. Feeding the child establishes initial contact with the mother, and it is in eating, swallowing, and biting that the meaning of being dependent on others and the joys of receiving are learned.

Freudian theory suggests that the primary source of the child's pleasure shifts from the mouth to the rectum during the anal psychosexual stage. During this time of toilet training, a mixture of gratification, frustration, and reward are used by the socializing agents to obtain expected behavior. These experiences of parental approval and disapproval form an important part of the psychological makeup of the growing child. At

this time, he learns the psychological meaning of possessiveness—of giving and withholding and of jealousy about loved ones and material objects—and acquires a sense of will, purpose, and autonomy. As Baldwin (1967) notes:

When the child reaches this stage, the problems of socialization change . . . He can also now do things that are destructive and irritating: He must learn not to do them. In general terms, the child must learn to be autonomous, not completely dependent, but he must also accept limits to his autonomy and must learn to obey rules and commands (pp. 361–362).

The phallic psychosexual stage precedes the achievement of full, mature, adult sexuality. This stage begins when the center of physical pleasure shifts to the genital area. Sexual intercourse comes eventually to be the arena of encounter in which the most intimate of human interpersonal relations will be experienced. As the developing child moves to that objective, he must learn how to deal with his sexual impulses and feelings and be socialized in the ways of expressing this impulse in a socially approved manner. What he learns of sex and how he reacts to the socializing forces shapes his adult personality and determines much of his social fate.

These psychosexual stages were originally conceived by Freud to be immutable, fixed, human stages of evolution and thus an inevitable part of human experience. Later theorists have rejected this theory of a fixed sequence of stages and have shifted the research emphasis to those elements of socialization and development that involve fixed biological progression in life and more social and interpersonal influences. Freud established a fairly rigid theoretical notion of the nature of man and how he is formed; others have tempered that view by adding an emphasis on the social and interpersonal influences that shape the mature adult.

Freud's view of stages of growth connected to biological and social developments in the maturing organism resembles many modern views suggesting that growth is an orderly progression. However, modern theorists have increasingly shied away from Freud's underscoring of impulse systems in the formation of the adult and have emphasized instead the role of the self, or *ego*, in individual development. This new *ego psychology* does not contradict early psychoanalytic theory but complements it and expands its usefulness. Recent theorists have modified some aspects of Freudian theory, but these changes do not violate the basic form of the original theory.

Mental Development

For Freud, as the infant grows, he moves from an irrational mode of thinking dominated by unconscious processes to an adult ability to deal with life in a conscious, rational fashion. The mental organization of the infant is dominated by what Freud (1933, 1949) designated as the *primary process*—a condition in which self and non-self are indistinguishable, cause and effect do not exist, such terms as "before" and "after" are meaningless, and desire is predominant even at the expense of protecting the self from danger or destruction. The infant is thus motivated by a set of violent and unreasoning urges, which Freud called the *id*. Logic has no place in such a scheme, and contradictory or incompatible ideas and feelings can exist together without conflict.

As the child grows and has more contact with the external environment, he experiences frustration; all his desires cannot be satisfied at once in the real world as they are in fantasy. This frustration stimulates learning how to distinguish self from non-self and reality from fantasy. At this point, a strict system of controls over the asocial behavior motivated by the id begins to develop. At first only represented by parental disapproval, these controls become internalized in the individual. Freud termed this morality principle the *superego*.

This primary process mode of thinking and problem solving gives way to *secondary process*

forms of thinking and reasoning because the child must learn how to balance the demands of the id against the pressures of the superego, formed through his interaction with the world and the people in it. The result of this learning process is the formation of the *ego*, or the reality principle, which is the conscious part of the self enabling the child to adapt rationally to internal and external stimuli in ways that promise the greatest gratification with the least risk to the integrity and well-being of the self.

However, not all children can at all times adapt to reality and handle the pressures of both the id and the superego. The child distressed by the contrast between the way things are and the way he wants them to be may resort to *defense mechanisms* in order to maintain the integrity of his personality as a system. A variety of mechanisms, such as rationalization, projection, and fantasy, are available to the child defending himself against reality, but all of them offer solace to his damaged ego at the cost of an unrealistic appraisal of the way things really are.

Ideally, for Freud, the process of socialization should ensure that the child will grow to an adult with as little distortion of the real world as possible. However, even though rational, conscious thought ought to predominate in evaluating reality and making the important decisions about how to conduct one's life, the adult is never really free of either the insistence of primary process thinking or the influence of the unconscious when he is under severe pressure from the environment.

AFTER FREUD

A host of minor researchers have tinkered with the theoretical mechanics of how man becomes human, but these men have always labored in the shadow of the giants in the field— Erik H. Erikson, Robert R. Sears, and Jean Piaget. The contributions of these three men to the theory of socialization have been analyzed by

Henry W. Maier (1965). Maier chose the theories of Erikson, Sears, and Piaget for analysis and comparison because all three deal with "personality development as a continuous and sequential process, starting with a child's status as an infant and dealing with each subsequent stage of psychological growth: early childhood, childhood, and adolescence" (p. 6).

In combination, these three theories are concerned with the basic events involved in human socialization: cognitive functioning, learned behavior, and emotional processes. Piaget pioneered in the study of cognitive thought, Erikson expanded Freud's psychoanalytic teachings into the realm of ego psychology, and Sears and his colleagues combined learning theory and empirical data to produce a modern view of socialization techniques. Although each theorist stressed a slightly different facet of the developing child, the observations of all three are needed to trace the complicated path of socialization.

Erik H. Erikson

Erikson's writings show that the psychoanalytic point of view can be modified in productive directions. Erikson extended Freud's thinking by shifting its emphasis away from his concern with the individual's management of the id to the framework of socialization in the family and in the wider social setting. This new emphasis has made classic psychoanalytic formulations more applicable to daily modern life and has opened the door to controlled experimentation that promises to shed additional light on the nature of man's development.

Freud's model of biological energy and of its transformation into psychological processes remains valid for Erikson, but he tied physical growth more closely to certain psychological events; these reflect the organism's level of biological maturation and are in part determined by it. Thus, the individual's state of bodily growth and capacity is mirrored in his psychic experience. These intertwined psychological and biological aspects of growth and development occur in a social and cultural setting that finally fashions the adult.

The child evolves via a series of biological, social, and psychological events described by Erikson as phases in which one central problem is paramount. The stages and ages of child development, then, consist of a "series of childhoods" that mold the adult personality. The early stages of growth are theoretically consistent with Freud's original notion of psychosexual stages of development, yet Erikson placed more emphasis on the essentially inseparable connection of each stage to the next one and the one before. Thus, personality development has continuity and a basic regularity often recognizable by the chronological and socio-cultural groupings characterizing a particular stage of growth. Even though personality development is regular according to this theory, it allows for considerable variation in individual personalities. The particular social institutions with which the individual comes in contact as well as his state of psychological and biological readiness at the moment some aspect of socialization is proceeding all influence the shape of his personality.

For Erikson, each child must successfully negotiate a series of developmental crises from which will issue a basic sense of the world and his personal place in it. During infancy, childhood, and adolescence, the individual should acquire a sense of basic trust, autonomy, initiative, industry, and identity. The tasks to be completed during adulthood include acquiring a sense of intimacy, generativity, and integrity. Obviously, the psychological tasks of socialization and development require a total lifetime to be completed.

Progress through Erikson's stages and phases is both continuous and cumulative in that the foundation of all of an individual's later development rests squarely on the outcome of the earlier stages. The example Maier (1965) uses is that of acquiring basic trust while overcoming basic mistrust. The helpless newborn infant must discover whether the world is a safe or an unsafe place in which to live, and his decision is undoubtedly made in response to the kind and dependability of physical care that his parents give him.

Once the child feels physically safe, his sense of trust can be extended to the whole range of new psychological experiences that will crowd in on him day by day. Mistrusting and frightened, the child faces a series of critical phases of life that he will meet only haltingly and timorously, if at all. The egocentric infant is forced into contact with harsh reality, and, within the limits of his biological functioning and of the support of his socio-cultural environment, he learns patterns of response and modes of behavior that will characterize him throughout his life.

After basic trust is established, the child can begin to acquire some autonomy. His growing biological and psychological reach can now set the stage for an expression of personal will and a movement into the environment to shape it into a desirable form. With independence can come a beginning sense of initiative, a growing awareness of the autonomy of others, and a feeling of guilt about the form that his behavior may take. The regulation of his initiative and freedom of choice is formed in great part by his contact with his parents, his peers, and other important people in his life.

As autonomy and initiative subtly merge into a sense of industry, the child learns to feel capable as a human being. Physical growth and accomplishment combine to give him a feeling of well-being, which begins to fashion a sense of personal identity. "Who and what am I?" becomes a question that must be answered during this period.

Erikson thus modified the stages posited by Freud and freed them from their reliance on biological assumptions that overwhelmed considerations of culture and personal psychological states. In Erikson's view of socialization, the influence of the culture—both consistent and contradictory—is a lively component of total development. The American culture, whether through "momism," the degree of support and independ-

"As autonomy and initiative subtly merge into a sense of industry, the child learns to feel capable as a human being."

ence given children, the "moratorium" between childhood and adulthood, the changing role of the father, the absence of long-standing tradition, or the shifting positions of family life, produces a particular and unique form of the adult—just as every other culture does. Thus, for Erikson, the psychoanalytic view of man remains relevant once it is modified with a perspective including more of the context in which man grows.[1]

Robert R. Sears

Sears's primary contribution to the study of socialization came with his urge to test psychoan-

[1] For a more full account of Erikson's work, see these writings: Erikson, 1945, 1946, 1950, 1954, 1956, 1958, 1959, 1962, 1964.

alytic theory empirically. Sears was an eclectic at a time when eclecticism was necessary if a wedding of experimental and clinical views of development and socialization was to take place. Like Erikson, Sears applied Freud's psychoanalytic concepts to child rearing. However, unlike Erikson, Sears approached this problem with a learning-theory bias unique in his day.

Sears started with measurable overt behavior in order to make explicit the learning sequences that produce learned behavior. In the simple formula of stimulus and response, Sears found the reason that parent-child interaction produces patterns of adult behavior. Given an initial drive (most often biological) and reinforcement for some patterns of response rather than for others, new, learned drives (secondary drives) come to rule human behavior.

Thus, for Sears, the biological source of human behavior is less vital than the direction in which parent-child relationships steer behavior. Dyadic interaction is an important part of learning, and the mother and child form the most important unit of social learning. An essential part of this learning is the child's initial dependence; an autonomous organism would have little need for—and would be little responsive to—the learnings relevant for a helpless one. The development and socialization of the child become, then, functions of the child rearing practices devised to channel the basic biological drives into socially acceptable patterns of behavior.

Too much or too little, too soon or too late are also important dimensions in the socialization process. Sears used all the classical (that is, Freudian) aspects of psychological and social growth (weaning, toilet training, feeding, dependence, and so forth) to show that the timing and balance of child rearing is as vital to proper growth as what is done. Thus, development was for Sears curvilinear rather than cumulative.

According to Sears, the broad patterns of behavior are established through permissiveness and its opposite. For example, he criticized punishment as a technique of socialization, for he demonstrated convincingly that punishment fails

in its purpose—the extinction of various forms of unacceptable behavior. The child responds to punishment, but that response is often a resentment of the punisher and a continued repudiation of the desired patterns of behavior.

Sears felt that some of the most fundamental learnings occur in the social management of the urge to aggression, and he conducted an important part of his research in this area. Sears's commentary on the expression of aggressive impulses is telling. ". . . as much by accident as by design" (Maier, 1965, p. 167), aggression appears as a vital aspect of the socialization process. Anger, rage, and resentment are mirrors of the socialization process and the form that it takes.

"Dyadic interaction is an important part of learning, and the mother and child form the most important unit of social learning."

By accident the infant learns to associate aggression with the lack of satisfaction of his needs. They can be gratified through aggression, and, thus, he learns a fundamental lesson of living. Consequently, learning to direct aggression into socially acceptable channels is a basic part of socialization.

Although the child learns secondary motivation systems from the "caring people" in his environment initially, his later exposure to the wider peer culture imposes complications on the early, basic learnings. Finally, the society at large differentially reinforces these systems. In this way, rudimentary behavior becomes more sophisticated with time and additional experience, and each person grows in a continuous pattern of ever expanding awareness and knowledge. Nonetheless, the basic process of learning remains the same and, according to Sears, accounts for how each generation becomes sufficiently civilized to be allowed full admittance into the society.

Jean Piaget

The Swiss theorist Piaget has devoted most of his life to studying cognitive development—how "normal" man learns about the world, its contents, and its rules. In Piaget's attempt to discover the "embryology of intelligence," he moved naturally to observation of the thought processes of childhood. As Maier (1965) has described him, "Piaget might be compared to an explorer who sets out to investigate unknown territories, but who ends up discovering a new continent" (p. 80).

For Piaget, cognitive development occurs in a consistent fashion and takes place in five distinct phases extending from childhood to adulthood. This development proceeds from simplicity to complexity; the steps from physical to social knowledge of the world begin in the pure egocentrism of the infant and culminate in the more realistic position that most adults finally come to

"In Piaget's attempt to discover the 'embryology of intelligence,' he moved naturally to observation of the thought processes of childhood."

occupy. Through sheer activity with objects, the child learns that things fit into time and space and have properties that are enduring and dependable.

From these modest beginnings issue the complicated forms of social life involving the notions of ethics, justice, conscience, and social reciprocity. The seemingly universal regularity of cognitive development—at least in Western man —provides a number of guidelines for timing the socialization of the child. According to Piaget, the growth of intelligence is more than a quantitative accretion of layer after layer of the same material; it is the acquisition of qualitatively different ways of thinking that develop at various ages and stages of growth. Thus, each new phase of growth involves the evolution of a primitive thought pattern into a more sophisticated and age-relevant means of responding.

These phases are, for Piaget, roughly divided by age and function. Between birth and about two years of age is the *sensorimotor phase*, in which the infant's physical experiences and perceptions of the real world become assembled stage by stage into a primitive but meaningful whole. The ever expanding cognitive environment of the growing child begins to combine simple reflex actions into more complex and prolonged action sequences. Becoming able to differentiate one object and experience from another and to generalize about them establishes the groundwork for later intellectual and emotional growth. With these developments comes the capacity to anticipate events, to delay reactions to them, and to experiment with the varied ways of responding in time and space. Invention is now possible, and the child is ready to enter the period of preparation for conceptual thought —the *preconceptual phase*.

Between the ages of two and about 12, the child's interaction with his social world broadens. His growing command of speech provides an essential tool for the development of an ability to assimilate the involved world of symbols, ideas, logical thinking, and values. These and a number of other intellectual tasks are achieved as a prelude to the phase of cognitive thought.

After the ground is prepared for learning about rules of conduct and reciprocity in social affairs, the youth enters the *conceptual phase* and becomes increasingly involved in reasoning "beyond his realistic world and his own beliefs" (Maier, 1965, p. 135). He is able to form intellectual hypotheses about things as they might be in addition to being able to think about things as they are. At this juncture, the human organism becomes capable of abstract thought and can immerse himself in a social life of complicated rules and regulations (Piaget, 1924, 1926, 1927, 1936, 1941).

Morality, Piaget (1932) said, is essentially a system of rules; moral behavior is respect for them. In contact with play and school groups of peers, the child learns morality. As he becomes more mature, he will (1) cease to follow rules blindly and literally just because they exist; (2) temper rule following with an understanding of the reasons supporting those rules; (3) internalize sensible rules, so that they become part of his moral code; and (4) add his knowledge of the intentions of others to his interpretation of the rightness and wrongness of their actions. These steps in learning vary from child to child in being learned well or less well and in the age at which they are accomplished.

Because of such individual differences, socialization efforts that attempt to present a child with tasks incorrectly selected and timed can only end in disappointment for the eager parent. Moreover, socialization and intelligence level are intimately related, although we can only speculate about the exact relationship between the two. Children of low intelligence must be socialized in a manner different from that used for children of superior intelligence, so that no simple formula can be furnished for the teacher or the parent. Nonetheless, Piaget's work does suggest a regularity and predictability in the development of intelligence; simplicity becomes complexity, and the child's capacity to absorb the lessons of socialization expands to meet the demands made on him.

THE SOCIAL-LEARNING THEORISTS

The *objective*, or *stimulus-response*, theory of learning began with the behavioristic movement espoused by John B. Watson at the turn of the twentieth century and has continued to make an important contribution to our understanding of child development and socialization. Behaviorism has for years been described as a "black box" experimental and theoretical system because it ignores feelings, sentiments, thoughts, and other forms of mental activity while concentrating on the visible, measurable behavior of the human organism.

Nonetheless, a number of theorists, using such tenets as classical and instrumental conditioning, habit, operant and respondent reactions, inhibition, extinction, reinforcement, discrimination, and generalization, have assembled massive evidence on the importance of the learning process in socialization and development. Clark L. Hull, B. F. Skinner, John Dollard, and Neal E. Miller are among the most important researchers in this area. Robert R. Sears, discussed earlier, must also be classified as a S-R theorist, even though his theoretical base is strongly Freudian or Neo-Freudian. Most recently, the research of Richard H. Walters and Albert Bandura has stirred renewed interest in social-learning theory.

Early social-learning theory was an attempt to apply the stimulus-response concepts to the older psychoanalytic idea of how the child learns and becomes civilized. Although this initial attempt was successful and stimulating, it drew clear lines of conflict among theorists over the value of psychoanalytic theory as a basic model for the study of the child.

Most recently, social-learning researchers have emphasized the learning of social responses in the adult-child interchange. Beginning with an exploration of the early, dependent relationship between mother and child, these theorists have tried to delineate the mechanisms that can account for not only dependence but also its opposite, independence, and for related systems of behavior—that is, aggression, conscience, and self-control. Some of these mechanisms are differential reinforcement, shaping, imitation, and identification. The form, pattern, and sequence of the parent's responses to the child are an additional and complex aspect of the total child-parent learning experience. Models of social

learning can account for parts of this process, but a complete explanation has not yet been achieved. As Baldwin (1967) says, social-learning theory is a "theory in the making" (p. 471) in which alternative explanations of observed events are still very much alive and in competition. This theory is one that "leads to empirical studies which modify without destroying it" (p. 473).

Social-learning theory has brought an objective and experimental viewpoint to the study of socialization. This approach shows great promise but is not free of deserved criticisms. These theorists' very conscientiousness and strict adherence to the scientific method has perhaps made them excessively and sometimes blindly critical

"There is certainly more to child rearing and socialization than the limited facets that can be reproduced in the laboratory."

of other methods and theories for the study of developing man even before their own progress has reached a state of full coherence and acceptability. Rigor is to be valued if it does not become the rigidity of a closed mind.

Another, related criticism of social-learning theory should be mentioned, although others could be detailed at some length. So experimental in form, social-learning theory has neglected the historical and observational studies on which so much of present-day knowledge is based. A laboratory demonstration that, given a certain controlled environment and a managed set of stimuli, aggressive or conscience-laden responses can be produced is not the same as the discovery and description of the complex conditions in the natural setting of the home that produce a similar set of responses in the average or not-so-average child. There is certainly more to child rearing and socialization than the limited facets that can be reproduced in the laboratory. The evidence that hypothesized events in a child's experience match up to what really happens seems to be a next vital achievement for social-learning theory.

ALFRED L. BALDWIN—A CONCLUSION

In Baldwin's (1967) comparative analysis of six theories of child development, he points out that there are few issues on which any two theories confront each other directly. Each of the theories is more concerned with nonoverlapping aspects of child behavior than with competing explanations of the same aspect. There seems to be little reason that these theories could not be assembled into a single theory of the developing child. The first step toward assembling that theory would have to be the establishment of some common, neutral language. Until all these theorists can agree about the meaning of the words that they use, they will never know whether they are all talking about the same events.

Once such a language is established, combining the various theories into a single one seems possible, for all modern theorists agree on certain basic elements in the socialization process. One of these elements is that human functioning regularly occurs at a multitude of levels in the personality. For example, certain cognitive processes seem routinely to dominate and often seem to control the sensorimotor levels of human functioning. This complex kind of learned, voluntary functioning tends to become characteristic of the adult even though he begins life in a primitive, noncognitive state.

Most modern theorists also agree on the importance of emotion and motivation in the developing human being. Any theory of the developing child must acknowledge powerfully felt motives, impulsiveness, emotion, and little civilized control over behavior. Because the child learns socially acceptable patterns of behavior in a variety of ways, the notions of stimulus and response, reinforcement and pleasure, drives, tension, deprivation, frustration, and satiation are all relevant to a final common theory.

Baldwin (1967) indicates that the basic and much-proven theories of conditioning must be part of any all-encompassing theory of child development and socialization. A well-established process in human learning, conditioning deserves greater recognition in modern theories. Nonetheless, some theorizing is necessary on how man acquires new behavior patterns that have no precedent in human experience. Imitation, identification, stimulus and response, and related theories still seem inadequate to account for this miracle of humans learning. We know it happens, but we cannot fully explain how.

Finally, the concept of maturation remains central to any view of socialization; certain growth events are clearly tied to an internal scheme of development that can be influenced by (but is not dependent upon) external events. Because each stage in the process of maturing does happen at a particular chronological age, maturation remains a vital but mysterious aspect of the total puzzle of development and socialization.

Baldwin feels that we should assemble what we have in order to move forward in the areas in which we have little. Without such a consolidation, the study of child development and socialization could well remain confused and lacking in needed self-discipline. Nonetheless, even given these problems, Baldwin remains convinced that we have traveled a great distance toward understanding human development and socialization if only we can decipher the code that tells us exactly how far we have come. He observes:

In retrospect, the theories do not turn out badly. In many ways they support each other, and, in total, suggest a kind of prototheory of child development which, although obviously incomplete, badly defined, and surely wrong in some respects, is a feasible and workable basis for further research and for more refined theory building (p. 599).

Perhaps this is all we can ask of theories on child development and socialization—that they reflect progress and offer hope for more.

SUMMARY

Important theories of socialization are primarily based on the efforts of Freud, Erikson, Sears, and Piaget. Although each of the four addressed his theorizing to different but related aspects of socialization and growth, these men provided the broad guidelines followed by research today.

Freud's description of the unconscious and its effect on human thought and decision making and his emphasis on the importance of socialization in the early, formative years have been particularly valuable contributions to theory.

Erikson broadened psychoanalytic theory. By abandoning its reliance on biologically determined motives in man, he placed psychoanalytic theory more squarely in the mainstream of family, social, and cultural life and its influences. Erikson's outline of the phases and stages of life and the lessons learned during each one inserts the culture and its pressures into the process of socialization.

Sears applied modified psychoanalytic insight to learning in the family setting and tried to test the limits of his theory empirically. According to Sears, socialization takes place in the parent-child relationship, in the coping with the tasks of weaning, toilet training, feeding, and learning independence, and in the use of punishment and reward to manage sexual and aggressive urges.

Piaget studied the way in which the child learns about the world and the people in it (his cognitions) and the way in which he learns the rules of moral living. Piaget, too, saw child growth as proceeding through an organized sequence of stages divided roughly by age. From the child literally following rules as though they were dicta from on high to the adult who abides by rules because he understands the reasons for their existence is essentially a description of effective parental and peer group socialization.

The social-learning theorists, who take an objective, behavioristic, and experimental approach to the study of the child, have emphasized the social environment in which the child grows and learns. They view the socialization transaction between mother and child as basically a stimulus and response process of learning. These theorists have probed the various mechanisms by which learning occurs and have demonstrated models of such learning in the laboratory. Social-learning theory has added a necessary rigor and reproducibility to the study of socialization.

As Baldwin has noted, although the various theories of socialization do not always deal with the same issues, the degree of agreement between the theories is a substantial and promising one.

The purpose of examining the process of socialization is to be able to make generalizations about why human beings behave the way they do. In order to make those generalizations, the social scientist must study cause and effect in human behavior (Grünbaum, 1952). In looking for these causal, or functional, relationships (or their absence), the social scientist manipulates one set of events in order to study the effect of the manipulation on a second set. If he does not find a measurable and predictable causal relationship between events, he cannot formulate laws of behavior. And even if he does identify what he considers a significant relationship, the conclusion that he draws from his experiment cannot be considered reliable until other researchers, following his directions and performing the same experiment, verify the results. Thus, in performing and describing an experiment, the social scientist must make careful use of the *social scientific method*.

THE SOCIAL SCIENTIFIC METHOD

The social scientific method is the key to the accumulation of knowledge about human behav-

The social scientific method and the study of socialization

ior. This method consists of at least six steps (Marquis, 1948).

1. Formulating the Problem

No one can view the developing child dispassionately without wondering why his development occurs in the way it does. However, the social scientist's asking of a question differs from the lay person's wondering in the scientist's way of formulating his question and in his subsequent establishment of the conditions necessary for a controlled examination of the question. A scientific question must be formulated in precise, researchable terms; no scientific investigation could answer a question posed in the general and undefinable terms of popular language.

2. Reviewing the State of Existing Knowledge

The researcher intent on answering a question must examine the scientific labors preceding his own endeavor; it is unusual to encounter an aspect of child development that has not been touched on by some scientist. Leads uncovered in the past may indicate that the question will be productive or that it should be modified.

3. Making Preliminary Observations

A good scientist must be something of a hoarder of facts, observations, descriptions, and insights. Using this collection of odds and ends gathered by reviewing what is already known about the question that he is asking, the scientist begins to probe about, collect his observations, and organize some tentative notions about the meaning of what he has observed. This process frequently consists of a *pilot study*, in which the scientist uses crude and approximate methods for

testing a small population of subjects in order to determine whether these first observations and formulations make enough sense to warrant further investigation.

Preliminary observations amount to a rough first test of ideas that have just begun to jell. For example, the test may suggest that the ideas have merit but that the actual research situation is much more complex than its original conception led the researcher to believe. For such reasons, those first ideas are usually greatly modified by the time the final research plan is put into action.

4. Constructing a Hypothesis or a Theory

After the researcher has formulated the problem to be studied, has reviewed all that is known or has been thought about it, and has made his preliminary observations, he is ready to make a hypothesis, which is actually no more than an educated, scientific guess about the relationship of one thing to another. When the researcher assembles a *series* of related hypotheses into a coherent and far-reaching *system* of hypotheses, he has a theory. Such a system, taken as a whole, suggests a general law that has an application reaching beyond the original hypotheses. Thus, you may have a hypothesis about why an apple falls down rather than up; when you generalize this formulation and come up with the notion of gravitation, you have a theory. What remains is the verification of the original hypothesis or theory through experimentation.

5. Verifying the Hypothesis or the Theory

In order to verify a hypothesis or a theory, the researcher must test it with techniques approved of by other social scientists. Under the current rules of science, he cannot rely on magic, on the authority of past researchers' conclusions,

THE SOCIAL SCIENTIFIC METHOD

Step 1: Formulating the Problem

Step 2: Reviewing the State of Existing Knowledge

Step 3: Making Preliminary Observations

Step 4: Constructing a Hypothesis or a Theory

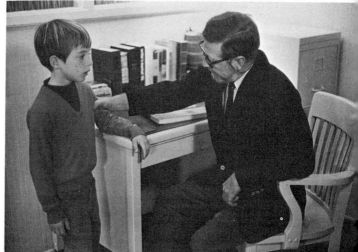

Step 5: Verifying the Hypothesis or the Theory

Step 6: Translating the Verified Hypothesis or Theory into Action

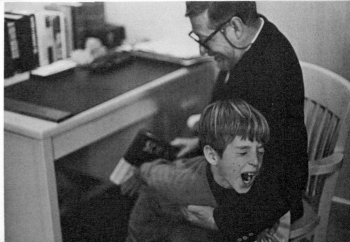

or on logic alone. Rather, he must conduct controlled experiments in which there is some assurance that the question asked will be answered in a trustworthy and repeatable fashion.

The approved technique must also be appropriate to the experiment. The selection of the technique appropriate for a particular research approach depends, in part, on the nature of the investigation being conducted, on the population of subjects available, and on the kind of answer being sought. For instance, the researcher studying socialization may choose the controlled observation method appropriate for his experiment. There are at least two kinds of controlled observation. He might decide to control the child's environment and observe its effect on the child's total behavior, or the researcher might select only certain elements of the child's behavior to observe. Depending on the experiment, the researcher might decide to use a combination of these two methods.

Any choice of a technique is not easy; the current approaches and techniques for the scientific study of socialization are jumbled together and hard to separate into clearly defined categories. Any one of a number of techniques may be either appropriate for or required by a particular approach, and a single technique may be useful for a number of approaches. Part of the reason for this confusion is that data on human beings can always be studied and interpreted in more than one way; so much of it is unobservable and thus known only through inference. Even sophisticated statistical association methods cannot eliminate this aspect of social science, so that many "verified" hypotheses and theories will remain only close approximations of ever elusive psychological truths.

6. Translating the Verified Hypothesis or Theory into Action

This final step is a controversial one. The behavioral scientist intent on maintaining his image of his own integrity claims that the application of his findings is of no concern to him. He insists that he has pursued truth for its own sake and that its application is a corruption of the meaning and intent of true science. This view is the philosophy of the amorality of science, or ethical positivism. Furthermore, some scientists argue that if they were to assume responsibility for what man does with truth, they would be inviting political control of science as a means of regulating its application. Other scientists feel that the findings of pure science are valueless if they are not used for the betterment of man. The issue is a complex one for which as many solutions have been proposed as there are epochs in man's history.

USING THE SOCIAL SCIENTIFIC METHOD

Following one research project through each of the steps Marquis lists as necessary for the scientific study of man would make the application of the experimental method clearer. The project used here is a team research by Walters, Parke, and Cane (1965). This one was chosen because it deals with an important issue in socialization—methods and timing of punishment.

Step 1: Formulating the Problem

Walters, Parke, and Cane were concerned that, despite all the theoretical discussion of the role of punishment in socialization, few successful laboratory studies of punishment had been conducted. These researchers wondered whether teaching a child to inhibit certain kinds of behavior might not be a function of the timing of the punishment—that is, whether the child is punished as he *begins* the forbidden response sequence or *after* he completes it.

Step 2: *Reviewing the State of Existing Knowledge*

Walters, Parke, and Cane did a particularly careful job of reviewing the relevant literature. The theoretical discussions of Church (1963) and Solomon (1964) suggested that punishment might be more effective than most psychologists believe it is and that a simple "yes" or "no" answer to this issue must take into account many complex aspects of giving and receiving punishment (Aronfreed, 1964; Bandura and Walters, 1963; Martin, 1963; Solomon, 1964; Walters and Demkow, 1963). Walters, Parke, and Cane found that the broad theory of timing is based on the attachment of a particular fear response to a particular set of stimuli. Punishment after the act, these researchers theorized, attaches fear to responses that are occurring at that moment; for example, punishing a criminal while he is spending stolen money would attach a fear response to the spending rather than the stealing. Thus, it would seem, the earlier a child is punished for committing a deviant act, the greater will be the association of fear with that act and, consequently, the greater the inhibition of it.

After the researchers explored the literature on the consequences of observing punishment administered to others for a deviant act (Bandura, 1965; Walters and Demkow, 1963; Walters and Parke, 1964), they concluded that a child can learn to inhibit his own deviant behavior simply by watching someone else being punished for similar behavior. By the same token, reward for a prohibited act might signal permission to violate rules that would otherwise be observed. Thus, for instance, a child taught not to aggress against others might well change his behavior if he sees others acting in the prohibited way and being rewarded for it.

Step 3: *Making Preliminary Observations*

Walters, Parke, and Cane's preliminary observations were made over a number of years. Each successive experiment provided observations that triggered new views of the problem and stimulated new patterns of research. Thus, each experiment was a kind of pilot study for the next research task. Had this research project been the first exploration of the problem rather than an expansion of their own and others' efforts, it would have been sensible for the research team to spend time observing natural situations in which the timing of punishment varied and in which the opportunity for children to observe others violating rules would be frequent enough to give cues to the children's typical responses.

Step 4: *Constructing a Hypothesis or a Theory*

The researchers' review of previous work and their preliminary experiments led them to formulate these hypotheses: (1) The earlier the punishment for a deviant act, the greater the inhibition learned for future temptations to deviant behavior, and (2) a child who has observed a model punished for committing deviant acts will resist similar deviation on his own part. The converse of the second hypothesis was also thought to be true: A child will engage in greater deviation after he observes another child either not punished or rewarded for a prohibited act. Of course, the second hypothesis and its converse are based on the assumption that children are capable of learning simply by watching others. This assumption necessarily constituted a third hypothesis tested in the final experiment.

Step 5: *Verifying the Hypothesis or the Theory*

In order to test these hypotheses, Walters, Parke, and Cane designed an experiment with 80 first grade and kindergarten boys as subjects. In the part of the experiment involving early and late punishment, the child was allowed to express interest in an attractive toy—only to be told that it belonged to another boy. This punishment (denial of access to the preferred toy) was accomplished verbally and done quickly in the early-punishment condition only after the child had picked up and handled the toy. In the part of the experiment dealing with a child's inhibition of deviant behavior through seeing others punished for that behavior, the researchers showed children a series of films in which reward, punishment, or no consequences at all followed for a child who played with prohibited toys.

After both kinds of training sessions, the child was left alone with the attractive toy for 15 minutes as a test of his ability to resist engaging in the forbidden act. An observer hidden by a one-way screen measured the child's behavior during that period. The measures used included the length of time before he broke the prohibition, how many times he engaged in this deviation, and how long he indulged in it.

From the results of the experiment, the research team concluded that early punishment does indeed produce more resistance to deviation than delayed punishment does. Children who were exposed to early-punishment training in the experiment and who watched a film in which a model was punished were most inhibited about committing deviant acts. This successful experiment paved the way for an even more detailed exploration of the exact conditions under which these events occur.

Step 6: Translating the Verified Hypothesis or Theory into Action

Walters, Parke, and Cane surely feel that their findings would be valuable to parents trying to discover correct and effective socialization methods—even though this experiment dealt with only a limited aspect of the total process of socialization. Indeed, these researchers' findings do not even encompass the entire realm of interpersonal relations implied in punishment and reward. Di-

mensions such as the "sequencing and scheduling of rewarding and punishing events, the strength and nature of the punished response, the relative status of the agent and the recipient of punishment" (p. 10) all have yet to be explored for a full understanding of this complicated human exchange.

THE PROBLEM OF BEING "SCIENTIFIC"

The classic meaning of being "scientific" has always implied an objective, emotionless state that assures clear vision and bold confrontation with the truth. Attaining that state is probably relatively simple for the physical or natural scientist. The chemist who devotes his life to the study of one class of chemicals rather than another may do so for a variety of reasons, but not one of them would involve emotionally valuing that class of chemicals over another. Being "scientific" is harder for the social scientist to achieve; most of human behavior is not emotionally neutral. The social scientist must always be aware that his particular set of values may determine which problem he selects for study in the first place. These values may make it difficult for him to separate belief from fact in the conduct of his research.

Furthermore, as Lowe (1959) notes, the psychologist is increasingly called upon to leave his laboratory and move into the world of practical service to mankind. And, when he leaves the laboratory, he must leave behind the physical or natural scientist's immunity from life contacts with others and from interpersonal values. As a scientist in the search for truth, the social scientist has one set of prerogatives; as a practitioner, he must be concerned less with what *is* than with what *should* be.

It is this encounter with real life that poses ethical issues for the psychologist. The industrial, educational, or clinical psychologist works for others and, as a consequence, must compromise some of his values. Moreover, his own values may influence those of other people. For example, every choice of a therapist involves an implicit acceptance of some set of values (Williamson, 1958), and patients who improve through therapy seem to revise their values to resemble more closely those of the therapist (Rosenthal, 1955). The psychologist's responsibility is thus an awesome one in a complex society that has no single, simple set of values but rather a multiplicity of competing sets.

SUMMARY

It is the hope of the modern social scientist that experimental methods will furnish more reliable guidelines for the socialization of future generations of children even though the study of child socialization will continue to consist of overlapping approaches and techniques. However, the social scientific method does provide a framework for that study. The social scientific method consists of these six steps: formulating the problem, reviewing the state of existing knowledge, making preliminary observations, constructing a hypothesis or a theory, verifying the hypothesis or the theory, and translating the verified hypothesis or theory into action.

Carefully controlled scientific observation remains the cornerstone of social science. The perfecting of computers has permitted substantial advances in statistical studies of the association between various classes and elements of observation. Nonetheless, even these methods do not eliminate the special experimental problems of applying the methods of the natural and physical sciences to human beings who have values and who can modify their behavior to suit environmental circumstances as well as the ethical problems of the social psychologist in professional contact with others.

Part two

The agents
of early
socialization

The family begins with pregnancy and birth. The purpose of the family as a social institution in all societies, whether simple or complex, is to perpetuate the society by providing it with new members, to protect the child until he is able to take care of himself, to train him in socially acceptable behavior, and to care for the aged. Although every family serves these basic societal functions, the functions of the individuals within the family and the structure of the familial relationships can vary widely from culture to culture and even within the same culture (Kluckhohn, 1960).

PATTERNS OF THE FAMILY

The Family in Primitive Societies

In primitive societies, the individual's primary function is to contribute to the physical and economic well-being of the community. In accordance with this scheme, the structure of the family in a particular society is the one that best serves the economic activities of that society. Thus, in many primitive societies, a child is valued as a future contributor to the society's welfare, and

5

Socialization in the family

special emphasis is placed on fertility in such societies. In some cases, a woman's proven fertility determines her acceptability as a marriage partner; in other cases, a barren wife can be returned to her parents as a defective product (Bossard and Boll, 1966).

This view of the child as a utilitarian organism dictates, of course, the nature of his socialization. The child in the primitive society has few complex social and psychological nuances to learn; he is trained only to fill the role of producer, which he will assume very early in his short life (Bossard and Boll, 1966). The temporary economic liability that the child represents during this training period is considered likely to be repaid many times over during his productive years.

The Family in America

In some ways, the structure of the family in Colonial America resembled that in primitive societies. The ordinary American family at that time was primarily concerned with sheer physical survival and, beyond that, its own economic prosperity. Thus, the child was valued in terms of his productivity, and he assumed the role of producer quite early. Until he fulfilled this role, his position in the structure of the family was one of subordination, and his psychological needs and capacities received little consideration.

As American society became more complex, the status of the child in the family and in the society became more important. In the complex, technological society that America has become, each member must fulfill a number of personal and occupational roles and be in constant contact with a great many other members. Consequently, viewing the child as a potentially acceptable and necessarily multifaceted member of society means that he is regarded more as a person in his own right than as a utilitarian organism. This acceptance of the child as an equal participant in the contemporary American family is reflected in the variety of statutes protecting the child's rights and

in the social and public welfare programs devoted exclusively to his well-being.

This new view of the child and the increasing contact between the members of society has also resulted in a surge of interest in child rearing techniques. People today spend a considerable portion of their time conferring on the proper way to bring up children. It is now possible to influence the details of the socialization of another person's child by spreading the gospel of current and fashionable theories and methods of child rearing.

The socialization of the contemporary American child is a two-way transaction between parent and child rather than a one-way, parent-to-child training program. As a consequence, socializing the child and living with him over a long period of time is for the parent a mixture of pleasure, satisfaction, and problems. The parent can find satisfaction and joy in just having a child of his own, in the child's companionship, personality, and intellectual characteristics, and in watching him progress satisfactorily through various school and social relationships. But the parent is also confronted with many problems: the demands of routine child care, the child's relationships with his siblings and other relatives, and—not unexpectedly—the features of personality, school, and social relationships that go in directions not to the parent's liking. The father and mother do not always receive the same amount of pleasure or concern from a particular aspect of rearing their child; each views him with a different set of anticipations, and each has a different role in caring for him (Tasch, 1955).

Parent-Child Relationships

Even though the child in the modern American family is generally regarded as a person in his own right with his own needs and capacities, the degree to which he is so regarded—and, thus, the structure of the relationship between parent and child—can vary considerably from family to family. That structure may range from *autocratic control* over the child in some families to *democratic interaction* among all members in other families (Radke, 1946; Baldwin, Kalhorn, and Breese, 1945).

Subpatterns also occur at various points along this range. For example, democratic families may be divided into these categories: (1) pseudo-democratic families, in which the child is allowed to participate in only those decisions that are not truly important; (2) scientifically democratic families, which rigorously but impersonally adhere to the principles of democracy; and (3) warmly democratic families, which practice democracy out of concern for the child and with warmth and affection.

Other dimensions in the always complex relationship between parent and child add a number of further possible variations in family patterns. For example, two families might be equally democratic but may exhibit different degrees of acceptance (rapport with the child, affection toward him, child centeredness of home) or of indulgence (general protectiveness, babying, solicitude for the child's welfare, intensity of contact with mother). Naturally, pigeonholing a phenomenon as complex as any individual family is not always possible. Thus, some families can only be described as casually indulgent or casually autocratic.

Whatever the structure of the relationship between parent and child in a particular family, the kind of structure determines the socialization techniques and, consequently, the shaping of the child's personality (Clausen, 1966). For example, the child raised in a democratic home—where the reasons for the decisions regulating his behavior are explained to him—is an active, outgoing, competitive, and open-minded individual. Such children become leaders—even though they do not always lead in the direction that society cherishes most. On the other hand, the child raised in an authoritarian family that imposes clear and arbitrary restrictions on his behavior is more obedient, conforming, dependent on others, and less likely

"It is now possible to influence the details of the socialization of another person's child by spreading the gospel of current and fashionable theories and methods of child rearing."

to become a leader (Baldwin, Kalhorn, and Breese, 1945).

Other dimensions of family pattern besides the authoritarian-democratic one can, of course, influence socialization methods and, consequently, the child's personality. A pattern of indulgence and overprotection in the parent-child relationship can be particularly disastrous for the child. An overprotective mother in a democratic, loving family can be so attached to her child that she fails to make those socialization efforts that produce independent children. Probably the single most important accomplishment during these years is becoming independent. Forbidding the

"Probably the single most important accomplishment during these years is becoming independent."

child to explore his ever expanding world, treating him as though he will never grow up, and watch-dogging his every move will make him a perpetual infant. The child who has been treated in this way is often a social misfit. He is demanding, manipulative, tyrannical, impossible in peer relations, and disobedient to his mother, who, of course, feels compelled to indulge his every whim. The same kind of overprotection in an autocratic family produces a child who is shy, inhibited, withdrawn, fearful, and unable to establish gratifying relationships with his peers.

Family Composition

The relationship between parent and child is not the only factor influencing the pattern of the family. Most American families include other siblings and at least a few relatives, who are more or less on the periphery of the nuclear family. The number of siblings, their ages and birth order, and the possible influence of the relatives all help determine the pattern of the family, its socialization practices, and, consequently, the personalities of the children involved. For example, in large families, the simple mechanics of managing several children of different ages dictates authoritarianism (Elder and Bowerman, 1963). Such families place a high value on internal organization and its concomitants of cooperation, conformity, and division of labor (Bossard and Boll, 1966).

However, carrying out the details of socialization in these families may be less structured than in families with only one or two children. The parents can spend only a limited amount of time with each child, and, therefore, many of those details are given over through default to the older siblings. A child reared by siblings must become a different kind of adult from the child reared in the sole company of adults or in a setting in which there is one sibling quite a bit younger or older. For the child in a large family, "an older sibling may be caretaker, teacher, pacesetter, or confidant" (Clausen, 1966, p. 19). An older sibling will clearly be a less mature model than the parents whose role he has displaced. Moreover, the self-concept of the younger child may be determined in important ways by the reflected appraisals that he receives from the older sibling rather than from his parents (Sampson, 1965).

The Human Variable

A final complicating factor in patterns of the family is the human variable, which assures that no two families will ever be exactly alike and, indeed, that no one family will ever be rigidly patterned in the same way throughout its existence—or possibly even over the space of a year or two. Every parent is an individual who brings something special and unique to his marriage; the personality of each parent, the compromises achieved in the marriage, the final set of values shared, and the dynamics of the timing of the children's births all help shape the pattern of the family and at the same time keep it more or less fluid.

This human variable affects, of course, the process of socialization. Parents are human beings who satisfy and control children with the long-range goal of making them acceptable to the rest of society. However, human beings tire of the task, have their own needs that demand gratification, and sometimes act on impulse in what would clearly be a highly inconsistent fashion in the view of a child rearing "expert."

Complicating the humanness of the parent is the humanness of the child. If every child were a simple machine capable only of responding to parental admonishment, every parent could more easily become an expert in child rearing. As it is, however, the child's primary goal is doing what he wants to do when he wants to do it, and efforts to socialize him are always an interference in his ongoing activity. He resists these efforts to the degree that he is able, and, thus, conflict between the parent and the child begins. Then "a shift in parentmanship is countered by a shift in childmanship" (Loevinger, 1959, p. 149), and the struggle continues.

Nonetheless, every child learns in the family, whether through insight, identification, or reinforcement, the beginnings of a more or less successful adjustment to society. The pattern of the child's family and the complexities of the relationship between him and his parents influence the way in which he learns. Although it is doubtful whether any parent always uses the same method for teaching his child, all parents interact with their child with some idea of the correspondence between their own action and the child's response.

Thus, the parents in an autocratic family regulate the child's behavior through a rigid system of punishment and reward. Such parents, subscribing perhaps unconsciously to the theory of learning as reinforcement, assume that the child will continue to be bad if no pain is attached to forbidden acts and no reward to desirable ones. Indulgent parents who gratify their child's every whim may believe that the happy child one day gains through insight an understanding of the importance of rules and regulations. Other, permissive parents probably count on the process of identification to make the child learn how to be like them in values, attitudes, and behavior (Loevinger, 1959). Regardless of the method used, however, the parents are fulfilling one of the functions of the family—teaching the child socialized behavior.

LEARNING IN THE FAMILY

The family's role in socializing the child involves teaching him about the real world, about the behavior expected of him in it, about who and what he is, and about what other people are like. Learning about these things on a reasonably sophisticated level requires language; thus, socialization is, during most of childhood—and, indeed, beyond it—a matter of words. The essence of human development is perhaps man's command of the symbol and the spoken word. Without language, the human being is little different from his animal cousins and can communicate and respond only in a primitive, animal way. Consequently, one of the most important roles of the family is to teach the child language.

Learning Language

The attempt to account for the efficiency with which children the world over learn complicated grammatical and linguistic structures has led to many theories of language development. Some theorists think that language learning may have a biological base peculiar to human beings (McNeill, 1966). A more common explanation is the process of imitation (Brown and Bellugi, 1964). Regardless of the explanation, however, any child with the necessary intellectual and neural equipment can learn how to speak. In order to learn language, the child must be able to make cognitive judgments about the world around him, to tell one speech sound from another, to reproduce these sounds, and to comprehend their meaning in relation to himself.

Environmental influences are also important in the development of language. For example, the kind of adult speech to which young children are exposed affects the speed of acquisition of language and of grammatical structure. An experiment conducted by Cazden (Ervin-Tripp, 1966) compared experimental and control groups of Negro children aged 28 to 38 months. These children were exposed to two and one-half hours of treatment a week in which adults responded to them in full and grammatically correct sentences. This rich verbal stimulation produced the predicted improvement in the experimental groups. Training of this sort lets some children enter the world of language sooner and better equipped than others. Operant conditioning of language has also been attempted by some researchers (Rheingold, Gewirtz, and Ross, 1959).

When speech first appears, it is no more than a new device for extending the pattern of behavior that characterized much of the child's earlier life.

However, as he grows older, he is exposed to a rapid succession of learnings; "He learns about bad men and ghosts and rockets and magic and football and religion and war and surgery and wild animals (some gentle and some fierce)" (Church, 1961, p. 97). In order to talk about all these things—or even understand them—the child needs language. Thus, when he learns it, he learns a system of responses for both communicating with others (*inter-individual communication*) and facilitating his own thought and action (*intra-individual communication*) (Carroll, 1964).

With the acquisition of speech, the child's ability to learn cognitive skills becomes organized, and his active interaction with the adults in his environment is made possible (Luria, 1961). In this process, the child develops what can be called a *verbal self*, with which he discovers and denotes himself with descriptive words in his search for his identity. An important part of this self-image is furnished by the verbal feedback that he receives from those who approve and those who disapprove of his actions, thoughts, and feelings. In accordance with this development, the parents abandon physical punishment for deviant behavior and substitute the psychological pain of criticism.

By this stage in the child's development, language has become both the primary means by which parents socialize the child and the primary means by which the child responds in the advancing parent-child and peer-child dialogue. As the percentage of childhood egocentric speech decreases and the frequency of socialized speech increases, there is a parallel alteration in the kind of socialization efforts exerted by the parents. Age and increased language capacity signal an onset of new and greater demands for socialized behavior on the part of the child. As Watson (1965) reports, there is probably a cause and effect relationship between these two developments; "it is plausible to believe that the change from egocentric to sociocentric speech partly stems from rewards for such speech from persons in the child's environment whereas egocentric speech is simultaneously discouraged. The socially oriented verbalizations that the child learns bring with them rewards" (p. 326). In turn, this shift in speech patterns aids the socialization process:

. . . When the child can understand instructions, when he can ask and answer questions, when he can defend a course of action, when he can tell what he is doing, then he is in a position to profit expeditiously from the socialization efforts of those around him. Every parent knows how much more facility there is in controlling a child's behavior when his understanding of spoken language improves (Watson, 1965, p. 326).

The course of socialization will vary on an individual basis simply because of the normal range of silent to verbose children and the frequent differences in the age of the onset of clear verbalization and in the speed of comprehension of the spoken word. These individual differences serve as the upper and lower limits of the use of language in socialization and determine the timing of attempts to regulate various aspects of the child's behavior.

After the child has acquired basic learnings (perception, cognition, motor skills, and so forth)

and rudimentary language skills, the parents can begin to fulfill another function of the family in socializing the child—teaching him *role behavior*. In doing so, the parents are equipping him with a structural base for social interaction.

Learning Role Behavior

Learning role behavior includes acquiring "an understanding of the society's status structure and of the role prescriptions and behavior associated with the different positions in this structure" (Brim, 1966, p. 5). Although there is much conceptual and terminological disagreement about the exact meaning of "role" (Bell, 1961; Fichter, 1957; Johnson, 1960; Krech, Crutchfield, and Ballachy, 1963), it can be said that the concept of role is complementary to the concept of *status*. "Status" refers to one's social position and the rights and obligations that accompany it. "Role" places more emphasis on the holder of the status and how he behaves in terms of the expectations that go along with that status. Thus, role behavior

"The essence of human development is perhaps man's command of the symbol and the spoken word."

UNTIL THE ARRIVAL OF TROOPS FROM AMERICA

can be viewed as both expected behavior and actual behavior (Dewey and Humber, 1966). The expectation of the behavior for a particular role may be either explicit or implicit.

Roles and appropriate behavior are learned in interaction with other people who reward or punish the learner. The child is forced to anticipate how other important human beings will react to his behavior in order to fashion a guide to the behavior that he can make public and visible to them. Good and bad behavior evoke positive or negative responses in others. By play-acting a variety of roles, the child sorts through those most fitting to his basic temperament and abilities and finds one (or many) that suits him well and promises him the reward and approval of others. In these actions (*role rehearsal*), the child learns the limits of what he can and should do to merit acceptance by those vital to his emotional well-being. When these do's and don'ts are practiced in play, they constitute an exercise in a safe environment—an exercise free of the criticism that accompanies "playing for real."

Role playing in the early years is only a crude approximation of the finesse and polish that will be demanded of the child as he matures. In fact, some of the most charming parental anecdotes issue from observing the child who acts out in play adult forms of behavior and seems to know "the words but not the music" of life. The child can only guess at real life, and if his guesses are amusing, it is because he is too literal and simplistic in his conviction of how it really is.

An important aspect of learning about real life and its accompanying roles is the learning of *sex roles*, which are an integral part of social behavior. Learning sex roles well determines much of the individual's successful personal and social adjustment.

Sex roles. The learning of sex roles begins very early in the child's life. Most children of three or certainly four years of age are aware that human beings are of two sexes (Seward, 1946). As soon as the parents are aware that their child has recognized that, they begin working diligently to shape the child's behavior to conform to the social and sexual role that he must occupy. This teaching continues throughout the years that it takes for the child to realize the full meaning of differing sexuality. Some children learn that meaning clearly and early in life, while for others the dimensions of this difference remain obscure throughout childhood.

Children must be taught which sex they are, they must come to prefer that sexual role over the other, and they must learn all the behaviors deemed proper for each sex. *Sex preferences* come early in life, although the age at which they develop differs substantially from child to child and helps to determine how long the child will have to practice the role that biology assigned to him. Boys prefer the male role more than girls do the feminine one. Further, when children are pressed to discuss preferences that go beyond the male-female role—that is, being a mother or a father—more of them say that they would rather be a father. This tendency for girls to reject their natural sexual role must be countered if they are to become sexually and socially adjusted. Nonetheless, even among adults, more men than women seem to prefer their sexual status.

Many factors, including the parents' sexual adjustment and the family pattern of democracy or authoritarianism, affect the development of sex role preference and successful adjustment. A father's anxiety about sexual matters influences the positive development of masculinity in boys and femininity in girls as early as age four. Fathers who show great affection for their girls and assume a high degree of responsibility for their care tend to masculinize their daughters. When severe socialization practices are instituted early in the child's life and later coupled with a physically punishing mother and ridicule, both boys and girls become more feminized (Sears, 1966).

The composition of the family also makes a difference in identifying with the proper sex role. At various ages, boys who have brothers are more masculine than those who have just sisters. In the same fashion, girls with sisters rate higher on femininity than those who only have brothers (Sutton-Smith and Rosenberg, 1965).

Complicating these factors—and thus increasing the difficulty of learning how to adjust to the sexual role—is the emergence of a new cultural pattern of femininity and masculinity. "One of the more significant psychosocial developments of contemporary American society would appear to be the relatively fluid state of the sex roles of individuals. Within a single generation, significant changes have taken place in the traditional conceptions of what is masculine and what is feminine" (Brown, 1958, p. 232).

If this convergence of sex roles continues to increase, role behavior will, of course, change in important ways. Male and female roles may become less rigidly differentiated, the boundaries between them more permeable, and the overlap between them greater than that in any other century. What was once clearly labeled male (work, tools, sports) and clearly labeled female (housework, cooking, sewing) may lose their labels and differences of a secondary sort (who does what) decrease for both males and females. Thus, male-husband-father and female-wife-mother may no longer dictate so much of the individual's total behavior as in the past.

It is difficult to know whether this development will be an advantage or a disadvantage to our culture. Certainly the rigid definitions of masculinity and femininity made in the past were arbitrary and based on a concept of the natural superiority of men in a fashion that cross-cultural studies have described as meaningless. The new cultural pattern will probably be, like most social changes, a thing of mixed blessings. We will gain new perspectives and new freedoms, but we will lose some of the stability and predictability of past eras.

Nevertheless, whether this new cultural phenomenon continues or not, now and in the future the child must learn to accept his proper sex role in order to maintain his own psychological well-being, to which the approval of other people is crucial. Others in the culture still respond to the supermasculine girl and the effeminate boy in a negative fashion. For example, even as early in a child's life as kindergarten, the more masculine a boy is, the more likely it is that his teacher will think him mature, constructive in play, physically able, and possessing social virtue. These differences in the teacher's perception of children continue; a masculine boy in the first grade is generally rated by his teacher as a better reader (Anastasiow, 1965).

If the child learns both sexual and social roles easily and well, his parents and society will reward him. The child will also derive gratification from this learning, for the flexible individual who is capable of assuming whatever shape that society demands of him can find fulfillment in his adaptation. Learning how to become flexible involves occupying a progressively greater number of social

" 'Within a single generation, significant changes have taken place in the traditional conceptions of what is masculine and what is feminine.' "

roles as well as the sexual one. The concomitant of this progression may be *role strain*, which must be met by the growing child.

Roles and strain. Role strain begins early in the child's life and is a natural accompaniment to his development. At many of the transition points in development and socialization, the role that the child is expected to play is an odd mixture of parts of the role he is abandoning and parts of the new one he is assuming. For example, the familiar complaint of the youngster in his early teens is that he must pay adult prices to attend the movies but is not allowed to see movies designated "For adults only." Role conflict is also inevitable because, as the child grows older and his world expands in stages from being just the family to society at large, he must continually reorganize his role obligations. In this way, priorities of responsibility are established (Toby, 1952). For instance, among teen-agers, attachment to the peer group scrambles the previous hierarchy of priorities, in which parental dictates always came first.

Other factors are also sources of role strain, and more than one may operate at a single time. Role distress can occur if an individual's personal characteristics (abilities, attitudes, and so forth) are simply not suited to the demands of a role. Moreover, a role may provide too little reward for the amount of energy expended in fulfilling it, or various roles may make conflicting demands on him. Finally, not all role prescriptions are perfectly clear to begin with or remain clear over a period of years. *Role ambiguity* (Kahn, Wolf, Quinn, Snoek, and Rosenthal, 1964), in which the individual's actions do not always produce predictable consequences and in which other people do not react dependably to role behavior, can bring high stress.

The strain of fulfilling a role drives the individual to seek some means of strain relief. In order to find it, he must make, either consciously or unconsciously, bargains and compromises. The individual, whether a child or an adult, may play some roles with great vigor and emotional investment while meeting others in only a minimal

"Role distress can occur if an individual's personal characteristics (abilities, attitudes, and so forth) are simply not suited to the demands of a role."

fashion (Goode, 1960). Thus, for example, he may curtail social and civic activity in order to concentrate on the work role. The individual may also eliminate some of his roles when he finds himself compelled to play too many (Goode, 1960). In this case, he might delegate certain roles to others, so that an assistant handles his social engagements and his wife manages the family budget.

The proper performance of certain roles essential to the conduct of organized society brings more strain than do personal, casual roles. Consequently, to avoid embarrassment, for example, which is viewed as disruptive to social interaction and proper role performance, society has established strict mores and taboos on certain kinds of personal behavior in the performance of a socially oriented role (Gross and Stone, 1964). Thus, a drunken judge, who would be unable to perform the related courtroom roles, is socially viewed with horror. Political figures must stand foursquare for God, Mother, and Country, and teachers are expected to be morally cleaner than most people. So long as beliefs, attitudes, and behaviors that do not fit the social role are kept personal and private, they are tolerated.

Thus, society most clearly prescribes those behaviors necessary to the conduct of vital public and social roles. At the same time, society permits relief from the strains of such roles when the individual is removed from public observation. Society further provides for strain relief by dictating a protocol for how others should respond to public roles. People high in the political, economic, or managerial hierarchy, for example, are usually surrounded by associates who run interference for them and control the form of interaction that they must undergo. When the governor of a state sets aside time to meet any citizen who wishes to talk to him, that action is recognized as a departure from the usual pattern of governor-citizen interaction. Such a governor has, in essence, declared that he is free of role strain and is willing to abandon the usual devices designed to protect him.

SUMMARY

The function of the family in every society is to perpetuate the society by furnishing it with new members, to train and protect the child, and to care for the aged. However, the functions of the individual members of a family and the structure of their relationship can vary widely from culture to culture and within the same culture. For example, the function of the individual in primitive societies is to contribute to the physical and economic well-being of the group. This attitude determines the socialization of the child, which consists of teaching him his responsibility to the group and the few skills that he needs to carry out that responsibility.

On the other hand, in contemporary American society, the socially acceptable individual must fulfill many personal and occupational roles, and his socialization is the preparation for being able to fulfill them. This emphasis on the child as a developing person means that he is accepted as an equal participant in the family. The degree of acceptance does, however, vary from family to family and helps to determine the structure of the relationship between parent and child in a particular family.

These variations in American family patterns can range from authoritarian control over the child to democratic interaction among all the family members. Other dimensions of family pattern include acceptance, indulgence, family composition, and personality variables. All these factors, of course, influence the socialization method that the parents use and thus influence both the shape of the child's personality and his acceptability to society.

Two of the most important functions of the family in training the child are to teach him language and role behavior. Language facilitates his own thought and action as well as enabling him to communicate with other people. The shift in language patterns from egocentric babbling to socialized speech also means that the child is both subject to greater demands for socialized behavior and able to derive more profit from the lessons of socialization.

After the child has learned rudimentary language skills, he begins learning role behavior, which involves understanding the society's status structure and the role prescriptions associated with each status. Role rehearsal is the means by which he learns. The child also learns about sex roles at this time. Many factors, including his parents' sexual adjustment, the family pattern, and cultural values, help to determine how successful his adjustment to his proper sexual role will be.

Because the child is required to fulfill a progressively larger number of roles as he grows older, he will be subject to role strain. Role strain may arise when the child is beginning to assume a new role but has not completely grown out of the old one, when assuming new roles requires a reorganization of role obligations, when he must assume a role that he cannot fulfill, or when he experiences role ambiguity. Even though these kinds of role strain are inevitable, there are psychological and social mechanisms that can bring strain relief. Compromises made by the individual and social provisions for avoiding embarrassment in social interaction are two of these mechanisms.

Most of us conceive of the family as a universal feature of any society, and we assume that as an institution it has certain universal characteristics. Surprisingly, studies of family structure in the past in a great number of societies cast some doubt on this assumption. The selection of sexual partners before and after marriage has not always been subject to a uniform set of strictures in every family in all societies, the biological facts of parenthood may or may not have been directly relevant to family life, the inheritance of property has been known to take any of a number of complicated forms, and family authority has been centralized in one dominant figure or dispersed to many others. Thus, there has never been a unit called the family that can be identified solely by a particular pattern of relationships among its members or by a particular style in which it is organized.

However, regardless of how the family is structured, it has always been designed to inculcate an acceptable pattern of beliefs, attitudes, and behaviors in the young. The children born each year to families in every society represent a kind of invasion by a horde of barbarians who must be civilized before they can be admitted to full citizenship in the culture (Malinowski, 1930). Socialization is the process by which such

6

The structure of the family and its effects on socialization

acculturation is achieved, and the family is the active instrument in its accomplishment. Society makes this training role legitimate by investing in the parents power over the life and rights of their children.

THE EVOLUTION OF FAMILY STRUCTURE

The Extended Family

During the early stages in the development of many societies, the structure of the family was that of *the extended family*, which consists of a group of relatives who live together and accept a common authority. The very size of the family unit requires the invention of a complicated set of regulatory mechanisms to determine the rights, privileges, and responsibilities of each member. Thus, membership and rank in an extended family may be determined by using lines of descent— the family line of the father rather than that of the mother, for example. Once membership is established and family status and rank determined, where one will live, whom one can marry, whose authority must be respected, and what role one must play may all be rigidly prescribed.

The extended family was an effective social device in societies that led a nomadic existence or farmed just enough to care for their basic nutritional needs. This device also served well when cooperative home industry welded the family into an economic unit in which the contribution of each member promoted the welfare of all. With the advent of urbanization, industrialization, and technological dependence in modern society, the world of work left the home, the authoritative and dominant role of the head of the family was substantially eroded, and family members became mobile and independent. The family pattern effective in a rural society was simply not viable in a world of machines, factories, complicated finances, and complex legal and political restrictions (Zelditch, 1964). Then the task that the

extended family was expected to accomplish—and at which it failed—was "to accommodate its structure and processes to those norms of the society that govern marriage, sexual gratification, reproduction, inheritance, residence, production, distribution, consumption, and, to a lesser extent, education" (Mogey, 1964, p. 510). Because the extended family was not suited to this task, *the nuclear family*, which was better able to meet the challenge, evolved.

To be sure, the nuclear family did not emerge as totally different from the extended family. In some respects, we still have a modified extended family system. Our children follow occupations unlike those of their parents and move away to lead lives physically separated from their families of origin. These acts of independence do not, however, free the children from all responsibility to or continued contact with their parents. Although daily contact with relatives is reduced, a sense of loyalty to others and an acceptance of familial obligations is clearly apparent at certain times—marriage ceremonies, graduations, house warmings, festivals and holidays, deaths, and the like. Care for the sick, the elderly, and the financially distraught and concern about the welfare of members of an extended family continue to exist even if in a less urgent form. Moreover, the extended family still provides a sense of belonging to the individuals who have strayed from it and provides emotional ties that bind more closely than those of neighborhood, acquaintance, occupation, or social class.

The Nuclear Family

Our society uses the institution of marriage to establish the conditions under which a man and a woman are allowed to have sexual relations, to have children, and to pool economic resources. In our society, the husband, wife, and children have become a nuclear family and are no longer really members of an extended family of two or more nuclear families bound together by kinship.

The nuclear family has an identifiable structure and specifiable functions that it must perform to meet its cultural responsibility. The function of the nuclear family unit is to guard the physical and psychological welfare of its members and to train the young to fit comfortably into social and economic roles in the culture. The structure of the nuclear family is based on the relationships within it. These are organized around the role and status of each member. Thus, if the role of the father and that of the mother are distinct and unambiguous, the child of each sex can internalize values and attitudes and learn the patterns of behavior appropriate to each sex. Learning the fine points of role behavior and the reciprocal relationship between roles becomes most important in acquiring a sex identity that other members of society can accept.

The nuclear family in contemporary America is not so closely knit as in the past. In our industrialized society, with its stress on physical mobility (factories are located in cities), technological skill (computer programming is not a family task), and education (even the neighborhood schools of the recent past have given way to busing students to a school at some distance from their homes), the togetherness of the farm families of the past has disappeared. Early in the child's life, he is exposed to the influence of people other than family members, so that even parental impact is soon weakened. He later marries, moves away from his family, and raises children in his own fashion.

The contemporary American family, then, has been shaped by the industrialized and technologically oriented society in which it is embedded. Although the family still performs the function of producing properly socialized citizens, the family has become increasingly nonfunctional for the individuals that it contains. As Dager (1964) notes:

Symbolic of this non-function is the increasing reliance by families upon many secondary agencies: social security, industrial retirement programs, care of the aged, a plethora of welfare agencies, care for the young in the form of day nurseries, play schools, nursery schools, prekindergartens, and baby-sitting, fringe benefits, and so on. The passing of these activities from the family to other agencies . . . has occurred by default, not design (p. 776).

Fathers still possess more family authority than mothers, and sons and daughters remain subordinate to both. The family still works out a division of labor among its members that usually acknowledges male superiority. And educational and occupational achievement are still highly valued indicators of successful family management. However, the family has been caught up in a society in transition, so that the structure and function of the family must change steadily in order to meet the demands of new times and new social needs.

One fascinating aspect of the shift in the structure of the family over the years is the altered relationship of married couples and their in-laws. When an extended family system held sway, in-laws possessed rights and privileges that were not abandoned when young people got married. In-laws in those days, Bernard (1964) notes, might limit the alternatives and choices available to the married couple. They might, for example, continue to decide what responsibilities the husband owed to the family of his origin, determine where he must live, dictate the contribution that he must make to the economic welfare of his relatives, and even influence the number of offspring he created. Modern family units maintain certain ties with their in-laws, but the kind of in-law influence has changed considerably. Because young married couples are mobile and by custom establish a place of residence separated from the parental families, the young people are free to work out a new style of married and family life by themselves.

This modern arrangement, however, is not a perfect solution to the in-law problem. As Duvall (1954) reports, the complaint that in-laws meddle in and dominate some parts of their lives is still common and chronic among young marrieds. This complaining about in-laws occurs most frequently among wives. The heavy in the script is the husband's mother. One startling revelation in Duvall's study is the next most frequent complaint about in-laws. Those newly married couples who did not gripe about interference seemed to resent the lack of attention that in-laws paid to them; that is, they complained that an indifferent set of in-laws seemed not much interested in the recent marriage and failed to dance attendance on the newlyweds.

Nevertheless, in the first years of marriage, the in-law problem is resolved in one fashion or another, so that its immediate impact on newborn children may be minimal. The transformation of in-laws into grandparents may produce new consequences for the child in the modern family, but much of the direct and immediate impact typical in the past has disappeared with the decline of the unique set of rights and privileges characteristic of the extended family.

"The heavy in the script is the husband's mother."

The Family, Technology, and Urbanization

Technology and industrialization are clearly major forces in the shift from an extended family system to the current nuclear family. Mobility is one of the most important contributors to this shift. Newlyweds escape the influence of the extended family by moving to their own residence, redistributing authority and responsibility, interpreting the culture in their own way, and raising their children to fit an industrial society that extends privilege to the individual based on his occupational status rather than his lineage, kin, cult, clan, or family. Consequently, the means by which the parent earns a livelihood and where he works (away or in the home) are essential to the kind of interaction that occurs between the parents and their children (Dager, 1964).

The occupational structure of a society has an indirect but significant impact on the lessons that the child learns within the confines of family life and shapes the values that he will subscribe to in his encounter with the society. The shift from small to big business in our society has tolled the death knell for those psychological characteristics most suited to personal enterprise and entrepreneurial endeavors and has encouraged instead the formation of those characteristics that make the child sensitive to the needs of others, capable of "getting along" with all kinds of people, and able to keep his nose clean via submission in a bureaucratically organized society (Miller and Swanson, 1958).

Technology also makes demands on the individual members of a society. An occupational structure dominated by a continuous succession of technological innovations designed to raise individual productivity must of necessity be serviced by a new or modified breed of adult adapted to survival in such a world. These demands are translated into socialization practices that more or less successfully produce new generations ready to move the society closer to its aims. Thus, because machines and automation have increasingly replaced manual labor, education and technical training have become requisites for survival. Education by its very nature demands that the individual be capable of postponing immediate gratification in order to achieve greater reward at some later date. Therefore, the ability to tolerate this delay and to assess future gain must become essential ingredients in the socialization process if the child is to enter the culture easily and to desire and labor for the rewards available to him.

Marginality and Alienation

Two consequences of urbanization, technological advance, and industrialization are marginality and alienation. The family who has failed to socialize the child to a proper fit in modern culture may produce what has been labeled a *marginal man*—a man who is best described as living on the periphery or margin of the society. He is isolated from others and so forced to maintain an identity without the emotional support that most of us receive from fellow citizens. Such a man does not participate fully in the society either because he was not taught appropriate skills and attitudes as a child or because he has been rejected by the other members of society. If the origin of marginality is incomprehension of the cultural traditions or inability to follow the prescribed forms of behavior, that marginality is expressed in the form of behavior repugnant to others, so that public censure and punishment are the usual outcomes.

Some forms of marginality are not so visibly antisocial and obviously damaging to the continuation of the culture. For example, some of our citizens are marginal by choice. They have examined the values espoused by society, considered their own reaction to them, and decided for themselves the degree to which they can actively support those values. Moreover, there seem to be many citizens in our complex society whose public facade suggests that they are in complete accord with the social, political, economic, and moral values of our culture while their private opinions and behaviors suggest that these men are more marginal than they appear to be. These kinds of alienation may, of course, be valuable; if all fami-

lies practiced child rearing in perfect accord with the existing mores and standards of society and always produced new citizens happy with the status quo, our culture might well cease to move forward.

Marginality of a different sort occurs for those members of our society who live constantly on the brink of economic misfortune. If the father in a family can contribute little or nothing to its economic and social status, he may lose the authority that normally accompanies the role of husband and father. If he does, the children focus on the mother as the primary source of support, succor, and control. Marginality in this instance influences the kinds of socialization lessons that the children learn and thus the kind of adults that they eventually become.

Marginality of either the quite visible or less visible sort implies an estrangement or alienation from vital parts of the society and its members. However, the alienated individual is not necessarily marginal in his interactions with some members of society. Moreover, he may be productive but disenchanted about the meaning and value of his actions, or he may perform well but seek psychological and emotional satisfactions in hobbies or interests that remove him from the mainstream of cultural life. Feeling that he cannot be an approving part of what is happening in the society or finding himself neutral about what others seem to value highly, he shrinks his life sphere to fit personal pursuits that free him from involvement with the rest of society.

Of all those who may be alienated from society, probably only a few have the material or psychological resources to permit a dignified withdrawal into other absorbing activities and interests. For the factory worker laboring to provide for his family living in a sprawling, crowded, dangerous city, the sense of alienation may also contain an unmistakable feeling of helplessness and victimization. He may feel that his identity is composed of little more than a series of digits. His personal feeling of ability to produce a meaningful impact on the broad course of society may be near zero, and this feeling may be coupled with an equally great sense of powerlessness about altering even those immediate events that most influence his life and that of his family. As Sechrest and Wallace (1967) said:

It is scarcely any wonder then that so many people feel that their vote doesn't count, not really, when the total even in a large city may run to millions. . . . Prices go up and down, schools are built or not, automobile styles change, and wars are fought whether the individual likes it or not and seemingly without reference at all to his opinion or will (p. 566).

If vital decisions are made at unknown times and at places psychologically distant from the individual, he cannot have a sense of where he fits into so complex a structure.

Perhaps these problems of marginality and alienation are inescapable concomitants of modern society. Perhaps no family can read the lines of cultural tradition clearly enough for its socialization methods to produce a new citizen absolutely compatible with things as they are in the society—much less things as they will be.

Family Developmental Tasks

Another way to view the family as a structural unit in society is to examine the *developmental tasks* that each family is called upon to perform. In this sense, family functions are the services that the family must provide as a part of its responsibility to the larger society. The core tasks that families are asked to perform include, according to Duvall (1962), control over reproduction, physical well-being, protection, education and socialization, recreation, status conferring, and affection giving. In each stage of the child's development, one or more of these tasks is most salient while others are secondary to his well-being.

Exactly when these stages appear and how precisely they can be defined have yet to be worked out fully in theory. Many of the stages, for

"Feeling that he cannot be an approving part of what is happening in the society or finding himself neutral about what others seem to value highly, he shrinks his life sphere to fit personal pursuits that free him from involvement with the rest of society."

example, merge indistinguishably into one another. However, this theoretical conception at least allows us to put into rough order the tasks that the family must face as its age and composition change.

In addition, each of these tasks falls into a different context depending upon whether the family situation is one of *expansion, contraction,* or *stability.* The child experiences these stages differently if he is the first child of young marrieds (expansion), the middle child in a large and aging family (stability), or the last child to leave the nest (contraction). Viewing the family in developmental terms treats it as though it were in itself a growing, changing, adapting organism.

The family developmental history can be divided into more complicated phases. Hill and Rodgers (1964) use seven stages for this purpose: establishment, child bearing, preschool family, school-age, adult trainees, middle years, and aging years. Points of transition between these phases can be determined each time the oldest child shifts from one significant age category to another (enters school, graduates, gets married). As each of these events occurs, the major goals of family life begin to change as the members of the family reorganize their relationships to one another and to society.

An example of these changing relationships is the findings reported by Conner, Johannis, and Walters (1954) in their study of conflicts between parents and adolescent children. Launched (left home), female, adolescent college students reported that most of their conflicts with their parents had been and continued to be focused on the issues of dating and mate selection. Between the high school and college ages, however, parent-child conflicts of all sorts declined in frequency. These conflicts were a reflection of the attempt to perform a developmental task common to most families. The background characteristics (age, education, place of residence, family size, parental occupation) of those studied was not significantly related to the fact of conflict with the parents.

Another example might add definition to this theoretical conception. As more children are born to each family, the family composition shifts, and the role of siblings in influencing child development changes accordingly. Each new child changes all the relationships of the others to one another and, in turn, affects their relationship to him.

The firstborn finds himself in the hands of young, inexperienced parents who are on their own for the first time. He occupies center stage in the family play, but the parental players are learning new roles. When his first sibling arrives, everything changes. Relationships predictable in the past cease to exist, and new patterns must be learned very suddenly. He may feel abandoned, rejected, and unloved; he may resent the intruder; and he will react in accord with his feelings by becoming hostile and competitive.

What the first child will perceive and how he will react will depend in great part on the age and stage of his personal development when the second born joins the family and on how his parents respond to his reaction to the intruder. The reaction of the parents will, in turn, partly depend on their age, the nature of their marital relationship, their socio-economic status, their previous experiences with their own parents, and a host of other variables.

It is this incredibly multidimensional, moment-by-moment shifting and changing of parent-child relationships that makes accurate and unqualified prediction so difficult; with even the addition of each new sibling, an entirely new set of forces is added to the dynamic nature of the family. It should be apparent, then, that family developmental tasks are an abstraction that lets us make only beginning sense of the phenomenon called a family.

This theoretical conception of family functions that are altered as structural changes occur in the family (addition of children, entry to and exit from school, young adult launching, and so forth) needs to be fleshed out with a great deal of research exploration. The concept does, however, provide a framework that can help us understand deviations from the model nuclear family and the particular and unique family developmental tasks that each deviation might pose for family members.

THE ROLE OF THE FATHER

The structure of the contemporary American family does not often conform to the model nuclear family. The conditions peculiar to our technological society have increased the mother's domination of family life and the rearing of children. Labor-saving devices have freed the mother from domestic chores, so that she has more time for training and pampering her children, while the father is so immersed in economic pursuits that he has abandoned much of his own role in rearing the children (Gorer, 1948; Kluckhohn, 1949). Labeling contemporary American society a "mother-land" would not be a great exaggeration; even the educational system is almost totally dominated by women teachers (Ostrovsky, 1959).

Because the role of the father is now primarily limited to teaching the child skills for work and recreation and because these lessons are usually carried out only during the child's school years (Sunley, 1955), the young American male has difficulty in achieving a mature concept of virility. His development at home and in school is molded largely by women, who promulgate a code of masculine behavior closely resembling the standards espoused for young girls (Elkin, 1946). Thus, one of the father's primary socialization functions is to give young boys an adequate identification with the masculine role (Parsons, 1947), and close contact with the father very early in the child's life is crucial to development.

The mother spends the greatest amount of time with children of all ages (the father is gone an average of 10 hours a day in urban society), she interacts with them most frequently, and she is usually the one to mete out reward and punishment. Her omnipresence makes her the most likely object for identification during the formative years for children. This influence must be balanced for both boys and girls by exposure to the male sex role and the attitudes and values usually attached to it.

Any factor in family life that leads to strong identification with the mother or weak identification with the father may tend to produce antisocial behavior on the part of the male child. After he becomes aware of the cultural demand for adult masculine behavior, he may overcompensate with excessively masculine behavior as a reaction against his early identification with his mother. For this child, badness becomes masculine because goodness is so closely associated with mothering and femininity.

The overt behavior stemming from this symbolic assertion of being a man is often coarseness and toughness or juvenile delinquency. Young lower class males are especially prone to expressing their masculinity through delinquency, for the father in these families is frequently absent either physically or psychologically (Cohen, 1955). Nevertheless, the sex role conflict in boys raised primarily by women is culture-wide, so that its expression in violence and crime is the result in other social classes as well (Miller, 1958; Bacon, Child, and Barry, 1963).

These results of the male child's being deprived of adequate early contact with his father are underlined by studies of a special and extreme case of the absent father—military service during World War II and the Korean War. In one of these studies, Sears, Pintler, and Sears (1946) examined the effect of such deprivation on the aggressive behavior of preschool children, as expressed in doll play. The hypothesis of the study was that there would be a reliable difference between boys and girls in the frequency with which they use the father doll as an object of aggression when compared with the amount of aggression acted out using the mother doll (the father normally serves as both an aggressive model and a frustrator to the son, but this role is less explicit with the daughter). The researchers found that boys whose fathers were absent displayed less difference from girls in the frequency of aggression than did boys whose fathers were at home. In fact, the doll-play behavior of boys and girls whose fathers had been absent for a substantial period was hardly distinguishable. The boys seemed to be less conscious of their masculinity, and sex typing —knowing whether one is a boy or a girl and what the role of each is—was delayed.

The same research technique was used by Bach (1946), who examined the fantasies that children have about their fathers when the fathers had been away from home for some time. The children studied consisted of 10 boys and 10 girls, between six and 10 years old, whose fathers had been away in the armed forces when the children were between one and three years of age, who

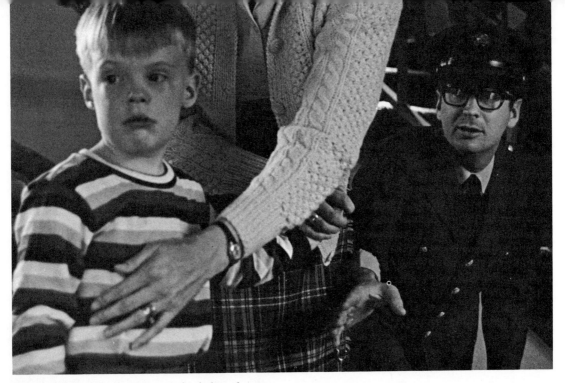

"In a manner quite distressing to the father, the un-comprehending child often refused his attentions and sought to escape contact with him."

belonged to the lower middle class, and who possessed average intelligence. These children, expressing their feelings by playing out life themes with dolls, tended to produce an idealistic and feminized fantasy picture of their fathers. The influence of the mothers' attitude toward the fathers, which was obtained through interviews, was seen as crucial to the establishment of this view in the children.

In this kind of situation, the returned father has difficulty in establishing his role as father, and the child has difficulty in accepting him as father. A study conducted by Stolz *et al.* (1954) examined the families of 19 men who returned to Stanford University after the Korean War. In each of these families, the father was away during the pregnancy of the mother and returned after the first child was at least a year old. These families had a total of 35 children, 19 of whom were the firstborn and 16 of whom were born after the father returned.

In interviewing the fathers and the mothers, in observing the children in social situations with peers and adults, and in observing the children in play situations of a "projective" kind, the research team discovered that the father returning to his role as parent faced major adjustments in becoming the head of the family. The firstborn child had to adjust to an unknown man who suddenly invaded the family, took a dominant position, and upset routines to which the child had been accustomed for years. In a manner quite distressing to the father, the uncomprehending child often refused his attentions and sought to escape contact with him. Not infrequently, this pattern of response evoked resentment in the father, who in anger would be tempted to become more insistent and more demanding about the behavior of the alienated child.

The firstborn child also identified more closely with the mother than with the father, was less independent, showed a greater number of fears, revealed more overt expressions of tension, and lacked skill in dealing with his peers. These personality characteristics were frustrating to the father—particularly if the child was a boy. The father's disappointment at what he felt to be his son's lack of masculinity was, the researchers felt, communicated to the child and would eventually produce a form of psychological development that might make his later adult adjustment more difficult than it would be for his counterpart who had grown up with a father in the home. This prediction has been substantiated in terms of antisocial behavior by a recent study (Siegman, 1966), which found more antisocial activity in a group of adult males whose fathers had been away in the armed services during early childhood than in a group whose fathers had not been away.

For the girl child too, absence of the father has an impact during the early years. Mothers in father-absent families tend to assume parts of both the father and the mother role and to be more concerned about their children and more overprotective of them. Girls are not affected so deeply by the absence of the father as are boys but do become more dependent as adults and more exclusively like their mothers than would be the case if they learned the adult role in a two-parent family. The absence of a male model is most likely to have an impact on later male-female relationships, such as dating and choosing a marriage mate.

The simple presence of a father in the home is, of course, an inadequate guarantee that the girl will learn appropriate lessons about what the grown male of the species is like, what he values and believes, and how he tends to react in male-female relationships. However, it is clear on logical grounds that the mere presence of a father will, in most instances, temper the form of the lessons presented to the child and alter the dimensions of her learning. This tempering may take the form of shaping some of the girl's interests, of exposing her to a different range of experiences, of clarifying her own role as a female by contrasting it with that of the male, or of modifying attitudes acquired from the mother alone.

Thus, when the model arrangement in the culture is a husband and wife who live out their lives together and children who live with the parents until maturity, separation becomes an important psychological event for the children. To them, separation, whether the result of military duties, economic pursuits, or failure of the marriage, is a threatening deviation from what is "normal."

THE BROKEN HOME

Because the divorce rate in our society is high (one out of four marriages), divorce has become the chief source of discontinuity in the lives of an increasing number of children. It is frequently insisted that such problems as money, sex, and religious differences are the most common causes of divorce. However, an exacting appraisal of the marriage relationship reveals that the underlying impetus for most divorces is the emotional immaturity of the participants and their consequent inability to adjust to each other when beset by the inevitable difficulties that follow the honeymoon (Finch, 1960).

One way to make sense of the divorces that alter our model conception of the nuclear family is to view them, as Jessie Bernard (1964) does, in terms of divorce as an outcome, as a strategy, and as a process.

In some marriages, divorce as an outcome is fated from the inception of the marriage. Here, the mismatch is so apparent that the issues of the when and how of the divorce are the only relevant ones. Marriage has a required discipline all its own, and those unsuited to it because of immaturity, inadequate socialization, or emotional disturbance may be unable to make it last even for a brief period.

For a number of those seemingly not so handicapped (their second marriage takes after the first fails), the outcome can be interpreted as a strategic failure. According to Bernard (1964):

For some reason or other, one or the other partner "played his cards wrong" or became "cornered" or "boxed in" or was maneuvered into a position where divorce seemed the only alternative. . . . Divorce in such cases is almost accidental, in the sense that a modern war might come about by accident, neither side really wanting it (p. 722).

Making each other totally miserable can assure that the outcome will be divorce because alternative solutions simply become too costly to afford emotionally and psychologically for one or both of the marriage partners. Divorce, then, may be the outcome of a basic incompatibility, it may be an accident of timing and stress management, or it may reflect the kinds of interpersonal strategies employed by one or both of the marriage partners.

Strategies for dealing with marital strife are not, of course, limited to divorce; divorce is only one of the alternatives available. An uncounted number of married couples adopt strategies that involve living together while avoiding open interpersonal confrontation. Through the investment of energy in activities external to the marriage itself—children, travel, community service, entertaining, work, drugs, and sexual affairs—acknowledging basic incompatibility can be avoided.

If divorce becomes the only sensible alternative, it can be used as a strategic means of maximizing gain and minimizing loss for each of the partners. Cold and calculating as this approach to divorce may be, it is likely that it becomes an essential ingredient in the process of divorce when alternative solutions have finally been abandoned. As Bernard (1964) indicates, from beginning to end in the strategy of divorce, values can change. This change can influence the emotional tone of the outcome as far as children are concerned. The mother in love with someone else and intent on remarrying as soon as the legal hurdles are overcome will communicate a quite different view of the divorce process to her children than will the mother essentially abandoned by a husband who is seeking a new way of life for himself.

In divorce as a process, "A disagreement may begin with only a moderate amount of hostility present, but each parry or thrust adds to the hostility of the other and leads him, in turn, to increase his own hostility, and so on, in a process that has come to be known as escalation" (Bernard, 1964, p. 724). Thus, any of a series of misbehaviors by one partner may trigger a process

of interpersonal hostility that escalates to the point where each has accumulated an extended list of grievances against the other. Continuous exercise of these grievances in arguments acts to alienate each from the other until both partners occupy a psychological position that admits of no alternative except divorce.

Some theorists have suggested that married couples need to be trained to argue and fight constructively. "Constructive," in this context, means that disagreements can be nonescalating and can call on alternatives short of divorce. As we have seen, however, escalation is only one of the many prime movers in divorce. And whether outcome, strategy, or process is to be made the culprit in this explanation of the breakup of the nuclear family by divorce, it always has an impact on the innocent bystanders—the children. The problem posed by divorce is not that two people cease to live together, but that the separation results from a *continuous process of failing adjustment* that stretches over time and waxes and wanes in severity. Thus, for the child, divorce is the formal conclusion to a long-lasting disturbance in the family structure.

Although divorce may actually be less stressful for a child than the continuous bickering and quarreling that precede the actual breakup of the home, it inevitably creates special problems for him. Among the possible problems are these: (1) the conflict created in the child who is deeply attached to both parents, (2) the continuing awareness of the parents' marital problem, which the child may carry with him for the rest of his life, (3) the need to deal with the consequences of having had parents who could not agree on what constitutes the proper balance of freedom and restraint, (4) the inevitable comparison of his life with the lives of children from normal homes, (5) the development of emotionally disturbing points of view toward his parents, (6) the possibility of facing the transition from being a product of a broken home to being a stepchild, and (7) the strain of shifting between households with different sets of standards (Bossard, 1948).

This variety of possible problems and their

dependence on the family structure and pattern and the personalities of all the individuals involved means that no child who undergoes the breakup of his home will display a single or particular type of emotional reaction to it. For example, feelings of resentment, distrust, suspicion, and dependence are bound to vary with the child and with the particular status that he occupies when the divorce occurs. The age of the child also affects his reaction; younger children tend, on the average, to adjust with greater ease to the fact of divorce than older children do. Older children have a greater awareness of what has taken place and have more memories to contend with over the years. Finally, other members of the family influence the problems that the child faces. Siblings of various ages and dispositions add their reactions to the total mix of interpersonal relations. Do-gooder relatives and advice giving friends—as well as third parties for either parent—may create additional conflict and so intensify his problems.

Moreover, the child's problem of emotional adjustment does not end in the few months after the divorce but may continue throughout his life. For example, the remarriage of either parent may be an emotionally crippling experience. The child inevitably compares the step-parent to the one that he lost. If the relationship with the original parent was pleasant, then the child will naturally be resentful and distrustful of the new parent, whom he inevitably views as an intruder (Podolsky, 1955). The child may have a powerful need to lean emotionally on the remaining parent. If he does, the need to exclude the interloping step-parent is intensified.

The task of forming a successful relationship with the step-parent as well as adjusting to the trauma of divorce may simply be beyond the child's resources. The step-parent's successful resolution of these problems would require his mental health and emotional adjustment to be exceptional. And if he is inexperienced in dealing with children (or children of a particular age), then the problems of mutual adjustment may be compounded in an incredible fashion.

Another continuing effect of divorce on the child is the possibility of guilt. The child may feel that the divorce happened because of his own failure to be what his parents expected him to be. If the child senses, consciously or unconsciously, that he is the cause of the divorce, the consequence for his self-esteem is so disastrous that he may be burdened with guilt for the rest of his life. That guilt may be expressed in his choice of a mate or in the nature of the interpersonal relationship that he establishes with the mate. This consequence of guilt is particularly liable to occur if either of the parents tried to justify the divorce by constructing an elaborate case in which he was the innocent victim of an evil partner. After all, it is only through the relationship with both the male and the female parent that the child comes to learn an acceptable pattern for future responses to other males and females. If the child becomes convinced that one of the sexes is untrustworthy, the pattern of all his future male-female relationships may be altered.

Finally, the parent's guilt over the divorce may have a lasting effect on the child's emotional adjustment. This guilt is the result of the cultural belief that parents have a high degree of responsibility for the child (Johnson and Medinnus, 1965) and that divorce produces emotional mal-

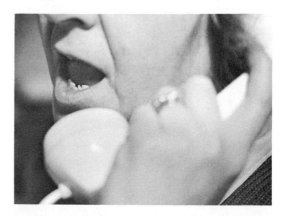

"Do-gooder relatives and advice giving friends—as well as third parties for either parent—may create additional conflict and so intensify his problems."

adjustment in him. The parent usually expresses his feeling of guilt in the form of anxiety about the future welfare of the child. The parent may also rationalize his guilt feelings by asserting that remaining married would have been harder on the child than the divorce was (Goode, 1956). This guilt and the parent's attempt to rid himself of it have, of course, an impact on the child. Whether or not the parent succeeds in losing his guilt, he will probably continue to make fumbling and often misguided attempts to "smooth things over" for the child. And that may do him further harm.

This common parental guilt is one indicator of our strong cultural orientation toward the family. We become civilized and socialized human beings within the confines of the family, and the feeling that family life is an integral part of our growth and development is perpetuated there. Thus, it is natural for us to feel that separating the child from one or both of his parents brings emotional damage to him. However, there is little evidence to suggest that our method of child rearing is superior to other ways. In fact, radical experiments in communal child rearing, such as those undertaken by the Hutterites in America (Eaton and Weil, 1955) and the kibbutzim in Israel, seem to have produced young people singularly free of delinquency and emotional disturbance.

THE KIBBUTZ—AN EXPERIMENT IN SOCIALIZATION WITHOUT PARENTS

The kibbutz experiment is a deliberate attempt by well-educated Europeans to rear children in a group fashion calculated to make them independent of their parents from early life. As infants, the children in the kibbutz live in groups of a dozen or so, and adults who are replaced regularly during the course of their early lives take care of them. These substitute parents are trained and free to devote themselves exclusively to child care without the worries of the harried housewife

typical in America. Perhaps even more important, these workers are less likely to have the common parental anxieties about "their own" children and so can use greater objectivity in child rearing. However, because most kibbutz babies are breast-fed, the intimate, personal contact of mother and child is not sacrificed in early infancy (Bettelheim, 1964).

When the child of the kibbutz becomes a toddler, he leaves the nursery cottage each day to spend part of the evening with his parents and is with them during most of Saturday. Yet he still lives with a small group of other children of the same age until after high school graduation. This peer group provides most of the assistance to and supervision of one another. The parent, who would normally respond to the child's night cries, is replaced by a peer who calms his fears or sees that he gets attention if it is necessary. Thus, the peer group members become substitute mother and father to one another. Because of this cooperative living, each member learns early to live by the group code and submit his personal needs and desires to the will of the majority or the group leader. In this way, he learns to live as a member of a group throughout his life, to participate in the activities of the group, and to coordinate his needs and impulses with those of others.

Living with peers does not mean that the children are cut off from adult society; in many respects, the kibbutz allows children to have much more direct and intimate contact with the adult world than contemporary America does. Just as in the small rural town in our society of the eighteenth and nineteenth centuries, children in the kibbutz have access to a great deal of informal teaching by the elders in the community and are made to feel welcome where the adults work. Because of this sense of community, these children "belong" in a way that many of our children do not. When the children mature, they are free either to accept adult membership in the kibbutz or to leave it for a different way of life, but few of the children raised in this group style choose to leave the kibbutz when they attain maturity (Bettelheim, 1964).

According to reports by a variety of observers, the children of the kibbutz grow up to be different from children raised by our method and in our urban society (Rabin, 1958). Although not all of these Israeli young people grow up to be secure, self-reliant, and unneurotic, we might profit by re-examining some of our own traditional assumptions about the one and only proper means of rearing children. We tend to accept on faith what is as an indicator of what should be.

SUMMARY

The family is the social unit designed to inculcate an acceptable pattern of beliefs, attitudes, and behaviors in each new generation of citizens. When our society was primarily rural, any extended family system was workable. This kind of system gave way to a nuclear form of the family to meet the new demands of the urban, industrialized, technologically sophisticated culture of today. Socialization in the nuclear family is oriented toward producing those personal characteristics in children that will assure their later successful encounter with the occupational and role playing structure of the society. However, training children to be what they need to be is not always successful; marginal or alienated man can be the outcome.

Each nuclear family, then, must perform certain developmental tasks from the time when marriage initiates the family until the exodus of the children completes it. The complexity of family life and the influence of this complexity on socialization can be seen in even a bare outline of the stages and phases that each family member must undergo as the family composition changes, its participants age, and a number of significant transitions are made. During each of these stages and phases, the socialization practices change. Thus, the socialization experience will be different in some respects for each child in a family because he enters it in a unique context.

The nuclear family is in every society subject to deviation in its structure. An absent father, for example, can alter the role learning of male and female children in a variety of ways. The achievement of a proper sex identity seems most affected by being reared in a fatherless home. A home broken by divorce exposes the children to a unique form of socialization connected closely to the pattern of conflict and how it is managed by the parents. The child of divorced parents faces strains not present in the life of a child reared in an intact nuclear family.

Finally, in some societies, a deliberate attempt has been made to modify the form of the nuclear family and to alter the pattern of socialization to produce an adult suited to the way of life of the culture. The kibbutz experiment is one example of a meaningful departure from the model of the nuclear family current in our society.

Part three

The components
of socialization

Intelligence is "the capacity of the individual to act purposefully, to think rationally, and to deal effectively with his environment" (Wechsler, 1944, p. 3). Teaching the child how to deal purposefully, rationally, and effectively with his environment in terms of a certain set of values is the goal of socialization. Intelligence thus makes an incalculable difference in the individual's continuing ability to comprehend and absorb the lessons of socialization. Intelligence, broadly defined, probably sets the upper and lower limits on the socialization of the human being throughout his life span.

HEREDITY AND ENVIRONMENT IN THE DEVELOPMENT OF INTELLIGENCE

According to most psychologists, intelligence is an innate capacity that is modified and developed by environmental events that assist or stunt its growth. Inheritance probably sets the upper limits on intelligence. The environment and the nature of the socialization process may affect the development of intelligence and the way in which the individual uses it, although psychologists do

7

Intelligence and socialization

not agree on the extent of environmental influence.

The theorists who assert that heredity is the major determinant of intelligence point to the correspondence between the child's physical growth and his intellectual growth as evidence for their claim; as the child grows physically, he becomes more capable of intellectual performance that can be tested, measured, and labeled as intelligence.

At the earliest stages in the child's growth, intelligence tests are limited to measuring physical coordination and development. Thus, for example, testing the intelligence of a two month old child involves finding out whether he can make such minimal adjustive movements as fixing his eyes on a stationary object, following a moving object with his eyes, and lifting his head. Such movements are necessary if he is to be aware of and alert to his environment. By ten months of age, the child must be capable of poking about in his environment and exploring it, even if he is not very mobile. Six months later, he should be able to demonstrate some of the skills that he has acquired, such as pointing to objects on request, naming a few objects, and following simple orders.

As the child grows older, the testing setting becomes more prescribed and formalized. The two year old should be able to name common objects when shown them, designate parts of his body, build towers with blocks, and combine words into short, functional sentences. Just six months later, the child is expected not only to designate objects that the examiner names but also to name an object after being told its use. Moreover, he must be able to fit blocks into forms cut out to receive them, and he must be more facile with language.

For the child of three and a half years, the tasks are even more complex. Now he must have a picture vocabulary (name objects in a picture) of about 15 words, consistently obey simple commands, and be able to demonstrate comprehension by answering questions with properly controlled language. Shortly thereafter, by four years

"Intelligence thus makes an incalculable difference in the individual's continuing ability to comprehend and absorb the lessons of socialization."

of age, the child must be able to demonstrate physical skill in manipulating objects (drawing pictures), to discriminate between various forms, and to identify objects by memory.

When the child is about six, intelligence testing begins to assume form as a measure requiring considerable facility with abstract thought and language. Then the complex activities required of the child involve using numbers, defining words, identifying missing parts of pictures and absurdities in them, and identifying things that are alike and things that are different (Sawrey and Telford, 1958).

This correspondence between physical and intellectual growth suggests, naturally, that both qualities are inherited and, perhaps, that each has genetic limits set on it. Other evidence also seems to indicate that biology and inheritance largely determine intelligence. For example, high correlations in intellectual performance exist within families. These correlations increase with the degree of relatedness between the children; that is, the I.Q.'s of identical twins are very close, those of fraternal twins are less close, and those of ordinary siblings are least close. Moreover, a recent study (Shields, 1962) found no significant difference in intelligence test scores between identical twins raised in different homes, so that environmental influence on intelligence would seem to be negligible.

However persuasive this kind of evidence may be, the environment does clearly shape intelligence to some as yet unknown degree. For example, in an environment lacking stimulation, the measured intelligence of children regularly declines (Jordan, 1933; Skeels and Fillmore, 1940). Furthermore, extreme cultural disadvantage may cause sharp drops in intelligence, as two detailed studies of children in culturally impoverished areas indicate. According to one of these studies, the average I.Q. of Kentucky mountain children dropped from 84 at seven years of age to 60 at 15 years of age (Asher, 1935). The other study was carried out in isolated communities in Georgia, where children showed I.Q. losses of 24 points between the ages of seven to nine and 14. The I.Q.'s of some even older children had dropped from 100 to 70 (Edwards and Jones, 1938).

Such findings suggest that differences in I.Q. may be related to socio-economic class. And, indeed, the test scores of children from the lower classes regularly average below those of children from the middle and upper classes; the difference may run as high as 15 to 25 I.Q. points (Herrick, 1951). Such differences in test scores do not, however, mean that all lower class children are less intelligent. Rather, intelligence tests have a built-in cultural bias that automatically penalizes lower class children in a reflection of the cultural differences among the classes (Davis and Gardner, 1941; Davis 1948).

Standardized intelligence tests were designed to measure in school only one of the various kinds of problem solving ability, and the questions in these tests are almost always based on middle class culture, from which our school system arose. For example, a typical test question is this one: "A symphony is to a composer as a book is to what?" The answer choices are these: "(1) paper (2) sculpture (3) musician (4) author (5) man." In one administration of a test in which this question appeared, 81 per cent of the children from the upper and middle classes answered

it correctly, while only 51 percent of the lower class children did (Davis, 1948). Moreover, when any test item is expressed in an academic form or bookish words, the difference among the social classes becomes increasingly apparent. And, as would be expected, this differential performance is more obvious in older rather than younger students (Davis, 1951).

Thus, intelligence tests are probably very useful for separating bright students from dull ones in the middle socio-economic white classes but are unacceptable for measuring the intellectual capacities of lower class children. Intelligence is more than being facile with language and being able to solve middle class problems. However, even if there were an intelligence test that reflects the experience of lower class children, their motivation and "set" for test taking would be inadequate. Indeed, the very taking of the test would be alien to these children, for they are unaccustomed to that much pencil and paper activity— particularly when it is focused on abstract conceptions of the world.

In order to sort out these effects of a culturally disadvantaged environment on intellectual performance and be able to measure actual intellectual capacity, attempts have been made to develop "culture-free" tests. For example, Rosenblum and Keller (1955) studied 30 boys ranging in age from 10 years and two months to 13 years and eight months who had scored low on the Wechsler Intelligence Scale for Children (WISC) and the Stanford-Binet Intelligence Test. The I.Q.'s of these boys ranged between 55 and 75, with a mean of 67.57. The researchers hypothesized that the subjects would score higher on the Davis-Eells Culture Fair Games, which is a nonverbal test based on experiences common to all children and designed to reduce the effect of cultural influences. However, the boys did no better on this test than on the other two.

The same factors that cause lower class children's motivation and "set" for test taking to be inadequate cause their general academic achievement to be poor. Children reared in families in which the parents themselves cannot read or regard reading and the school curriculum as unimportant can scarcely receive the kind of preparation necessary for achieving both good academic performance and high intelligence test scores. This sort of family attitude makes even the idea of attending school a difficult adjustment for lower class children to make; school is unfamiliar ground for them, whereas, for middle class children, school is an extension of the home in that school rewards and punishes them for about the same kinds of performance (Havighurst, 1951). After lower class children begin attending school, their exposure to middle class values does not often improve these children's motivation significantly. It might improve with careful teaching and proper learning conditions, but most lower class children attend the ill-equipped schools staffed with ill-prepared teachers that characterize the poorer districts in most cities.

These factors are usually augmented by other concomitants of low socio-economic status, which, of course, help to determine the motivation and achievement of lower class children. Their parents may provide few books or magazines and limited opportunities for travel and other social experiences. Parental ignorance or neglect may cause problems in health and nutrition; many of these children have auditory, visual, dental, and other health difficulties. Family disorganization, marked by steady unemployment, broken homes, crime and delinquency, frequent changes of address, and inadequate housing, produces modes of thinking and perceiving quite different from those of children reared in the more stable environment of the middle classes. The culturally disadvantaged child with this kind of family background usually becomes an adult whose socialization has been inadequate—at least according to middle class values—and we cannot wholly correct the effects of his socialization or the lack of it.

Our socialization practices are designed to be effective for middle class children with average I.Q.'s. We also cannot properly fit our socialization methods to children whose native intelligence and learning ability fall in the far ends of

the distribution of intellectual capacity. Degree of intelligence makes its greatest demands on the kind and timing of socialization lessons. The gifted child acquires socialized patterns of thinking and behaving much sooner than the average child, while the retarded child still struggles with Lesson 1. For both the gifted and the retarded child, discordance comes from the inevitable incongruity of chronological age, stage of physical development, and ability to comprehend the meaning of what is being taught.

GIFTEDNESS

Giftedness is a complex phenomenon that does not depend upon a particular score on an I.Q. test or upon outstanding intellectual and professional achievement. In fact, any attempt to quantify giftedness may be futile, because children·who are clearly gifted differ as much in quality of ability as they do in amount. For example, a gifted child might possess one or more of at least three kinds of gifts: a literary or abstract kind, a mechanical or technical kind, and a concrete or practical form of both giftedness and creativity (Burt, 1958). Thus, perhaps the most useful view of giftedness is the social view—that gifted children are those whose performance in a potentially valuable line of human activity is consistently remarkable (Witte, 1958).

Another reason that the social view of giftedness is the most valuable is that *creativity*, which is an important dimension of giftedness, does not depend upon measured intelligence alone. Relatively dull as well as very bright children may be creative. Furthermore, creative thought itself has several dimensions, which may appear in different degrees in different children. Some of these dimensions are the following: (1) fluency, or the number of ideas produced in a particular length of time; (2) flexibility, or the variety of ideas produced; (3) originality, or the degree of uniqueness in the ideas produced; (4) elaboration, or the amount of detail with which the

" . . . *gifted children are those whose performance in a potentially valuable line of human activity is consistently remarkable.*"

intelligence. These operations, according to Guilford (1956), include processing the raw materials of information by (1) understanding them, (2) retaining the basic information, and (3) engaging in either divergent or convergent production of ideas from this information. Divergent production is the invention of new information from the basic information given and is measured in terms of the variety and the quantity of the output. Convergent production is the formation of unique contributions with the given information and is thus a qualitative measure of creation. The final operation is evaluation, in which measures of adequacy, suitability, or worthwhileness are applied to the creation.

Identifying the Gifted and Creative

Identifying a child as gifted presents special problems for both the parent and the educator. Merely labeling a child "gifted" is giving him a burden because that label changes the way in which other people perceive him and, therefore, changes his perception of himself and his relationships with his peers, his parents, and his teachers. Although the label "gifted" may produce jealousy among peers, it almost always evokes new interest in the child on the part of parents and teachers (Torrance, 1965).

The educator may use one or several indicators to identify the gifted child. Common criteria used to identify giftedness are these: teacher judgments, group and individual intelligence tests, school grades and achievement records, and interviews with the child and his parents to determine the extent of his social and emotional adjustment. To these criteria should be added tests of creative thinking and observations of the child's behavior; using these additional measures would prevent the now common confusion of giftedness with conformity, social adjustment, and talent (Torrance, 1965). In order to identify truly gifted children, these criteria should probably all be used in combination. Relying upon a single index of

original ideas continue to be enhanced; and (5) sensitivity to modifications of the original ideas, or different or unique ways to apply the ideas (Guilford, 1956).

These dimensions of creative thought are expressed by means of the *operations of applied* giftedness, such as intelligence tests—which will probably nevertheless continue to be heavily emphasized—often results in not recognizing gifted children.

Next to intelligence tests, teacher judgments are a notoriously poor basis for identifying the gifted. Teachers are often misled by glib, winsome, or attractive children who make the most of their talents but are not gifted. Moreover, teachers often base their judgments on classroom performance, which is not always a valid indicator of giftedness (Hoch, 1962; Taylor, 1964). More often than not, the gifted child expresses his gifts in ways that run counter to the teacher's goals and his idea of what a gifted child is. If the gifted child does not happen to be attuned to either, denial of giftedness and conflict may ensue. The teacher whose efforts are directed to the average child in class may, for example, respond badly to a gifted member of the class who suggests that the teacher "needs to be a more firm disciplinarian if he wishes to gain the respect of the class."

The Nature of the Gifted Child

The popular image of the gifted child is that of a small and sickly bookworm who wears glasses. However, gifted children are actually on the average bigger, healthier, and better looking than other children are (Terman, 1925). This physical superiority continues throughout adulthood (Terman and Oden, 1959). The reason for this superiority is that gifted children usually come from homes with a relatively high cultural and educational status, where the standards of child care are generally higher than those in the average home (Goodenough, 1956). Thus, the gifted tend for economic and social reasons to be physically superior to any other *unselected* group of children; gifted children are not statistically bigger and healthier than ordinary children if the ordinary children come from the same kind of home (Laycock and Caylor, 1964).

This kind of home nurtures the intellect of the gifted child as well as his physical development. The parents, who are usually professional or managerial people, are in general better educated than other people, so that the gifted child grows up in an environment more intellectually stimulating than most. Naturally enough, such parents expect the child to attend college as part of the normal course of affairs, and, indeed, three-quarters of the gifted students from such homes do plan to attend (Stouffer and Shea, 1959). Partly as a result of this intellectual stimulation, the gifted succeed in the academic world regularly and easily.

The socio-economic difference between gifted and nongifted children also influences the social acceptability of the gifted. There is evidence to suggest that they are more socially acceptable than children of lower intellectual and socio-economic levels. Further, the peers of gifted children tend to choose them as leaders. The gifted seem to have less need to conform to peer group pressures, although that is probably more a reflection of socio-economic status than of intellectual ability.

An example of the phenomenon of giftedness in children should help to make the above description more concrete. The author's research work brought him into contact with a family with three children who would be classified—by any measure selected—as gifted. In terms of measured intelligence, the least bright among them had at nine years of age an I.Q. of 155. The brightest had an I.Q. of 165.

The mother of this family is a registered nurse and President of the League of Women Voters in a city in which the membership of the league is made up almost exclusively of women educated considerably beyond the average in our society. Far from the stereotype of the hard-driving, masculinized, intellectual woman seeking an escape from motherhood and wifely duties, she is warm, affectionate, reliable, dedicated, hard-working, bright, and capable of dealing effectively with demanding personal and social relationships of all sorts. She is an omnivorous reader and a critical thinker who can never seem to get her fill of the thought processes and opinions of her fellow human beings.

Her husband is a university professor who shares her variegated interest in civic, social, and political events. Successful in his own right, he has been elected to a number of presidencies within his own professional group and has served in a variety of civic and social capacities. He also has a wide circle of friends, but his inexhaustible energy allows him to juggle this variety of interests simultaneously.

The eldest child is a boy who in 1966 was 16 years old. This boy's elementary school and junior high school teachers saw that he was different from the average child but provided no coherent plan of educational stimulation for him. Consequently, he soon withdrew from the educational pattern prescribed for the average student and developed his own curriculum outside the school. For example, on weekends he regularly retreated to the basement, where he had constructed a complete miniature society subject only to his own rules of conduct, which were supplemented with suitable social reinforcements. Each of the people in this society had a personal history, an assigned task in life, and the tools necessary to accomplish that task. At the age of eight, this boy had invented in one evening a mathematical system that he christened "Quay-Doddy." Quay-Doddy turned out to be an independent invention of the system known as "long division." At the age of 16, he began doing advanced work at the university while he was still in high school.

The second child is also a son, who was at 15 years of age taller and heavier than the average American adult male, popular among his peers, and a natural leader. Even at that age, he was responsible, independent, and sensitive to the personalities and needs of other people. As a freshman in high school, he made the varsity football team, won a city-wide leadership prize, and received both an athletic and an academic award. He worked by his own choice and thus had a workday beginning at 6 A.M. and ending at 7 P.M. after football practice. What remained of his evening was devoted to homework. His life was as organized as an adult's, and he pursued his goals in a systematic and calculated fashion. Although the older boy was detached from everyday life and immersed in a world of symbols and abstractions, this one achieved a remarkable balance between the social, intellectual, and personal spheres of living.

The youngest child, a daughter, was at the age of 10 writing several plays, reading almost continuously (even at every meal), running for various school offices, participating in every extracurricular school activity, maintaining at least a dozen different hobby collections, and complaining bitterly that she was incredibly bored by the gross lack of activity that life offered to her. Her friends were on the average two years her senior, but that seemed totally irrelevant to her success in achieving leadership among them. Her native intelligence was coupled with an unusual verbal capacity, so that her brothers responded to her not as a 10 year old female but as an intellectual peer who challenged their understanding of the world and its contents. Both boys, therefore, "picked on her" at every opportunity; the evening meal sounded like a spirited town hall meeting in which the parents acted as moderators to limit responses that became excessive. Interestingly, the most devastating insult that could be launched by one child toward another was the accusation of stupidity or ignorance. Thus, the daughter referred to her brothers as "mental retards."

Some generalizations can be drawn from this case study. It was fortunate that those parents were matched with those children. The three children were immersed in a psychological and intellectual life suited to stimulate them to take advantage of their basic capacities. Under other circumstances, the native capacities of these children could have been stifled by a restrictive atmosphere imposed by parents who failed to recognize their children's gifts. Even in an environment that was tolerable but did not stimulate the children to achieve close to their potential, their level of achievement could have reached no more than average heights. Clearly, even though typical child rearing procedures may work very well with average children, something less typical is required for gifted ones.

Educating the Gifted and Creative

American society is committed to the notion that everyone should be given equal opportunity to develop to the limit of his potential. Therefore, different educational approaches and methods should be used for students with different intellectual abilities (Lucito, 1963). Nonetheless, our society has not responded in great measure to the educational needs of gifted children. In 1961, for example, only 11 percent of the nearly 0.75 million school-age gifted children were to encounter anything even resembling special educational opportunity (Sprague and Dunn, 1961; Mackie and Dunn, 1962). These estimates are sheer guesses, of course, and they assume a nonexistent scientific agreement about who the gifted are or are not.

Many of the so-called "programs" for the gifted have been no more than limited attempts to give special training to a few children on a part-time basis. Part of the reason for this limited response to the needs of gifted children is, of course, the acute shortage of specially trained teachers. The consequence of this shortage is that both kinds of children learn from teachers trained to teach only the average child, and most gifted children thus receive basically the same sort of intellectual stimulation that ordinary children do.

One danger in teaching gifted children in this way is that teachers without special training may try to make the gifted fit an artificial idea of what the gifted child ought to be. And the goals of the teacher are vital in determining the educational experience of any child, gifted or not. Unfortunately, the goals of many American teachers are, at least according to one extensive study (Torrance, 1965), ones that are liable to cripple the expression of giftedness and creativity rather than foster it. In this study, Torrance compiled the views of over 1,000 teachers from several

different states on the ideal gifted student. The teachers noted on a check list of 62 characteristics those that should be encouraged in pupils and those that should be discouraged or punished. From these teacher ratings, Torrance formed an index of desirability and undesirability.

Of the 10 personality characteristics that these teachers rated as most desirable, consideration for others was the single most important one. However, creative students do not always snugly fit this view of the way to behave. When creative people become absorbed in their work, they may have little thought for those about them. Placing such a high premium on consideration for others smacks of the urge to produce conformity in those having the least need for it.

The characteristic rated second in importance was independence in thinking. It is reassuring that teachers prize this characteristic, for thinking independently, making judgments based on this thinking, and standing by these judgments despite the pressure exerted by others who disagree are vitally important personal characteristics. Nevertheless, independence in thinking must be coupled with the courage to defend one's ideas, and courage is not rated very highly by either parents or teachers. Courteousness, industriousness, obedience, energy, and so forth are all valued more highly.

The characteristic that the teachers thought next in importance was determination. As Torrance notes, "Someone has suggested that the truly creative personality is likely to be the first to give in but the last to give up" (p. 15). Oddly enough, however, it is this characteristic that is liable to bring the student into conflict with his teachers; they value determination provided that it does not subtly cross over into the realm of antagonism or resistance.

The fourth-most-important characteristic was industriousness, which is, of course, a quality that all teachers hope to instill in all children. It is questionable, however, whether this quality can really be taught to the gifted child because his curiosity tends to drive him to labors far exceeding those of the average child. Indeed, for the gifted, they do not appear to be labors because the pursuit of truth cannot be labeled work or play for him.

Torrance's sample of teachers thought a sense of humor fifth in importance. Although it would be comforting to assume that all gifted children possess a wry or droll but intellectual sense of humor, some of the gifted unfortunately assume the role of the class clown or act in a silly or crazy manner in their attempts to deal with the inner tensions that they are experiencing in social living. The other five characteristics in the list of the 10 most valued were these: being curious, being sincere, being courteous, doing work on time, and being physically healthy. Clearly, the entire list is discouraging. Few of us in the less gifted majority are capable of meeting the emotional, intellectual, and social challenge of giftedness.

Torrance's findings are only one indicator of our failure to alter drastically and inventively our approach to educating gifted children. One reason for this failure is that we are the victims of our own conformity to tradition; there is security in our familiar habits. Another, much more crucial, reason is the tendency of educators to reflect the cultural confusion over the proper kind and degree of privilege to be accorded to intellectually superior individuals. The philosopher, poet, writer, artist, and musician are still regarded with suspicion because of their apparent idleness in the work-a-day world. This public uncertainty is echoed in the schools, where disagreement remains about the degree to which students of high potential should be allowed to deviate from the average educational pattern.

These difficulties must be eradicated and an educational experience appropriate to the needs of gifted children designed. Some of the requirements for a new design can at least be outlined. Whatever the curricular plan, the first ingredient in the overall design must be a provision for motivating the children to use their gifts. Second, if we are to foster creativity as well as technical ability, any design must demand these characteristics from students (McNeil, 1960):

"The philosopher, poet, writer, artist, and musician are still regarded with suspicion because of their apparent idleness in the work-a-day world."

1. An insatiable urge to inquire into the nature of the world around them.

2. A willingness to be skeptical of man's most cherished beliefs and immutable laws.

3. A capacity to pursue this inquiry in the face of opposition from other people.

Third, the current trend toward grouping students according to ability and achievement must be accelerated. This emphasis on custom-tailoring education to fit the individual's capacities and needs and the raising of standards of performance for able students cannot help but improve both the curriculum for and the performance of the average student as well as the able underachiever.

Finally, there must be some provision for the enrichment of gifted children's comprehension of their own and other people's psychological workings. Learning the way to emotional stability and self-insight is an integral part of acculturation in general and education in particular. This kind of learning has been ignored through the devotion of educators to goals of intellectual and academic accomplishment, although a crippling emotional conflict can undo the most thorough and energetic attempts to sharpen a student's intellect and creativity.

RETARDATION

At the other end of the continuum of intelligence are retarded children. Despite our advances in knowledge about retardation, we cannot explain the cause of 90 percent of the cases of retardation. There are, however, theories that try to account for it. For example, some theorists maintain that stimulus deprivation is a primary cause of mental retardation. Most of these theorists designate the largest group of retardates by the term "cultural-familial." This term suggests that the cause of retardation is a complex interaction of environmental and hereditary factors. The advocates of this position point out that retardates come from families in rural or urban slum areas, where emotional, intellectual, and social stimulation is often severely deficient.

Other theorists claim that the cause of retardation is genetic or biochemical. Early advocates of this position believed that most of the brain damage resulting in retardation was produced by birth injuries. However, it is now suggested that factors present at the time of conception or arising during the first three months of pregnancy produce an abnormal fetus, which, in turn, produces after-the-fact birth difficulties (Masland, 1958). And, indeed, there are recognizable pathological conditions in 60 percent of the children with I.Q.'s below 70. For example, abnormalities in the chromosomal structures, abnormalities of gestation, dietary deficiencies of the mother, metabolic disorders, virus infections in the mother, blood type incompatibility of the mother and fetus, or the mother's inhalation of carbon monoxide or other poisonous fumes may be cited as the cause of retardation.

Although the cause of all kinds of retardation is unlikely to be purely biological, some kinds are clearly the result of physical damage of an originally sound brain and nervous system. For example, one of these kinds, the direct result of brain damage, is called the "Strauss syndrome" or the "Strauss-type child." This type of child exhibits the following biological indicators of brain injury: slight neurological signs, a history of neurological impairment, and no history of mental retardation in his family. These are, of course, coupled with patterns of behavior that issue in intellectual inadequacy. These patterns include perceptual disorders, perseveration, thinking or conceptual disorders, and behavioral disorders (Strauss and Lehtinen, 1947). Nevertheless, even given these criteria for identifying the Strauss syndrome, distinguishing a Strauss-type child from other types of retardates is still difficult.

Classification of Retardation

In order to determine whether or not a child is retarded, two criteria are commonly used. One is the *social criterion*, which is a measure of ability to conform to the laws and customs of society and of ability to take care of oneself in the context of everyday life. The other is the *psychometric criterion*, which is a measure of performance on a standardized intelligence test. This criterion is much too restrictive to be an accurate appraisal of something as complex as retardation but has been a popular basis for classification.

The traditional way of classifying retarded children is to place them in one of three categories—*idiocy, imbecility,* and *moronity.* These categories are based on a loose combination of social and psychometric criteria. According to this type of classification, idiocy is the most severe form of retardation. About 5 per cent of those classified as retarded fall in this category. On a standardized I.Q. test, idiots receive a maximum score of 20. Consequently, their potential mental age cannot quite exceed that of an average three year old child. Thus, the kinds of dangers that the world holds for a two or three year old exist in equal measure for idiots. It is almost impossible to teach such persons even to control elementary bodily functions. Because they cannot take care of themselves or even respond slowly to simple spoken commands, idiots are helpless in our society. Therefore, idiots are custodial, and nearly all live in institutions.

The next-less-severe form of retardation is imbecility. The I.Q. range of imbeciles is between 20 and 50, so that their maximum mental age is the equivalent of a six or seven year old child's. Imbeciles are capable of learning a minimal degree of bodily care and, under ideal circumstances and adequate supervision, can learn to perform some simple, routine tasks. Thus, imbeciles are trainable, but they cannot be expected to move into everyday life, marry, earn a living, or manage themselves except in the simplest fashion. They also cannot be educated; they are incapable of learning the fundamentals of reading, writing, or spelling except for the simplest of words. Arithmetic is beyond them.

The least severe form of retardation is moronity. Morons may have I.Q.'s as high as 70. They can take care of themselves reasonably well and are usually educable. However, morons cannot do schoolwork above the sixth grade level, and they learn very slowly. In many social and work situations, the intellectual simplicity of morons is only a modest handicap—they respond with emotions appropriate to the situation and

are accepted and often protected by others. Morons are often recognized as people with intellectual limitations who yet are accorded a satisfactory social niche by those who are not far removed from them intellectually.

One difficulty in the exclusive use of this classification system is that the two criteria for deciding whether an individual is retarded may not be weighted in the same way throughout his life. Thus, for example, during an individual's school years, an impaired ability to learn and the consequent low I.Q. score would classify him as one of the three kinds of retardates. However, this same individual may as an adult be able to maintain a home and family or at least earn a living reasonably well. Such an adult would then not be considered by society as retarded, but rather "slow." Conversely, the child who seems to rank close to average children in school may be unable to lead a normal life as an adult and would therefore be classified by society as retarded during his adulthood.

Moreover, using these two criteria at all implies that there are only two kinds of children, retarded and normal. Dividing children into these two categories leaves no place for those who are not mentally retarded but who need special treatment and understanding. For example, one type of child who is neither normal nor retarded is the *pseudo-retardate.* This condition is primarily triggered by physiological factors in the child's brain and nervous system (Burks, 1961). The pseudo-retarded child

"demonstrates severe academic deficiencies, particularly in reading. He can be shown to possess a general intelligence rating above that accepted as a criterion for placement in a class for the mentally retarded. He may or may not be a so-called behavior problem, but he does commonly exhibit such symptoms as distractability, impulsivity, and restlessness. He is often uncoordinated. The teachers call him immature. Usually the child demonstrating this syndrome is a boy (Burks, 1961, p. 65).

We are not always able to distinguish this condition from true retardation.

Finally, this three-part classification is subject to two other objections. First, so many degrees of retardation are possible that lumping all retarded children into one or another of only three categories is misleading. Thus, most psychologists prefer to use the more descriptive labels approved by the American Association of Mental Deficiency. These labels are *borderline, mild, moderate, severe,* and *profound* retardation.

Second, the categories of idiocy, imbecility, and moronity are inadequate for the educator because they do not sufficiently designate degrees of educability. Consequently, most educators rely on another three-part division: *educable,* those with an I.Q. between 50 and 75; *trainable,* those with an I.Q. between 30 and 50; and *custodial,* those with an I.Q. below 30. Educators have assumed responsibility for the educable and limited responsibility for the trainable. The educable can at least become literate; the trainable cannot be expected to achieve more than minimum literacy, but they can be socialized enough to learn rudimentary skills in self-care and in language.

The educable mentally retarded constitute about 2 percent of the school age population. The intellectual development of these children is only about one-half to three-quarters of the average child's. By the time that they are 16 years old, their mental age ranges from eight to 12. Most of the educable retarded are incapable of doing schoolwork above the fourth or fifth grade level (Dunn, 1963). However, in some school systems, there is no immediate attempt to differentiate between retarded and normal children; only after two or three years of failure are the educable retarded recognized as such and referred for placement in a special class or school.

Perhaps, as our cultural emphasis on academic excellence grows, special educational services may be provided for children with I.Q.'s as high as 80 or 85 at the beginning of their school careers (Dunn, 1963). If that happens, children who are therefore considered educable mentally retarded may constitute as much as 15 or 16 percent of the school population.

Trainable mentally retarded children develop intellectually at about one-third to one-half the rate of the average child. As adults, their mental age is between five and eight years old. The retardation of the trainable is so great that, on the average, they cannot be expected to do academic work beyond the fourth grade level—the minimum standard for literacy. Thus, the trainable retarded can benefit from participation in the regular public school program, but they are not educable in the academic sense.

The trainable retardates rarely read for pleasure, are not able to take care of money, and so forth, but they are able to dress and feed themselves. They can learn to talk and to carry on simple conversations, and, if the trainable retarded are protected, they avoid common dangers and perform simple chores. As adults, they are not socially or economically independent; they need care or supervision throughout their lives, and they seldom marry and raise families or even set up homes of their own. These retardates usually require the care of some social agency or residential facility for the retarded.

Regular or Special Classes?

During the last two decades, the number of special classes for both educable and trainable retarded children has grown rapidly. However, at the same time, a great deal of argument and research has accumulated over the efficacy of these classes. Neither regular nor special classes have been universally satisfactory for even the educable retarded (Dunn, 1963), although at present the great majority of these children attend regular classes. This arrangement will probably continue. Nonetheless, advocates of special classes state that educable retarded children placed in regular classes find themselves confronted with a standard of achievement so far out of reach that they are unable to make a reasonable evaluation of their own capacity. Thus, if they can work in a setting in which the rate of learning is consistent with their ability, their appraisals of themselves would become more reasonable and healthy (Jordan and DeCharmes, 1950; Meyerowitz, 1962).

However, the difficulty with unequivocally advocating a special class for the retarded child is that it can also have a negative effect on his self-concept; obviously, a youngster's opinion of his own value would drop when he found himself pulled out of a classroom of friends and placed in a different room or, perhaps, in a different school. Moreover, special classes accumulate troublesome, disturbed children who have had a great deal of difficulty in regular classes. The child is asked to adjust to peers who may be at his intellectual level but who are physically or chronologically distant from him. If the class is housed in a regular school, then he must also be prepared to respond to the attitudes of normal children, who soon learn that this is a special class with special characteristics and that the children in it are either dumb or have caused problems in the regular classroom.

The retarded child's recognition of his deficiency affects his self-concept even when his retardation is not severe—that is, when his I.Q. is between 60 and 85. One study (Meyerowitz, 1962) found that educable retarded children as young as two and a half to three and a half years old have some notions about social expectations of acceptable behavior and that children as young as three and a half to four years old have what seems to be a consistent self-concept that can be measured. Meyerowitz measured the self-concepts of 120 first grade children with I.Q.'s between 60 and 85 by means of the Illinois Index of Self-Derogation. This index is made up of 30 items, and each item consists of two sentences. One sentence describes a child who is socially undesirable—that is, some children do not like this child; the other sentence describes a socially desirable child—that is, many children like this child. After the subjects listened to the description of the two imaginary children, they marked on a score sheet the child that they regarded as most like themselves. Thus, this test measured how the children differentiated between socially desirable and undesirable alternatives. Meyerowitz concluded that

segregating retarded children into special classes—and so officially recognizing them as retarded—makes them tend to develop very clear and very negative self-concepts.

There has been prolonged argument about whether or not the trainable mentally retarded should be put in either regular or special classes. Perhaps the trainable are not properly the responsibility of the school system, for it can be said that the unique function of the schools is to educate children who can learn. The trainable mentally retarded do not have the ability to learn skills for abstract reasoning, judgment making, and problem solving and will never return in full measure to society what society has invested in their schooling. Moreover, placing trainable children in regular classes sets up false hopes for their parents and puts an unnecessary burden on teachers who are without the preparation to give these children a rudimentary socialization. On the other hand, special classes may not be the answer, because children of this sort may learn as much at home. And it has been maintained that, considering the shortage of teachers and schools, these children should be kept there (Goldberg and Cruickshank, 1958).

However, regardless of whether either kind of retarded child is put in any class or kept at home, he must be taught by his parents or his teachers how to achieve a minimal personal and social adjustment. Without that training, he is rejected by other people because of his frequent antisocial behavior, such as fighting, swearing, cheating, and bullying. In turn, the child reacts to his lack of acceptance by expressing hostility, aggression, defiance, or withdrawal. This sort of behavior causes further rejection. Because he is unable to understand why others treat him so badly, he may try to influence the others' opinion of him by bragging, bribing, threatening, or stealing. And so the vicious circle continues.

Such a child, having no particular ability or skill that would help to make him a desirable member of the group, is continuously rejected not only by normal children but by other retarded children as well (Johnson, 1950; Johnson and

Kirk, 1950). Nonetheless, the trained parent or teacher can do much to socialize the most visible and least acceptable aspects of the child's behavior through direct, concrete, and repeated instruction and demonstration.

The need to help the retarded child achieve a minimal social and personal adjustment is one reason that psychotherapy as an adjunct to the socialization of the retarded has been frequently discussed (Abel, 1953; Burton, 1954; Sarason, 1959). However, most therapists believe that the effectiveness of psychotherapy on the retarded is not worth the effort put into it. These therapists feel that retarded people will not voluntarily seek psychotherapeutic help because they are unaware of the existence, severity, or meaning of their emotional problems. Moreover, psychotherapy relies heavily on the development of insight and understanding as a prerequisite to the modification of behavior, but the mentally retarded lack enough intelligence to manage the necessary insight and understanding.

Although these objections to the use of psychotherapy are certainly valid, some success with it has been reported. For example, Heiser (1954) tried psychotherapy on an individual basis with 14 children over a period of one year, and, even though their I.Q.'s changed little, both the behavior and the adjustment of the children improved. Fisher and Wolfson (1953) also reported general success in psychotherapy with 12 female subjects. However, most of these studies are clinical reports uncontrolled along dimensions such as chronological age, mental age, the kind of institution in which the patients were confined, how long the patients stayed in the institution, what kinds of behavior were manifested by the patients at the time that the psychotherapy was undertaken, and so on. Thus, the quality of the evidence of improvement may be less than ideal. But certainly the quantity of it suggests that psychotherapy might help some of the mentally retarded. If it is to help more of them live in society, however, the traditional psychotherapeutic methods must be modified to fit the limitations of the mentally retarded.

The Retardate in Society

If mentally retarded children are given the appropriate socialization, education, and skills, many such children can grow up to be reasonably well-adjusted members of society. Here, for the educable mentally retarded at least, special classes do seem to help. According to several studies (Boboroff, 1956; Dinger, 1961; Johnson, 1957; Phelps, 1956), after graduating from special classes, most of the retardates studied found employment in an unskilled, semiskilled, or service type of work. They married, established homes, purchased goods, and blended indistinguishably into society. The majority of these graduates invested in insurance, maintained bank accounts, and negotiated loans. Compared with the general population, however, the retarded group had a great number of legal offenses and poorer driving records, participated less in community and club activities, and took less interest in voting.

Nevertheless, some later studies are not nearly so encouraging as these earlier ones. For example, Lee, Hegge, and Voelker (1959) found that, of the group that they studied, only 61 percent of the graduates of special classes and 28 percent of the residential training school graduates had made even a minimal social and economic adjustment in young adulthood. Moreover, a considerable percentage failed to abide by the laws, and a large proportion of the girls were sexually delinquent. This study casts some scientific doubt on the adequacy of earlier studies, which may have suffered from an optimistic bias.

The moderately mentally retarded may also live reasonably well-adjusted lives. Of this group, at least according to one study (Clarke and Clarke, 1958), the majority of both males and females make a successful social adjustment in a community, marry people with higher intellectual capacities, and have children who are average in intelligence. As many as 80 percent of this group may get married (Charles, 1953).

As would be expected, the trainable mentally retarded do not lead such nearly normal lives even after having attended special classes. For example, in one study of 84 young adults with I.Q.'s below 50 (Delp and Lorenz, 1953), none of them had established his own home; most of them still lived with their parents or in residential facilities. Most of those who were living at home were socially accepted in the neighborhood and were useful about the house. The majority of these retardates were able to get about the neighborhood, eat in restaurants, go for groceries, attend movies, and enjoy other kinds of entertainment. However, out of all 84 subjects, only 10 had ever been gainfully employed, and only two had ever held full-time jobs. Delp and Lorenz conclude that special classes had been important in training all of these retardates. Although this conclusion is a little difficult to justify because there was no control group against which to compare these findings, the results correspond to those of other researchers who have studied trainable retardates with I.Q.'s of 40 to 50.

On the other hand, trainable retardates with only slightly lower I.Q.'s are predictably much less independent—even though they may have attended special classes. One study (Tasdall, 1960) reports that, of 126 retardates with I.Q.'s between 30 and 40 who had been enrolled in special classes for the trainable mentally retarded, one-fourth were at home and receiving no formal training, another quarter were still in special classes, and a fifth were in parent-sponsored classes for school age trainables. The remainder were in institutions, working in sheltered workshops, or attending classes for the educable mentally retarded. Only three of these subjects had managed to find gainful employment in the community, and only one of the three received a regular salary.

Clearly, a crucial factor in both the educable and the trainable retardate's successful personal and social adjustment is economic usefulness. Some jobs are, fortunately, open to retardates; these jobs require only minimum literacy and practically no academic skills. Moreover, the individual's I.Q. is no predictor of success in these jobs, for any I.Q. between 40 and 80 seems sufficiently high provided that the job selection and the employment conditions are adequate and appropriate. The important criteria for employment seem to be good health, coordination, and appearance. There is no reliable evidence that work habits or personality have an effect on employability. The number of years in school also has no apparent effect upon retardates' employability, although the individuals who have spent a long time in special classes are probably more successful than those who have not attended any special classes (Kolstoe, 1961).

However, after the retarded have been hired, they still seem to need some special help—at least initially. For example, in the first few months of employment, the retarded have a number of common problems, such as a lack of acceptance by fellow workers (manifested through teasing and practical jokes) and a lack of social and job sophistication (disregard for proper dress and punctuality, failure to report an absence, inability to handle a time clock, ignorance of cafeteria procedures, or inability to communicate a problem to the foreman). Furthermore, such problems as the inability to budget and spend money intelligently, the lack of responsibility and initiative coupled with an inability to read notices, work tags, and instructions often results in guessing or bluffing rather than seeking help (Peckham, 1951). This tactic, of course, creates more problems. It is obvious that specific skills must be taught in school to the retarded if they are to be helped by our educational system.

SUMMARY

The process of socializing human beings is aided, distorted, and limited by the fact that man is a thinking animal. This biological capacity to think, reason, and solve problems makes the process of socializing the child an enormous task. Complicating this task is the uneven distribution of intelligence; special techniques are required to socialize the small percentage of children who are either gifted or retarded. An additional complication is that the two factors of heredity and environment set limits on the quality of the child's intellectual response to his lessons in socialization.

For the average child, chronological age, physical development, and intelligence grow apace, so that the developmental tasks of socialization are a reasonable assignment. For the gifted and the retarded, however, typical socialization and its timing are inappropriate. Our methods of socializing the young are designed to be effective for those in the middle range of intellectual func-

tioning. We have yet to adapt these methods to fit those at either end of the distribution of native intelligence.

The several degrees of severity of retardation have posed special problems for our complex industrialized society; daily life may be bewildering even for those with normal intelligence. Assimilation of the gifted into our culture has proved to be a less pressing social problem, but the waste of intellectual resources has been a particularly costly one.

No model of socialization is applicable to all of the children in our society, for each child grows up in a unique psychological, social, and physical setting. Thus, the social class and the racial or ethnic group to which the child belongs—as well as his family pattern and structure, his sex, and his intellectual capacity—influence the shape of his personality and his adjustment to society.

SOCIAL CLASS

For analytical purposes, the social classes are usually broken down into the *lower-lower*, the *upper-lower*, the *lower-middle*, the *upper-middle*, and the *upper classes*. However, in practice, this breakdown is sometimes difficult to identify. The rigidity of the class structure and the percentage of the population in a particular class vary from community to community. Moreover, the class structure itself is less clearly defined in newer communities than in older ones (Bernard, 1962); it takes time for people to detect the criteria that differentiate one person from another. Finally, of course, growth and technological and social change alter the class structure in any community.

8

Social class, race, and socialization

However, regardless of the class structure in a community at any one time, the social status of an inhabitant can be estimated by using a number of indexes. These indexes include the individual's education, his occupation, the amount and source of his income, the district that he lives in, and the kind of home that he has. The members of a particular social class also have a similar life style and set of values (McNeil, 1960). Thus, other indicators of the social class to which an individual belongs are the kind of people that he is most free to associate with, the kind of clothes that he wears, the organizations to which he belongs, and the ways in which he spends his leisure time.

The Lower Classes

Members of the bottom half of the lower class may include between 15 and 25 percent of the total population. They are identifiable by their minimal formal education and their jobs, which are not very secure or well paid. Unstable marriages are another characteristic of this part of the lower class. Girls of this class marry early, they may indulge in common law marriage, and their husbands often desert them. Because these girls usually marry again, calling lower-lower class marriage "serial monogamy" (Hollingshead, 1949) is not a great exaggeration. Lower class religious taste runs to fundamentalist persuasions of a Baptist or Catholic form.

Lower-lower class people often have socially maladjusted parents, live in inadequate homes in deteriorated neighborhoods, have low incomes, and move frequently (Kvaraceus, 1954). These living conditions contribute to conflict with the legal authorities and arrest, which are frequent among members of the lower-lower class. For example, in the sample for one study (Hollingshead, 1949), about half the men had been convicted of habitual public drunkenness, 12 percent were charged with property offenses, 9 percent were charged with sex offenses or family neglect, and 30 percent were charged with miscellaneous offenses.

The amount of social contact between members of the lower-lower class and members of the middle class is minimal, in part because of the difference in values and life styles. Thus, for example, lower-lower class adults participate very little in community affairs. There sometimes seems to be a kind of running warfare between the two classes in which the members of the middle class complain that lower-lower class people do not participate in community affairs, while the members of the lower-lower class feel that they have been excluded. These people, aware that they lack the proper education or information about the world around them and the proper clothes or manners, feel that they would be shunned by members of the middle class.

The upper segment of the lower class shows all the signs of beginning middle-classness. In this group, which constitutes between 20 and 40 percent of the total population, is a mixture of lower class and middle class habits, values, and attitudes. These people, a mixture of skilled and unskilled laborers (blue-collar workers), even usually look like the middle class picture of respectable, honest, clean, hard-working, sincere people. Moreover, although they may live on the edge of financial insolvency and carry a steady burden of car and appliance payments throughout their lives, they do not get financially behind in the same way that members of the bottom half of the lower class do.

However, even though members of the upper-lower class are respected and trusted by those in the lower-middle class and seem superficially like them, the upper-lower class members remain effectively without political power. Their religious affiliations are Catholic, Lutheran, Methodist, Presbyterian, and Congregational. Another distinction is that they seldom engage in civic affairs except for those connected with labor unions. Finally, even the social clubs that the members of the upper-lower class belong to (Odd Fellows, Masons, and Knights of Columbus) are ones almost exclusively composed of people in their own social class.

The Middle Classes

The middle classes are supposed to be the backbone of and controlling force in our society. These white-collar classes are composed of skilled workers, managers, salesmen, clerical workers, foremen, school teachers, and other people in similar occupations. However, it is not always easy to identify a particular individual as being middle class; even middle class people are confused about who should be included in this category (Cuber and Kunkel, 1954).

Members of the lower-middle class live in small but well-furnished and well-kept homes located in respectable residential areas. These people marry later than those in the class below them, their children are born in hospitals, and desertion, separation, and divorce are less common. Both children and parents recognize the value of education; the children become their teachers' favorites because they work hard in school, consider it important, and seldom create disciplinary problems. Lower-middle class children go to college as a necessary way to improve their social status.

The religious affiliations of the lower-middle class are Catholic and various Protestant denominations. Church attendance is higher and more regular in this class than in any other. Brushes with the law are minimal; they account for only about 8 percent of the total number of arrests in this country. However, it is perhaps in social and civic life that members of this class are most distinguished. They are the active ingredient in welfare activities, PTA's, and fraternal and service groups.

Of the people in the upper-middle class, about half have moved up from a lower status. These are the successful executives, professionals, and administrators. Their homes are built on spacious lots and are almost obsessively well furnished, well kept, and well insured. Because the energies of these people are devoted to community activities, they have little time to spend with their children. The children are perhaps overorganized and spend a great deal of their time doing things that are character forming or skills building in groups specially designed for them (Bernard, 1961).

Education is, for the members of the upper-middle class, almost compulsory; the very idea of their children's not getting good grades elicits great anxiety. The children quickly absorb this attitude toward education and thus strive excessively to excel. They get the best grades, they take college preparatory courses, and they fare well on conventional measures of social adjustment and intelligence. The good schools in the neighborhoods where these children live make a vital contribution to their preparation for the future. Consequently, their schooling may be determined almost solely by being born into a particular family with upper-middle class status. And then these schools feed the children into occupations that match their social status (Davie, 1953).

The Upper Class

Only about 3 percent of our population belongs to the upper class, and only a few of its members have been studied very thoroughly. Their status is an inherited one. Thus, "family" is important to them. Wealth is less important because, although it was once used to gain status, it is not necessary to acquire more wealth or even to maintain it in order to keep social prestige. The children go to college and join the right fraternities, but not all of them graduate because, according to these people, being a college dropout is not very disgraceful. Further, not many of them go to graduate school; most education beyond a bachelor's degree is "trade" training and thus inappropriate to members of the upper class.

THE IMPLICATIONS OF SOCIAL CLASS

An individual's membership in a particular social class has important implications for his socialization, his personality, and his life style. Being born poor, for example, affects one's development and socialization in ways that are deep-reaching and all-pervasive. "Members of different social classes, by virtue of enjoying (or suffering) different conditions of life, come to see the world differently—to develop different conceptions of social reality, different aspirations and hopes and fears, different conceptions of the desirable . . ." (Kohn, 1963, p. 47).

The individual's conception of the desirable determines, of course, the qualities that he wants to instill in his children. Although members of all the social classes have the same broad child rearing values, members of different classes emphasize these values differently. For example, all parents in general value obedience, neatness, cleanliness, self-control, curiosity, happiness, and consideration. However, lower class parents emphasize the first three qualities, while middle class parents emphasize the last four (Kohn, 1963). Thus, lower class parents value overt conformity to the external

prescriptions of society, and middle class parents value self-direction. These different emphases are in part the result of the different occupations of each class (Kohn, 1963). In addition to the difference in education required, in stability and amount of income, and in prestige, middle class jobs involve the manipulation of interpersonal relationships, ideas, and symbols, whereas working class jobs involve the manipulation of things. Moreover, middle class people direct themselves, whereas working class people are directly supervised by others.

The values supporting the patterns of behavior required to do these jobs are instilled in children through different methods of punishment and reward; "working parents are consistently more likely to employ physical punishment, while the middle-class families rely more on reasoning, isolation, appeals to guilt, and other methods involving the threat of loss of love" (Bronfenbrenner, 1958, p. 424). Thus, identification with the aggressor is a characteristic child rearing device for

"Being born poor, for example, affects one's development and socialization in ways that are deep-reaching and all-pervasive."

lower class parents, while anaclitic identification is more typical for middle class parents (Hoffman, 1963).

The timing of and reason for punishment and reward also contribute to the establishment of these values in children (Kohn, 1963). Working class parents are likely to punish when they find the immediate *consequences* of their children's acts intolerable. In contrast, middle class parents punish when they interpret their children's *intentions* as intolerable.

Finally, the operation of these different value systems can be seen in mother-child interaction, which helps to reinforce a particular set of values in the child. Lower class mothers interact with their children much less than middle class mothers do. When the former do interfere in their children's activity, the mothers do so in order to criticize and thereby to redirect that activity into more acceptable, or obedient, behavior. In contrast, middle class mothers interfere in their children's activity in order to teach them by structuring the activity in such a way that it will stimulate them both to think independently and to assume responsibility for the consequences of that activity (Merrill, 1946; Bishop, 1951; Schalock, 1956; Zunich, 1961; Walters, Connor, and Zunich, 1964).

These two sets of child rearing values and techniques produce, of course, two very different kinds of personalities in children. Even as early as four or five years of age, the middle class child is verbal, boisterous, aggressive, and curious. The lower class child, on the other hand, is withdrawn, nonverbal, and indifferent. He may seem aggressive, but that is the result of his predilection for erratic, acting out behavior rather than of the healthy behavior of an energetic and extroverted child.

The personality pattern of the child provides the base for personality development throughout adolescence and adulthood. However, because of the values instilled in the lower class child so early in his life, his personality is not likely to grow in constructive directions; being poor affects personality development in deep-reaching ways. The lower class child as a youth has a poor self-image, fatalistic view of life, and an orientation toward the present rather than the future (Pearl, 1965). His primitive, anti-intellectual attitude contributes to his highly unrealistic expectations of what life holds in store for him (Miller, 1958; Lewis, 1961; Deutsch, 1963).

The lower class youth also suffers a great deal more social humiliation in our culture than the middle class youth does; the middle class youngster has a future if he is patient and does the right things at the right time, but no such option is offered to the lower class youth (Pearl, 1965). His natural reaction to such hopelessness may be demonstrated by placing rats on a jumping stand and forcing them to solve an insoluble problem. The reaction of the rats is neurotic behavior. When there is no way out, human beings respond in the same way (Lewin, 1951).

These effects of being a member of the lower class can be at least partially alleviated early in the child's school years. His teachers can help him by recognizing such factors as these: (1) Lower class pupils often cannot or will not respond in the same manner to the teacher and the curriculum as middle class children do. (2) Broad generalizations about "the average child" make little sense when the differences between the classes are as great as they seem to be; the concept of the average child must be replaced by the concept of the average child belonging to a particular social class. (3) Children must be informed very specifically about the kinds of behavior that teachers expect them to learn; good citizenship is not the same to middle class students as it is to lower class pupils. (4) Some appraisal of the reasons for the learning difficulties of lower class children is necessary (Shapiro, 1960).

Other members of our society can also help lower class children in school. We can ease the difficulties faced by lower class pupils in simply staying in school by reducing the hidden costs of education, such as books, gym fees, laboratory fees, special uniforms, club dues, and so forth. In addition, the direct study of social class and its implications at every level in school might decrease some of the present discrimination to which lower class children are too often exposed (Bernard, 1962).

Despite the viability of these suggestions for helping the lower class child, we should not assume that merely helping him to stay in school will change his lot significantly. The whole life of the lower class youth militates against his emergence from his subculture through education. His educational disability begins early in school and assures his failure when the work required becomes more complex. Moreover, concentrating on the vocational classes in the public schools is an inadequate alternative; vocational training in high school is usually a mockery because it is tacked on to the preferred curriculum.

Thus, for the modern poor, there is no way out. In the past, Horatio Alger effort and thrift could lead to an escape from poverty. In today's technological society, changing an unskilled laborer in the space of a few years into an engineer is impossible. Indeed, even starting a small entrepreneurial enterprise—the one-man business needing little capital investment—is no longer possible for a member of the lower class. The only solution to this dilemma is, unfortunately, a long-term one that will not have much effect for at least a generation or two. Only improving the lives of the poor—and thus changing their attitudes and behavior—and then upgrading education can truly erase the effects of being poor.

SOCIALIZATION AND THE NEGRO

Hopefully, the day will arrive when the color of one's skin is irrelevant to an account of socialization. Today, being a member of a racial minority makes a difference in how one grows up and in what one learns about the world. In this culture, therefore, the Negro child learns lessons that the white child does not. One of the most persistent of the Negro child's lessons is his exclusion from white society.

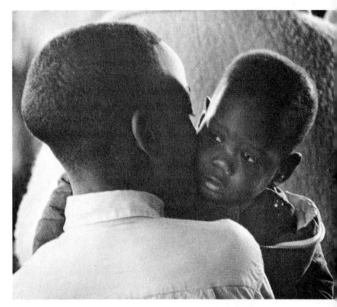

"Today, being a member of a racial minority makes a difference in how one grows up and in what one learns about the world."

The Roots of the Problem

Our present racial problems assumed their basic shape through the particular form that American slavery took. In this system of slavery, the slave had no protection. He was cut off from his past, and he had no hope for the future. He, his "wife," and his "children" were considered to be property and could therefore be treated in whatever manner the whim of their owner dictated. Laws forbade him from learning to read or write, practicing religion, assembling with his fellows, or seeking freedom. Thus, the creation of a dependent, servile class of people was deliberately undertaken. This condition produced in the Negro a personality adapted to survival in the face of absolute authority. Because the reward system for good behavior was contingent on absolute and unquestioning obedience, this type of personality developed without enterprise or the need for achievement.

"One of the most persistent of the Negro child's lessons is his exclusion from white society."

The historical effects of this system on the Negro can be illustrated by comparing it to the system in other countries. In Brazil, for example, a slave had certain social rights. He could marry legally, he could protect his family from being broken up and sold indiscriminately, he had guaranteed days of rest, and he could earn money to buy his freedom. As Glazer (1963) remarked, "the Brazilian slave knew he was a man, and that he differed in degree, not in kind, from his master." Consequently, even though slavery existed longer in Brazil than in America, the Brazilian Negro now feels accepted—without anger and distrust—as a full member of society.

Although American slavery ended, of course, with the Civil War, it was only after Reconstruction that the formation of the Negro family began to take place on a large scale. The setting in which the family developed, however, differed substantially from that typical for the white American family. Jim Crow was invented to reinforce the notion that the Negro is basically inferior. Segregation destroyed the fundamental masculinity of the Negro male, fashioned him into a weak father figure, and forecast the powerlessness of the Negro family system.

Had the American society remained rural, the fate of the Negro family might have been different. Negroes became urban dwellers in greater proportions than the whites and, naturally, lived principally in slums. Slum life destroys family unity for any human being. Because Negroes had little in their past history to cement together family relationships, the erosion of slum dwelling was catastrophic for family unity.

Another prime contributor to family dissolution today is the unavoidable fact of Negro male unemployment. During most of this century, twice as many Negroes as whites have been unemployed. Being unemployed produces stresses that are destructive of family life (Bakke, 1940). First the family's credit is exhausted. Then the wife enters the labor force because she is more employable than her husband. The female thus becomes the bread winner, and another female, the social worker, intervenes to plan the continued existence of the family. The consequence is a reduction of the male to a menial position and an assault on his masculinity. The only way that he can remedy this situation is to find work. However, the Negro male remains the last hired and the first fired.

The differential employment of Negroes—70 percent of Negro employees are women—is to reverse the roles of male and female considered typical in the United States. Moreover, Negro females are better educated than Negro males. Thus, Negro females typically marry people less educated than themselves. These two factors inevitably breed feelings of inadequacy, inferiority, and lower ability or intelligence in the male Negro, who does not always passively accept such feelings as normal. His social and sexual behavior may be in part a form of rebellion against his feelings. The resultant emotional relationship between him and his wife is bound to be reflected in the values transmitted to the children. It is in this crucible that pathology is forged.

This breakdown of stable marital relations is reflected in the disproportionately high rates of divorce, separation, or desertion and illegitimate births among Negroes. Of the urban Negro families, nearly one-quarter are not living together. In some urban centers, such as New York City, the percentage in some years has been as high as 30

"Being unemployed produces stresses that are destructive of family life."

percent—even without including official divorces. In the last 30 years, the rate of illegitimate births has increased for both the white and the non-white population. However, between 1940 and 1963, for example, the Negro rate rose from nearly 17 percent to nearly 23.5 percent, while the white rate rose from 2 percent to 3 percent.

Put another way, by the end of this period, there were 11 more illegitimate births per 1,000 among whites, while there were 68 more per 1,000 among nonwhites. These discrepancies in rate are even higher in certain urban areas of the country.

This combination of high rates for desertion, separation, or divorce and illegitimate births has produced a rising number of families managed by females alone. In the last decade, the number of such families has increased among whites, but this increase is half of that for nonwhites. Nearly one-fourth of all Negro families are headed by females. Thus, only a small number of Negro children will have lived *all* of the first 18 years of their lives with both parents. Further, the large number of broken homes and illegitimate births plus the high rate of Negro unemployment means that many Negro children are on welfare or receive charity at one point or another during childhood; 56 percent of the Negro children are on welfare roles, while only 8 percent of the white children are. The consequences of this way of life for the psychological and social development of the children are incalculable.

Three centuries of exploitation by the white majority have clearly left their mark. This exploitation has influenced not only the form of the Negro family but the basic structure of the Negro society as well. The Negro community is beginning to divide into two groups, a small, stable, middle class group and a disorganized, disadvantaged, lower class group, which are cut off from each other by their economic and psychological differences (Frazier, 1962). The Negro middle class, whose level of stability and conservation of its resources even exceeds that of the white middle class, is improving its social position, while the position of the lower class group is deteriorating.

The Socialization of the Negro Child

One reflection of the separation of Negroes into two distinct social groups is the difference in their socialization practices. It is this difference in the socialization *practices* of lower class Negroes, not in their values, that accounts for the relative inability of members of the lower class to behave in conformity with middle class standards. Negro middle and lower class mothers share the same set of child rearing values—that is, honesty, happiness, obedience to parents, and a good education. However, the lower class mothers emphasize these values in terms of obeying people in authority, being liked, and conforming to external rules of respectability; middle class mothers underscore the same values in terms of the internal qualities of consideration and dependability. The consequence of these different emphases is that middle class mothers are more responsive to their children's emotional needs than lower class mothers are and initiate a significantly greater number of interactions with their children than lower class mothers do.

In these interactions, lower class mothers use more *unilateral techniques* of influencing their children—that is, orders without explanations—

"Three centuries of exploitation by the white majority have clearly left their mark."

than middle class mothers do; the latter use more *bilateral techniques,* such as "consulting" with the children about their behavior. Thus, the lower class mothers more often "bribe, order, or coerce" their children, while the middle class mothers "explain, use psychological manipulation, or sensitize the child to the mother's feelings about his behavior" (Kamii, 1965). In keeping with these techniques, middle class mothers more frequently reward their children, while lower class mothers more frequently set limits for their children's behavior.

Because the nature of the relationship between mother and child as reflected in her socialization practices and values is different for the two groups, punishment occurs in different contexts as well. The middle class Negro child, who is dependent in his relationship with his mother, finds punishment a severe threat to the equilibrium of this relationship. Punishment does not have the same impact or meaning for the lower class child because he does not always view punishment as a threat to a highly gratifying interpersonal relationship (Sears, Maccoby, and Levin, 1957; Bronfenbrenner, 1958; Fraiberg, 1959; Swanson, 1961; Hoffman, 1963; Kahn, 1963; Kamii, 1965).

For both groups of Negro children, however, the psychological and emotional experience of socialization is completely different from that of white middle class Protestant children. The lessons that Negro children learn at the parental knee are supplemented by exposure to their fellow Negroes, both peers and adults. Their peers make up one-third of all the youths in training schools for juvenile delinquents; Negro adults are arrested for 3 out of every 5 instances of murder, manslaughter, aggravated assault, and forcible rape. (This crime rate is not an account of Negro hostility against whites but primarily a record of discord within the Negro population itself.)

There are other important departures from the model of socialization, which is white and middle class, for Negro children in both groups. However, perhaps the most crucial is that, even though Negro children are separated and alienated from the white population (only one Negro in nine is attending school with white children), the families of Negro children are no longer teaching them that in "the white man's country" they must accept inadequacy, inferiority, and dependence as a way of life. Negro children are finding a new model—one never dreamed of by their fathers. Catapulted from obscurity to prominence in the eyes of society, Negro youths must find a new path to self-regard. According to Jones (1965), Negro youths are now seeking a new image, and they are seeking it with a new confidence in their prospects. The Negro young people no longer feel that they are only a part of a helpless and hopeless minority; they are beginning to see their long-term relationship with all the "persons of color" in the larger world.

Jones insists that, in the quest for a new image and full participation in society, Negro youths can select from a number of distinct ideological orientations, or identities. For example, one of these is the *Accommodators.* These are young people who accept the growing improvements in the Negro's status and, being educated, tend to fill the ranks of traditional occupations. The Accommodators do so with satisfaction and a sense of fulfillment. What Jones calls the *Transcenders* are those who study hard and focus on self-development in an attempt to take advantage of the new opportunities being opened to them. Their goals for the good life are the same as those of the Accommodators, but the Transcenders are traversing a set of paths only newly opened to them.

The *Social Activists* work with white youths in activist campaigns designed to achieve political, economic, and educational equality of opportunity. The members of this group vary in terms of the kinds of motivation and of fulfillment that they derive from the activist role.

An additional category is the *Apartheids,* who are Negro youths accepting the Black Muslim ideology. This category may include subcategories, such as the *Identity Seekers,* who wish to segregate themselves from the whites in order to find a distinct identity. For this group, the prerequisites of that identity are often reformation and

The Transcenders

The Social Activists

The Apartheids

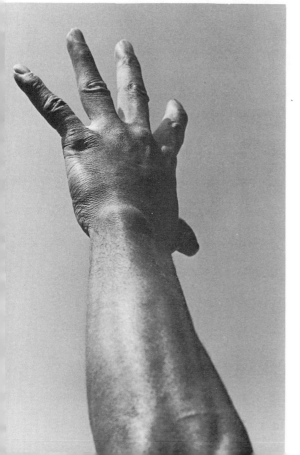

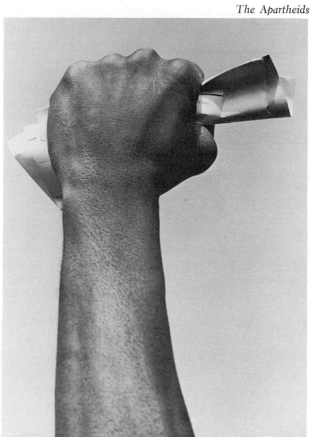

avoidance of temptation, or a clean mind and a strong body. These are prerequisites because they are viewed as the only way to battle the influence of the "white devil." The Apartheid group may also include the *Acter-Outers*, who are committed obsessively and violently to aggression against all white people.

Finally, what might be an extension of the Apartheids are the *Black Worlders*. These consist of Afro-American youths with an activist, black internationalist philosophy. They feel that white versus black must one day become a struggle of international proportions with the planet as the prize.

A vital issue raised by this description of the Negro youth movement resulting from Negro socialization and the social and economic context in which it takes place is why some children become Accommodators, some Transcenders, and others Black Worlders. The answer, in truth, is that we are uncertain of the details of how life styles and values are planted in childhood and thrive throughout adulthood. It would, of course, be possible to try to modify the theoretical model of middle class, white socialization in such a way as to fit it to the double indemnity of lower-classness and Negroness, but that would be a less-than-honest scientific move. Socialization in the Negro family in white America represents a new frontier for research—a frontier as wild and woolly as any explored in the past.

The Negro Child in School

The American family has passed the responsibility for the later socialization of the child to the professional educator. This shift in responsibility was a social decision that has worked imperfectly, for the educational system has yet to grapple adequately with the problem of the culturally disadvantaged. The culturally disadvantaged child has adopted values to deal with his immediate life situation that do not enable him to achieve in school. This failure to adapt to formal education is not a function of inadequate intellectual capacity. Although whites generally receive higher average scores on intelligence tests than Negroes do, there is little evidence to support the hereditary interpretation of Negro-white differences. Rather, there is increasing evidence in favor of an environmental explanation (Anastasi, 1961; Kennedy, Van de Reit, and White, 1963; Klineberg, 1963). Thus, the practice of standardizing tests on white subjects and then using these tests to measure Negro intelligence might be responsible for the lower average scores of Negroes.

The Negro child's failure to succeed in school is, instead, a function of motivation. Motivation as a determinant of intellectual achievement encompasses these factors: (1) the degree to which the child values competent performance in a given area, (2) his expectations of success or failure, (3) ,the minimum level of achievement with which he can be satisfied, and (4) the extent to which he sees himself or others as responsible for his success or failure (Crandall, 1963). Because the Negro child develops under the heritage of slavery, he develops under conditions that retard his ability to internalize these aspects of motivation (McClelland, 1961). Whatever motivation the lower class Negro has is external rather than internal, as the motivation of middle class whites is (Battle and Rotter, 1963); the degree to which an individual perceives himself as able to obtain the rewards that society offers influences his feelings about personal control over his life.

Consequently, the middle class formula for success (hard work, perseverance, and slow gains) seems alien to Negroes—both children and adults. This conclusion is supported by a study of minority groups in New York (Stuart, 1962). The study is a report of efforts to recruit Puerto Ricans and Negroes from ill-paid, unskilled jobs to be trained for higher-paid and more skilled positions as sewing machine operators in the garment industry. This attempt met with poor results in spite of encouragement by union leaders, employers, and public schools. There was a greater response to this program among Puerto Ricans than among Negroes. Some of the Negroes who offered a reason for not wishing to move into more skilled positions said that they did not aspire to the social and cultural level of the garment workers and that most of the efforts to become more skilled seemed pointless to them. This sort of attitude is, of course, transmitted to their children in the socialization process.

Thus, Negro children, poorly (or differently) motivated as they may be, enter a middle class educational system ill suited to meet them on their own ground. For example, the 6.5 million nonwhite children in our society learn to read and write from books that scarcely acknowledge their existence (Larrich, 1965). Moreover, the nearly 40 million white children who read those books can only learn that they are members of a majority group untroubled by even the existence of human beings with a different skin color.

The vast majority of children's books published in America are lily-white. Of the 5,200 children's trade books issued by 63 publishers during 1962–1964, only 6.7 percent include one or more Negroes. Those firms that publish the majority of books for children tend to be the worst offenders; the inclusion of Negroes in the best-selling books of these companies is one-third less than in those of lesser-known publishers. Even the books that "include" Negroes often refer to them either only in terms of the "slave era" in America or in such a way that their skin color is almost unnoticeable. Moreover, nearly 60 percent of those books that do include Negroes are distributed only outside the continental limits of the United States. Only four-fifths of 1 percent of the books tell stories of the Negro in modern America, but many of these books show the Negro in illustrations without any textual reference. The degree of unrealism in these stories about the modern Negro is best revealed by the absence of any reference to civil rights marches, cattle prods, police dogs, and church bombings.

Consequently, the Negro child learns only about white society in the schoolroom, and he usually learns that he does not belong and that he is mistrusted and disliked. Such socialization of the Negro as takes place in school, therefore, tends to be a series of open conflicts between value systems and to culminate in an even greater whittling away of the Negro's self-image. As long as he can, he resists this interpretation of himself and his life by seeking solace in the peer group; when he leaves school, he withdraws from that interpretation, but he bears toward it a life-long fear and enmity.

The Negro's alienation from the educational world retards his inclusion in white society. Our society has just recently begun to realize that and to compensate for it. One result of this attempt to compensate is the new counterstereotype of the American Negro, in which he is portrayed as a beyond-perfect example of middle class morality. He works hard, smiles a lot, is polite, does very well in school, never loses his temper, and is loved by all, especially whites. Another, more constructive, result is the new programs designed to mitigate the effects of cultural disadvantage.

COMPENSATION FOR CULTURAL DISADVANTAGE: PROGRAMS

For culturally disadvantaged children starting school, the lack of identification with significant adults, the lack of an adequate self-concept, and poor language development lead to and reinforce failure beginning in the first few weeks of the first grade. Middle class children have the skills to deal with the material that they are given in school. These children's successful experiences lead to feelings of competence, which promote continuing success and positive attitudes toward school. However, the failures of culturally disadvantaged children lead to feelings of incompetence and, eventually, to lowered motivation. These children give up. Their parents do not have the time to discuss this problem with their children, and there is no one to prove to them that they can succeed if they want to. Unless a teacher or counselor can work with culturally disadvantaged children and provide them with some of the basic tools necessary for achievement, these children will become early dropouts and/or slow learners.

In order to help culturally disadvantaged children, there are now guidance programs and enrichment and remedial courses in operation throughout the country. One such special program, which was held at Oberlin College, was for seventh and eighth graders. The directors of the program felt that children of this age would be more amenable to change than older ones would be. None of the students participating in the program had a positive attitude toward school, nor had they achieved an educational level commensurate with their ability. The purpose of the program was to provide these children with an educational and cultural experience that would enable them to broaden their horizons and to become more sensitive to the world around them. The experience, it was hoped, would raise their levels of aspiration and "make them develop a more positive attitude toward themselves, toward people, and toward education" (Antes, 1964, p. 21).

The curriculum was arranged so that the pupils could explore a particular subject that interested them. A number of lectures and field trips were arranged, the staff and the students lived together, and the staff was accessible to the students 24 hours a day. All who worked with the program felt that the children became more interested in academic subjects during the summer. For many of the children, this was the first time that they could be sure of three meals a day and a warm place to sleep at night. And, for many, it would probably be the only time. One of the counselors who still receives letters from the children and occasionally sees some of the others noted that all the children soon reverted back to their old language habits and seemed reluctant to talk about school even though they were still enthusiastic about the summer. After participating in this program, these children were isolated by many of their peers, so that the reversion to old language habits was perhaps a defense against ostracism.

In 1956 a program called Higher Horizons

was begun. This program has served as a model for the Great Cities Improvement Project. The aim of the Higher Horizons experiment is "to identify, stimulate, and guide into college channels able students from low socioeconomic homes" (Riessman, 1963, p. 98). The project was later broadened to include all levels of students and now serves about 12,500 pupils.

Higher Horizons stresses a number of features:

1. A variety of instruments, including a nonverbal I.Q. test, were designed in order to stress the ability of the students.

2. In order to encourage motivation and to enhance the pupils' self-images, pictures of Negro and Puerto Rican doctors, nuclear physicists, and journalists were displayed in the classrooms.

3. Special remedial reading classes were kept at a maximum of five or six pupils so that each child could receive a maximum of individual attention. Each teacher, regardless of what subjects he usually taught, spent the first 10 minutes of his class in conducting drills in reading.

4. Book fairs and circulating libraries of paperbacks were started in the schools in order to stimulate reading.

5. A counseling service was established in order to provide guidance on college and career possibilities.

6. An intensive cultural program was initiated in order to acquaint the children with "good" music and to broaden their tastes. The children were prepared for these cultural experiences in advance.

7. Classrooms were kept open after school hours in order to give the children who came from crowded, noisy homes a quiet place to study.

Cleveland's Hough Community Project coupled with the "Cleveland Now!" plan are concerned with both parents and students. Project workers visit each student's home within three days after his enrollment to encourage his parents to want to keep him in school and to want him to receive as much education as he can. These efforts are coupled with parent education through informal group meetings at the schools.

For the students, the project includes a reading improvement program, part of which is an effort to show the project teachers new ways of teaching reading; a broad range of health services; counseling services to help build self-confidence and hope for the future; and an extensive recreation program. Part of this recreation program is a one-week summer camp that exposes many of the students to their first taste of discipline and gives them routine living experiences.

The programs discussed have four common factors:

1. Awareness that the culturally disadvantaged child lacks skills in communication and therefore fails in other subjects.
2. Discovery and utilization of community resources.
3. Willingness to experiment with different types of teaching materials and to present these materials in new and more meaningful ways.
4. Extensive in-service training programs for the teachers, whose attitudes are wholesome and enthusiastic.

Although changing methods and curricula are important factors in this way of teaching the disadvantaged child, the teacher's attitude seems to be a crucial factor. The teacher who expects achievement and believes that his pupils are able to be educated conveys these feelings to the pupils in a convincing way. In most of the programs is still another important factor—the use of people in the slum neighborhoods to help bridge the gap between their inhabitants and the schools.

One other program not only encompasses these general principles but also exhibits a pro-

"The culturally disadvantaged child may have no one to trust or identify with."

found awareness of the psychological effects of cultural disadvantage—the lack of identification with significant adults, of an adequate self-concept, and of adequate language development. The program is in the form of a clinic, called the Educational Therapy Center. This name suggests that the program is more school oriented than psychotherapeutic. However, the program implies that the word "education" means much more to the founder, Hertha Riese, than the traditional reading, writing, and arithmetic usually associated with school. The culturally disadvantaged child may have no one to trust or identify with. And there may be no one to help him recognize himself as a meaningful individual. According to Dr. Riese, when this child enters school, the teacher will be talking over the child's head because he cannot be ready for a formalized learning situation until he has been exposed to experiences allowing him to discover that he is an individual.

The homes of the children treated by the Center are characterized by two significant conditions: *They are crowded with people but barren of objects.* These conditions seriously handicap the personality development of the children. Under the first condition, the child's home is a constant mass of ever changing faces. As a consequence, he becomes "totally confused as to who all these people are, whether they are related or not, and if they are related, to whom they belong" (Riese, 1962, p. 69). One of the contributors to this condition is the ever-changing sex partner of many of the mothers. Of the children treated, 60 percent were from one-parent families resulting from death, desertion, divorce, separation, common law marriage, or illegitimacy. Thus, in families with no real father, the adult male is often a transient, so that the child is exposed to a series of "daddies" and "uncles" with little or no opportunity to identify with the male role as family head and provider. As each new "daddy" disappears, the boy again faces confusion in his sex role.

Moreover, both boys and girls face other problems resulting from life in this sort of home. In these families, a young grandmother is often the head of the household.

"While the teenage mother is avid for sex gratification, the thirty- to thirty-five-year-old grandmother is an insatiable consumer of grandchildren, regardless of what it does to the child. Overprotection and neglect will alternate, and the basic realities such as available space, food, or privacy will be disregarded" (Riese, 1962, p. 60).

The second condition, a lack of object stimulation, often dulls the child intellectually. When he is not dulled completely, he may experience a "will-of-the-wisp agitation, an aimless search, an obsession to touch and resourcelessly release everything; or the child is under compulsion to handle and 'experiment' with everything promiscuously in the most inappropriate and dangerous manner" (Riese, 1962, pp. 71–72).

When there are no objects in the home, the child has not had, of course, the privilege of owning things. Consequently, he has difficulty in learning the concept of ownership. The obsession to *touch* things is often followed by the obsession to *take*. The searching, touching, and taking of objects fulfills the child's need for self-definition and clarification of his awareness of existence. However, his need leads to rejection because his "taking" is viewed as stealing by the adults in his family, who do not recognize his needs and so attempt to reform him.

Dependent on a concept of ownership are, moreover, the need to share objects with others and the need to protect objects for future gratification. The child must see an object in the light of both its future gratification to him and sharing, or its potential for usefulness to someone else. To the child who has been deprived of objects, sharing is a threat to his existence. By destroying the object, he can deprive and punish the child who is competing for the ownership of it. Because he can depend on only the present moment, the child equates delaying his gratification with deprivation.

Language is another area of the child's development that fails to mature because of the lack of stimulation:

Due to the intellectual, emotional, and socioeconomic status of the parents, the children referred . . . know language not as a bridge between people but as a moat in a shooting war. Either the drawbridge is raised completely and the child is taciturn, or it is lowered only in order to send across a steady stream of words to attack the opposing forces. It is a means of coping with emergencies (Riese, 1962, p. 312).

Such a child needs the support of an adult who not only *watches* but *listens* to what the child is saying. When an adult listens willingly to what a child is saying, he begins to lose his feeling of inadequacy. Thus, in the first days of school, he is explosive and unable to delay his speech. However, as he discovers that the adult cannot hear what he wants to say, he learns to modulate his voice, articulate more distinctly, and express his thoughts with greater care and clarity.

Besides treating such children, the clinic gives therapy to mothers who have previously been considered untreatable. These are "the mother who has given up striving altogether, the discouraged, depressed, and neglectful woman, the one who indulges in promiscuity to the exclusion of any action and any constructive life" (Riese, 1962, p. 179). If, after every effort has been made, the child is unable to make progress and still remain in his home, he is placed in a well-selected foster home.

The Educational Therapy Center creates a milieu designed in part to counteract the one in which the disadvantaged child spends most of his waking hours. Thus, a variety of stimulating objects are available to the children and a guided, nonpunitive experience in the using and sharing of things is an important part of the therapeutic curriculum. One of the primary lessons, delaying gratification, uses toys as a vehicle for learning.

Members of the staff not only listen to the child and understand the feelings that he is trying to convey but help him to convert his feelings into language that will make his efforts at communication effective. Staff members attempt a kind of limited repair of the vehicle of speech in order to make it capable of carrying a greater load of feeling.

Methods such as these are not unique to the Educational Therapy Center, nor do they represent a radical departure from a commonsense base. They are attempts, really, to provide disadvantaged children with the experiences that the parents of the more favored young in our society take for granted. These educational therapy methods give the disadvantaged child a glimpse of the world most alien to him and a world view necessary for success in his coming encounter with the educational system.

Riese's attempt to remedy the effects of cultural alienation or disadvantage in a middle class educational world is a splendid example of how the best in therapy and the best in education must be skillfully combined if we are to correct those conditions that limit the worth of the educational experience for an important percentage of our youth.

SUMMARY

The model course of socialization in our society is altered by the individual's social and racial status. The life experiences of lower, middle, and upper class children are apt to be quite different from one another, and the different attitudes, values, beliefs, and patterns of behavior issuing from those different experiences produce class conflict within our culture. Being both poor and Negro disenfranchises the individual from full participation in our society. Education is a means of social mobility, but this avenue is closed to Negroes and members of the lower class; neither can compete on an equal basis with middle class whites.

The differences in socialization practices between the classes are less a function of values and goals than the means by which these are achieved. Thus, both middle class and lower class parents have the same broad child-rearing values but relate to their children in a different manner and use different methods of punishment. The psychological differences in these socialization relationships produce different results in the children and prepare them well or less well for their encounter with the middle class educational system.

Our society is now attempting to compensate for being poor and/or being Negro, for these people have been demanding their fair share of society's pleasures and rewards. However, we may have responded too slowly to meet the needs of these people; we have only recently become aware of the massive psychological damage that socialization in these circumstances can produce. Remedial efforts are outlining the extent of what is yet to be accomplished, and through these it is apparent that we must ultimately alter the kinds of socialization experiences to which the poor and the Negro are exposed.

It is evident that examining the interaction of the particular person in his particular environment is the only way to account for the final pattern of his behavior. Thus, the individual's physical constitution and his experience with other people during his infancy are two additional factors that contribute to the uniqueness of his socialization and personality.

Infants differ from one another in a variety of ways: Some are continuously active, while others are placid or lethargic; some are easily able to adjust to alterations in the regimen of child care, while others are fussy and actively resist being scheduled into a regular pattern; and some withdraw from new stimuli and new experiences, while others seek them out and enjoy them. These regularities in reaction patterns have sometimes been labeled *temperament*. This term describes a series of innate differences in infants that are reflected in their adult patterns of adjustment.

Each of these children needs socialization practices fitted to his individual characteristics. In much the same fashion, children whose physical state or early socialization marks them as people apart from the model or ideal held by their society undergo a socialization process and interpersonal experiences different from those of "normal" children.

9

Physical variations, early deprivation, and socialization

" . . . *children whose physical state or early socialization marks them as people apart from the model or ideal held by their society undergo a socialization process and interpersonal experiences different from those of 'normal' children."*

PHYSICAL VARIATIONS

Our culture is devoted to an impossible concept of physical normality, which means uniformity to us. We value uniformity in almost all aspects of physical appearance and constitution (except for those deviations that we find to be useful or currently fashionable), and we are psychologically ill prepared to deal with any variations beyond those minute ones considered to fall within the range of "normal." However, beyond these "normal" variations are at least three com-

mon forms of deviation: *temporary and chronic medical disorders, physical limitations,* and *sensory defects.* The impact of any of these variations in physical condition on the child may alter the course of his socialization.

Temporary and Chronic Medical Disorders

Illness, for most children, causes a minimum of emotional disturbance. Indeed, illness may even be a constructive grappling with fate and thus an important growth experience for the child if he is emotionally stable to begin with and if his parents handle the fact of his illness properly. Nonetheless, any physical illness that he may have, no matter how trivial, has a unique meaning for both him and his parents (Langford, 1948; Newman, 1963). That meaning can be devastating to the child. When he becomes sick, he is aware he does not feel the way he usually does, but he does not know why. His normal wondering about his physical condition can easily turn into intense anxiety if his parents feel that they have contributed to the illness or have failed to prevent it and are then unable to hide their own anxiety from the child. The child may also form a psychologically damaging opinion of the reason for his illness. He may believe that he broke his leg because he did not heed his parents' advice, that he got a cold because he did not wear his rubbers, or that he got an upset stomach because he did not eat properly. This belief that illness is a punishment for misdeeds is a common reaction. Moreover, if the child has to be hospitalized, he may be too young to understand why and feel that he is being sent away because he was bad. Finally, the sick child must submit to all kinds of mysterious and sometimes painful medical procedures, and, as Anna Freud (1952) has suggested, he may be unable to distinguish between the discomfort of the disease and the suffering needed to cure it. Thus, if the medical treatment for the illness is painful, the child may see that treatment as another deserved punishment for his misdeeds. If the child's parents reinforce this sort of belief by saying, "I told you so," we have all the necessary ingredients for psychological complications.

Another concomitant of illness that may cause psychological problems is the subtle change in emotional climate that often comes over the home when sickness strikes. The child, previously told what to do in no uncertain terms, may suddenly be showered with increased attention, indulgence, and concern. For the young child totally engrossed in the process of becoming independent, nursing care can be a severe threat to whatever level of self-determination he has achieved by the hard work of childhood. The loss of that status, coupled with the irritability and restlessness occasioned by the restriction of his activity level and bodily movement, may produce an emotionally loaded situation.

One of the psychological consequences of this stressful situation is regression—the return to an earlier and much less mature level of adjustment. The more prolonged and traumatic the illness is, the more severe the degree of emotional disturbance and consequent regression may be. And, of course, the younger the child, the more quickly this regression occurs and the greater the difficulty in dealing with him. Other aspects of the overall psychological reaction to illness also vary from child to child. Some children become quite dependent on adults; these children become whiny and demanding and need extra affection to feel secure. In contrast, other children act rebellious. They express their resentment of sickness by lashing out and blaming others for their condition. Still others become chronic invalids. These children, who have overconcerned and highly anxious parents, can drag out the recovery process long after there is any need for either parent or child to be worried about the illness. After their recovery, these children may be saddled with a life-long obsession with their bodily functions.

Hospitalization for an illness shapes a set of responses and of patterns of behavior different from that of illness in the home. Removal from the home and hospitalization is particularly painful for the very young child, for admission to a hospital deprives the child of the warm, intimate, and stable relationship he has established with his mother. If the child is less than three years of age, he seems most susceptible to the emotionally destructive aspects of hospital care. Thus, he may exhibit depression and various disturbances of feeding, sleeping, and toilet behavior. However, the most common form of his adjustment to hospitalization is regression.

If the child is only slightly older, or less than four years old, his reaction to hospitalization takes the form of three distinct phases. The first phase is protest, in which the child vehemently demonstrates his grief at the separation. Next to occur are feelings of despair. During this stage, the child is less active in displaying his acute need for his mother and instead expresses a sense of hopelessness. Finally, during the third phase, the child becomes withdrawn and apathetic; he makes no demands on others because he has withdrawn into himself for solace.

This final stage is sometimes erroneously interpreted to mean that the distress of the child has lessened because in this phase he may even appear stable, sociable, and more interested in his surroundings. However, this interpretation is a superficial one. Theorists now feel that the child manifesting this kind of behavior is making a defensive attempt to adjust to the uncompromising fact of hospitalization. That attempt may be reflected in a defensive attachment to his temporary surroundings; thus, the child may not recognize his mother when she visits, or he may weep uncontrollably when he leaves the hospital.

The older the child is at the time of hospitalization, the greater is the likelihood that his reaction to diagnostic procedures and treatment will resemble his typical response to punishment. Thus, the child who adjusts most successfully to hospitalization is the one who has the most satisfying relationship with his parents—particularly with his mother (Bowlby, 1951; Robertson, 1959). Not every child, of course, is permanently and horribly marked by the experience of hospitalization. However, hospitalizing very young children may be only partly rational; it may make treatment easier, but it may also be psychologically damaging. Hospitalization can be a constructive rather than a destructive experience if the issue of physical health does not submerge all consideration of psychological well-being. Unfortunately, medical doctors are rarely exposed to anything but the most superficial insights about the psychological experience of hospitalization.

Just as important as the preparation for the child's hospitalization and the response to him while he is hospitalized is the care that he receives upon his return home; the child returning from the hospital is not psychologically the same one that left the family some time ago. The attempt to restore his life to what it was before may eventually be possible, but doing so is difficult. How the family reintroduces the child to his relatives and peers, what the family does about the attitudes, feelings, and beliefs that he has developed while hospitalized, and how the family deals with his response to further treatment are all central to the success of the child's long-term adjustment.

The child learns how he should view his illness, his hospitalization, and his current state of health by observing the reactions of others to him. If his every whim is catered to with a clear sense of urgency and if an unaccustomed tomb-like silence falls over the house, the child might well become anxious. But his anxiety may not be based on an understanding of his physical condition, its prognosis, or possible complications and dangers. It may only be a feeling contracted from the nervous adults that surround him. If he is well cared for but responded to casually, his view of his illness can be that it is no more than a temporary detour on the road of life.

Physical Limitations

Society's attitude toward the typical and the familiar makes anatomical variation an important issue for socialization. No direct and simple connection exists between the anatomy of the individual and his personality or pattern of behavior, of course. Yet bodily structure does have a significant effect on psychic functioning. So many of our personal and social reactions to others are dictated by their physique that a new word and a new field of exploration were invented—*somatopsychology*. The concerns of this area of endeavor extend even to the fact that girls with generous chest measurements tend to behave differently from girls who are less well endowed.

Every person varies anatomically from every other person and has physical limitations of one sort or another. This fact, in itself, has no more meaning than the statement that a rock differs from a tree. However, our society is intolerant of a noticeable physical limitation in the individual and communicates that intolerance to him. Thus, he becomes aware of a difference that makes a difference to other people. That his limitation is negatively valued by others becomes important to him only if he cares about what others value. If the individual does care, he may begin to perceive himself as handicapped. This new concept of himself will, of course, influence his feelings and actions (see Figure 2).

Thus, the individual's physical difference becomes a disability only through the subjective value judgment made by the other members of his society. Variations in physique, therefore, have little meaning outside the frame of reference in which they are evaluated. For example, a short Pigmy male and a strapping Okinawan woman are considered normative in the societies to which they belong. However, in our society, the Pigmy would be considered ludicrous, and the Okinawan woman would be considered unfeminine—particularly if she revealed her ability to row boats, hoe fields, and haul in fishing nets. In the same way, the tall, skinny fashion model of our society would be an object of wonder and pity or contempt in other contemporary societies.

In our own society, the height of an individual is particularly subject to value judgments—even when it falls within the range "normal" for the sex of the individual. If, for example, a man's height is near the top of the 5.5-to-6.5-foot range, he tends to receive greater socio-economic rewards. Thus, railroad presidents have generally been taller than railroad station agents, university presidents taller than presidents of small colleges, and bishops taller than small-town preachers (Gowin, 1927). Of course, the social class into

"So many of our personal and social reactions to others are dictated by their physique that a new word and a new field of exploration were invented—somatopsychology."

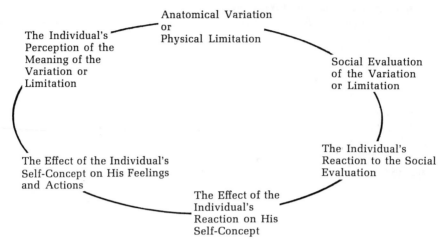

FIGURE 2

The Effect of Bodily Structure on Psychic Functioning

which the individual was born is a factor in his success, for members of the upper-middle and upper classes are more likely to become railroad presidents than members of the lower class are. However, members of the middle or upper classes are also likely to be taller and healthier than members of the lower class are—perhaps because of the difference in standards of child care and nutrition. Thus, members of the lower class tend not only to be shorter but are also more likely to be crippled and to have cardiac, auditory, and visual defects (Mayer and Hauser, 1953). The lower class individual who has one or more of these disabilities is even less likely to be socially viewed with approval than a healthy member of the same class would be.

Fortunately, the individual concerned about society's reaction to him can alter his physique to some extent if he wants to. Weight lifting pursued with devotion can develop physical structure. Giving children a proper diet helps them to grow taller than their parents and outstrip them physically in almost every way. Other variables besides exercise and diet can also influence physique. For example, physical sexual characteristics as well as

interest in the opposite sex can be altered by the injection of sex hormones.

Nonetheless, physique and the social judgments that it brings nearly always influence personality development. The child who is taller and heavier than what is typical for his age group tends to be a leader, to be more popular, and to be better adjusted than the smaller child is (Barker, Wright, Meyerson, and Golnick, 1953). The child with a noticeable physical limitation experiences rejection by others (Woods and Carrow, 1959; Elser, 1959) and before long accepts this social evaluation as the proper, correct, and reasonable one; that is, he comes to believe that he *is* inferior and therefore begins to judge himself in those terms. He then learns to act the part of a handicapped person. This behavior serves to reinforce the others' original perceptions of him. And so the child's conception of himself as inferior becomes stronger.

This negative self-concept may be intensified if the child has had to be hospitalized for his disability; most children who are hospitalized believe that they got sick because they were bad. Thus, the child's physical limitation in itself is less relevant than his psychological response to that limitation and the conditions in which it exists. His response actually determines the degree to which he will be incapacitated by his limitation.

Because other people's acceptance or rejection of the child's physical condition are so crucial to his personality development, they are crucial in determining the direction that his socialization takes. The child's parents, who are in the closest contact with him, are the most important determinants of the extent of his physical limitation and of his later social adjustment. However, the handicapped child can be a severe test of the stability and maturity of his parents and their marriage. For example, he imposes a financial strain on his family and influences the relationship between his parents as well as the relationships between his parents and the other children. Indeed, the toll that a severely limited or handicapped child may exact from his family cannot easily be measured; that toll may involve everything from the additional time and effort needed for his physical care to the need for his parents to withdraw from an active social life.

The cost for the parents in tension, anxiety, or guilt is similarly incalculable. Guilt, psychological injury to the parents' self-esteem, and anxiety about feelings of rejection for the child may all occur. The parent whose personal adjustment is already overtaxed by life may find this additional burden too difficult to bear.

Sensory Defects

The infant has a massive agenda of things to learn in the first two years of his life. If he follows the normal course of physical and motor development, he learns during that period to speak, to use all his senses effectively, and to attach meaning to the sights, sounds, and sensations that will abound in his life. Naturally, sensory defects would make him unable to acquire these skills. If he cannot acquire them, his later socialization will be impossible or, at best, imperfect.

One of the skills that the infant must learn is how to tell whether he is upright and how to stay that way. Part of this skill is being able to tell whether he is tilted at an angle instead of being straight up and down and, in general, how much he is tilted and in what direction. The infant learns this skill in at least two ways. First, the force of gravity furnishes clues; he must make a great many small adjustments in his posture in order to stay upright. Moreover, he is surrounded by all kinds of objects that are vertical or horizontal. These visual clues plus his postural adjustments to gravity establish a baseline for knowing whether he is upright or lying flat on his back.

Suppose, for example, that a child's sensory system was doubly impaired by vision severely restricted by cataracts and by Meniere's syndrome (a disease of the labyrinth of the inner ear that is accompanied by deafness, dizziness, and rapid involuntary eye movements). Learning the seemingly simple task of knowing whether he is sitting tilted or upright would be, in this instance, an incredibly complicated task. The failure to learn this lesson would, naturally, make more complex every learning task to follow.

Another skill that the infant must learn is depth perception. When he becomes mobile, he must learn to detect the difference between a little down and a lot of down. Anyone who has ever spent much time around very small children knows that it is necessary to protect them from falling off things when the children begin creeping or toddling. When the child can avoid tumbling over the various small cliffs that life presents to him, he does not do so because he has fallen frequently and has thus learned from experience; some of the tumbles would have been fatal and therefore nonrepeatable. Somehow, the child comes to perceive what depths are dangerous. This awareness is not a function of learning alone.

The child acquires depth perception, according to one study (Gibson and Walk, 1960), as soon as he can crawl. Gibson and Walk demonstrated that depth perception first makes its appearance then by using a visual cliff. This artificial cliff had two parts, a high cliff and a low cliff. These were constructed by suspending a board covered with a patterned material on top of a sheet of thick glass. On one side of the board, the patterned material was directly beneath the glass, so that the material looked like a continuation of the board. On the other side, the patterned material was several feet below the glass. Thus, one side of the board was a low cliff and the other side a high one.

Gibson and Walk tested 36 infants ranging in age from six to 14 months. Each child was placed on the center board, and then his mother called him from the deep cliff side in an attempt to make him leave the board and venture out across the glass. Then she called him from the shallow side to see whether he would leave the center board and crawl to her. The children crawled to their mothers if the material was right beneath the glass and so looked like it was on a level with the board. However, they would not try to cross the apparent chasm on the deep cliff side. This reaction is clearly a visual phenomenon because the children often peered down through the glass on the deep side and then backed away from it. Moreover, some of the children also patted the glass on the deep cliff side with their hands and, despite their awareness that the glass was solid, refused to cross it. Many of these children would have fallen over the deep cliff side of the board if the protective glass were not there. However, that was not the result of poor depth perception but of their level of physical coordination, which was not nearly so good as their visual acuity.

Absence of vision in one eye, for example, makes impossible depth perception of the usual variety (seeing an object through eyes separated in the skull—each seeing a matched but slightly different part of the object). Other cues in the environment can be used to make this judgment of depth, but this learning takes longer to accomplish and is never as accurate as that possible with two eyes. Moreover, a child with vision in only one eye might, for example, experience a greater number of painful falls and might, as a conse-

quence, be more tentative in exploring his environment, take fewer risks, and learn the nature of his world at a slower pace.

As the infant learns the limits of his body and the dimensions of the world around him, he is working toward an active mastery of his environment. During this period, the nature of his environment and the stimulation that it provides him are vital to his ability to venture into that world. If the infant is deprived of crucial elements in his environment, his psychological growth may be severely impaired.

EARLY DEPRIVATION

Deprivation in early infancy is one of the most dramatic means by which the process of socialization can be short circuited. In particular, depriving the infant of his mother or the parent figure who provides him with a warm, basic relationship with another human being seems to be disastrous for his socialization. However, it is difficult to generalize about the specific characteristics of the deprived infant, for there are many different kinds and degrees of deprivation (Yarrow, 1964). For example, an infant may lose his mother and then be subjected to a sequence of mother substitutes who may be good or bad, consistent or inconsistent, accepting or rejecting. Another infant might lose his mother and be cared for consistently and well, so that he never experiences deprivation. Thus, psychological deprivation is not always produced by separating the infant from his natural mother.

Moreover, there are different kinds and degrees of separation, each of which may produce a different effect on the child. Separation may be brief and followed by reunion with the mother (trips, hospitalization, school, and so forth); a single, permanent separation (death or permanent disability of the mother); or a series of repeated separations (a succession of foster homes where emotional bonds are established only to be destroyed again). And, for some children, separation is not a single event but rather, from their point of view, a series of psychological separations that may never end (Yarrow, 1964).

The effects of separation in infants and children are both immediate and long-term. The immediate reaction reported in infants under two years of age is highly regular. The sequence usually is violent crying followed by a steady and progressive withdrawal from people and surroundings. Moreover, physical as well as psychological damage occurs. The children in one series of studies (Spitz, 1945; 1946) were grossly underweight, small for their age, quite subject to infection, and generally retarded in the acquisition of the expected developmental skills. The physical damage is progressive, and, after five months of separation, the progression cannot be reversed. However, children separated from mothers with whom they had had a poor relationship in the first place show much less disturbance, as do infants who are rapidly provided with a good substitute mother.

The above conclusions on the effects of separation from the mother should, however, be viewed with caution. Most studies have dealt with children placed in public institutions. Thus, no all-inclusive generalizations can hold, for institutions differ substantially in their patterns of response to abandoned infants. Further, most of these studies dwell on the extreme instances of serious intellectual, emotional, and behavioral retardation in such children, but not all infants suffer to the same degree. In institutions that provide adequate stimulation for the children, these problems are appreciably reduced. Nonetheless, the individualized relationship of parent to child that occurs in the normal family simply cannot be duplicated in an institution, and so the uniqueness of the child is inevitably crushed.

The same caution should be observed in interpreting the connection between early events and adolescent or adult behavior. For example, in one classic study (Bowlby, 1944) of 44 juvenile thieves, the researcher selected 14 whom he diagnosed as "affectionless characters." When he searched through their life histories, he discovered that at least 12 of these 14 had been separated in infancy from their mothers. The lives of the 12 were full of pathogenic events. Some of these thieves had been hospitalized for unusually long periods, some had been institutionalized, and some had lived in many different foster homes. Bowlby concluded that institutional life seems to produce psychopathic behavior, inadequate control over impulses, and inability to relate to other people in an emotionally normal way. However, the connection between early experience and later behavior was difficult to demonstrate in a clean and crisp manner. Other studies (Goldfarb, 1943, 1944) of children who spent their early years in institutions also report that important intellectual and personality malfunctions occur as the result of institutionalization. Although personality organization, such as superego development, seemed most subject to distortion, learning disturbances, inadequate intellectual functioning, poor impulse control, and the like were common. Such damage is, however, best described as a highly frequent but *not* inevitable consequence of separation from the mother.

Giving the child adequate care after he has been separated from his mother can prevent such severe physical and psychological malfunctions. A special case of this child rearing technique is *multiple mothering*, or a number of substitute mothers caring for the child with no one mother having primary responsibility for him. In some societies this communal child rearing is the norm, while in others the children grow up in an "extended family," in which relatives or fellow villagers feel a sense of responsibility for all the children. Such children may even learn to trust more people and to be less dependent on a single mother figure for emotional support than the child raised by his natural mother does. Regardless of whether the child has one mother or many, however, he must experience an adequate interpersonal relationship with whoever is rearing him in order to develop free of damage to his personal and social adjustment. In order for that relationship to be adequate, it must include *physical and emotional interaction* and *learning experiences*.

Deprivation of Interaction

A mixture of common sense and clinical evidence suggests that children who lack proper maternal care suffer critical damage to later personal and social development. In fact, syndromes such as autism, marasmus, and sexual deviation may be traceable to deprivation during infancy. However, the mother-child relationship cannot be exploited experimentally to reveal the conditions that produce wreckage of such a severe sort. The closest that researchers have come to true experimental control of the conditions of child rearing has been in experiments with man's near cousin the rhesus monkey. Monkeys can be raised in isolation, provided with inadequate mothers, deprived of mothers completely, and issued siblings as the experimental conditions dictate.

In a series of carefully designed experiments, the Harlows (Harlow, 1958, 1959; Harlow and Harlow, 1961, 1962), studied the effect of deprivation of interaction on the development of the affectional system in young monkeys. First, Harlow raised male and female rhesus monkeys in total social deprivation during the first two years of their lives. Although these monkeys grew and developed (slowly), they were unable to make a successful adjustment to other monkeys. The deprived monkeys were frightened, interacted little with the others, were uninterested in sex, and remained unable to defend themselves from smaller and weaker monkeys two years after the isolation experience. The longer the deprivation lasted, the greater the social damage was. However, contact with human beings helped bring adjustment even if monkey companionship was denied.

Another group of monkeys was reared in wire cages from which they could see and hear other monkeys but not touch them. Two other groups of monkeys were raised under similar conditions, but one group had access to a wire surrogate mother (a cylindrical, monkey-sized, wire form welded in a semiupright position and topped by a crude wooden head), while the other group had a surrogate mother covered with terry cloth. The monkeys in all three of the groups developed abnormal patterns of behavior including fixed staring into space, injuring themselves, rocking back and forth, and being unable to mate.

In mechanical terms, the terry cloth surrogates were ideal mothers. They always provided milk and warmth (a light bulb was inside), and they felt soft. Moreover, they never scolded or hurt the young monkeys and were available 24 hours a day. The only flaw in these surrogates was their inability to interact with the infant monkeys. As a result of this flaw, the young monkeys grew up to be incapable of appropriate sexual response. Further, when those raised by surrogate mothers played with monkeys raised by monkey mothers, the former were obviously socially inferior in a variety of ways. Finally, when some of the surrogate-raised females had babies of their own, they proved to be totally inadequate mothers and failed to make the proper maternal responses. Either the babies were ignored, or they were attacked, beaten, and punished. Interestingly, the abused infants returned again and again to seek physical comfort from their mothers.

There is no fully trustworthy, easy translation of these observations of the effect of rearing conditions on monkeys into observations on the parent-child relationship for humans. It may well be that the human infant is much more dependent at birth than the monkey is and thus much more susceptible to psychic and developmental damage by an inadequate, cruel, or rejecting mother. Nonetheless, this pioneering research is provocative for the consideration of the critical question of the timing of proper stimulation in producing appropriate emotional response in the young.

Part of the stimulation that will produce the ability to respond emotionally to another human being is the physical contact that characterizes adequate mother-child interaction. It seems logical to assume that being hovered over, picked up, and handled would be terrifying to the infant. However, this assumption is erroneous, for a provocative series of studies has indicated that this kind of treatment is crucial to the infant's development. In order to test that assumption, Levine (1960) studied the effect of subjecting a group of infant rats to electric shocks scheduled to occur at the same hour each day. Levine placed other infant rats in a cage but did not shock them. A third group of infant rats were left in the nest and not handled or molested in any way. Levine and his co-workers anticipated that the shocked rats would display emotional disorganization when they reached adulthood. The researchers were surprised to discover, however, that the rats that were never handled displayed the most peculiar kinds of behavior. The actions of his shocked rats were indistinguishable from those of the rats that had been handled but not shocked.

Levine used these insights as a basis for his later studies of infancy, in which he subjected infant animals to a variety of stresses and intensities of handling. Again and again, he found that the groups of animals not handled by the researcher were the ones that exhibited the greatest deviations in behavior and physiology by adulthood. When these animals were placed in unfamiliar but otherwise nonthreatening surroundings, they crouched terror stricken in a corner, while the fondled animals found it easy to explore the space about them. The animals that were handled in infancy also developed faster. They opened their eyes earlier, they achieved motor coordination sooner, their body hair grew faster, and they weighed significantly more by the time they were ready to be weaned.

The effects of stimulation can be approached from a different beginning point. Some researchers, using a physiological approach to experimentation, have surgically destroyed the septal region of the brain in infant animals. Ordinarily, when this part of the brain is destroyed, the animal becomes hyperexcitable and vicious and reacts to stimulation with rage. When this operation was performed on both manipulated and nonmanipulated animals, the researchers discovered that the animals manipulated in infancy were far tamer after the operation than the nonmanipulated animals.

"It seems logical to assume that being hovered over, picked up, and handled would be terrifying to the infant."

These experiments underscore a vital point. The character of the early infantile experience is an important determinant of individual differences in animals. Organisms simply do not grow in a vacuum; even their early handling in a laboratory produces a kind of stimulation that has important consequences for their later behavior. Nonetheless, research with animals does not provide a definitive answer to the question of exactly when physical contact in the mother-child relationship is most crucial for the physiological and psychological development of human infants.

Deprivation of Learning Experiences

A fairly recent theoretical approach to understanding how the child develops is the notion that there are certain periods critical to his development. According to this approach, the child is better able to learn at certain times during his childhood than he is at others. Thus, if training occurs before or after these periods, the effectiveness of instruction is greatly reduced. For example, two such periods seem to be critical to the child's development of independence from his mother. The first period is when the child is about eight months of age and the second when he is between two and three years of age. If during these periods the child's attempts to explore his environment are restricted, he may become overdependent on his mother and display a much less mature pattern of interaction with others (Stendler, 1952). This theory of periods critical for learning has led to the deduction that the retardation observed in institutionalized children is chiefly the result of the institutions' providing very few opportunities for the children to learn (Dennis and Najarian, 1957). If this interpretation is correct, it should be possible to improve the intelligence test scores of institutionalized children by giving them supplementary learning experiences.

In an examination of this hypothesis, Dennis and Sayegh (1965) tested 31 foundling children between the ages of four and 12 months at the Creche in Beirut, Lebanon. These children's mean developmental age on the Cattell scale was six months; 10 infants between seven and 12 months of age scored below the four-month level. These children could not even maintain a sitting position when placed in that posture on a flat surface. To these 10 subjects were added three who were more than a year old but could not yet sit unaided. Then the 13 subjects were divided into an experimental group of five and a control group of eight. These two groups were alike in chronological and developmental age at the beginning of the study.

The experimenters decided to train these children to sit in an upright position, to have an interest in objects, and to develop skill in manipulating them. In the training sessions the researchers helped each child to sit erect and at the same time presented him with an interesting object. As soon as the child lost interest in one object, another was presented to him. Among these objects were a red plastic ashtray, small plastic medicine bottles, plastic multicolored discs with perforated centers dangling on a chain, small cardboard boxes, shiny metal box tops, a plastic fly swatter, a shiny copper bowl, pieces of colored sponge, and freshly cut flowers. Each of these objects could be manipulated by the smallest child.

The experimental subjects spent approximately an hour a day in the training room. During this period, all five children were simultaneously present. The members of the control group were not stimulated in any way during the training period except by seeing the experimenters when they came to the dormitory rooms to pick up and return the experimental subjects.

Each subject in the experimental and control group was given the Cattell test three times. The first test was given during the five days immediately preceding the training period. The training sessions took place five days a week for three weeks. Then the second test was given on the two days immediately following the training period. The third test was given six weeks after the completion of the second one. Thus, one month elapsed between the first and second tests, one and a half months between the second and third tests, and two and a half months between the first and third tests.

Dennis and Sayegh found that all five experimental subjects gained in developmental age in the month between the first and second tests. The mean gain was 1.9 months of developmental age. Some gain would, of course, be expected even if there were no special training. However, the rate of gain of the experimental group during this period greatly exceeded their rate of gain before training was begun; before training, the average rate of gain was about 0.43 of a month of developmental age for every month of chronological age. It is difficult to assess the statistical significance of these findings because the results are based on a study of only five children. Nonetheless, in the time between the second and third tests, when no training was given, two of the five experimental subjects gained in developmental age. Thus, the significant rate of change in the experimental group during the training period was followed by a period of nonsignificant change when training was discontinued.

The control group gained more in developmental age than would be expected on the basis of the first test, even though the gains were smaller than those of the experimental group. It was difficult to understand why the control group improved as much as it did. What Dennis and Sayegh suspected was that the caretakers in the institution had watched the training sessions through a curtained window and tried out the experimental techniques on the control group children when the researchers were not present. Moreover, by sheer coincidence, several outside groups of people began giving the Creche children more attention at the particular time that this experiment was in progress. Junior Red Cross clubs from secondary schools and civic groups visited the Creche, picked up the children, gave them toys, carried them about, and played with them. Because visiting hours were in the afternoon and the training sessions were in the morning, the experimenters were unaware of these activities until the experiment was over.

As if these problems were not enough, there were two other contaminating factors. A professor in the medical school of the American University of Beirut initiated a nutrition experiment at the Creche soon after the training period began. That experiment involved, of course, increased weighing, measuring, and handling of several of the infants. In addition, a pediatric congress brought to Beirut doctors who examined and handled some of the infants. All four factors make up the catastrophic kind of accident that regularly plagues experiments however carefully they may be planned. Nonetheless, the developmental improvement in the experimental group is still dependable and helps to confirm the theory of periods critical to the child's learning.

The proper physical and emotional development of the child is clearly rooted in the family and in the mother-child relationship in particular. Without the close personal interaction and the learning experiences that this relationship provides, the child may well develop into a mental and emotional cripple. A dramatic and unusual form of that crippling called *infantile autism* underlines what can happen to the child who is deprived of those necessities.

Infantile Autism

Infantile autism was first described by a psychiatrist named Kanner (1943). The children in his study came from families in which there were almost no signs of mental disorder. These children showed no appreciable evidence of physical or neurological defect yet clearly had a behavioral disorder for which there was no certain cause and no positive cure.

A few autistic children seem to shake the effects of this psychological disturbance. However, of those few, some continue to function at the level of an idiot or an imbecile, while others demonstrate remarkable mental powers as adults. For example, there are reports that at least one autistic child became a mathematician, and that another became a meteorologist and part-time composer. These are, of course, exceptions. Most of the victims of infantile autism are inmates of institutions designed for the retarded or the emotionally disturbed.

Infantile autism primarily afflicts male first-born children. No particular complications of pregnancy are reported, and the infant is frequently exceptionally healthy, attractive, precocious, and alert. He does, however, show one peculiarity. When a normal infant is about to be picked up, he seems to anticipate it and responds with "readying" movements. The autistic infant remains inert and so provides something like the difficulty of trying to put galoshes on a child who is not helping or even paying attention.

Other symptoms begin to appear when the child is between four and 18 months old. He may rock back and forth in his crib or bang his head against the side of the crib at the same time that he shows no interest in his surroundings. In other cases, the opposite sort of behavior may appear. The child may be acutely aware of his environment, insist that it remain unchanged, and get upset if it is altered. When this symptom predominates, the child engages in play that repeats itself over and over again.

When the child is between a year and a half and two years old, what has been called "autistic aloneness" may also occur. In this state, the child sits motionless for hours and stares into space as though wrapped in deep thought. It is impossible to attract his attention during that time. This sort of behavior is particularly distressing because he seems to display an almost complete lack of interest in people. He acts as though other people do not exist—inanimate objects, yes; people, no. Thus, such a child can become attached to mechanical devices in a way that he never becomes attached to people. He may even run up to a recently parked car and embrace it in order to feel the warmth of the engine.

By this time, other problems have also occurred. For example, nearly all autistic children have strange eating habits. In one case, an autistic child loved chocolate but would eat it only when it was cut into squares; chocolate in a round form was regularly rejected. Another child would eat only sandwiches that she had made herself. This quirk began when she was only three years old. Finally, one autistic child lived entirely on milk for the first six years of his life. Such children also tend to have odd habits about liquids—refusing to drink water, drinking water only out of a transparent container, drinking water only at a precise temperature, and so forth.

By the time that the autistic child is about two years old, the parents seek professional help; anyone confronted with this strange array of symptoms would reasonably begin to suspect that some defect was hampering the child's development. Among the first suspicions is that the child is deaf. Another might be that the child

is mentally deficient. However, neither of these conclusions is substantiated by the child's appearance and abilities, so that both conclusions are soon discarded by the experienced psychological examiner. These children tend to be very skilled in tasks requiring coordination and do not look retarded. They lack the dull, vacant look usually associated with feeble-minded children. Instead, they always appear to be concentrating on something other than what is occurring in their immediate environment. Moreover, their memory is sometimes truly phenomenal. For example, some autistic children can recite at the age of two the names of all the presidents, and some are able to reproduce exactly an aria in a foreign language after hearing it only once.

Many autistic children also acquire language skills very early, but these skills have not developed in the normal way. Some autistic children can write but can not speak, some can read aloud accurately but do not seem to know what the words mean, and some can communicate only through writing. Moreover, some of the children can use complete sentences at one year of age when there is no evidence that the words that make up the sentences have ever been used before. Naturally, the parents of such children view them as potential geniuses.

The trouble with this early acquisition of speech is that the speech is generally of a peculiar kind. The words are pronounced in an unfamiliar monotone, for the emotional expression that usually accompanies speech is missing. Further, the words "I" and "yes" are absent in a very striking and highly consistent fashion. Sometimes these children also repeat obsessively what seem to be meaningless words. And some children are fascinated by radio and television commercials and repeat them endlessly.

The prognosis for the autistic child tends, strangely, to be closely connected to his speaking ability. In follow-up studies of 63 autistic children, for example, it was found that 32 of them could speak by the age of five. Half of the 32 "speaking" children were able to achieve *fair* to *good* social adjustment, while only one of the 31 nonspeakers reached even the *fair* level of adjustment. More than half of the 63 children had to be institutionalized, and, so far as we know, therapy of any sort has not influenced their condition (Eisenberg, 1956; Kanner and Lesser, 1958).

Although the exact cause of infantile autism remains unknown, it seems to be the result of either early parental disaffection, a constitutional defect, or an institutionalization-like response to the environment. The scientists who feel that the cause must be psychogenic, or attributable to the form of the transaction between parent and child, have examined the backgrounds and personalities of the parents and have discovered that they are most often brilliant, well-educated people. The fathers are psychiatrists, lawyers, chemists, professors, businessmen, or engineers; the mothers are usually college graduates. Many of the grandparents are listed in *Who's Who in America* or *American Men of Science*. The relatives of autistic children are seldom mentally ill, are virtually never divorced or separated, and are bright and socially distinguished. Nonetheless, the parents are rational and objective to an extreme—humorless, detached, bookish, and, perhaps, cold or unemotional. Regardless of whether this sort of personality has crippled the parent-child relationship and has caused the child's autism, it is clear that parental attempts to socialize the child have failed in some incomprehensible fashion.

SUMMARY

The model course of socialization must be altered to accommodate children with physical variations, such as temporary and chronic medical disorders, physical limitations, and sensory defects. Any one of these variations can distort the individual's personal and social adjustment. Nonetheless, because our culture has little tolerance for those who are physically different, we have given little consideration to the effect of social intolerance on the self-image of the variant person.

The process of socialization can also be distorted early in the child's life if he is deprived of elements in his environment that are crucial to his physical and psychological development. Among these elements are an adequate relationship with his mother, emotional and physical contact with other human beings, and properly timed learning experiences. The deprivation of these elements often causes severe psychological damage; infantile autism may be a result of such deprivation.

Part four

Education, the socializer

The terms "education" and "socialization" should be considered synonymous in our society, for education is the primary means of socializing all children after they reach the age of five. Our children now spend the bulk of their time in groups of about 30 strange peers dominated by a professional teacher in a building specially erected for that purpose. This educational system socializes children by teaching them the knowledge and intellectual skills essential to full participation in society as well as the mores and habits of its members.

Because the instructor teaches techniques that will ensure adequate social adjustment, education is a mixture of *instruction* and *indoctrination*. This function of indoctrination results in society's concern over the loyalty of teachers to their culture. Society prefers educators to be technical drill sergeants who shape children's outlook to fit the existing social norms. Regardless of how loyal an individual teacher may be to those norms, however, there is always bound to be some variance between what the parents of any child would like him to learn and what the instructor is willing to teach. Moreover, all parents fear that teachers will indoctrinate children with attitudes and values that the parents do not share. Consequently, parent-teacher associations were invented

10

The nature of education

"The role of the teacher in the classroom is highly complex . . ."

as devices allowing the parents to keep tabs on the educational process and, in a subtle way, to influence it. Through such social institutions as these, certain kinds of information are systematically withheld from the young in order to ensure their satisfactory adjustment to society.

THE TEACHER

The role of the teacher in the classroom is highly complex, in part because that role is defined in different ways by all the different people with whom she comes in contact—colleagues, pupils, parents, and administrators. Indeed, in her classroom alone, the teacher may be viewed in as many as 30 different ways by her 30 different pupils. For example, one of the pupils may view his teacher as a parental surrogate. The child, experienced with authority figures in the form of parents, may generalize to all others who seem to occupy a similar role and so come to view the teacher as similar to the parent. Consequently, the patterns of acceptance and rejection that the child experiences in his interaction with his parents can become the model that he expects his teacher to follow. Another result of viewing the teacher in this way is that the child may try to manipulate his teacher in the same ways that he does his parents. If the child's expectations of the teacher's behavior are grossly in error, he is liable to adopt methods of relating to her that are inappropriate to the classroom situation. It is at this juncture that it is vitally important for the teacher to understand the task that she faces and to devise workable means of dealing with it.

A child may also view the teacher as a model citizen. Parental and community attitudes reinforce this view to such an extent that it is no wonder that, for the child, the teacher may become the epitome of all that is right and pure. The susceptible child is, of course, particularly prone to glorifying his teacher beyond all reason. The teacher can only find this hero worship flattering and may in certain circumstances be reduced to playing the hero role in spite of herself.

Nonetheless, the teacher can make a conscious decision to avoid being influenced by others' perceptions of her and cast herself in another role. Of course, probably the most useful one is to view herself as the official dispenser of knowledge. This role is more likely to be adopted by teachers in junior high or senior high schools, in which the self-contained classroom has been abandoned in favor of an emphasis on the content of what is taught rather than on the process of learning and the characteristics of the learners. The teacher should, however, also view herself as a group leader capable of setting the educational tone and atmosphere—the educational esprit-de-corps—because the classroom is a social group. In accordance with this role, the teacher must be knowledgeable about the nature of individual interaction in groups and about the way in which groups influence individuals if she is to educate the whole child (Sawrey and Telford, 1958).

In practice, however, many teachers view themselves as professionals with specialized training in and knowledge of the field of teaching and taking care of children. A common accompaniment to this self-concept is the view that parents are people who lack such a background and therefore cannot understand the teacher's problems. In fact, according to this view, the parents' entering the school is always potentially dangerous (Becker, 1953).

In spite of this self-satisfaction common among teachers, many of them do not feel confident in handling disciplinary problems and students who do not fit the common mold (Hunter, 1955).

These teachers are often particularly annoyed by the child who behaves in a way that either violates their personal standards or challenges their role as leader, disciplinarian, or instructor (Kaplan, 1952).

Such teachers with such shortcomings are the people with whom the child is most in contact during most of his childhood. While the child learns, he interacts with his teacher. Most of these interactions may not be particularly noteworthy, but some of them involve discipline, and the teacher-child disciplinary interaction is one of the most potent forces helping or hindering the socialization of the child.

THE CHILD IN SCHOOL

The Nursery School

The newest facet of our educational system is the nursery school, which is thought to provide the child with an organized, group experience that is beneficial to his physical, emotional, psychological, intellectual, and social development. However, each nursery school child has already formed a particular set of attitudes, beliefs, and feelings, has lived in a unique home environment, and has been in contact with his parents, siblings, and peers, all of whom have exerted a unique influence on him (Marshall, 1961). His previous experience in large part determines how efficacious attending nursery school will be for his development. Clearly, if the child is exposed in nursery school to learning experiences that he has not been exposed to at home, his development may be accelerated (Riessman, 1962).

This factor of the uniqueness of each child's experience, plus the problem of providing adequate experimental control for all the other factors besides nursery school attendance, makes conducting definitive research on any aspect of the nursery school experience difficult. For example, one study (Wellman, 1943) concludes that children who attend nursery school seem to show gains in intellectual functioning. However, this finding remains controversial because a number of other investigators have been unable to duplicate these results. A thorough study of this aspect of nursery school would have to include a detailed analysis of both the nature and content of the school program and the expectations that might reasonably be held for intellectual change in the child (Swift, 1964). Some nursery programs may contribute to intellectual development, while others may have no measurable effect (Bird, 1940; Lamson, 1940; Jones and Jorgensen, 1940; Goodenough and Mauer, 1940).

The same sort of research problems makes generalizing about the effect of nursery school attendance on individual social development difficult—even though the contact with peers of the same age should help every child's social development. Parents send their children to nursery school in the hope that the socializing experience of associating with peers in a controlled setting will contribute to the ease of future social relations. Some early studies (Joel, 1939; Horowitz and Smith, 1939) do report that, through attending nursery school, many children become more mature, independent, and socially outgoing and learn adequate social techniques. However, many such studies did not always use appropriate control groups; any study of social development must separate the effects of natural social motivation from the effects of forced contact with other children in the nursery school (Vitz, 1961). Nonetheless, even though studies that utilized control groups (Jersild and Fite, 1939; Brown and Hunt, 1961) report an improvement in social relations, the results of these studies are still not perfectly clear (Allen and Masling, 1957; Bonney and Nicholson, 1958). In part, the problem is that no two experiments use exactly the same dimensions of social adjustment and that the chil-

"The newest facet of our educational system is the nursery school, which is thought to provide the child with an organized, group experience that is beneficial to his physical, emotional, psychological, intellectual, and social development."

"Parents send their children to nursery school in the hope that the socializing experience of associating with peers in a controlled setting will contribute to the ease of future social relations."

"Nursery school, according to some parents at least, should also teach the child to conform to the group . . ."

" . . . at the same time that he learns how to maintain his independence from it."

dren and teachers as well as the situations in any two nursery schools are seldom exactly equivalent.

Nursery school, according to some parents at least, should also teach the child to conform to the group at the same time that he learns how to maintain his independence from it (Jersild and Fite, 1939). Although most of the responses learned at home are just reinforced in nursery school, new lessons are always present for the child to learn, so that he can become aware of the contradictory alternatives available to him. Thus, the child interacting with a large group of other children is very likely to become more independent than his non-nursery school peers.

Readiness for School

In our society, all children enter school when they are five or six years old. However, at that age, children are better able to learn some things than others. Thus, it is important to determine which learning experiences are most appropriate for an optimal level and rate of learning; that is, when is it most advantageous to teach children to read, to write, to do arithmetic, or to learn foreign languages? When are children ready to learn? This concept of *readiness* means that a child's physiological and emotional level of maturation, his general mental ability, and his experiential background must mesh if he is to learn effectively.

Other factors are also crucial to the child's readiness to learn. For example, his needs, goals, ideas, and skills all contribute to his level of readiness at a particular age (Cronbach, 1954). Moreover, the materials and methods of instruction must be appropriate to his level of readiness if he is to learn effectively (Blair, 1954). In fact, the longer that researchers study readiness, the longer becomes their list of elements crucial to readiness. Some researchers do, however, claim that readiness is highly amenable to stimulation, direction, and control. Thus, teaching the child useful skills at home before he begins school and using appropriate teaching methods once he is in

school may make him more ready to learn certain kinds of material than he otherwise would be.

We are all sensitized today to the difference between privileged children's readiness for school and that of disadvantaged children. This difference can be bridged by the nursery school experience, according to Bottrill (1967). In his experiment, however, it required 70 hours a week in a day care center to bring the under-privileged children to a level equal to privileged children who had spent 10 hours a week in a nursery school.

In this respect, the nursery school or day care center and the experiences that they provide are remedial. The implication is that in the preschool years it is yet possible to ready the child for what lies ahead in his academic endeavors by providing practice in the skills, attitudes, ideas, and responses most necessary to achieve success in the tasks that our educational system will ask him to perform. Most schemes designed to ready the child for school have one of two qualities—firming up skills prerequisite to any learning or early practice with future tasks or their components.

Nonetheless, in practice, it is still difficult to determine any group of children's level of readiness and then give them appropriate learning experiences. Even among children at six, some are advanced and some are retarded in various kinds of abilities. Thus, any curriculum, lesson, or learning plan devised to accommodate all six year olds must on the face of it be in error. Moreover, as the children grow older, the absolute differences among abilities increase steadily, so that chronological age becomes a less and less trustworthy criterion for determining proper learning experiences. Increasingly refined measures are therefore needed to determine the level of each child at a particular moment.

Despite such problems, determining the child's level of readiness is important, for the frustration that would accompany a learning experience for which he is unprepared may turn him against new learning experiences. And a failure to learn a basic skill would retard the child in acquiring a variety of new skills. Nonetheless, in our educational system, the educator obviously cannot

The Child Enters School

"*School, for most children, marks the first prolonged separation from the mother.*"

School, for most children, marks the first prolonged separation from the mother. Deliberately or not, the school assists in weaning the child from his home and fosters increasing independence in him. In school he must respond to and obey a different adult who requires that he do a series of things that may not be rewarding to him. Hopefully, the child learns to enjoy doing them, for they determine his successful adjustment to society. The educational system tries to teach him what is required for full membership in society by exposing him in school to planned, systematic experience with success and failure. The child, of course, knows about having and going without and about achieving and failing, but he has never before devoted his entire day to activities so heavily flavored with winning and losing.

The child soon discovers that success and failure may have little to do with actual accomplishment but usually refer to the psychological distance between his accomplishments and his own and other people's goals, expectations, and aspirations for him. Thus, he must also face the truths that (1) his own goals, expectations, and aspirations never seem to be stable but change as he develops and comes into contact with new people and (2) in general, the significant peers, parents, teachers, and other adults in his life hold quite discrepant views of what his goals, expectations, and aspirations ought to be.

The child's success and failure are measured in terms much more precise than those that he has experienced in the past or may experience in the future. The measurement of success and failure in school is frequent, public, final, and an important influence on the nature of his peer group membership. Moreover, if the child is a member of the middle class, academic work is for him the single measurement of his acceptability to his parents and other important people in middle class society. Any child, however, despite the other desirable characteristics that he may

wait until he is certain that all children are ready for a particular learning experience by delaying it until past the time of readiness for all children. Perhaps his only recourse is to make sure that an appropriate learning situation and a properly trained teacher will at least help those children whose readiness is different from most of the other children's.

possess, is considered a failure if he does not achieve academically. The adult can balance failure in one area against success in another and so escape being held accountable to a single standard of performance measured along one rigid dimension. For the child in school, life is not so generous or forgiving. His performance is measured solely by a grade in one form or another, for society is convinced that childhood is the once-in-a-lifetime chance to learn the system of social reward and punishment.

This socialization technique works, for children begin to show its effects soon after they start attending school. One careful series of studies (Stendler, 1951; Stendler and Young, 1951) examined the changes in the behavior of 212 children during their first year in school. In order to ascertain those changes, the mothers of the children were interviewed at three different times—before the children entered school, after they had been in school for two months, and after they had been in school for eight months. In the first interview, nearly all the mothers insisted that their children anticipated school with favorable attitudes, which the children had acquired through their parents, older brothers and sisters, and friends. In the second interview, 86 percent of the mothers reported that their children's view of themselves as well as their behavior improved. Most mothers also reported that their children became more independent. Thus, within the short period of two months, the children were beginning to show the effects of the socialization efforts that school makes.

Finally, in the third interview, the mothers compared their children's present behavior with what it had been before they started school in terms of these dimensions: maturity, self-control, helpfulness, patience, self-confidence, responsibility, obedience, and ability to get along with playmates. All of the mothers reported improvement in all these characteristics except for obedience and patience, and 60 percent of the mothers said that their children were easier to handle this year than they had been the year before. Of course, it is possible that the year that elapsed accounts for the increased ease in handling these children. Yet most researchers believe that school contributes to the development of more mature behavior.

Despite such socializing effects of school on children, however, it remains true that some children object to school, some resist it, and some find it a very disturbing experience. Thus, for some children, the school experience is a threatening and frightening event that provokes a crisis of considerable proportions. And trouble in school means disciplinary difficulties.

DISCIPLINE

The contemporary view of discipline is that it is vital not only to the education of the child but also to his psychological well-being. Discipline is not just a means of controlling delinquency or managing destructive classroom behavior but a way to establish in children positive attitudes toward education. In this sense, the word "discipline" refers to the way in which productive habits and patterns of work are produced in children. Thus, all the educational-mental-health efforts of the teacher or the school system tend to be fired in the crucible of discipline.

However, discipline can be judged healthy or unhealthy only in terms of the reaction that the discipline produces in the individual child. There is no rule of thumb for disciplinary action that can be applied to every child; it is this absolute individuality of discipline that makes it such a difficult problem. As a way of approaching this problem, imagine that you are continuously interrupted by someone who screams loudly, persistently, and irritatingly. After tolerating this interference for a while, you decide to remove it by having a few words with the screamer. Therefore, you walk over to him and ask him, in the nicest way you know how, to be quiet. He points out, however, that he is not screaming out of sheer perversity or malice but because his foot is caught in a bear trap from which he is unable to extricate himself. He knows his screams are annoying, but he screams because he must.

Children, who lack the sophisticated verbal tools of adults, must communicate their agonies by whatever means are at hand. This communication usually takes the form of disturbed behavior, which is at best difficult to decipher. Nonetheless, disturbed behavior is most often a direct translation of the victim-with-a-foot-in-the-bear-trap, which is the child's way of communicating to the outside world that he has run out of possible solutions to his problem. Disturbed behavior is thus the scream of the child who has exhausted all his personal resources; it is a kind of cry for help.

Teachers seldom recognize disturbed behavior for what it is and so do not respond to it properly. They generally view defiance, disobedience, disrespect, and derogation of academic duty as a fundamental threat rather than a cry for help. As a consequence, even well-intentioned discipline usually initiates a chain reaction of resentment, rebellion, additional discipline, and steadily deteriorating interpersonal relations.

Only a small percentage of children clearly reveal their reaction to conventional methods of discipline. Most children who have just been disciplined do not overtly behave in a rebellious way and present instead an appearance of shame, embarrassment, or sullenness. The most important outcome of discipline is, however, the internal and invisible one. If the teacher fails to understand that the important effects of discipline are these hidden, internal ones, she is liable to continue using disciplinary practices that harm rather than help. Such practices may foster resentment, reinforce the child's feeling that life is treating him unfairly, and damage his sense of adequacy. These effects of discipline are too high a price to pay for conformity and apparent obedience.

Disciplinary methods producing those harmful effects are nonetheless common in classrooms today. These practices are also often carried out in public—in part because so little other opportunity is available to the teacher—even though that, too, may be harmful to the child. Indeed, teachers have evolved an infinite variety of public punishments. These may range from tying children to their chairs and putting scotch tape over the mouths of the more verbal ones to forcing them to sit in a corner. Although teachers seldom use the dunce cap today, some make an offending child wear a placard proclaiming the nature of his offense. However, probably the most frequent and the preferred method of public criticism is the "chew out" concept of group control; anyone who walks through the halls of any school in America can hear the shrill and exasperated shrieking of the teacher at the end of her rope. It is always difficult to determine in such instances whether the true value of such behavior is "ventilation therapy" for the teacher or correction for the children.

Educators must evolve sound methods for handling such behavior as disrespect, defiance of the teacher's authority, peer aggression, calculated rejection of the school's goals, and destructiveness—all of which are prevalent today. Although these disciplinary problems are more evident in central urban complexes, similar behavior occurs in suburban and rural areas as well. Intensified pressures for academic accomplishment produce more failure and frustration, and the many daily examples of raw aggression prevalent in society encourage impulsive acting out. At the same time, there is a realignment of the socializing forces in our society; the family influence is diminishing, but schools and other community agencies have not yet found a way to take over the family's role in the socialization of the child.

The Mental Hygiene View of Discipline [1]

Modern discipline has become in theory inextricably intertwined with the *mental hygiene view*. However, that marriage has not been a happy one, for this view of school discipline stays one jump ahead of chaos. Some advocates of this

[1] The material presented here is adapted with permission from W. C. Morse, "The Mental Hygiene Viewpoint on School Discipline," *The High School Journal*, 1965.

view cling to the simple-minded hope that affection and acceptance will conquer all; others are certain that the only way to manage recalcitrant youths is to get tough and kick them out when they do not respond. Such a primitive dichotomy, based as it is on vastly oversimplified notions of how to influence behavior, is no longer worthy of serious students' attention.

The primary problem is that the mental hygiene movement is still dominated by concepts that, although valid in themselves, are remote from the Monday-morning-to-Friday-night routine of schools with thousands of children who must be controlled in the social world of school. Mental hygienists speak a language peculiar to themselves in describing the salient features of the child's psychic structure, and this language is seldom translatable into the action terms needed by teachers when they must make disciplinary decisions. Thus, for example, a therapist may indicate to the teacher that a pupil misbehaves because he has a "damaged self-concept" or suffers from "low self-esteem." From a mental hygiene point of view, it would be beneficial to the child if the teacher were to take this state of affairs into consideration at those moments when discipline is called for, and it would also be helpful if the classroom experience itself could be designed to alter the child's view of himself. At this point, the teacher and the therapist may be in complete accord about the ideal circumstances for this child's continued healthy psychological development. The trouble comes when the teacher tries to translate these observations into action to take with the child.

Neither the teacher nor the therapist is able to specify exactly what kinds of experience will be positive, negative, or neutral for the child's self-esteem or to estimate their precise impact on the child. In addition, the teacher is not sufficiently trained in mental hygiene concepts to be able to adapt them easily to the multitude of daily confrontations that she will have with the child. Should she reward effort rather than accomplishment? Should she abstain from punishing him? Should she let him disturb the class more than

she would allow other children to do? Should she assign him special leadership roles? Should she temper the grading system in terms of his emotional problems? Should she demand the same, more, or less of him than of other pupils?

In short, the mental hygiene viewpoint may be a valid blueprint of the psychic life of the child but is useless as a guide to the management of the disciplinary relationship between teacher and child. The teacher directs a group of children bent on accomplishing the tasks of education; she is not a psychotherapist working exclusively with one pupil. The dilemma is that we have sensitized the teacher to the views of mental health specialists without providing the means by which these concepts can be made an integral part of the ongoing conduct of the classroom. One attempt to solve this problem has been the development of the *life space approach* to discipline.

The Life Space Approach to Discipline

The phrase *life space* was coined by Kurt Lewin of The Massachusetts Institute of Technology to describe the total set of phenomena that constitute the real world for a person. One's life space thus includes the pressures, needs, and motives in operation in a situation at a particular moment—it is a way of describing the things and events in one's life. Therefore, according to the life space approach, discipline can only be effective if it is predicated on an analysis of the fields of force (using a physics analogy) that exist at that moment for all participants in the disciplinary situation.

The life space approach to discipline begins with an examination of the major forces operating in the misbehaving child's milieu. Thus, the nature of the task in which the pupil is involved must be analyzed because the task may contain the seeds of acute frustration, which would lead directly to misbehavior. The group relationships must also be analyzed because they may generate forces producing unacceptable behavior; a group may put strong pressure for certain behavior on the members or make one or more members into the group scapegoat. Moreover, the authority relationship may contain the source of misbehavior, so that the adult-child interaction must be scrutinized; a youngster who is rejected or feels that he is rejected by the teacher may act out to get a response. Finally, the child's parents, siblings, neighborhood, and so on must be studied because they are all forces influencing his behavior.

These forces alone, however, do not produce behavior; they filter through a particular self. Therefore, knowing about the child's self-esteem, aspirations, and role also helps educators to discover appropriate disciplinary measures. Plans for changing the child's behavior can then be directed at both his self and the field of forces operating upon him. Thus, the educator may be able to change the child's behavior by modulating the tasks assigned, the group involvements, or the authority relationship. Through counseling, it may also be possible to change some of the perceptions that contribute to his misbehavior.

Environmental manipulation may not significantly alter the child's self. However, the educator may be able to adjust the environmental forces to a level at which the child can learn to cope with them. The child who learns coping skills for managing difficult situations is able to maintain himself within the range of acceptable behavior. These skills can be taught to many students through proper handling at times of crisis. Nevertheless, our schools often handle tense situations in a way that encourages or consolidates unfortunate coping—we generate anger, we pile on rebuke, we belittle the child's intention and capacity to adjust—and we do all these things in the guise of motivation and support. Building coping strength is not easy, but the most significant way to change undesirable behavior—as well as to prevent it—is to expose the child to an environment reasonable for him, and work through the steps until he is able to accommodate more stress (Bower, 1964).

Although this life space approach is not a panacea, it is a framework that helps make sense of some of the most vexing discipline problems. For example, one of these is "accepting the child." Is it accepting the child to exclude him from the classroom or the school? To restrict his freedom? To put high demands on him for compliance? To give him a chance to try something that we know he will fail? The answer to each of these statements is both "yes" and "no"; psychological acceptance is not a set pattern of adult behavior but depends upon the nature of each child and upon what will help him to learn. Helping him to learn requires *differential diagnosis*, or looking behind the symptom to his own basic pattern of behavior. Therefore, we accept the child psychologically only when we react in the way that best teaches him what he must learn.

Thus, for instance, all children do not learn to control their impulses in the same way. An adolescent with a minimum of conscience learns little of how to cope with his impulses from permissive acceptance because he exploits permissiveness. He needs to know that his environment will always be less rewarding if he misbehaves. Therefore, gratifications must be denied him, although never with hostility. With a youngster of this sort, words are largely wasted; clear action is necessary. He is accepted by being restrained. In fact, accepting him may even require physically holding him. An anxious child, on the other hand, needs to talk and work his problem through. Therefore, accepting him follows another pattern even though his behavior may have to be drastically curbed. The variety of patterns of acceptance in effect matches the variety of personality patterns in children.

Discipline—Cookbook Style

One of the difficulties in administering discipline is that the educator usually looks for some cookbook-style rules to guide him. However, problems of discipline have no simple solution; discipline always involves a trade-off of good and bad effects. For example, suppose we ask the question

"Should I punish in anger?" Any adroit psychologist or teacher could defend both sides of this issue equally well. First, let us answer this question by flatly stating that one should never punish in anger. The punisher's anger affects his judgment, so that he tends to overdiscipline and inflict physical or psychological injury that was unintended. Because he may make such errors, the child may well misunderstand the reasons for disciplinary action; he may feel that his teacher always hits him or criticizes him because she is angry rather than seeking to help him lead a better life. After all, each time the child is disciplined, his teacher is angry. The reinforcement provided by such a series of experiences makes an unmistakable impact upon the child's psyche.

Discipline conducted in anger is also antieducational. No educational goal could be achieved by such methods; no one would teach a course in a flaming rage. Imagine, for example, your feelings if you were in court and found that the judge assigned to your case was rabid in his detestation of the crime of which you had been accused. You would hardly expect reasonableness and justice from him. Thus, anger tends to convert discipline into punishment and makes a personal vendetta out of a corrective experience. It is not an appropriate educational device because its side effects (whatever the romanticism we may have about our own experiences with "tough but fair" teachers) are too damaging.

Suppose we answer the question in the opposite vein: "Yes, discipline should be conducted in anger." The reason that it should be is that, for the child, the issue is soon lost. Behavior worth criticism is a temporary thing in the mind of the child. Therefore, disciplining him for something he did even a relatively short time ago seems to him inappropriate—ancient history, in fact. Moreover, the child would be subjected to double jeopardy. He would not only have to pay for his crime but also suffer anticipatory guilt and deal with the anxiety produced by exaggerating in his own mind the kind of punishment that he will receive. Finally, waiting to discipline is like waiting an hour to yell "Ouch!" after hitting one's

thumb with a hammer. The adult who disciplines a child in this manner seems to him machine-like, cold, and infallible. It seems more logical that the child has a right to know the emotional impact of his actions and so learn that the feelings of others are essential ingredients in the total stew of interpersonal relations.

Thus, there is no cookbook solution to the problem of discipline. It is an interpersonal transaction that must be played by ear in order to contribute to the mental health of the child. In any disciplinary transaction, however, it is necessary to abandon the script of the disciplinary conversation typically used with children. The conversation goes like this: "Don't you know you are not supposed to do that?" "Yeah." "Then why do you do it?" "I don't know." The traditional conclusion is an ad lib moral lecture on the fundamental worthlessness of the child and combines an assault on his self-esteem with statements on behaving better in the future. These traditional methods are without merit as a corrective device; they produce only resentment and rebellion and, at best, blind conformity to a system that is without the grace of logic.

The next step in approaching discipline properly is to eliminate the crime and punishment or cops and robbers definition of discipliner and disciplinee. As long as discipline is viewed as a game in which one protagonist commits a crime and the other plays Sherlock Holmes, the sensible goal of final internal control of behavior on the part of the child will always be elusive. The aim of discipline is not just to correct present behavior but to inculcate in the child a sense of responsibility that will give him control over himself in the future.

Viewing discipline in this way gives the teacher an edge; she can now employ strategy. The teacher, knowing in advance that the child will repeat the behavior that he has indulged in for so long, is free to analyze the nature of this behavior and to anticipate its occurrence in the future. In that analysis, the teacher must be committed to searching for the bear trap—the why of the child's behavior. If the child detects that the teacher is not interested in the reason for his behavior, he will feel that she is not to be trusted and will therefore react with even greater defiance and violence. Thus, the teacher must develop a one-to-one relationship with the child. Doing so may seem like an additional burden to the already harried teacher, but it is profitable in the long run.

Finally, it is important for teachers to use one another as a resource. Too often teachers restrict themselves to superficial social exchange; they isolate themselves in their own classrooms and are reluctant to draw on the experience and methods of teachers in the same school who have dealt successfully with similar problems. In discipline, two or more heads are better than one.

SUMMARY

In our society, the educational system is the primary agent of socialization for the growing child about to be weaned from home and family. However, we are not certain of the exact role that the teacher should play in this process—stimulator of independent thought or reinforcer of cultural values. The child's experience with school usually begins with nursery school and an early exposure to socialization by a group of peers in a setting away from the home and family. After he enters grade school, he begins to reflect the school's pressure for socialized behavior and so appears changed to his parents—mostly for the better.

Part of the socialization process in school are disciplinary encounters with the teacher. According to the modern view of discipline, the nature of the psychic experience of the child being disciplined is essential to the success of his socialization. Thus, the most productive approach to discipline is the life space approach, which involves analyzing the forces in the child's life, knowing the self through which these forces are filtered, and intervening in the total life situation.

Any discussion of the role of education in the socialization of children leads ultimately to the age-old wish for a cookbook that would direct the process, make it less complex, and guarantee results each and every time. Such a cookbook will never appear; the myth of its possibility is a hope borne only in the minds of those who insist that man is a simple, stimulus–response-bound organism. Intelligent, effective discipline will remain a matter of difficult judgments made in situations in which not all of the relevant forces and pressures are usually known.

After the child enters school, he must learn an enormous array of complex things in order to receive full membership in adult society. Trying to learn them will probably be highly frustrating to him. This frustration and his attempts to master it constitute a major part of the child's development. If he is unable to master his frustration, emotional disturbance may well result.

THEORIES OF FRUSTRATION

The scientist can approach frustration in three different ways. First, it can be treated as an inner state of the organism. Such states are, of course, inaccessible to direct study, so that the researcher must depend solely on the report of the organism experiencing the emotional state. Second, the researcher can look at the overt behavior of the organism and, using his own experience as a baseline, make judgments about what the inner experience might be like. Finally, the researcher can view frustration as a hypothetical construct that relates antecedent and consequent behavior. Viewing frustration in this way means that an organism's frustration can be measured and as-

11

Emotional disturbance and education— The problem

151

"*The classic example of displaced aggression is the situation in which the boss (who holds life-and-death economic power) criticizes the employee.*"

"*Because the employee wants to retaliate but fears that he would jeopardize his job, he displaces his aggression and lashes out at his own underlings—his wife and children.*"

sessed in terms that can be relied upon by other investigators.

One of the classic theories based on the third approach is the *frustration-aggression hypothesis.* John Dollard and his co-workers at Yale's Institute of Human Relations theorized that frustration is produced by interference with the achievement of some end or goal. This frustration always increases the organism's tendency to respond aggressively. Thus, the fact of aggressive behavior is evidence that frustration has occurred.

Dollard and the others elaborated on this theory with a series of qualifications. According to one of these qualifications, the strength of the tendency to respond aggressively to frustration depends on "the strength of the goal-response sequence interfered with"—that is, on the intensity with which the goal was being sought in the first place. Although it is difficult to define "amount" in a reasonable fashion, the researchers suggested that the total amount of interference with the goal seeking bears a direct relationship to the tendency toward aggressive response. By the same token, the more times that actions are frustrated, the greater is the tendency to strike out aggressively. Thus, in its simplest form, this theory makes the commonsense suggestion that the more severe the frustrations, the greater the likelihood that aggression will be the outcome.

The condition of punishment also affects the relationship between frustration and aggression. Both children and adults are punished for lashing out at the environment and the people in it. Thus, punishment or the anticipation of punishment inhibits aggression. Knowing how much aggression will follow how much frustration depends upon knowing how much punishment is liable to or expected to ensue in retaliation for the aggressive outburst.

Not all aggressive behavior is direct and focused on the source of frustration. In some instances, the real object of an aggressive assault may be a dangerous target capable of retaliating. The classic example of displaced aggression is the situation in which the boss (who holds life-and-death economic power) criticizes the employee. Because the employee wants to retaliate but fears that he would jeopardize his job, he displaces his aggression and lashes out at his own underlings—

his wife and children. Or he may use an even more abstract target—people in general.

A final consideration is that aggression may be useful in that it serves to release tension in a variety of ways. Aggression may not only provide catharsis but also force the environment to yield —which is the goal of aggressive behavior.

Another theory of frustration is the *frustration-fixation hypothesis,* which was developed by Norman R. F. Maier (Maier and Ellen, 1951; Maier, 1956). Maier began by stating that frustration produces in an organism a fixated and unproductive pattern of responses. Thus, frustrated behavior is not subject to typical theories of learning and motivation and might better be identified as "behavior without a goal." Fixated behavior is an end in itself and, therefore, is not the same as problem solving behavior.

Maier developed this theory through experiments with rats and a Lashley jumping stand. A Lashley jumping stand is a simple apparatus consisting of a platform from which a rat can leap through either one of two windows, each of which is covered by a piece of cardboard with a design emblazoned on it. The purpose of the apparatus is to teach the rat to jump at the window displaying the insignia that the experimenter wants the rat to recognize. He does so by locking in place the cardboard in front of the "wrong" window. Then, when the rat makes his choice and jumps, he strikes either a movable cardboard that allows him to land safely on the other side and be fed or a fixed one that makes him bounce off it and fall into a net suspended below the apparatus. Making the correct choice lets the rat avoid the unpleasant fall from the perch and achieves a food reward for him.

Maier, after teaching his rats which cardboard was movable, made the problem impossible to solve by locking both of the cardboards in place, so that, whatever cardboard that the rats jumped at, they fell and received no food. When the rats naturally refused to jump at all, they were forced by a blast of compressed air or a sharp rap on the tail to jump whether they liked it or not. Thus, no form of goal oriented or adaptive behav-

ior worked, but the rats had to respond anyway. Maier had created total frustration.

As a result of this frustration, about 80 percent of the rats began to jump only toward one window regardless of what design was presented to them. Other rats began jumping at just one card regardless of its position. When the cards were shifted on a random basis, so that the rats could not figure out a pattern of response that would assure reward, then the rigid solution of always jumping in the direction of a particular card or window would mean that the rats would be successful 50 percent of the time but would never solve the problem of how to increase the frequency of success.

Once these stereotyped forms of response were firmly established in the rats (jumping at the same window or the same card each time), Maier set the apparatus so that either response resulted in failure 100 percent of the time. Then, the frustrated rats continued their inappropriate behavior even though shifting their tactics would have resolved the dilemma. Thus, behavior in rats —and presumably in humans—can become fixated even when the consequence is all punishment and no reward.

Another theory of frustration is the *frustration-regression hypothesis,* which attempts to relate frustration to the development of the child. Freud first suggested that frustration can force an individual to regress to patterns of reaction that were useful at an earlier stage in his development. The classic test of this hypothesis was made by Barker, Dembo, and Lewin (1941). Their experiment examined the way in which children learn motivation and adult forms of responding to it. This examination involved assessing the degree of motivation that the children had already attained, exposing them to frustration, and comparing the maturity of their response after frustration to their prefrustration level of maturity. The researchers estimated the children's "maturity" in terms of the "constructiveness" of their play with a standard set of toys.

In order to establish frustration, Barker, Dembo, and Lewin exposed the children to a play situation with a standard set of toys and then exposed them to a much more fascinating set of toys. After that, the experimenters took away the fascinating toys and returned the standard ones. When the researchers dropped a wire barrier between the children and the highly desirable toys, so that they could see the toys but not play with them, the experimental frustration was established. The children responded to their frustration with regression, which is thus an alternative to fixation and aggression.

These theories did not deny the possibility of alternative responses to frustration but simply neglected that aspect of frustration. Other theorists have taken a closer and more sophisticated look at frustration. They have broadened the experimental base of frustration theory and have attempted to relate it to general behavior theory. These efforts have produced a reconceptualization of the frustrating situation itself. The new concept emphasizes the idea that there is *no unique* overt behavior characteristic of all frustrated organisms (Lawson, 1965). For example, Child and Waterhouse (1952) revised the frustration-aggression hypothesis by noting that a clear statement of alternative responses available to the frustrated person must be catalogued before a prediction of aggressive response can reasonably be made; aggression *may* follow frustration but *need* not.

EMOTIONAL AND BEHAVIORAL PROBLEMS

The American school system was not designed for emotionally and socially frustrated children. Some of these children are so disturbed that they cannot remain in the regular classroom even with supportive services. These children, who are unacceptable to peers, adults, and themselves, engage in behavior disruptive to the rest of the class. The overt behavior may range between the extremes of aggressive destruction and massive withdrawal.

Besides exhibiting these kinds of behavior, the emotionally disturbed child "needs an unusual amount of prodding to get work completed, is inattentive, indifferent, apparently lazy, has nervous reactions such as nail biting, thumb or finger sucking, stuttering, extreme restlessness, muscle twitching, hair twisting, picking and scratching, or deep and frequent sighing." Moreover, he "is actively excluded by most of the children whenever they get a chance, fails in school for no apparent reason, is absent from school frequently, dislikes school intensely, seems to be more unhappy than most of the children, achieves less in school than his ability indicates he should, and is jealous or overcompetitive" (Kough and DeHaan, 1955).

Children like these are not uncommon in the schools; special educational provisions are needed for at least one out of every 200 children in the school age population. Further, 10 to 12 percent of all school age children need psychiatric help, and one child in 2,000 needs full-time intensive treatment. Finally, 0.5 million severely disturbed youngsters are expelled from school (Pate, 1963).

Emotional disturbance is not, however, equally distributed throughout the population. For example, age and sex are both variables affecting the distribution of emotional disturbance. Boys in early puberty display the greatest degree of emotion disorder and generally outnumber girls four to one in admission to mental health clinics (Bahn and Norman, 1959). Among 14 to 16 year old boys and girls, psychotic and personality disorders seem to be most prevalent, while psychoneurotic disorders are most prevalent among 10 to 13 year olds.

Occupational status is another factor in the distribution of emotional disturbance. Families in which the father's occupation is a service or semi-skilled one produce more than twice as many emotionally disturbed children than would be expected in terms of the proportion of these families to the rest of the population. Conversely, families in which the father has a professional, managerial, clerical, or sales job produce fewer emotionally disturbed children than would be expected (Bower, 1961).

Violence in the Schools

Violence, which is always disruptive to the regular and orderly processes of society, presents a particular problem for the educational system. However, it is difficult to report accurately the direction and quantity of violence in the schools, for much of school misbehavior is "kept in the family" and not reported to the general public. An admission of such difficulties is to the educator an admission of failure.

One thorough survey has, however, been completed by the National Education Association (1956). For this survey, the Association sent a list of 18 kinds of misbehavior to a sample of 2,987 urban and 1,283 rural teachers in elementary, junior high, and senior high schools. Each teacher in the sample was asked to evaluate how prevalent each kind was then and how prevalent each kind was 10 years ago. Over 50 percent of the school districts reported that the most serious forms of misbehavior (carrying knives, guns, or other weapons, gang fighting, using narcotics, and engaging in physical violence against teachers) were nonexistent both at the time of the study and 10 years before it. However, 25 percent of the districts reported an average increase in these kinds of behavior, although a matching decrease in other districts balanced out this rise.

Thus, because the relative frequency of these types of misconduct remained at much the same level, the correct conclusion is that serious misconduct increased only *in certain districts*. These districts were those with a million or more population. Rural and small urban districts had relatively fewer increases in serious types of misbehavior, although these districts did note an increase in both impertinence and failure to do homework. Such less serious delinquencies also increased in the larger districts. Of these, 70 percent reported an increase in impertinence, more than 42 percent reported an increase in the use of obscene and profane language, and nearly 58 percent reported an increase in the destruction of school property.

These increases in both serious and less serious delinquency in urban districts result from a steady decline in the conditions under which the pupils live. These children live in neighborhoods in which there are a high percentage of families on relief, low rentals, foreign born or Negro heads of households, and a low percentage of home ownership. Those are the conditions of social disorganization and decay. The families living under these conditions are characterized by instability, erratic discipline, rejection of offspring, and disregard for legitimate authority. Families like these in turn produce maladjusted children. Such social conditions produced the Italian and Irish gangs of two or three decades ago and are now producing a modern counterpart in gangs of urbanized Negro and Puerto Rican youths (Shaw and McKay, 1942; Glueck and Glueck, 1950). However, these socio-economic factors do not always produce maladjustment; both model citizens and chronic offenders come from the same neighborhoods. For both kinds of children though, school may be the only stable influence that they experience and the only way that they can extricate themselves from the slum culture.

In order to help those who are socially maladjusted, some special schools and special classes have been established in the major cities of America. However, only a beginning has been made. Only a few of the 50 largest cities have special classes for the maladjusted. Among those that do exist, some are no more than dumping grounds for problem children—the troublemaker classes of America.

Ordinary schools tolerate the delinquent child—but just barely. For this child, the socialization process in the school is hardly deserving of the name. Little is done to socialize him, but a great deal is done to reject him, demean him, and diminish his image of himself as a worthwhile person. The child tolerates this treatment with very little grace, and drops out of school as soon as he can legally do so.

The Dropout

The dropout problem in education is not restricted to the intellectually limited segment of the student body. In our society, 40 percent of the children drop out of school before high school graduation. In addition, tens of thousands of those who physically remain in school have mentally dropped out, for they achieve far below their measured intellectual capacity.

This problem is also not limited to children in the lower class, as one thorough study (Lichter, Rapien, Seibert, and Sklansky, 1962) indicates. These researchers studied 105 white middle class adolescents of average mental ability who were referred by the Chicago public high schools as potential dropouts. The adolescents were divided into a treatment group of 33 girls and 37 boys and a nontreatment group of 35 others. Clinical analysis of the treatment group revealed striking similarities among the members. These children were not only presenting disciplinary problems but also failing academically. These educational problems produced, besides extreme parental pressure, resentment, shame, and declining self-esteem. Under such stresses, the children felt that it would be impossible to alleviate their educational problems and so believed that dropping out was the only alternative. Thus, "the dropouts left school because they were motivated to *run away* from a disagreeable situation; they did not feel impelled to *run toward* a definite and positive goal" (p. 247). What plans they did have were unrealistic, aimless, or vague.

This desire to drop out of school was indicative of emotional and personality disturbances, which seemed to have begun before the children entered school; "apart from the large issue of severe emotional disturbance, no other single factor could be isolated to account for school malfunctioning and premature leaving of school" (p. 253). The personality development of 76 percent of these children was grossly immature. Consequently, they cracked under the strain of the competition in school, which became for them a focus of conflict, resentment, and rebellion.

There were, however, sex differences in the time that these educational problems began. The boys were unable to perform academically as early as grammar school and responded to the academic challenge of high school passively and ineffectually. The girls, on the other hand, had been good —if somewhat conforming—students in grammar school, and it was only when they entered high school that rebellious acting out, class cutting, and failing to do homework appeared. Thus, the high school behavior of the boys was consistent with their earlier maladjustment. The massive rebellion of the girls was a new and startling pattern of behavior.

"The massive rebellion of the girls was a new and startling pattern of behavior."

Some of these children's parents were also examined in the study. Only a fourth of the parents availed themselves of the treatment and consultation offered because three-quarters of the parents did not last longer than five interviews. Of the one-fourth studied, the majority were immature and dependent. The fathers were weak and helpless, and about half of the mothers were aggressive and demanding. The response of each parent to his child's difficulties in school was uniformly negative, unconstructive, or confused. Such responses reflected unhealthy parent-child relationships. These inadequate parents had difficulty in dealing with their offspring during childhood and now found themselves overwhelmed by the pyrotechnics of adolescence. The consequent hostile interactions of parent and adolescent triggered further rebellion in the girls and even greater ineffectiveness in the boys.

Nonetheless, the assistance offered by the study produced significant results in the treatment group. Of this group, 48 percent improved in emotional or personality functioning, and 60 percent of the 40 students remaining in school improved in school adaptation. As might be expected, more of the youngsters judged to be most mature improved in personality functioning. Further, although both girls and boys showed emotional improvement, more boys than girls remained in school.

This study suggests that schools, social agencies, and communities can help to alleviate the dropout problem. A primary role of the schools should be to detect emotional problems as early as possible, so that they can be corrected before they become chronic. Schools are not mental hygiene clinics and cannot reasonably be asked to substitute therapy for education. However, schools are not helpless. They can detect emotional disturbance in children, alert their parents to its existence, make adjustments in the educational experience of these children, and refer them to social agencies for treatment.

In order to fulfill this role, teachers and school administrators must learn more about the nature of emotional difficulty and its relationship to motivational and attitudinal problems. Teachers today recognize social and emotional maladjustments in children more often than teachers in the past did (Stouffer and Owens, 1955). However, they still do not seem to gain much basic understanding of children's behavior from experience in teaching (Gaier and Jones, 1951); teachers are still likely to recognize children as seriously disturbed only if their disturbance issues in behavior that threatens the orderliness of the classroom (Wickman, 1928; Henning, 1949; Clark, 1951; Stouffer and Owens, 1955). Mental hygienists would consider to be much more important the less threatening symptoms of anxiety or withdrawal, which may signify a much more serious personality disorder.

Social agencies must also become more responsive to the needs of disturbed children in the schools. The divorce of child therapy agencies from the educational system has been so complete that few agencies have staff members adequately trained to deal with the problems peculiar to the experience of school. Therapists must learn more about the schools and become much more familiar with the minute-by-minute and day-by-day classroom experience of their patients.

However, even if the social agencies working together with the schools can develop special services and special classes for disturbed children, the level of community support for such provisions is inadequate. Moreover, some children will drop out of school no matter what precautions are taken or services provided. Thus, communities must devise appropriate means of meeting these children's needs as well. Leaving school does not end the dropout's contact with our society, so that we must plan to make dropping out less tragic for him.

It is, of course, easy enough to recommend that schools, clinics, and communities become more effective in detecting and treating the potential dropout or the potential delinquent. The doing rather than the recommending is painfully slow and difficult. Nevertheless, constructive attempts are being made to solve the problem of the disturbed child in school.

TRENDS TOWARD EDUCATIONAL MENTAL HEALTH [1]

Schools have increasingly been held responsible for what is amorphously called the "whole child." Because this term refers to the child's personal and social—as well as intellectual—development, the crucial issue in educational mental health is the degree to which the schools are prepared to deal with the whole child. Teachers have been expected to foster adequate adjustment in the child, his parents, and the culture around him as well as to teach him.

Consequently, as the schools have realized that mental health is part of dealing with the "whole child," they have responded to meet the challenge. The nature of their response was dictated by two factors: (1) the way in which they had solved previous demands for assuming added responsibility and (2) the existing social design for dealing with mental health problems. Factor 1 determined that the schools would add to their staffs specialists in mental health as well as specialists in physical education, health, and home economics. Factor 2 determined that the role of the specialist would be like the one that he had already established in the child guidance clinic, the development center, the hospital, or the family service agency—that is, providing one-to-one diagnostic and therapeutic services for disturbed children.

This transplanting of the clinical design to the public schools cannot be overstressed as a factor bringing us to our recent state of despair about overcoming the problem of educational mental health. These have been the consequences of the transplant: (1) a continuing allegiance to what Redl (1959) has called "pressure chamber treatment," in which the child is removed from his classroom habitat, subjected to a special kind of laying on of hands (termed "being seen"), and then returned (repaired?) to the classroom for another go at it; (2) the perpetuation of clinical

jargon as a means of describing and understanding children in the classroom, where this jargon has little real (or even translatable) meaning; (3) the establishment of empires of influence and hierarchies of power concerned with the issue of who is really responsible for the management of the "whole child"; (4) the development of interprofessional enmity and various levels of citizenship among professionals dealing with children in schools; (5) an abrogation of the teacher's opportunity for feeling competent to deal with her charges; (6) the domination of mental health in education by mental health professionals who give little attention to the basic educational issues raised by the programs; and (7) a stultification of efforts to develop programs that would meet the unique problems of the moderately disturbed child in school.

That this design is inadequate has gradually become apparent to educators and, to their everlasting credit, to the mental health professionals themselves. A flurry of activity in instigating both research and programs has occurred, the most striking portion of which involves a major shift in the philosophy underlying programs in school mental health (Biber, 1958; Allinsmith and Goethals, 1961; Ojemann, 1958; Jersild, 1955; Berman, 1954; Morse, 1961). Most of these new approaches to educational mental health are attempts to put more life and practicality into teachers' training in mental health. If mental health is to become a reality in the classroom, the teachers themselves must have the understanding, skills, and attitudes that contribute to a hygienic classroom climate. Thus, the teachers will have to be recruited into the mental health effort as responsible co-workers fitted for a special role in helping to prevent mental health problems from occurring.

Other researchers have arrived at similar conclusions. Talbot (1958) argued that cultural influences on learning have been neglected by both educators and mental hygienists. Wall (1960) cited public pressure and apathy, poor teacher selection and training, and lack of referral sources as impediments to good school mental health

[1] The material in this section is adapted from Cutler and McNeil (1963).

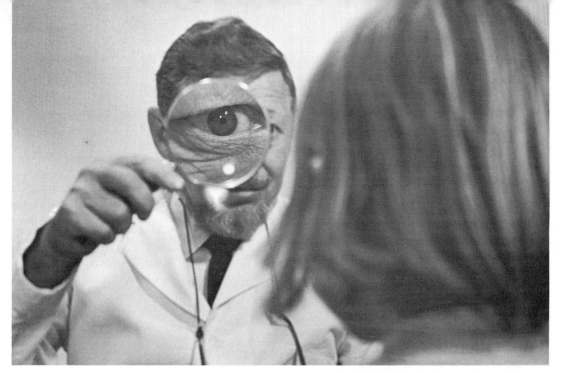

"This transplanting of the clinical design to the public schools cannot be overstressed as a factor bringing us to our recent state of despair about overcoming the problem of educational mental health."

programming. Liss (1958) offered educators and mental hygienists a common ground based on psychodynamic views of the teaching and therapeutic processes. Biber (1961) stressed that school provides a unique opportunity to develop basic ego skills and positive self-concepts in children. Redl (1959) described the life space interview as a technique to be taught for behavior management and personality change in the classroom. D'Evelyn (1957) and Dreikurs (1960) offered a series of practical suggestions to teachers for dealing with classroom behavior problems.

Extensive programs in teacher training in mental health have been conducted with growing frequency and impact. A child study program, for example, was sponsored by the Institute for Child Study at the University of Maryland (Prescott, 1957). The purpose of this program was to develop clinically oriented teachers—ones who understand the individual child, not just children in general. Although the program was not designed to make teachers into psychotherapists, it did stress a clinical approach to teaching. In small group meetings throughout the year that were attended by consultants, voluntary groups of teachers gathered to study the dynamic individual and the group forces that contribute to behavior. Moreover, reading and discussing research material was coupled with studying individual children. Although many teachers' attitudes toward children were changed through this approach, a significant number of teachers were not affected. Further, translation of these changes in teacher attitudes into measurable alterations in children's classroom behavior has not yet been demonstrated.

A different approach to training teachers is exemplified by the Teacher Education Program at Bank Street College in New York (Biber, 1958). The stress here is on giving the teacher knowledge of both mental health problems and herself through participation as a student assistant in classrooms and through individual counseling of the teacher. This approach is designed to increase the teacher's insight into her personal assets and liabilities as well as her insight into the process of being a teacher and of solving classroom problems.

Other programs work directly with children as well as teachers. Among the best known is the Human Relations Program at the State University of Iowa (Ojemann, 1958). The assumptions of this program are that children in elementary and secondary grades can learn to understand the dynamics of behavior and that they can apply this learning to their relations with others; that is, children can learn about the causes rather than merely the surface characteristics of behavior. In accordance with this view, the teachers are trained to teach such materials to children as well as to practice a causal approach to interactions with them. By both example and the use of prepared narratives for class discussion, the program is intended to teach children a different perception of human behavior and, consequently, a substantially altered response to it.

Another approach to school mental health is the Forest Hill Village Project (An Evaluation of Four Projects, 1951). This Canadian approach trains selected teachers for a year in the principles of mental hygiene. After this training period, the teachers are expected to return to their communities and there act as a link between other teachers, the children, and the children's families. The project also includes a clinical team (a psychiatrist, a social worker, and a psychologist) that directly treats disturbed children. In addition, the Forest Hill Village Project arranges for parent education through discussion groups focusing on the study of mental hygiene. Finally, the program operates "human relations classes" for selected grades in the schools. These classes meet an hour a week for group-determined discussions of personal emotional experiences. The catharsis provided by these discussions converts them into something closely resembling traditional group therapy.

A more specialized mental hygiene project has been established at a public school in New York City (Adlerblum, 1950). This project is treating kindergarten and first grade children who display such symptoms of maladjustment as shyness and overaggression. The program consists of parent interviews, small-group play with the children under observation, work with groups of five children each week, and conferences with teachers. The children have been removed from their regular classrooms and are being treated in a clinic. However, the clinic maintains continuous communication with the children's teachers. This program is the forerunner of the current movement to establish special classes for emotionally disturbed children.

SUMMARY

The key to the emotional disturbance exhibited in the classroom is the frustration that disturbed children experience as they try to grapple with tasks beyond their psychological capacity. If estimates are correct, between 10 and 12 percent of our school children need psychiatric help. Without this help, disturbed children are liable to abandon education, and dropouts have no effective plan for life and no place to go.

Teachers and mental hygiene workers have not learned to view emotional disturbance from the same vantage point, so that their efforts to resocialize disturbed children have often been at cross-purposes. Thus, attempts to remove these children from the classroom for treatment in the clinic have proved to be inadequate. But during the last decade a number of new approaches to the problem have appeared. These efforts have principally focused on preparing the teacher to manage the task of resocialization in the classroom.

Emotionally disturbed children should be viewed as those whose socialization was mismanaged, distorted, or incomplete. Because learning in school presupposes successfully learning the curricula of infancy and early childhood, the unsocialized child can be taught only imperfectly. Teachers and the public school system must resocialize the faulty behavior that appears in the school child, advance his socialization to meet the new demands that life will make on him at each age, and correct the distortions of emotion and cognition that interfere with his education. Thus, for such a child, the classroom must become a center for both therapy and learning.

PROJECT RE-ED

One approach to the problem of making the classroom a center for both therapy and learning is Project Re-ed (Project for the Re-education of Emotionally Disturbed Children). The conceptualization of this project began with Nicholas Hobbs's visits to Scotland and France. In Glasgow, he found that teachers who had had two years of on-the-job training (and were called "school psychologists") were used to staff guid-

12

Emotional disturbance and education— Solutions

ance and treatment centers in the city. These centers provided an excellent range of services for disturbed children. In France, he found small residential treatment centers staffed by *educateurs* (specialized workers) who, in turn, received support from mental health specialists. Both of these programs were based on the assumptions that mental health is a community affair and that manpower shortages exist and will continue to exist.

Project Re-ed is based on this recognition that services for emotionally disturbed children cannot be provided by one-to-one relationships. Thus, Project Re-ed does not view itself as the agency solely responsible for the child but as the organizer of the school and community forces needed to arrange significant aspects of the child's life. Project Re-ed combines these forces by sending the child to a residential school that works with him on an around-the-clock basis, five days a week, for about four months. The aim of the project is to bring him in that time to a state that will enable him to return to the community as a reasonably functioning member. No "cures" or even "treatments" are intended.

Underlying this general objective are certain philosophical assumptions, both implicit and explicit, about the nature of the child, the community, and society at large:

1. There is a learning bias. It is assumed that the child is not suffering from mental disease but that he has acquired bad habits; he has learned to view the world as a world that has rejected him. Thus, the task of re-education is to help the child learn new and more effective ways of viewing himself and his world and to learn habits that lead to more effective functioning. The child must learn how to learn.

2. There is a time bias. The passage of time alone may result in improvement in many cases needing therapy.

3. There is a growth bias. The years between 6 and 12 are years of steady growth on all fronts for the child. During this period, he is malleable, both physically and psychologically. Thus, corrective experiences can be most productive during these years.

4. There is a social systems bias. After we have abandoned the concepts of "cure" and "intrapsychic processes," we cannot merely substitute other labels such as "individual adjustment," "relations between child and family," and so forth. We must focus on the total system of which the child is a part. Thus, we must change the mother, the father, the teacher, the minister, and the policeman on the corner.

5. There is a bias away from dynamic psychology and its concern with psychoanalytic concepts. Interpretation and insight are considered to be unnecessary processes because re-education aims at more immediate, effective functioning.

From these working assumptions and biases, Project Re-ed has developed specific tasks necessary to accomplish with each child. One of these is the development of trust. In his dealings with adults and in his ability to learn from them, the disturbed child has been impaired. He cannot trust adults. Re-education must establish the conditions that make trusting relationships possible.

Gaining competence is a second aim of re-education. Any child must feel that he has ability —at least in some areas—not only for his own self-esteem, but also in order to gain acceptance from others. Thus, the child must become competent in the school subjects that he could not master before. However, competencies are not limited to school matters alone; one important effort in re-education is to help each child develop his own special ability (or abilities), so that he can assert his uniqueness.

A third aim is the control of symptoms. Symptoms are themselves important and should be dealt with directly, for the child has usually been rejected on the basis of the symptoms of disturbance that he has displayed. These, therefore, must be unlearned as a first step in the process of being restored to the community. The behavior—not its source—is of prime concern.

Learning middle class values is a fourth aim. As contradictory as it might appear, Project Re-ed supports the notion of instilling middle class values in its children.

A fifth aim is "gaining cognitive control for today and tomorrow." The child is helped to come to an understanding of what his behavior is like, whether others view it as "good" or "bad," and how it might be changed or improved. Thus, the child is helped to gain intelligent control over himself and his environment, although the intent is not "insight" in the psychoanalytic, therapeutic sense.

The development of community ties is an important sixth task. Hobbs argues that children need to identify with the neighborhood and thereby learn that social institutions are there for their own welfare.

A seventh aim is "physical experience as a basis for greater awareness of self." The basic notion here is that the clearer the differentiation of the physical self, the clearer the definition of the psychological self. Project Re-ed gives each child a full round of physical activities in order to achieve this aim.

A final aim—and perhaps the most intriguing one—is the knowing of joy. Joy is important, and, in some fashion, the child must have his share of it. However, just as it is difficult to teach the child of this age to trust, so it is difficult to know how to bring joy to him.

MENTAL HEALTH CONSULTATION [1]

The Michigan Plan of Mental Health Consultation is a model of one class of approaches to dealing with emotional and behavioral problems

[1] The material presented in this section is adapted with permission from R. L. Cutler and E. B. McNeil, *Mental Health Consultation in Schools* (U. S. Office of Education) (Ann Arbor, Michigan, 1963).

"Joy is important, and, in some fashion, the child must have his share of it."

in school. The premises on which this plan was constructed, the principles behind it, the techniques employed in it, and its evolution over time illustrate both the nature of the problems typically encountered in school mental health programs and the way in which solutions are finally achieved.

The main purpose of this plan was to explore the effectiveness of approaching mental health in schools with an in-service consultation program involving both professional mental health workers and public school personnel. This approach is consistent with the increasingly evident trend toward recruiting and training larger numbers of teachers for on-the-line preventive work in mental health.

One of the reasons for this trend is the recognition that children do not have problems by appointment, so that it is imperative to have skilled help available at the moment when the child is facing difficulty. The economics of the school situation do not, however, permit having mental health specialists available on a standby basis. Thus, basic mental health skills should be available to the on-the-line worker—the teacher, for "emotional first aid" during moments of high stress is an effective tool in preventive and remedial mental health efforts (Redl and Caplan, 1961).

In order to turn the school personnel participating in the Michigan Plan into first-aid workers, we first attempted to introduce theoretical concepts fundamental to the child management process. These included the ideas that behavior is motivated, that remote events may influence the child's present behavior, that the child passes through a series of developmental stages, and that immediate situational factors often play a large part in determining the specific reactions of the child in the classroom. As it seemed indicated, we also introduced a version of the transference concept stating that the child tends to react to people in the present in terms of how he has learned to relate to significant people in the past. Occasionally, with the more sophisticated teacher, or where the management goals demanded it, we

would provide a more thorough dynamic explanation of the underlying causes of the child's behavior.

Second, we attempted to provide a framework for the diagnostic understanding of the child with whom the teacher is having difficulty and for the generalizing of this understanding to other children. For this purpose, we developed the life themes approach, which states that every person perceives and responds to the world in terms of a set of learned dimensions, along which he organizes his experience and reacts to the environment. These life themes can be described by familiar adjectives, such as fearful, aggressive, and status seeking. Further, we tried to teach the idea that these life themes, once established, tended to persist and to operate as selective forces in perception and response. We gave relatively little attention to the dynamic origins of these predispositions to respond because we preferred to stress their situational determination and management. We also attempted to show how interviews, the interpretation of day-to-day behavior, the examination of the child's productions in stories, "show and tell" periods, and so on can provide clues to his dominant life themes. Thus, we developed a description of child behavior drawing on areas familiar to the teacher and then attempted to provide diagnostic instruments from the natural productions of the child in the classroom.

Third, we tried to teach some principles of short-term management and some techniques for bringing about more lasting change in the child's school adjustment. In order to do so, we drew heavily on the milieu treatment concept and on Redl's reality interviewing and life space management approach. We tried to inculcate the basic ideas that friendship and understanding are not the same as indulgence and that the setting and maintaining of limits are not necessarily punitive. We often touched upon the use of physical management (particularly with younger children), and we tried to establish the concept of a planned, step-by-step program of authority, intervention, and control. Specific techniques for inducing self-control, for application to the demands of the classroom, or for effective group interaction were invented and applied when they seemed necessary.

Finally, when strong evidence accumulated that personal problems of the consultee were preventing the effective application (or, on occasion, even the acceptance) of suggestions about dealing with the child, we would attempt to deal with these on a short-term, ego-supportive basis. Or, when this technique proved to be ineffective, we would refer the consultee to appropriate sources of assistance outside the consultation program. We did not believe that the proper function of the school mental health consultant includes providing individual psychotherapy to consultees.

The moderately disturbed child's situation is quite different from that of the disturbed adult. First, the child's characteristic style of response is not likely to be so well established because he has not had a long time to rehearse and perfect it and because he is constantly changing in terms of both his physical and cultural maturation and the demands made on him. The behavior of this child is, therefore, much more susceptible to change. Second, the child has not perfected his verbal approach to the world to the degree that the adult has. Thus, the child's symptoms of disturbance are much more likely to be expressed in action. Third, because he is passing through a series of important life changes, he has repeated opportunities to acquire new means of dealing with his surroundings. Consequently, the teacher may capitalize on alternative problem solving methods by intervening in the child's action world at the moment of crisis. The alterations in behavior brought about in the child's life space by such intervention are more likely to have a pervasive and lasting effect. For these reasons, we believe that significant alterations in the child's basic approach to the world can be brought about by direct life space management.

Despite the advances made, only a few controlled experiments have tested the effectiveness of special education for disturbed children. The important studies are those that address themselves to the issue of long-term gains in emotion-

ally disturbed children, but short-term modification of behavior via consultation is not the same as a fundamental change in personality structure.

SPECIAL CLASSES FOR THE EMOTIONALLY HANDICAPPED [2]

Special public school classes for emotionally handicapped children are a relatively recent development. Typically, such programs are the last in the total spectrum of special services to develop, even though the public schools have been active on behalf of some kinds of emotionally handicapped youngsters for a long time. Now, however, experimental programs are proliferating, and most involve the "special class" concept. Nonetheless, it takes but one visit to one classroom in each of two different systems to recognize that there is little common conceptualization underlying these developments. Designs for the conduct of the special classes range from permissive, relaxed, "therapeutic" approaches to traditional educational programs in the context of tight controls.

Moreover, once such a class is established, the participating school and outside personnel are under heavy pressure to view it as successful. Thus, acclamations of success are commonplace —even when there is little in common among the programs for which such successes are claimed. In a parallel development, teacher training institutions have now undertaken to train special teachers for the emotionally handicapped. And, for the most part, all of these developments have taken place in the context of little hard evidence for the utility of the special class design.

To remedy this lack of hard evidence, programs of special classes for emotionally disturbed children were canvassed across the country. Of the existing programs, extensive data were col-

[2] The material presented in this section is adapted with permission from W. C. Morse and R. L. Cutler, *Public School Classes for the Emotionally Handicapped: A Research Analysis* (Council for Exceptional Children) (Ann Arbor, Michigan, 1964).

lected from a total of 54, representing 74 class-room teachers and more than 520 children. Visitors made on-the-spot ratings of various teacher and pupil characteristics and assessed the overall orientation and success of the programs. Finally, information was collected from the children themselves about their past, present, and future perceptions of their educational situation.

Basic Impetus for Programs

One fundamental reason for the development of special classes for emotionally handicapped children was, of course, the immense concern of the public schools for children, for whom the schools are responsible. But how this concern was translated into a specific program varied considerably. In addition to this basic concern for children, a wide range of other forces appeared to be at work. One of the most frequent of these was the need to relieve pressure on regular classroom teachers, who often felt that emotionally handicapped children produced such a drain on their own resources that they could not adequately serve the relatively normal children in their charge. Although such motives were typically altruistic, there were cases in which the regular classroom teacher had simply had it with aggressive, acting out children and wanted more than anything else not to have them in the regular classroom.

In several instances, parent groups generated pressure for providing such services. Typically, such parents had children who were disturbed, being treated, and often excluded from school. These parents' wish to avoid institutionalization and/or impossibly expensive private care caused them to push the schools into establishing programs and to express continuing interest in them once they were established. In some instances, parental pressure forced classes to be started before the school was really ready. Nonetheless, both the parents and the schools recognized that children who are excluded from school and taught at home become increasingly withdrawn and apathetic; emotionally disturbed children need the continuing social stimulation afforded by contact with other children—even though their response to such contact is not always ideal.

Finally, a few programs seem to have emerged from the shock created in both school and community by a particularly dramatic instance of emotional handicap. In one instance, a violent teen-age homicidal orgy created the feeling that the school might do something more effective in dealing with such children before their disturbance reached devastating proportions. In two other instances, violent assaultive tendencies in an adolescent boy and pregnancy in an early adolescent girl highlighted the growing number of children in need of special assistance.

Program Goals

The relatively primitive state of our knowledge about childhood psychopathology and its relationship to school behavior is underlined by the facts that program goals were stated very generally and that the same types of programs sought to serve many different kinds of children. In planning the development of their programs, very few of the responsible agents sought to draw upon the experience of programs in other areas. Most program developers felt that their own local situation was unique and that a specific plan had to be developed to meet their individual needs. Thus, pressed between the manifest need to provide help to emotionally handicapped children and an apparent lack of direction on how this help could be provided, most program developers and responsible administrators decided, in effect, to go it alone. They had a kind of faith that "something" would be an improvement over the regular classroom experience.

The difficulty with that sort of faith is that the child who is put into a special class may well have severe emotional problems; that is, he may be prepsychotic or psychotic, or he may be neurotic or sociopathic. However, it is the resultant behavior rather than the underlying pathology that gets him into the class.

Selection for Special Class Membership

The single most-time-consuming effort involved in establishing the programs was the screening and selection of pupils (see Figure 3). Mass screening was avoided in most systems because it was obvious to everyone concerned that such a procedure would turn up more candidates than could possibly be served. In the typical system, questionnaires were sent to the teachers, who were asked for nominations based essentially on classroom observations of behavior. Typically, children who were so referred were then subjected to a more intensive appraisal, sometimes consisting only of a review of his cumulative record and test scores and sometimes involving comprehensive diagnosis, including psychiatric evaluation.

At this point, a group decision was usually made that involved the regular teacher, the special class teacher, program administrators, special services people connected with the program, and outside consultants. At this conference, a diagnostic summary was presented, placement discussed, and a "plan" constructed. If all of the recommendations were positive, the child was likely to be placed in the special class. Parents were usually but not inevitably drawn into the process (Stages 3–5, Figure 3).

In any event, the screening process is a time consuming one and raises several problems. For example, there are often too many candidates for the facilities available, so that interpersonal stresses and political pressures develop. It is a rare program that uncovers just the number and type of student it "needs." As a consequence, early plans for the development of a special class for a given diagnostic group must be shelved, and the administrator is forced to respond to expediency rather than rational design.

Categorization of Program Types

A multitude of dimensions run through the various programs, so that they are difficult to classify in terms of a single set of categories. However, certain extremes are clear enough to make a rough classification scheme possible (see Figure 4).

1. *Psychiatric-dynamic.* In this type of class, the major emphasis is on dynamic therapy and pupil acceptance. The approach to diagnosis, decision making, treatment processes, consultation, and evaluation is psychiatric. Individual therapy is expected or required for each child, and therapy for his parents is stressed. Thus, education is less important.

2. *Psycho-educational.* Psychiatric and educational emphases are interwoven in classes of this kind. Thus, educational decisions are made with some consideration of the child's underlying motivation. The educational programs stress creative, project-type work, individual differences, and a benign but not necessarily permissive atmosphere.

3. *Psychological-behavioral.* These programs emphasize diagnosis of learning potential and administration of specific remedial techniques such as habit and behavior training. The classes are highly structured but nonpunitive and stress changing symptomatic responses through specific learning techniques.

4. *Educational.* The emphasis here is on formalized educational procedures, such as routine drills, workbooks, skills training, and inhibition of symptomatic behavior. Restrictive handling by the teacher is viewed as helpful, but the class atmosphere is unhostile.

5. *Naturalistic.* The teacher in a naturalistic class operates on a "green thumb" basis without a specific educational design. The work is

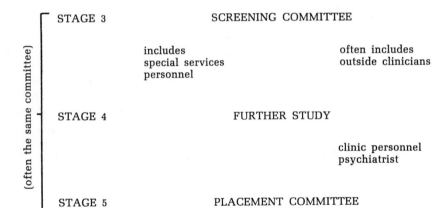

STAGE 1   NOMINATION OF POTENTIAL PUPILS

School Personnel   *Outside Personnel*

teacher   clinic personnel
principal   psychiatrist
special personnel   social worker
school consultants   psychologist
      parents
      private practitioners
      community agency referrals

STAGE 2   ADDITIONAL DATA COLLECTION

school   consultants for diagnosis
psychologist
social worker
guidance department

STAGE 3   SCREENING COMMITTEE

includes   often includes
special services   outside clinicians
personnel

STAGE 4   FURTHER STUDY

clinic personnel
psychiatrist

STAGE 5   PLACEMENT COMMITTEE

special education director

STAGE 6   ASSIGNMENT TO CLASS

(often the same committee)

FIGURE 3

Stages and Personnel Involved in Selecting Pupils for Special Classes

dominated by helping responses to individual academic and behavioral problems as they appear. The teacher frequently plays a benign, "kind but demanding" mother-teacher role and sometimes uses a joking, kidding method of control.

6. *Primitive.* In primitive classes, there is an overall coarseness in the handling of children, for the emphasis is on surface compliance for its own sake. Thus, the teacher is sometimes aloof and cold, and control means "no monkey busi-

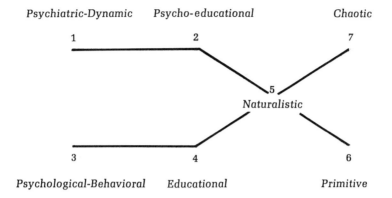

Psychiatric-Dynamic   Psycho-educational   Chaotic

1   2   7

5

Naturalistic

3   4   6

Psychological-Behavioral   Educational   Primitive

FIGURE 4

Paradigm for Class Categorization

ness." Children in these classes are encarcerated until they become passive enough to rejoin regular classes.

7. *Chaotic.* A chaotic class is one in which impulsive behavior is rife, and any semblance of order is momentary. In such classes, the teacher's extreme passivity and permissiveness may be justified by some rationalization on the beneficial effects of permissiveness.

Pupil Perceptions of Special Class

The research also investigated how pupils saw their assignment to the class in terms of their preadmission preparation, the reasons that they came, their present problems, and their likes and dislikes about the class, their associates, and the teacher (see Tables 1, 2, and 3).

Most of the pupils seem to "test reality" pretty well in that two-thirds of them saw both behavior and achievement as the reason for their placement in a special class. The number who believed that they came for academic help brings the total to over three-fourths of the students. Thus, less than one-fourth found it necessary to project or rationalize the responsibility for their own difficulties.

Nonetheless, many of the pupils were experiencing difficulty in their relationships with their peers. Peer relationships are a more serious problem in the special class because of both the in-

TABLE 1

Pupil Perception of Biggest Problem in Special Class

Type of Problem	Percent (N = 519)
Have no problems	8
General (for example, no fun)	20
Academic problems (Specific subjects 37)	49
Peers	13
Teacher	2
No response	8

TABLE 2

Pupil "Likes" about Special Class

"I Like Best"	Percent (N = 519)
Everything	13
Teacher	22
"Kids"	7
Help I get, success	20
Classroom activities	26
Nothing	4
Miscellaneous	3
No response	5

TABLE 3

Pupil "Dislikes" about Special Class

"I Would Like to Change"	Percent (N = 519)
Nothing	34
Teacher	7
"Kids"	15
Academic aspects	12
Classroom activities	4
Everything	9
Miscellaneous	11
No response	8

tensity of the relationships and the high saturation of children with problems. There are fewer "cushion" children to absorb the pathology of the others, and the more intensive interaction brings peer relationship problems into the open.

Teacher Perceptions of Class as a Whole

The teachers' perceptions of their classes differed greatly. However, in general, the teachers saw motivation and control of behavior as the major problems. These were especially trying problems for the teachers at the beginning of the classes; as one teacher noted, "The early weeks were hell."

After this initial period of struggle for control, the classes settled down and concentrated more and more upon motivational and learning difficulties and upon the particular problems of a few individuals. Thus, silliness, manipulation, and attention seeking behavior replaced the more unacceptable acting out, although in some instances, fearful, withdrawn children began to act out. Peer friction sometimes increased as the intensity of the group relationship increased and the children tested the limits for peer relationships. Competitiveness also increased. The difficulty with this reduction in problems of control is that, as one teacher put it, "It is harder to live with the annoying than with the traumatic—

when they behave really badly, you don't expect too much—but when they settle down, you begin to want them to achieve as much as the child in the normal classroom, and when they don't, you wonder what you're doing wrong."

Another problem was the difficulty of weaning children away from the intensive relationships of the smaller class and moving them back into the regular class. Moreover, highly disturbed children remained a problem both in terms of the teachers' relative uncertainty about what to do with them and the disruptions that they produced in the group operation. Teachers also felt strongly that they were differentially capable of working with different types of children.

Climate and Control in Special Classes

Classroom climate is the sum total of teacher and pupil attitudes, feelings, and behaviors. A central element in the climate in any classroom is the rule setting and rule-enforcing process. Each pupil reacts to this process differently, and his reaction may in large part determine his attitude toward both his class and his educators. For example, to one student, a strict, rule-bound classroom means onerous pressure against which he must rebel. On the other hand, another student may believe that the rules imply the adult's investment and belief in his recovery. Thus, physical control may be comforting to some, but others may interpret it as a manifestation of adult hostility.

The teacher's concern with rules is more or less balanced between matters of social behavior and matters of academics. According to Cutler and Morse (1964), in social behavior, physical aggression was the first item to be prohibited. One class had a "no fighting it out without permission" rule. Another significant item in many teachers' codes was verbal aggressiveness, such as name calling, irritating, and picking on others. Several teachers also indicated that blaming others was taboo, and some mentioned respect for the rights of others and a way of life in which fairness, self-control, and respect for every individual are goals. With some pupils, special matters required legislation. Of these, cigarette smoking was the most prevalent. However, several teachers also had rules about lying, carrying knives, swearing, stealing, gambling, and inacceptable clothing. Finally, for older pupils, drifting and being late was a favorite way of resisting, which resulted in numerous "be on time" rules.

Other social rules were concerned with enforcing the teacher's and the school's authority. One teacher approached the problem in this way: "At first I am the complete authority for everything. I make high demands. They think I'm cruel the first of the term when they must conform. Then it gets better. The teacher is boss, and this has to be made clear."

In addition to these areas of major concern, other matters often required rules. Such children often have trouble on the playground. They get excited and rowdy in free play. Silliness becomes mild hysterics, and hyperactivity is always just about to break through. The teachers saw these things as less crucial than physical aggression, but they induced severe group difficulties and had to be stopped.

It takes many laws to make order out of chaotic pasts. Thus, except for one teacher who applied pressure only to acting out behavior, the teachers had rules about academic work, too. Several said that their only requirement was to "do the best you can" and that this rule was flexible depending upon what kind of a day the student was having. However, two other rules were almost universal. One was that the pupil must learn before he can play. Thus, breaks, fun, or even gym and industrial arts were used on occasion as rewards for learning. The second rule was "Don't bother others who are working." An academically disenchanted child usually cannot stand the sight of others doing their work in the approved fashion. And if there is one thing that can upset a teacher, it is to see the disruption caused by

pupils talking, walking around, engaging in demonstrations of nonparticipation, or directly teasing the child who is finally getting down to his arithmetic.

All of these rules seemed to be enforced in one or more of three ways. One way was counseling, individual or group discussion, or some form of life space interviewing. This approach embodies problem solving, or learning to work out one's difficulties. One teacher used what she termed "cool offs" until rationality could be established. Cool offs may vary from benign moralizing and compulsive nagging to sophisticated interviewing that attempts to get at the causes of misbehavior.

A second general approach to control was through emphasis on individual and group responsibility—that is, introducing the idea that the students are their own watchdogs. Some of the teachers indicated that rules were set only after the group had discussed and planned them. In this approach, direction by the teacher was usually involved, although the amount of teacher control of the group or of the individual decision process was not clear. However, that control was probably dominant, so that the "group process" merely clarified what everyone knew the teacher expected of them.

The third major approach was indirect; the best method of control in any class is a good program and reasonable routines. In accordance with this approach, several teachers said that they disciplined through being an example and in that way portrayed the control expected of their pupils. This method may be, for example, deliberate demonstration of consistency and fairness for all. Other teachers used implied expectation rather than overt punishments for failures. By innuendo, through cues of some sort, the teacher said in effect, "I expect you to work." Other teachers stated a rule once and would not repeat it. This approach apparently reduces the students' desire to challenge the rule and sets an expectation that becomes part of the milieu. However, not every teacher has the ability to create a "pressure of expectation," for that ability operates somewhere between a tolerance for failure and an indulgence in the pupil's limitations. Moreover, creating the pressure must be managed in such a way as to instill courage rather than increase frustration.

Special Classes—An Appraisal

Research has revealed that the approaches to planning special classes for emotionally disturbed children are much less systematic and much more intuitive than expected. In part, this condition is a response to the variance in local situations, but it also reflects a confusion on the part of educators. We need a solid conceptual system for the understanding of psycho-educational problems, but such a system does not now exist, for clinicians and educators converse about those problems at different levels. We also need valid criteria for determining the success or failure of these programs. Judgments in this area are now painfully subjective.

Of course, the mere establishment of the programs does to some degree solve the pressing problems of teacher morale in the regular classroom, public pressure, and immediate pupil unhappiness. However, with the establishment of the programs, a second-level problem emerges immediately: finding a means to cope with the day-to-day crises and the continued academic difficulty of the children. Whereas the immediate problems are like a battle that may be won or lost quickly, the second-level problems are like a debilitating war of attrition in which a final decision is seldom forthcoming. It is these second-level problems that involve the school personnel. Although a few have given up, the vast majority continue struggling against the problems.

Another impressive factor is the degree to which these programs maintain a school-related focus. That is apparent to everyone—pupils, teachers, administrators, and clinicians. These programs must be relevant to education, for, to the pupils, success and happiness in school come from academic success, and improvement in adjustment and improvement in academic performance go together.

SUMMARY

The school's attempt to resocialize the child has taken several forms. One of the most radical of these designs is Project Re-education because it focuses on reorganizing the child's behavior along fundamental lines. The project tries to teach the child to view himself in new and more effective ways and to alter his habits. According to the theory behind the program, time and growth, with the cooperation of the rest of society, can bring about proper socialized behavior. Thus, Project Re-ed is concerned less with education than with reorganizing the child into a more acceptable form.

A second solution has been to provide classroom teachers with in-service consultation on the methods of resocialization. The intent is to give on-the-job training in behavior control to those who must daily make real decisions about problem children in the classroom. Consultation of this sort is based on the premise that there will never be enough fully trained professionals to deal with the increasing number of emotionally disturbed children in our classrooms, so that teachers must become the front-line workers administering mental first aid to disturbed children.

The current solution of educators is the establishment of special classes for the emotionally handicapped. However, this movement has proceeded more on intuition than on scientific conceptualization. Despite common goals, an incredible diversity of actual classroom situations has appeared, as have some highly unpredictable classroom populations and teacher methods. Because special classes for the emotionally handicapped are a relatively recent development, such problems are perhaps to be expected. Nonetheless, we have little reliable research to indicate that such arrangements are the best possible for all concerned—the teacher, the child, his fellow pupils, and the educational system.

Part five

The socialization
of youth

The adolescent entering the youth group of today is adequately socialized only for the role of a child. Nonetheless, he must now abandon that role as he prepares to move into young adulthood. The adolescent must begin to acquire the skills and knowledge suitable for adults and to align his beliefs, values, attitudes, and interests with those of grown-ups. At this time, society exerts inexorable pressure on him to abandon childish sentiments and accept the social responsibility of adult life. Moreover, as the young person's physique assumes adult form and glandular stirrings become insistent, the masculine or feminine role must be learned along with a new set of relationships with age mates of both sexes. Biology determines the timing of these changes, but the quality of the adolescent's existing interpersonal relationships limits the ease of his transition to independence.

In this transition, the adolescent must free himself from emotional dependence on his parents as he moves in the direction of economic independence. However, his parents continue their attempts to socialize him because they remain anxious that the job is not yet finished or has not been done well enough. Thus, they delight in evidences of successful socialization and despair the next moment to see signs of immaturity, sel-

13

Socialization and the youth group

"*The adolescent must begin to acquire the skills and knowledge suitable for adults and to align his beliefs, values, attitudes, and interests with those of grown-ups.*"

makes to the role of young adult is, of course, also influenced by the kind of surroundings in which he spent his formative years. Thus, "Trailer families as compared with apartment or home families, families that move all the time as compared with families that stay put, children whose mothers 'work' as compared with those whose mothers 'keep house,' children 'brought up' by maids as compared with those brought up by mothers, children of divorced parents as compared with those that have had the same two parents from birth, summer-camp as compared with summer-family children" (Murphy, Murphy, and Newcomb, 1937) all influence the shape of the individual.

For the young person being socialized to adulthood, that experience is usually a search for self-evaluation and direction. In fact, the severity of his behavior toward others in this period may be criticism of himself and anxious concern about the kind of person he is and will become. Uncertain of how he ought to evaluate himself and busy searching out a direction for his future, he appears unreliable and unpredictable, for freedom and self-direction must be practiced for some time before socialization to the young adult role is complete. As he over-reacts to the influence of his equally inexperienced peers, he violates adult norms and inevitably experiences guilt and confusion. For these reasons, socialization into the youth group is a major chapter in his life.

RITES OF PASSAGE

Deciding when an individual has stopped being a child and is becoming a young adult has been a matter of concern for every society. As a consequence, passing from one group into another requires something to mark the transition and to signify its importance to the participant as well as to the onlooker. Thus, nearly every society draws a line at common changes, so that birth, puberty, marriage, occupation, and death are surrounded by ritual. These ceremonies of transition, or *rites de passage*, have the singular advantage of clearing the air of social ambiguity.

fishness, excess, and bad judgment. This seeming inconsistency in adolescent behavior disconcerts the parents, who may then indulge in a sudden outburst of redoubled efforts at last-minute socialization in order to patch up the omissions of the past. The parents' discoveries that it is too late for the socialization practices of the past and that they are being retired as the primary socializers of the child require them to make difficult adaptations. In the process of adapting, the old companionship of the child is generally forfeit, the parents demand more of him, and practically any contact may be mutually irritating.

The kind of adjustment that each adolescent

However, our society has virtually abandoned concrete, observable *rites de passage* for the adolescent. In the past—particularly in other societies—there were rigid ceremonies to test the eligibility of adolescents striving for adult status; our society has retained only vestiges of such ceremonies in the confirmation rites of religion and in the coming out parties given for some girls. Where once children were differentiated from adults on physical and constitutional grounds, now the acquisition of mental skills more than physical ones signals the differentiation, as do psychological and personality changes.

The difficulty with not having concrete *rites de passage* is that the adolescent is in a state of limbo in which entrance and exit are ill defined. As a consequence, we face some problems with young people that are of our own making. Because neither parent nor child is certain of the exact moment at which the adolescent should have full adult status conferred upon him, access to adult privilege becomes a matter of continuous negotiation that is often marked by anger, resentment, and mutual misunderstanding. Adults, for example, are permitted to date as often as they wish and stay out as late as they care to. In contrast, the early adolescent must negotiate initially with his parents about dating frequency and time to return and then renegotiate this informal contract whenever he feels the time is right to improve its terms. Much of the adult–teen-ager conflict so deplored in our society results from the years of negotiated ambiguity in the adolescent's status.

DEVELOPMENTAL TASKS AND NEEDS OF ADOLESCENCE

Developmental tasks are the problems that individuals typically face at different periods in their lives. For example, the small child must master the complexities of learning to walk, to talk, and to control the elimination of the waste products of the body. In middle childhood, such skills as learning to play games and learning to read are of major importance. For adolescents, the developmental tasks are vital problems that must be met and solved during the transition from childhood to adulthood. These problems are not entirely unique to the adolescent period, but they are ones that the adolescent must solve if he expects to fulfill successfully an adult role. During this period, 10 tasks are particularly significant for the adolescent to complete: (1) achieving new and more mature relations with age mates of both sexes, (2) achieving a masculine or feminine social role, (3) accepting one's physique and using one's body effectively, (4) achieving emotional independence from parents and other adults, (5) achieving assurance of economic independence, (6) selecting and preparing for an occupation, (7) preparing for marriage and family life, (8) developing intellectual skills and concepts necessary for civic competence, (9) desiring and achieving socially responsible behavior, and (10) acquiring a set of values as a guide to behavior (Havighurst, 1953).

The adolescent also has a number of psychological needs that must be fulfilled before adulthood (Horrocks, 1962). The first of these needs is acceptance; the adolescent needs to feel that others respect and approve of him and that he is a worthy person. In addition, the adolescent has a need for achievement. He needs to do things, to prove himself, to attain objectives, and to acquire those evidences of accomplishment that society rewards with status and achievement. Allied to the needs for achievement and approval is another one—the need for recognition. Everyone, the adolescent included, needs to become known, to become an individual in his own right, and to be identified by others as distinct from those who surround him. A fourth need is for affection, being loved unconditionally for one's own sake. This need is tied closely—as is the need for achievement—to the need for approval but distinct from it, for being approved of is not necessarily an indication of affection or total acceptance.

Related to this need for total acceptance is the need to be understood—to communicate with other people and to express one's innermost thoughts and problems to others without loss of status. The adolescent must be able to let his hair down and have those to whom he confesses his doubts, fears, and anxieties understand the nature of the communication and feel sympathetic to them.

Belongingness is also a crucial part of the adolescent's need structure. Although one of the signs of maturity may be the ability to stand apart from people and to exist by oneself if necessary, for the adolescent it is vitally important to be part of an ongoing group, institution, or movement. In this way, he feels that he has a home base where he can count on approval, affection, and acceptance from others.

Conformity has reached the proportions of a need in young people, who are not yet certain of what the future might hold for them. Because the teen-ager seeks acceptance, affection, approval, and belongingness, he must avoid any marked

departure from what is typical or average in the customs of those who surround him. Although the adolescent's behavior, dress, interests, attitudes, and ideals may differ from those in adult society, they must still conform to those of his peers.

Other equally important needs help to explain the attitudes and behavior of the adolescent. Although one of his needs is to be free of external control by others, the adolescent has a complementary need to be able to ask for help and to depend on others for support and protection when necessary. It is this whipsaw action between dependence and independence that produces much of the conflict laden behavior so typical of the adolescent. Behind his attempts to balance these incompatibles lies the need for what Horrocks (1962) has called "mastery-dominance." This is the need to control, to lead, "To influence the behavior, feelings or ideas of others" (p. 507).

"Although the adolescent's behavior, dress, interests, attitudes, and ideals may differ from those in adult society, they must still conform to those of his peers."

A final need is the need for self-realization—the need to become what one is capable of becoming and to strive steadily toward increased accomplishment within the limits of one's capacity. This need is part of establishing an identity and relating this self-concept to the outer and inner environments. It is in this learning of proper self-assertion that the adolescent is most likely to engender conflict with the outer world. He makes what appear to adults to be clumsy attempts to manipulate the world (in a somewhat frenetic and desperate fashion) in order to wrest from it the prestige and dominance over others that is reassuring to his self-concept. Thus, what has been called a "drive to power" is a predictable and natural event in adolescence. However, failure in these attempts to manipulate the world is shattering to the adolescent's conception of himself and leaves him helpless in the face of adult self-assurance and competence in managing life.

Because few human beings can achieve what their fantasies dictate is important, a certain amount of acceptance of failure and of resignation to the facts of life is necessary. Adults faced with the need to temper their dreams to fit reality may seek refuge in hobbies or other escapes. The adolescent may turn to less desirable pursuits, such as delinquency, in his search for an answer to his unfulfilled expectations.

The arena in which the adolescent's developmental tasks are accomplished and his needs at least to some extent fulfilled is the peer group. With the onset of adolescence, the individual emerges from the confines of his family into full citizenship in the peer group, which both represents his first truly independent existence and becomes a powerful source of well-being, security, and belongingness. The peer group also confers a new form of prestige and reward, which sometimes conflicts with the parental reward system. Moreover, although the peer group may be even more severe in its judgments than the adult group from which the adolescent seeks to escape, the form and quality of the criticism differs from that of his parents. In this arena, the adolescent tries out the independence of adulthood, and here

adult attitudes, beliefs, feelings, and patterns of reaction are consolidated. Nonetheless,

In considering the attitudes and goals of adolescence it is necessary to remember that the adolescent is first a human, and only secondarily a member of a specific category of humans. . . . The essential bases of his motivations, the structural aspects of his personality, the mechanics of his attitude formation, the processes by which he learns do not differentiate him from other humans (Horrocks, 1965, p. 15).

PEER GROUP INFLUENCE ON PERSONALITY

The central event in the peer life of the adolescent is his acceptance or rejection by others. The way in which others view him as a person not only determines his role and status in the group but also helps to shape his personality. For example, children who are accepted by their peers are friendly and sociable (Feinberg, Smith, and Schmidt, 1958), while children who are rejected by others or forced to occupy a low status in the group are rebellious, hostile, or withdrawn (Northway, 1944; Smith, 1950). One of the major criteria that the peer group uses to judge an individual is his level of physical maturity (Clarke and Clarke, 1961).

Physical Maturation

In our society, the ideal for males is physical size and strength. Thus, achieving these attributes early in life suggests a level of maturity to which both peers and adults respond with increased respect and acceptance; the adolescent who is outsized for his age simply appears more grown-up. Conversely, appearing physically immature is bound to be a handicap for the adolescent pressing hotly forward in the drive to appear older. The resultant feelings of inadequacy, defensiveness, and insecurity produce what has been labeled "small boy behavior." Once this pattern of behavior is established, it may become self-sustaining and carry through into adulthood. That the reaction to late maturers may be misguided is irrelevant, for people react to what they see rather than to what they know. Thus,

if physical and physiological changes during adolescence were simply a matter of changing structure and function, one could simply describe and record them and then pass on to other topics. Actual structural or functional change, however, is only the beginning from which evolve social behavior, attitude towards self and others, and the entire constellation of values which give meaning and guidance to an adolescent's life (Horrocks, 1962, p. 311).

Because the timing of the marked physical changes of puberty is subject to wide individual differences, the early or late onset of pubescence has a substantial impact on personal and social adjustment. The personalities of early maturing boys are viewed in much more favorable terms by both peers and adults than are the personalities of later maturing boys. At age 16, the late maturers are regularly viewed by adults as being less physically attractive, less well groomed, less moderate in their behavior, and more affected and tense. Similarly, peers view late maturers as much more restless, less reserved, less grown up, and more bossy. Late maturers also demonstrate a more persistent dependence coupled, in an odd fashion, with a rebellious quest for freedom from restraint. In social activities, late maturing adolescents are also not selected as leaders. Thus, the lack of self-assurance and socially appropriate behavior among late maturers is clearly evident to both adults and peers (Jones, 1938; Jones and Bayley, 1950; Mussen and Jones, 1957).

However, it is only when early maturers are compared with late maturers that significant differences appear; there were few significant differences between early maturers and average maturers. Thus, although late maturation is an apparent handicap in the personality development of boys, early maturation may not always be an asset (Weatherley, 1964).

These personality differences between early and late maturing boys persist into adulthood long after the physical differences have disappeared. Late maturers are in later life much less capable of conveying a good impression to others, less self-controlled, less responsible, less dominant over others, and more inclined to turn to others for help (Jones, 1957).

Time of maturation does not have the same effect on girls; late physical maturation is an asset for girls, while early maturation appears to be a liability (Jones, 1949). The reason is again cultural, for the early maturing girl may tend to acquire a stocky and muscular physique, while the late maturer may be slimmer and therefore in keeping with the female ideal of our society (Jones and Mussen, 1958). Moreover, the early maturing girl is not only out of step with other girls of her age but also substantially different in physical status from the males of her age because boys in general lag about two years behind girls in puberty. However, with later adolescence, these physical differences become less marked and so interfere less with social development. Thus, the rate of physical maturation is less influential in personality development for girls than for boys (Weatherley, 1964).

Values and Peer Acceptance

As the adolescent undertakes the developmental tasks appropriate to his age, he enters the peer world burdened with powerful needs for affection, acceptance, and belongingness. He is ready to conform to peer values in order to garner the reward, prestige, and group status that are contingent on being the right sort of person. He does not yet know the exact dimensions of the values to which he must conform, but he soon learns. Communications from others about current, proper peer values are read in the positive or negative response of others via association (who seeks him out, associates with him, calls him up, and so forth). At first, this test of association is subtle and limited to school and neighborhood; eventually, who is included and excluded in after-school gatherings becomes the criterion of acceptance or rejection by various segments of the peer group.

These values do not conform to those underlying the school system, so that the adolescent's education is hardly preparing him to be able to fulfill his interests. In an attempt to assess adolescent values, Coleman (1961) asked boys whether they would rather be a jet pilot, a nationally famous athlete, a missionary, or an atomic scientist. The boys most often chose the nationally famous athlete, the atomic scientist ran a poor third to the jet pilot, and the missionary was almost totally ignored. Girls were more oriented toward traditionally valued roles; the girls' first choice was to be a nurse and their second to be a teacher. These choices were followed by actress and artist, in that order. However, as the school year wore on, the rating of glamorous model as an ideal occupation increased measurably. Similarly, being an actress or an artist increased in appeal while the nurse and teacher ratings remained constant.

Coleman also asked teen-agers how they would most like to be remembered in school. He gave boys the choice of brilliant student, athletic star, or most popular and girls the choice of brilliant student, leader in activities, or most popular. At the beginning of the school term, the boys selected the athletic star as the most attractive kind of memory to establish in school. This choice was followed by brilliant student and most popular, in that order. By the end of the school year, being an athletic star had increased in importance at the expense of being remembered as the most popular student. Being the most brilliant student shifted little over the course of the year.

For the girls, at the beginning of the school year, being a leader of school activities or being the most popular were about equally attractive, so that the brilliant student image came last. Some months later, the activities leader image gained slightly at the expense of the other two. When we recall that the primary focus of an educational institution is on studies and that it favors the brilliant student, we have a cultural paradox of no small proportions.

This cultural paradox is underscored by the dating preferences of both boys and girls. Coleman asked the boys in his study whether they would rather date a cheer leader, the best student, or the best looking girl in the class. In a similar vein, girls were given the choice of star athlete, best student, or best looking boy. A startling finding (at least from an adult point of view) is that the brilliant girl fared very poorly in terms of dateability. By the same token, the brilliant student was not an ideal date for girls. As time went on in the school year, the brilliant student lost even more of what little attractiveness he had to begin with.

When these young people were asked what they thought the parental view of their accomplishments would be, the boys believed that their parents would be considerably prouder if they were to make the varsity basketball team than if they were chosen to be a class biology assistant. The girls indicated, even more strongly, that becoming a cheer leader would be better received by their parents than being chosen as a biology assistant would be. However, comparing these responses with the attitudes of the parents made it obvious that some gross perceptual error existed on the part of either parent or child. Overwhelmingly, the parents said that they preferred both sons and daughters to be brilliant students. Thus, we have all the makings of a gross lack of communication between parent and child. Or have we? Perhaps children read parents better than parents read themselves.

Another aspect of adolescent values determined by the search for peer group approval is the automobile. Cars are an absolutely vital symbol to teen-agers. Having an automobile has become in our society one of the most distinctive criteria of the difference between childhood and adulthood. Thus, it is anathema to a teen-ager to have to be driven by his parents to athletic and social events. As soon as he has reached the age at which he is legally eligible for a driver's license, he exerts inordinate pressure for driving privileges and shortly thereafter for a car of his own. The excuse regularly used is that suburban living requires self-propulsion if he is to be properly educated. The adolescent who lives in the city, of course, experiences less of this sense of urgency for individual automotive transportation than his suburban counterpart does.

Another vital aspect of adolescent values focuses on becoming a member of the leading crowd in school. Peer groups are organized in cliques, so that it is of the utmost importance for a young person to be accepted by the in group. (This pressure is exactly like the anxiety rife among members of the adult community who judge their personal worth in terms of their acceptance by others.) According to girls, having a "good personality" is perhaps the most important criterion for acceptance. Of course, personal reputation, friendliness, good looks, good grades, neatness, good clothes, being well-to-do, and living in a good neighborhood are all part of having a "good personality." These criteria are a woeful commentary on the state of the adolescent world, but they are also faithfully reflected in the adult world.

When Coleman asked young people to tell him what it takes to get into the leading crowd in school, the answers included wearing just the right thing, having nice hair, good grooming, a wholesome personality, money, clothes, and a flashy appearance, dating older boys, and getting good grades. The criteria for one insightful student included "being a sex fiend," "dressing real sharp," having a car and money, smoking and drinking, going steady with a popular guy, having good manners, being clean, and being lots of fun. Personality seemed to come first, good looks second, and, for girls, being well dressed third. Clothes make the girl in that they promise success with the boys, and, at this stage in life, nothing is more important.

Although having a good reputation ranked fourth, it is an important route to acceptance by the in crowd. However, reputation is a dilemma.

"Cars are an absolutely vital symbol to teen-agers."

A girl must be popular with boys, according to adolescent culture, but she must still maintain a reputation of not being fast or easy. Being fast, in modern culture, suggests drinking, smoking, and the sexual character of one's public reputation. (Reputation, by the way, is no easy matter to maintain for a girl whose parents let her date widely and with boys of a variety of ages.) Moreover, public reputation and social status are closely related. Being born into the right family —that is, having money and the proper house, car, and clothes—is the best single way to achieve social status in our society, for social status is attributed not to personal behavior but to membership in a particular family.

For boys, how to become a member of the in crowd is not so vital an issue as it is for girls. Thus, for boys, a good personality, good looks, a good reputation, good clothes, money, and a house in the right neighborhood are all less important. Family background also matters less because a boy is to some extent permitted to cross the social tracks and select the crowd of his choice. Of all the things that a boy can have or do, athletic success seems to be the clearest and most direct way of becoming eligible for member-

"Only in America has it been possible to evolve a true youth culture—a culture devoted to the joys of being somewhere between childhood and adulthood."

ship in the in crowd, although a car, of course, can help.

These adolescent values are not intrinsically evil or bad in themselves. Rather, they represent a subculture devoted almost exclusively to a one-dimensional view of the nature of adult human relationships. Such values are, however, increasingly becoming the model for adult adjustment in our culture. Although more mature adults can easily dismiss such values as the products of childish minds, our population statistics have inevitably shifted in the direction of youth, so that we must be prepared to contend with youthful pressures that have never existed before. In fact, we may well be face-to-face with the ultimate outcome of science—a *youth culture* that will not be denied its role in adult affairs.

THE YOUTH CULTURE

Only in America has it been possible to evolve a true youth culture—a culture devoted to the joys of being somewhere between childhood and adulthood. However, our youth culture is not a rational, transitional blending of the values of childhood and adulthood; rather, it is a phase in which roles, values, and ways of behaving are distinct from those in the rest of the culture. Our youth culture is not always antiadult, but it is nonadult. The typical teen-ager has a kind of "double consciousness" in which he is in part oriented toward the adult world and at the same moment geared toward full participation in the youth culture.

One possible reason for the existence of this youth culture is that our society lacks adequate institutional devices to ease the transition from childhood to adulthood. The child in our culture is supposed to be submissive, nonresponsible, and obedient, while the adult is supposed to be dominant, responsible, and commanding (Benedict, 1938). The transition between these two stages must somehow be managed, and, if society provides no mechanism for doing so, youth must invent its own institutions to pave the way.

The institutions of youth weaken the bond of affection between young people and their parents as a first step toward achieving the emotional emancipation necessary for total independence. Achieving that independence requires the transfer of affection from the parents to peer associates; the symptom of this transfer is undying loyalty and conformity to the norms of youth institutions.

The first transitional institution of youth culture is the *clique*. In fact, the informal organization of urban society is composed in great part of a vast network of cliques and gangs, which constitute the basic institutions of socialization (Spaulding, 1948).

Cliques, which are a function of the habitual association present in the neighborhood play group, appear shortly after young people start school. This tendency to form cliques reaches its height when children are about 12 years old, but there is no chronological age at which it ends.

Membership in a clique is not determined by formal rules of recruitment, training, or rejection; acceptance is by mutual consent. Accordingly, the friend of a clique member may gradually be accepted. The kinds of meeting places or hangouts that young people use do, however, influence the structure of the membership of the clique. Thus, there may be church cliques, school cliques, community cliques, and recreational cliques (Hurlock, 1955). Cliques also tend to reflect the class structure of the larger society. Nonetheless, various highly valued parts of youth culture, such as athletic prowess among boys or glamour among girls, are sufficient to cut across social lines.

Cliques must have group solidarity. Thus, they coerce their members into a compulsive conformity in almost everything that the adolescent does and control his attitudes toward adults and their institutions. Because belonging to a desirable clique is the key to status and prestige in the youth culture, the informal sanctions of praise or admiration, abuse, ridicule, scorn, or isolation are the means of ensuring obedience.

Belonging to a clique has certain responsibilities, most of which are designed to encourage group solidarity. Thus, clique members may spend their time talking to one another in school, waiting for one another after school, and preferring the company of one another to that of others. Moreover, being a member of a clique may require rendering assistance when needed and resisting the pressures of both other groups and outside demands on the clique. Indeed, the clique is usually given preference over even the families of its members (Bossard, 1948).

The clique also performs certain functions for its members. For example, the clique is an important social device for helping young people to adjust to junior and senior high school. This close-knit group of friends with whom one feels some sense of commonality often gives meaning to the educational setting by redefining it as a place where friends are and where one can have a sense of belonging and participation. In addition, the peer culture in general and the clique in particular are probably the single most important channel for communicating sex norms and information; detailed communication about sex remains rare between parent and child. In fact, members of youthful peer groups start to communicate with one another about sex long before adults suspect that there is even the slightest interest in the topic.

This movement toward teen-age togetherness and away from the parents is intensified by the youth culture's deliberate attempts to seem different from the adult world. An adolescent may attempt to achieve distinction through clothing, hair style, jewelry, behavior, slang, social rituals, or any of a number of other ways. However, distinctive clothing is perhaps the most prevalent method. The actual design of the clothing, its fit, its color, and its style are all irrelevant. It is necessary only that the clothing be new and that it not resemble the clothing of adults. Of course, to the aging adult, it must seem that each year youthful clothing styles become more and more extreme, bizarre, and outlandish (Silverman, 1945).

For many years, clothing styles for boys were subject to only minor variation because boys were considered to be less clothes conscious and less subject to pressure from the leaders of style. However, ingroup boys have now become, in many cases, at least as clothes conscious as girls are; the "dandy era" has become a force in modern society. Altering external appearance through a combination of hair styling and clothing selection expresses defiance of the adult culture and deviation from it. Thus, long hair, lace cuffs, and frilly shirts—styles reminiscent of the days of Charles II—have reappeared in the violent demand that youths be perceived as different from adults (Gordon, 1957). Even the use of such cosmetics as hairspray, once a purely female practice, has become a male prerogative in the youth culture.

Another important characteristic that distinguishes the youth culture from its adult counter-

part is language. Speaking a language that is incomprehensible to adults serves as an additional barrier to communication and so as another way to keep adults on the outside of the youth culture. Slang, the language used in the youth culture, identifies its members as standing apart from the rest of the culture. Each variety of slang begins on the college campuses and finishes out its life cycle among the middle classes. However, each language cycle in the youth culture usually remains distinct from the continuing adult means of communication (Schullian, 1943).

This distinctively adorned youth culture with its alien language somehow is transmitted to successive generations of youth. Because there is surprisingly little communication between the older and younger generations of young people, the

"This movement toward teen-age togetherness and away from the parents is intensified by the youth culture's deliberate attempts to seem different from the adult world."

younger must emulate the behavior of the older without the benefit of formal instruction. In this loosely organized fashion, children are initiated into the youth culture, and, ultimately, youth is inducted into adult society. However, the concomitant of this social and psychological movement is often conflict between the different generations.

THE CONFLICT BETWEEN THE GENERATIONS

The task of the young male is to replace the old. When our society was rural, that succession was easier than it is today, for physical power was more important than theoretical knowledge. Thus, the strength of the young person fitted naturally into a sequence in which the older man used his wisdom but the younger man used his strength to move into a position of prominence. "Whenever there was no natural order to the ascendency of the generations, problems arose between them similar to those that are now typical for all in a machine age, when almost nobody's survival depends on physical strength" (Bettleheim, 1963, p. 68). If this ascendency is not a smooth and cooperative one, the older generation is likely to view the younger with suspicion.

Sources of Conflict

One of the most important sources of conflict between the generations today is the problem of independence. Independence means living life on one's own terms and pursuing goals in one's own way. The youth of the past could always run off to sea, join the army, or move west in order to escape from adults. The youth of today more often than not must battle the issue of independence while still economically dependent on his parents. Moreover, the American way of parent-

hood includes the ambitious ideal that children will accomplish more and do better than their parents.

As a consequence, both mothers and fathers often bring to bear on their children an enormous amount of overt and covert pressure to provide the experiences that were lacking in their own lives. Thus, the mother's pressure on her daughter to live out her own unfulfilled daydreams of popularity or to make a notable marriage can effectively block the girl's efforts to find an identity of her own and fulfill her own needs. The child cannot live his life solely to achieve what the parent could not, to be what the parent once hoped for himself, or to satisfy his parent's present needs and desires. Indeed, much of the rebellion of children in the middle class is a way of telling the world that they are the master of their own fate, whatever the cost may be.

Another source of conflict is the social and economic conditions that delay the adolescent's ability to find self-realization in work. Prolonged education for the youth has placed him in a marginal position in a society that no longer depends on his vigor for economic survival. Thus, many young people do not begin working full time until they are in their early twenties. And, as a consequence, youth has become the older generation's greatest economic liability. Someone must provide meaningful work for youth, but it is increasingly apparent that the older generation cannot do so.

Two other sources of conflict arise from the cultural emphasis on education. As higher education becomes increasingly widespread, more youths are outstripping their parents in educational accomplishments. These advances, of course, intensify the conflict between the two. Moreover, youths are not really considered to be full-fledged adults until they have finished their schooling. This attitude has produced an uncomfortable discrepancy in the timing of biological and sociological maturity; young people are ready for experiences that modern society does not yet want them to have.

Still another important source of conflict is

the problem of competition for authority, which is, of course, intensified by the adolescent's desire for independence. Most parents feel that their authority takes precedence over that of the schools. However, the schools, whether deliberately or not, work to wean the child from his parents. In this process, the schools reinforce competitive, middle class norms of behavior and serious values and tend to ignore cultural deviations from that norm. On the other hand, middle class parents define the period of youth as a time of irresponsibility, good times, athletics, and dating. When faced with this conflict, some children deliberately deviate from both sets of values in order to make the severance from the worlds of school and parents clearer and crisper.

Our culture has also produced a number of ways of excluding American youth from significant participation in adult activities. In turn, youth has established its own culture, which excludes adults. One of the methods of exclusion is the conspiracy of silence toward adults. By setting up barriers to communication with adults, the youth culture has excluded outsiders and safeguarded itself from adult sanctions or censures. This ritual of secrecy and deception is learned by having seen the ways in which adults in family, business, and political life deceive themselves and others (Smith, 1962). The tendency toward silence begins early in the child's life. Children soon learn to recognize what makes their parents anxious and subsequently avoid such subjects with great diligence. Certain topics are relatively or absolutely taboo in certain families. The children, who are sensitive to these things, enter into a subtle gentleman's agreement with their parents not to discuss those topics. Adolescents are perhaps most secretive about their heterosexual relations. Here youth assumes an attitude of outward conformity to adult norms and disguises secret violations. Adults, on their part, moralize against necking and petting, deny their existence, and assure themselves that only "other" children, not their own, participate. Yet peers know that such sexual behavior is indulged in with great fre-

quency and is part of the price of admission to the youth culture.

Probably the single issue that provokes the most difficulty between the generations is the young people's apparent lack of deep commitment to adult values and roles. Because adults feel that young people do not share their values and cultural expectations, a sense of alienation results. This alienation works both ways because, from the young people's point of view, the grown-ups are offering a dissatisfying adult pattern of life. If young people do not trust the adult world that they are expected to enter and view it as cold, mechanical, and emotionally meaningless, they must search for an alternative. Thus, some young people choose the cool life, with its detachment and lack of enthusiasm about life, as a means of rejecting adult values.

The irritant for the older generation is that the attitude of the younger seems to be one of ingratitude and irresponsibility. The younger generation appears to be overprivileged and overindulged when the older generation looks back to its own early life. But the recital of "When I was a boy . . ." is a tiresome recitation of adult hardship that falls on deaf and uncomprehending ears. Parents ought to understand that the "irresponsible generation" is always the generation that follows one's own.

For the young people, who are faced with rapidly shifting standards and points of view, it is difficult to accept blindly an outlook on life based on an era long since vanished. Thus, when parents become irrelevant as models for their children, the children turn to other sources in their search for a direction in life. It is not that parents have become incompetent or disinterested in their children; indeed, parents try very hard to understand and sympathize with young people. However, in order for parents to be a useful example for young people preoccupied with the future, the future would have to resemble the past closely. But our society is changing so rapidly that the past is not always an enlightened guide to the future.

Change and Activism

We have made the notion of continuous change the pivot of our entire society. This cultural addiction to change was fostered at first by the nature of our society, which had practically no traditional institutions or values geared to resist change. Moreover, our growing country did not have to cope with the conservation of one race, one religion, one tribe, and one history. This melting pot characteristic of America prevented it from being strangled by narrow tradition. Then, too, we moved very rapidly from a rural to an urban and from an unindustrialized to an industrialized nation.

Unfortunately, that early uncritical readiness to accept technological innovation was coupled with an unwillingness to do anything about limiting or guiding the direction of industrial and social change. Because there were no established institutions dedicated to resisting change or slowing its rate, change came to be enshrined as a way of life and as a way to salvation.

However, technological change always poses a threat to previously existing values because change leads to the new and yet untried. Thus, although we welcome technology with less reservation than any other culture in history, it also makes us uncomfortable. Our cultural stereotype of the mad scientist who destroys himself in some strange experiment may be one evidence of our mixed feelings about scientific advances (Keniston, 1963).

Because such contradictions make us uncomfortable, our society tends to ignore the most troublesome features of technological and social change. The consequence of ignoring them is an embarrassing gap between creed and fact in social life (Kenniston, 1963). For example, in every commencement speech, our young men and women are told that they must go joyfully forth into a rapidly changing world and meet the challenge of improving it. The natural conclusion to be drawn from these speeches is that social change is inevitable and that it is always for the best. However, they generally make little impression on young people; many of them are much too preoccupied with anxiety about the nature of the changing world they are being asked to wrestle to its knees. The future, to young people, must seem remote and uncertain, for it is almost impossible to predict social change in a society in which so little has remained constant. Thus, they face an unpredictable future in which the values and patterns of behavior that they have just learned may be irrelevant.

Moreover, in times of rapid change, youths must feel powerlessness on a social, political, and personal level. They must feel that they are incapable of having any measurable impact on a world that appears unsatisfactory to them. In addition, they may also feel that they will not be able to find a place in a world not of their making and not to their liking. The result of these feelings is the notion that to bow to the demands of society is to suffer defeat and to be sentenced to a lifetime of performing a meaningless, empty task. Therefore, rebellion in some form seems to be the only sensible alternative.

The most common way of rejecting what society expects the young person to become has been *privatism*. Young people subscribing to privatism tend to value the areas of their lives that are least involved in the wider society. These youths hope to find within their own peer group some of the stability and predictability that seems so absent in society. Moreover, because long-range, outside endeavors and commitments seem useless if there is a substantial possibility that the world will be enveloped in holocaust, such youths may cast life in terms of the immediate and so abandon concern with the past and the future. Immediate pleasure, even if transitory, can anesthetize the pain and anxiety of an incomprehensible future and induce temporary tranquility (Riesman, Denney, and Glazer, 1950).

Such feelings caused the student of the 1950s to be accused of apathy and a lack of commitment to the aims of the wider society.

"Youth is in all things the patron of excess."

However, the apathy so resented by editors of college newspapers has now been transformed into an intense concern with the national and international scene. The resultant plunge into civil rights and civil disobedience has produced a substantial embarrassment to college administrators, who hoped that involvement would be visible but insipid. The placard carrying, picketing, draft card burning, long haired, unwashed effervescence of "involved" young people was not what the older generation hoped for, but it was what they might have expected. Youth is in all things the patron of excess.

Regardless of whether the young people of today choose to escape or to become involved, our youth must still select from among the available people and institutions of the older generation and judge which are trustworthy as a guide for future encounters with the world. The most useful would seem to be those oriented toward change. However, having one eye on the future does not equally characterize all Americans. And, unfortunately, the impact of social change affects

some age groups more than others. The very young and the very old would seem least affected by rapid social change; the very young are not yet a part of the world, and the very old have retreated from it. The most affected would be the youths, who are caught up in the process of making decisions about the future. Those in transition suffer most in a transitional society.

SUMMARY

The socialization of the adolescent must be accomplished in concert with a sudden biological spurt and movement through the netherlands of mixed child-adult status. At this stage in his socialization, the adolescent abandons his emotional dependence on those most responsible for his socialization in the past and shifts his allegiance to the youth group. In the youth group, the values, attitudes, and beliefs that he acquired as a child are modified as he learns the proper sexual role, practices a new set of relationships with the opposite sex, and exercises a new-found freedom to make decisions for himself.

Socialization in the youth group focuses on learning about himself by contrasting the views that others have of him with the shifting evaluations that he makes of himself. Thus, for the adolescent, who is free for the first time to make his own choices, life can be like a cafeteria of skills, knowledge, attitudes, values, motives, habits, interests, and beliefs.

This transitional period finds the adolescent at the peak of conflicting yet pressing need systems that are fulfilled in the peer group. However, they frequently conflict with those of the older generations. The rate of physical maturation, the expectations and perceptions that others hold for him, and the natural anxieties of facing the demands of adult status all contribute to what appears to the adult to be excessive, emotional, and inconsistent behavior on the part of the young person.

The developmental tasks that the adolescent must accomplish are formidable, and the varied emotional and intellectual needs that become pressing at this stage in his life all seem to have an anxious and painful quality to them. This juncture in life between the child and the man is, therefore, one of the most difficult to manage. Nonetheless, success or failure at this time sets the stage for comfort or discomfort in the adult years.

The delinquent is a young person whose socialization has failed. If he has lived in a loveless world, where interpersonal relationships bring only pain and disappointment, he may have no choice but to define his world as one in which motivation is based only on reward and punishment and not on deep relations with others. For this individual, delinquency can be a satisfying way of life because it may provide him with gratification of his needs and impulses with the least possible delay. Moreover, at the same time, delinquency allows him to express his anger and contempt for those who have rejected and neglected him. Many delinquents pursue this way of life enthusiastically, not furtively, and the sense of accomplishment that they experience is indistinguishable from that issuing from a socially acceptable way of life.

Although delinquency is a form of social aggression, hostility does not necessarily issue in crime or delinquency. If an individual's control over his hostility is personally satisfying and socially acceptable, it presents no problem to him or to the other members of society. If his way of managing aggression does not satisfy the individual's needs but is socially acceptable, some form of inner disturbance may develop. If his handling of his aggression is satisfying to him but is socially unacceptable, one result may be crime or delin-

14

Delinquency— The failure of socialization

quency. If the control of angry feelings is neither satisfying to the individual nor socially acceptable, the outcome may be a form of neurotic or psychotic antisocial activity.

Nonetheless, delinquency is a legal rather than a psychological concept and so is defined in different ways in different places. The "delinquency" to which most people refer is the official delinquency reflected in court records and police files, although unofficial delinquency is much more prevalent. Our legal code specifies so many kinds of misbehavior that lawbreaking through ignorance or with deliberation seems unavoidable. Thus, the incidence of *hidden delinquency*—acts that are not noticed or recorded and go unpunished—by far exceeds the incidence of aggression against persons or property that comes to official attention.

The actual number of official delinquents cannot be estimated even when a single criterion, such as arrests, is used as a measure; estimates range from two out of every 100 children and adolescents to six out of every 1,000. Nonetheless, it is evident that the number of boys designated as delinquent always exceeds the number of girls. This proportion, which ranges between 70 and 90 percent in favor of boys, reflects the difference between the sexes that applies to almost any sort of overt expression of aggressiveness. Female delinquency most frequently takes the form of sexual promiscuity or stealing and rarely appears as destruction of property or violence. The occasional female delinquent who aggresses in the same way as the male delinquent is usually more seriously disturbed emotionally than the average delinquent of either sex.

THEORIES OF DELINQUENCY

A great many reasons have been advanced to account for the failure of some children and adults to fit comfortably into their society. For example, "at one time or another, crime and delinquency have been explained on the basis of race, defective physique, climate, capitalism, feeble-mindedness, poverty, mental illness, lack of recreation" (Martin and Fitzpatrick, 1964, p. 31). The difficulty with all these theories is that each has been promoted as the sole explanation of both problems. A major reason for this difficulty is that social theory is always time and culture bound; how a society at any time explains its delinquents is as much a commentary on the state of the culture as on the extent of its scientific knowledge. For instance, in a primitive society believing in magic, spirits, and a living devil, a misbehaving child is thought to have been invaded by the devil. Thus, he is treated accordingly —as a sinner. In a society believing in the scientific method, the view of the delinquent is bound to be different.

However, even in our scientifically oriented society, there are competing theories on the cause of delinquency. Geneticists look to heredity, psychologists insist on further research in the matter, sociologists ignore the individual to focus on the structure of the society, and psychiatrists look to pathology and mental illness. In addition, the equally vocal man on the street has his own, punishment-oriented point of view, which is not "scientific" but is effective in determining the kind of treatment that delinquents receive and in regulating the flow of public moneys to support the treatment.

The most productive of these viewpoints is a combination of psychiatric and sociological theories. The classic studies drew a distinction between environmental and personality factors in the causation of delinquency. A less static categorization of influences is to divide them into *macrofactors* (socio-economic status, family breakdown, emotional maladjustment) and *microfactors* (faulty child rearing practices, impulsiveness, negative self-concept) (Moles, Lippitt, and Withey, 1959).

These two sets of factors can, of course, be subdivided further. For example, delinquency is most often associated with low socio-economic status. A subdivision of the class macrofactor is

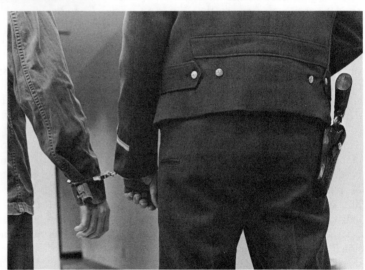

social mobility. A lower middle class child planning to enter college is upwardly mobile; an upper middle class child seeking to work in one of the skilled trades is downwardly mobile. Students who desire to move up in the social system are less involved in delinquent activities. Conversely, adolescents who perceive themselves as moving downward on the social scale are more involved in delinquency (Pine, 1965).

Further, delinquency proneness can be predicted on the basis of the two macrofactors of socio-economic status and emotional maladjustment. Behavior that is natural and innocuous for a lower class youngster can be very symptomatic of disturbance in a child of the same age but in a different social class. Thus, a middle class youngster who is doing poorly in school, has a tense or difficult family situation, is truant from school, and plans to quit at the earliest opportunity is on a macrofactor level headed for trouble. If microfactors such as personal passivity, suspiciousness, weak ego, and anxiety exist at the same time, a prediction of delinquency is a reasonable one.

For the lower class child, prediction of future delinquent activity relies on a different set of dimensions. If he runs with a gang that gets its prestige and status from violating the law, if he uses his school for delinquent depredations, if he defies adults and their rules and lives by his own, if he gets his kicks from the excitement of delinquent behavior, he is exhibiting all the elements leading to a final defiant break with society. For this child, an abundance of crippling macrofactors produces a set of values and a pattern of behaviors that do not need accompanying microfactors to explain antisocial actions.

Of course, these descriptions of delinquent and nondelinquent characteristics do not explain the cause of delinquency; such lists are not easily applied to any youngster, for each element listed can appear in different degrees in different children. And no check list of behavior is an adequate means of describing the psychic experience of any child. However, lists such as these do reinforce the observation that delinquency is a patterned response to internal and external pressures.

Other factors help to make the formulation of a comprehensive theory of delinquency difficult. With few—and very recent—exceptions, the delinquents used as research subjects have been institutionalized or convicted offenders. Institutionalized adolescents are far from representative of American youth. Moreover, they are usually members of the lower socio-economic classes. Arrest, conviction, and institutionalization occur more frequently for lower class than for middle class people. Thus, studies of institutionalized delinquents have only affirmed what we already knew—that the characteristics of members of the lower socio-economic classes are also characteristics of delinquents. Finally, delinquents make very uncooperative research subjects. They are suspicious, defensive, evasive, and easily provoked to anger and resistance. And among the delinquent population are some of the most accomplished, straight-faced liars imaginable.

DEVELOPMENT AND DELINQUENCY

Delinquent behavior is one stage in the process of continuous development that concludes with organized criminal behavior. As the delinquent child develops, he adapts the form of his delinquent behavior to his developing skills in very much the same manner in which the normally developing child learns conforming patterns of response. The behavior of young children, whether delinquent or conforming, is impulsive and covers a very short span of time. At this age, delinquent acts are mindless in that they are unplanned and usually dominated by the search for immediate gratification. Thus, they may even appear random to the observing adult.

The adolescent plans some of his delinquencies but may behave in much the same way as the conformist does. The delinquent as a conformist must plan, cooperate with others, and use judgment. These patterns must be learned and applied appropriately if a successful adjustment to

"Arrest, conviction, and institutionalization occur more frequently for lower class than for middle class people."

create may be much more serious and reach beyond annoyance. At this point, adolescents must decide on some issues that will determine much of their futures. One of these issues is whether or not to continue engaging in antisocial behavior. This decision is not, however, always a conscious, rational one. Some delinquents simply drift into the adult criminal way of life, and others may be forced into this pattern because they lack opportunity or emotional support for any other way of life. Being middle class or lower class, being a member of a gang or not, and many other factors all determine the final decision.

In social areas marked by high delinquency rates, it is as hard to explain why some children grow up to be nondelinquent as it is easy to document why some become delinquent. In some as yet unexplained way, the majority of children exposed to traumatic or delinquency producing environments are insulated from their influences and develop into responsible citizens. One suggested explanation is that nondelinquent boys more often feel that their parents are fair to them and concerned about them and that the relationship between their parents is fundamentally harmonious. In addition, nondelinquent boys think of themselves as good boys who will not fall in with bad companions or get into trouble with the police (Reckless, 1960). Once this self-image as a nondelinquent is established, it remains unshakable in the years to come. However, we still do not know how to assure that it will be established.

delinquency is to occur. If this adjustment is successful, the delinquent may be easily led into an organized, adult criminal life.

Most of us believe that the child's delinquency suddenly increases with the onset of adolescence. One of the reasons for this notion is that adolescents can plan much more serious and startling depredations against society than they could as children. Moreover, the apparent adult status of adolescents makes the social reaction to their behavior more violent; behavior equally delinquent is tolerated in the very young because it is viewed as a temporary detour on the path of development. The adolescent's actions are viewed as trustworthy predictors of the rest of his life (Cavan, 1962).

However, the most serious aspect of delinquency does not always appear when adolescence begins. Delinquent adolescents are annoying to the general populace, but their behavior is frequently no more serious or disrespectful than that of the high-spirited college student whom no one designates as delinquent. When adolescents are about to become adults, the trouble that they

The Home Life of the Delinquent

The home of the delinquent is usually dilapidated, crowded, poorly furnished, and located in a deteriorated area that is marked by social deprivation of every sort. Nonetheless, more crucial than the depressed physical conditions under which he lives are his relationships with his family and friends. In particular, the delinquent's emotional relations with his parents are far from healthy ones. Parental rejection, incompatibility, or emotional disturbance must leave its mark on the child.

Studies of the structure of the delinquent's family have not provided a perfectly clear and unchallengeable set of conclusions. The absence of a father in the home is regularly reported to be a vital factor in the failure of socialization (Gregory, 1965; Siegman, 1966). Yet the absence of the father may be the visible aspect of a much more basic pattern of rejection and conflict in the child's life, because the forces leading to separation or divorce may be the same ones that produce inconsistent or damaging socialization experiences for the child (Loeb and Price, 1965).

Such experiences produce, of course, personality maladjustment, which is often characteristic of delinquents. One of the classic studies of the personality of delinquents is that of Healy and Bronner (1936). They gathered extensive case history data on 105 juvenile offenders, each of

whom had a nondelinquent brother or sister near his own age. These nondelinquent siblings served as a control group that had been exposed to approximately the same environmental conditions. Despite this similarity in the environments of the two groups, 91 percent of the delinquents were unhappy with their lives or extremely disturbed by emotion provoking experiences or situations. Only 13 percent of the control cases displayed similar inner stresses.

Many of the delinquent subjects showed more than one type of maladjustment. The delinquent children, in contrast to their nondelinquent counterparts, felt rejected, deprived, insecure, and not understood by others. They had intense feelings of being thwarted in their need for self-expression and experienced a strong sense of inadequacy or inferiority. Confusion, unhappiness, and guilt also characterized them. For those nondelinquent children who showed a similar degree of emotional discomfort, there seemed always to

" . . . the apparent adult status of adolescents makes the social reaction to their behavior more violent; behavior equally delinquent is tolerated in the very young because it is viewed as a temporary detour on the path of development."

have been a set of counterbalancing satisfactions that blunted the edge of their distress.

The Delinquent in School

The delinquent child, deprived of appropriate models in his neighborhood and of emotional support and reward from his parents, gains even less gratification from his daily contact with school and the process of education. Although the average intelligence of delinquents is slightly lower than that of nondelinquents, the difference is not enough to account for delinquency or a negative reaction to schooling.

The typical delinquent is nonverbal, nonintellectual, and rejects traditional school subjects of any sort. This rejection of academic endeavor soon causes him to be held back in grade until he becomes the biggest, oldest, most hostile, and least interested member of the class. His response to failure to achieve in a situation from which there is no prolonged escape is uniformly an aggressive one. His teacher tends to return this hostile action in kind, and that rejection is congruent with all the other experiences in his life.

As the child's hostility mounts, the punishment for it increases accordingly, and he is driven to find an escape from the intolerable situation through truancy. Running away usually occurs after a long history of aggressive misconduct and always plunges the child deeper into his battle with rules and regulations. A truant child argues —with considerable logic—that his aggressive actions are provoked by the hopeless situation that society forces upon him. However, this reasoning falls on deaf ears; there are only two worlds, the world of adults and the world of children, and there is no provision for those who do not fit comfortably into either.

The delinquent child usually leaves school as soon as he can legally do so, but he seldom finds that dropping out has improved his lot. It is more likely that a feeling of helplessness will be added to his already existing anger when he discovers that he is not accepted as an equal in the world of workingmen and that he can no longer retreat to the world of age mates that he left behind. In an attempt to resolve this dilemma, the delinquent buys (or sometimes steals) a car, which is the badge of manhood and independence, and then hangs around the fringes of the educational system while remaining immune from its influence. By this time, he may have also thrown in his lot with a group of delinquents having attitudes similar to his own.

The Gang

The gang is the clique of lower class youths. However, gangs tend to be more integrated, more formal, last longer, and provide more tradition and morale than do middle class cliques. Although gangs have formal symbols, names, slogans, passwords, grips, or uniforms, membership in gangs is less exclusive than in cliques (Bossard, 1948). Yet gangs are made up of one sex. According to males in a fighting or conflict gang, girls tend to weaken gang loyalty, to interfere with activities, and to impair combat efficiency. Nonetheless, some gangs do have female auxiliaries, who serve as girl friends and sex partners. They may carry concealed weapons when combat is in order. *Delinquent gangs* form in neighborhoods integrated around a criminal subculture, whereas what have been called *conflict gangs* develop in disorganized slums in which violence provides the only route to social status (Cloward, 1960).

The measures taken by society to provide alternative paths to social prestige usually have little effect on delinquency; they fail to appeal to about 60 to 75 percent of the boys most in need of social assistance. Gang members have abandoned the rules of formal cultural institutions— community organizations, recreational agencies, churches, schools, and the economic and political-legal systems. And, unfortunately, the gang's rejection of social values provides a means for boys to become intimately acquainted with the most corrupt elements in the community.

Perhaps the most significant withdrawal of gang members from the standards of adult culture is that of leaving school. Half of the young people in gangs have not graduated from high school. Indeed, in a hard core lower class gang, the percentage may rise to 80 or 90. As one young gang member commented, "School is a place where they have to put us until they can get rid of us" (Crawford, Malamud, and Dumpson, 1950).

ACTING OUT

Acting out behavior is the translation of impulses into action. This kind of behavior ranges from the delinquent vandal, through the lunatic fringe of politics, to the sociopath who may one day trigger an atomic holocaust. In clinical use, the term "acting out" may refer only to a brief episode of expressing some unconscious impulse —for example, feeling frustrated or unloved and consequently indulging in an orgy of overeating or overdrinking. "Acting out" can also be applied to overtly psychotic behavior in which violently assaultive action issues from a delusional or hallucinatory experience. Hysterical people, too, have been designated as ones who act out. Their exhibitionism and histrionics are often viewed as translations of hidden impulses into overt behavior. In one sense, people who have amnesia are while in states of altered consciousness acting out impulses normally denied access to consciousness.

Those who act out may respond pathologically (with aggression against either themselves or others) at the same time that they appear normal to others about them. People who behave in this way most often ascribe the results of their behavior to accident or fate and do not see the cause and effect relationship in their actions. To them, their behavior seems appropriate, reasonable, and justified, and they will repeat it when the proper stimuli are presented again.

In some people, acting out involves the "fate neurosis" described by Alfred Adler. Such individuals are catastrophe collectors, continuous inno-cent victims of circumstances, and predictable failures. These people manufacture on an unconscious assembly line trouble for themselves or others. Examples used by theorists to describe the person for whom acting out becomes a way of life are the delinquent, the actress who remains the *enfant terrible*, the brawling, heavy-drinking playwright, and the absentminded professor who studiously lives out his accident-prone, forgetful role in life.

Related to these are the host of citizens in any community who maintain a steady outpouring of excitability, easy explosiveness, and aggression. Hasty, immature, volatile, they are people with few quiet periods in their lives, for they live in a constant state of upset that is a part of a total pattern of overactivity. This pattern of acting out is not, however, the same for those whose present behavior is a reworking of issues unresolved in early childhood and now finding unconscious expression in adult life. An example of this type of acting out is the man who had fought his father's authority and now repeats this battle again and again with employers. If people saddled with a problem of which they are unaware react immediately with overt behavior to every tension that they encounter, we have all the necessary ingredients for an acting out personality.

Acting out behavior is the province of the adolescent in our society. The fist fighting, drag racing, and violent enthusiasms of adolescence are part of the way in which the inexperienced young person reacts to the culture and its people. In his quest for inner security, the adolescent drowns himself in outer activity and displays the restless seeking and chasing that typify him. It has been suggested that this way of managing life has a genetic basis—that some individuals are predisposed to react in this fashion, to express it most clearly in adolescence, and to continue it into adulthood. However, there is little experimental evidence to substantiate this position.

Adolescent acting out may also be approached by placing it in the context of the general psychology of the adolescent phase of development (Josselyn, 1965). Adolescence is a time when the individual is experiencing change in a multitude of impulse systems (not just sexual) and an increasing intensity of impulse experience, and he must handle these changes with an ego that is not yet adequate to the task. Moreover, "Our society, at least theoretically, urges an individualized pattern of motivation, criticizes when that pattern does not take an acceptable form, smiles indulgently at many clumsy steps taken by the maturing individual, and offers little in structured guidance for the attainment of adulthood" (Josselyn, 1965, p. 70). Josselyn maintains that this psychological and social confusion inevitably results in confused, acting out behavior. Thus, acting out should perhaps be considered a normal facet of adolescence. According to this theory, the problem is not the acting *upon* impulse but the *acting out* of infantile conflict or impulses; some adolescents may be acting out on a characterological basis, while others act out only when confronted with stress that exceeds the ego managerial capacity.

In any case, it is evident that, in the development of the former sort of individual, past experience and ways of reacting come to dominate present behavior. It may be that for some people violent behavior is a means of preventing or warding off even more serious anxiety attacks or distorted behavior. Consequently, if the acting out person were to be prevented from expressing himself in this way, the outcome for his psychological organization might be disastrous.

In some cases, acting out may be valuable for society. For example, controlled acting out can be adaptive when it is revolutionary in character and forces social change for the betterment of society. In order to be psychologically useful, such acting out must meet the needs of those it serves and strike a responsive chord in the unexpressed impulses of many others. Picketing and planned civil disobedience are modern examples.

Acting out may also produce a positive social response. Even for those whose way of life is devoted to violent acting out, there are certain social rewards. Our society lauds those who live

out our unspoken impulses and get away with it. Moreover, as a nation, we are overcontrolled people who stand quietly in line and do little about the person who pushes boorishly ahead to get what he wants just because he wants it. Thus, not all those who act out are punished; most often they do well in a passive, conservative society whose members are taught not to take unnecessary chances. Although for some, acting out may issue in vandalism or narcotics addiction, for others, the result may be leadership in industry.

THE REPAIR OF SOCIALIZATION

The resocialization of the delinquent is handicapped by the difficulty of reversing established delinquency; that is, all delinquents do not become adult criminals, but the frequency of serious encounter with the law becomes more and more predictable the further that the adolescent ventures down the delinquent path. As a consequence, military service, which is the most thorough-going means of total control and resocialization that our society has invented, does not often transform juvenile delinquents into acceptable citizens (Roff, 1961). And even psychotherapy, which many people view as the only way to rehabilitate the criminal and the delinquent, is not always effective.

The Therapist and the Delinquent

Our society may have oversold the psychiatric and sociological viewpoint of delinquency and swung too far in the direction of proclaiming that delinquents are sick. However, if they are indeed sick, the difficulty of curing them is even more serious because there are so few professionals able or ready to treat them (Schmideberg, 1959). Most therapists do not work with delinquent children. The judgments that these therapists make about the degree of "sickness" in delinquents are primarily based on a private practice that deals almost exclusively with a carefully selected group of neurotic offenders. As a consequence, the therapists are tempted to believe that naughty children and adult criminals are only quantitatively different—although they actually differ substantially along qualitative dimensions. For neurotics, psychoanalytic therapy, insight therapy, or the permissiveness of supportive therapy may be very effective. For antisocial offenders, these methods may not work. In fact, they may make the patients worse, for in terms of impulse control, delinquents may represent the extreme opposite of neurotics. Therefore, as Schmideberg (1959) suggests, criminal psychiatry should become a subspecialty of psychiatry, and new therapeutic methods should be developed. It is not that psychotherapy does not help delinquents but that the therapist is often dealing with social and cultural upheavals rather than individual, internal complexes.

It is very difficult to interest psychiatrists, psychologists, or social workers in treating delinquents because such treatment has some highly unprofessional and unattractive features. The therapist who works with aggressive, antisocial, or delinquent children has to be prepared to deal with the police and the courts and to cope with personal violence. He may occasionally have things stolen from his office. And the financial rewards for such labors are meager indeed. Most professional therapists do not relish the thought of a life constantly immersed in troubles of this sort.

The treatment of delinquents demands that the therapist step out of his comfortable social and cultural milieu and frequent a part of society that is alien to him. Most delinquents come from the poorer socio-economic classes, where a particular set of attitudes, feelings, beliefs, and reactions is fashioned. These accompany delinquents into treatment. Thus, if the psychiatrist, psychologist, or social worker seeks assistance from the child's parents, he is liable to find resistance rather than cooperation. The level of defiance,

lying, irregularity, incomprehension, and lack of cooperation typical of such parents is frequently discouraging. The very way of life of the members of the lower socio-economic classes is reprehensible to most middle class, upwardly mobile therapists. And even if the therapeutic clan were able to surmount all these obstacles, it would still have to face the fact that verbal psychotherapy may be inappropriate for most delinquents. If the delinquent comes for help and finds that it does not materialize soon, his need for immediate gratification is threatened, and he abandons therapy in favor of the street.

The therapist who works with delinquents must, therefore, have a special temperament, special capacities, and special techniques. He must be able to establish a meaningful relationship quickly, which involves knowing the argot of the group, their mentality, their social background, and the probable legal consequences of their activity. Moreover, the therapist cannot be a passive observer. He must actively reach out to the patient's level of experience in order to make any contact at all. Treatment, which makes so much sense to members of the middle class, may be totally alien to members of the lower classes, so that the nature of the process must be cast in different terms. These patients need to understand why they do what they do and what its probable consequences will be. Thus, in order to "Motivate and constantly remotivate the very unwilling patient" (Schmideberg, 1959, p. 2), practical help rather than sugary verbal reassurance must be forthcoming. These children need jobs, need help with their emotions, and need assistance in keeping out of trouble. The emotions of the patient must be brought to bear on his life situation in order to short-circuit lawbreaking and initiate proper social behavior. Finally, because socializing the delinquent means making his behavior acceptable to middle class society, he needs to be educated if he is to become treatable. But in a very real sense, this education cannot be accomplished in the antiseptic office of the private practitioner.

A Critique of Current Methods

Traditional methods of remedy for these failures in socialization have proven to be inadequate along a series of dimensions. For example, a host of criticisms could be leveled at the way in which professionals are trained for the clinical management of socially disturbed and aggressive children. Perhaps the most damning charge is that tyro professionals are regularly and severely restricted to a limited assortment of actions and responsibilities with respect to the whole patient. The therapists who have been around longer regularly and passionately justify to one another the wisdom of placing working restrictions on the inexperienced, the untrained, and the unwashed. Thus, the child under institutional care or some related form of social control finds that, on the average, little of his day is occupied by contact with trained professionals whose efforts are directed toward his emotional and interpersonal reconstruction. "Treatment" of a formal therapist-patient variety also tends to be sporadic. Therefore, in most institutions such as hospitals, detention homes, children's homes, and training schools, he finds himself in enforced custody in only the company of peers whose adjustment is no more problem-free than his own.

In such cases, the concept of a *therapeutic milieu* is usually evoked to justify the social action of removing a child from his family and to make reasonable the substitution of peer-community living. Institutions are quick to claim that they have fashioned a benign atmosphere, which will correct the twisted emotional growth of the child's earlier years. However, constructing a therapeutic or mentally healthy social milieu is extremely difficult. Such a milieu is not simply a social system marked by the absence of brutality or other painful excesses in human relations; rather, it is an infinitely complex and subtle style of personal interaction that must be solidly based on a dynamic understanding of the emotional life and response system of each child for whom the setting is designed. As Fritz Redl has indicated, a therapeutic milieu, to be worthy of the name, must amount to more than "not putting poison in their soup." The establishment and maintenance of a therapeutic milieu requires both the careful indoctrination of all participants before their assignment to duty and continued observation and correction. Producing effective day-by-day participation by personnel and children in a therapeutic milieu is neither simple to teach nor easy to exercise.

Ideally, every setting dedicated to the care of disturbed or delinquent children should have exhaustive training programs. This ideal is generally given lip service but rarely achieved. Consequently, the attendant, cottage parent, counselor, detention officer, nurse, or ward worker—the person with whom the child has his most significant daily experiences—may present an unpredictable range of behavior for him to absorb. When a lack of appropriate training is coupled with poor morale, inadequate salary, limited experience with emotionally disturbed children, and ineffective supervision, the possibility of rehabilitating the child is remote.

These conditions result, of course, in further deterioration of the child's environment. One of the factors contributing to that deterioration is a phenomenon called "instant cynicism." The dedicated, inspired, novice juvenile officer comes dewy-eyed to his task and makes his first sincere but fumbling attempts to make sense of the frequently unpredictable behavior of his charges. He soon finds that the set of expectations that he previously found workable with normal children no longer seems to be effective. Without being able to comprehend the reasons for the unpredictability of these adult-child relations, he becomes easy prey to the ready-made cynicism of his more experienced co-workers and soon slips into their comfortable pattern of rejecting what cannot be understood. Thus, before long he categorizes all delinquent boys as hostile and incorrigible and believes that their behavior will change only in response to an adult reaction of a similar kind.

At this juncture, the juvenile officer has begun to travel down a road that has become familiar in the treatment of youthful misbehavior. Few human beings are equipped by either normal daily experience or early background to respond appropriately and therapeutically to disordered human behavior. When all of one's familiar overtures and responses prove to be nonfunctional, a normal defensive reaction is to counter with primitive actions calculated to restore one's previous sense of adequacy. And the task of abandoning old forms of response in favor of new ones can be painful in the extreme.

SUMMARY

A society survives and prospers if it can produce adults who share the values of the culture. When this socialization process fails, one of its visible forms is delinquency. The delinquent sets himself outside the influence of the attitudes, values, and beliefs of the rest of society in defiance of the intentions of those who socialized him.

In the search for the causes of delinquency, theorists have found that depressed environmental conditions and warped child-parent relationships often produce individuals who act out against organized society. Such an individual is sentenced to an unhappy life at odds with other members of society and is dissatisfied with a self that he cannot esteem.

Repairing failures in socialization is an unusually difficult task in part because we lack adequately trained therapists and in part because the ideal conditions for child training are no longer present. The child has become a half-man. Consequently, he is beyond simple punishments, independent of his parents, and emotionally little capable of acquiring the learnings that will make his life less laden with conflict.

Before the child in any society can be granted full membership in it, he must learn sexual attitudes, beliefs, and behaviors that are socially acceptable. However, the socialization of sexuality, which begins early in the child's life and continues through his adolescence, poses many complex problems. Many of these stem from the discontinuity of having to establish an asexual pattern of behavior in the child and then establish the opposite one when he becomes an adolescent. If the childhood pattern is reversed too early in life—that is, if the child begins to act in adult sexual ways before society thinks it proper—he provokes a great deal of anxiety in his parents. If the opposite kind of behavior appears—that is, if at maturity he fails to display interest in heterosexuality—attacks of anxiety are again the lot of his parents. Another difficulty apparent in any attempt to socialize sexuality is that, although the process begins early in the child's life, the success of the attempt is not really tested until some time in adolescence, when the time for dating and mating arrives. And, as a consequence, a successful adjustment to sexuality is another psychological task that teenagers must accomplish before they can be considered adults.

15

The socialization of sexuality

MALE AND FEMALE

Social sexual roles are clearly malleable; men and women learn to be what they are as a consequence of what their culture dictates. Anatomical and physiological differences are, however, usually of some consequence in shaping social and sexual roles. Thus, in many preliterate or nonliterate cultures, men gravitate toward work requiring muscular strength (warfare, metal working, hunting, mining, quarrying, boat building), and women tend to assume occupations centered on the home and children (basket making, gathering fruits and nuts, grinding grain, making pottery and clothes). Once these divisions of labor have been firmly established, they are strongly reinforced by taboo, ritual, superstition, prejudice, or any other form of social control available to the members of the society (Murdock, 1937).

On the other hand, the anatomical and physiological differences between men and women do not always help to determine social and sexual roles. The Arapesh, for example, are a mountain dwelling tribe that from our point of view seems feminine in its orientation. Arapesh men and women are more alike than males and females find comfortable in our culture; both may be passive, mild, domesticated, and gentle·and share the care of the children as well as other home duties. In this culture, the division of labor between male and female is hardly recognizable. The culture of Mundugumor is another in which men and women are more nearly alike than in our own culture. However, here the model personality for both men and women is one of ruthlessness, aggression, and violence.

Finally, the society of the Tchambuli is a culture very much like our own in that different roles are assigned to each sex. The differences in role are, however, reversed, so that the Tchambuli woman is the aggressive manager of business affairs and the dominant member in the marital relationship. The Tchambuli male is closely attached to his children and fulfills what in our society would be the role of the mother. He is

"The Tchambuli male is closely attached to his children and fulfills what in our society would be the role of the mother."

considered subordinate to and dependent upon his mate. The Tchambuli believe that this arrangement follows naturally from the "facts" of the biology of males and females; females, the Tchambuli note with confidence, are stronger than males. This role assignment is so thorough that when females give birth to the young, the males enter confinement, are attended by midwives, and have sympathetic birth pangs symbolic of the event of new birth.

Masculine and feminine social roles in American culture are of a very special sort. Men and women in our society may score equally well on tests of ability, yet women fall far behind men in terms of recognized achievement in and cultural acceptance of achievement oriented roles. For example, in 1903 Cattell (1903) compiled a list of 1,000 of the most eminent people in the world. This list contained only 32 women. In the early days of our culture, it was said that every great woman was a man—that is, to be a great woman requires the possession of male psychological characteristics.

In a more recent study by Lehman (1953), a list was constructed of 116 creative scientists who had done significant work in their fields prior to 22 years of age. This list included only three women. In another list of older scholars who were high achievers, no women appeared.

Although women have had a place in the culture, it has been highly restricted. The field in which women have accomplished most is in children's literature; 46 percent of the recognized authors were women at the time of the study. Women have also been sculptors and artists. In this category, women have represented about a fifth of those who are high achievers.

It is obvious that our culture has always offered men greater opportunities for achievement than women. Despite equal amounts of ability, men are encouraged and rewarded more than women are. Because men are expected to compete in the arena of achievement and women are excluded as a consequence of their sex, the social pressure motivating men toward achievement is substantially greater than that for women. In a culture where equal achievement is expected of both men and women, the results might be quite different.

Our society, then, has its own mythology on the rightful place for the male and the proper place for the female. These ascribed sexual roles influence the conduct of interaction between the sexes at all ages but have their greatest impact on our social pattern of dating and marrying.

However, these sexual roles are not so clearly delineated as they once were, for the American view of what is proper sexual behavior for males and females is changing. And this change is, of course, influencing our pattern of dating and marrying. As the frequency of premarital intercourse increases year by year, for example, the expectations of each dating or potential marriage partner shift to accommodate these alterations of the social view of male and female roles.

Today, as a consequence of these changes, parents are regularly distrustful of the casual equality that they observe between young people as they fondly recall the good old days of formal manners and proper comportment that were assumed to continue when the boy and girl were beyond parental purview. There was a day not so long ago when it would have been inappropriate for a girl to go to a man's apartment to cook his dinner and do his laundry.

THE SEXUAL REVOLUTION

A cultural ideal in our society is sexual chastity. Consequently, the sex taboo in America, which is quite general—officially, at least—maintains that only lawful, monogamous marriage is socially approved for sex release and for the propagation of the race. As Hortense Powdermaker (1950) has suggested, the standards of what can be shown in movies gives us an idealized view of what is publicly proper and improper in our culture. A decade and a half ago, the production code for movies decreed that there should be no suggestion of sexual intimacy and no reference to biological functions in films. Indeed, the code implied that the public should not be made explicitly aware that marriages are consummated sexually.

In very recent years, steady change has occurred in our censorship practices. Subjects once strictly taboo are now considered in frank detail, the human body and its sexual parts are exposed to public view in films and on stage, and there seems to be an open acknowledgment of what everyone already knew.

The traditional social ethic of sexual chastity relies on the belief that the sex drive can be sublimated or released on nonsexual levels. Thus, violation of sexual norms is assumed to be a failure of sublimation, and society punishes the offender accordingly. What is interesting is that 50 percent of the sexual outlets for the male population must then be socially disapproved and largely illegal. This means that about 95 percent of the total male population and perhaps 85 percent of the adolescents in our society could be convicted as sex offenders if the laws were stringently enforced (Kinsey, 1948).

In some parts of our society, these figures would be even higher because patterns of sexual behavior are different in different social classes. In general, men and women in the lower socio-economic classes indulge in more sexual activity and do so earlier than middle class men and women do. Comparisons between college students and noncollege students support these findings. For lower class males with only a grade school education, premarital intercourse makes up about 60 percent of their sexual outlet, while among males with a college education, premarital intercourse constitutes only 11 percent of the sexual outlet. Lower class sexual behavior thus consistently violates our society's sex taboos, which are essentially middle class. The result of this violation for the lower class youth is a moral dilemma.

However, such conflicts are not all peculiar to lower class youths. One source of conflict for members of all social classes is the middle class cultural ideal of romantic love. Subscribing to this ideal increases interest in sex, and this interest immediately conflicts with the social taboo on sexual relations before marriage. Among youths in the middle and upper classes, this is a particular problem. Kinsey (1953) reported that 60 percent of those married by 20 years of age had had premarital relations with the intended spouse. In general, rates of premarital sexual experience were about the same for females whatever their educational level or occupational background. Among males, rates of premarital sexual experience are significantly affected by social class membership.

At the time that the Kinsey reports were made public, a ripple of shock ran through society, for here in print and statistics was a blatant statement of what many had long suspected but had persisted in denying. The Kinsey reports led social scientists to take a closer look at the sexual revolution.

The Preadolescent Revolutionary

One aspect of the sexual revolution is that new norms have emerged for interaction between male and female preadolescent children (Broderick and Fowler, 1961). This change in norms is evident in the contrast between surveys of sexual mores in the 1930s and the 1950s and 1960s. The accounts of the 1930–1939 decade indicate that preadolescent girls were carefully excluded from participation in masculine activities (Furfey, 1930; Campbell, 1939). This exclusion constituted no real problem because the girls of those days held negative attitudes toward boys—which were returned in kind. What contact existed between boys and girls in the thirties was restricted to socially approved events such as games and dancing. Other studies done in the 1920s and 1930s report that the percentage of friendship choices extending across the sex barrier was nearly nil in the third and fourth grades and remained at a very low level until the children were eighth graders (Hsia, 1928; Seagoe, 1933).

This pattern of relations between the sexes is in sharp contrast to the behavior reported in a more recent survey conducted by Lewis (1958). Lewis reports that, although the pattern of avoidance may still be customary for some groups of young people, new patterns that promise to revolutionize boy-girl relationships are emerging. In the fourth, fifth, and sixth grades, boys and girls frequently vote for activities that range from folk dancing and table games to dating.

Other researchers (Broderick and Fowler, 1961) came to similar conclusions in a study of the friendship choices of 264 fourth, fifth, and sixth graders in a middle class elementary school in a Southern urban community. The children studied came from homes in the upper lower to upper middle classes. The age range was nine to 13 years for girls and nine to 14 years for boys. Broderick and Fowler found that nearly 52 percent of the children in the fifth grade and 38 percent of the children in the sixth grade chose one or more friends of the opposite sex when given the opportunity to indicate whom they liked best of all the children they knew. Thus, although preadolescent boys and girls still prefer the companionship of their own sex, an increasing number are now able to feel positive about members of the opposite sex. Indeed, Broderick and Fowler discovered that a great majority of the children in each of the fourth, fifth, and sixth grades claimed to have a sweetheart and maintained that this feeling was reciprocated by their chosen object. Today, the sweetheart knows, friends know, and even parents know of these early enthusiasms for members of the opposite sex.

In the past two decades, reports indicate an increase in early dating. Among the 10 and 11 year olds in the fifth grade, as many as 45 percent of the boys and 36 percent of the girls claim to have dated. In the seventh grade (12 and 13 year olds), nearly 70 percent of the boys and 53 percent of the girls claim to have had at least one date. Experience with kissing at these ages is also reported to be common (Smith, 1952; Lowrie, 1956; Cameron and Kenkel, 1960). This early appearance of sexual interest has social as well as biological roots. Our culture has changed, and that change has produced a shift in the standards for male-female relationships.

The Shifting Standards

The variety of social changes that our culture had undergone in the last quarter-century is re-

flected not only in the sex life of our citizens but in the altered relationship of male to female. In the 1960s, the American people were in the final stages of a sexual revolution. The economically self-sufficient family had all but disappeared, the traditional relationship of husband and wife had altered, and the family was no longer the center of recreation, moral guidance, and education, for these functions had in great part been relegated to social institutions outside the family (Schur, 1964). As a result of these changes, our attitude toward sexual behavior is changing as well.

Once women were allowed economic independence and had contraceptives available for regulating pregnancy, it was predictable that they would closely re-examine their view of sexual relations. Financial independence permitted the postponement of marriage, and effective contraception made pregnancy and parenthood a matter of choice. In addition, moral standards that were once fashioned in the close confines of the extended family were more often shaped by contact with an increasing number of people from a variety of walks of life. This exposure to moral standards different from those of one's parents also began to occur at an earlier age as our society became a mobile one saturated by an extended mass media.

Finally, values and moral standards changed when deviation from parental strictures was less easily detectable and increasingly difficult to punish. One news commentator opens his program each evening by saying, "It is 11 o'clock. Do you know where your children are?" In modern America parents often do not know. And the freedom of our young people multiplies the frequency with which they must decide for themselves about proper sexual behavior.

The argument over proper sexual behavior is at the core of the issue of shifting social values. Husbands and wives can relate to each other sexually and socially in ways that would have seemed alien to the citizen of the early 1900s. Manuals detailing sophisticated sexual techniques for married couples need no longer be purchased from beneath the counter of the local bookstore.

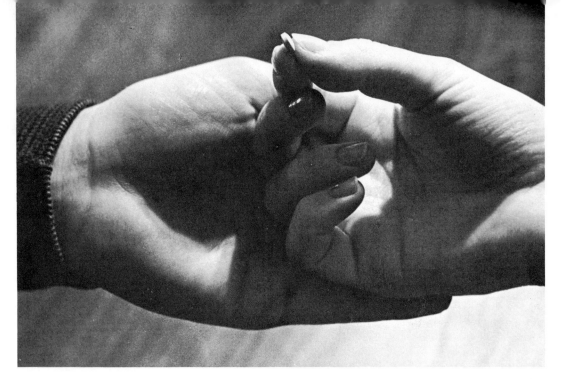

"Once women were allowed economic independence and had contraceptives available for regulating pregnancy, it was predictable that they would closely reexamine their view of sexual relations."

Rather, these manuals are advertised openly, quoted extensively in the widely circulated women's magazines, and no longer mailed to the home in brown wrappers. In addition, the modern husband and wife have been able freely to redivide family labor and marital roles with fewer restrictions anchored in a rigid definition of what is proper for males and proper for females. Even though this new kind of relationship is today greeted with reluctance and doubt, it is not subject to violent social disapproval. Thus, young people of dating and mating age can pattern their relationships along lines quite different from the traditional ones and find themselves subject to only moderate disapproval.

Nonetheless, our culture has always disapproved of premarital sexual experience, so that it is still difficult to find "respectable" voices to argue in favor of sex before marriage. Even the social scientists most responsible for the re-examination of our sexual mores listed 20 arguments against premarital coitus but could only muster up 12 reasons in favor of it (Kinsey *et al.*, 1953).

The arguments for virginity until marriage include pregnancy, abortion, venereal disease, forced marriage, traumatic sexual experience produced by an unsuitable setting for illicit love, guilt, loss of the male's respect for the woman, public disapproval, legal difficulties, and moral difficulties. The counterarguments include satisfaction of physiological need, practice in developing emotional adjustment to another person, training in physical expertise in sexual relations, and a test of married sexual compatibility. The argument over this issue still rages—particularly between the younger generation and the older.

However, the facts, at least according to Kinsey *et al.* (1953), do not support some of the arguments against premarital sexual relations. For women who participated in premarital affairs and later married, many of the arguments launched against premarital sexual experience do not seem to have an adequate basis. Fear of venereal disease, for example, seldom proved to be a deterrent, and much of the expected moral guilt failed to materialize. Even among women who had become pregnant before marriage, 83 percent registered little or no regret at having had this sexual experience. When the premarital experience was with the man whom the woman subsequently married, the percentage of women expressing regret declined even further.

Although the Americans of today clearly have seriously mixed feelings about sex, they are moving toward a new view of sexuality. Thus, for example, the literature of sex is more open, widely distributed, and casually acquirable than ever before. The difficulty with this new popular viewpoint is that the "official" view is still one of moralizing disapproval. This dichotomy suggests the need for a fundamental revision of our sex mores toward a new set of standards that will increase the degree to which sexual attitudes and beliefs coincide with both the physiological needs of individuals and the actual practices of males and females in our culture (Ellis, 1961).

LOVE

Western civilization is distinguished by the *romantic love complex,* which has a unique pattern in America. Romantic love dominates the social outlook of both youths and adults in our culture, but the youths are particularly desperate in searching for it. Although romantic love is primarily a middle class view of interpersonal relationships, the mass media have spread it throughout all the socio-economic classes. According to this view, love is a permanent and exclusive relationship in which all lovers are soul mates destined exclusively for each other by a heavenly design, brought together by a wise fate, and slated to remain united for eternity. Love at first sight is a particularly potent aspect of this myth; and is regularly reinforced by the love songs, stories, movies, and television shows that inundate American youth.

The myth of romantic love, of course, ignores the cold fact that the choice of a marriage partner is usually limited by social, racial, cultural, educational, and geographical factors. It is hard to see how the notion of romantic love squares with the fact that marriageable females tend to emphasize earning ability and personality as vital qualities in potential husbands, while men seek personal attractiveness in potential wives.

Romantic love has been described as a kind of emotional seizure stemming from an overwhelming sex attraction that causes each lover to be incapable of thinking of anything but the love object. And perhaps romantic love does contain something resembling emotional disturbance; romantic love is regularly referred to as being "crazy about someone." In this state, "The lover is subject to illusions, delusions, manic-depressive cycles, compulsions, and other systems of mental abnormality . . . [and] lives in a schizoid world of his own with his own private standards . . ." (Merrill, 1949, p. 37). Even our system of jurisprudence recognizes that lovers may suffer an emotional inflammation that may alter the soundness of their judgment.

Because romantic love is acutely monopolistic, the couple may become self-absorbed and socially self-sufficient; love increases the degree of their withdrawal from their families and from society. Moreover, an early, hasty marriage may be the outcome of a relationship marked by intense jealousy and possessiveness. Romantic love meets its only real test when confronted with the realities of marriage. As passion ebbs, romantic love may become bankrupt, so that the only recourse may be to change partners.

Another characteristic of romantic love is its obsession with glamour, a delusive glorification of a person based on sex. This cultural search for glamour, reflected in our concern over proper clothing and appearance, is a particular problem for the female in our society. Advertising, Hollywood, and television have all made glamour a prime goal for both youths and adults. Consequently, the college man's conception of the ideal girl tends to be a clear-skinned, blue-eyed brunette who is neat, clean, and healthy and has sex appeal (Folsom, 1943). Girls, of course respond to these demands with an almost obsessive concern with physical appearance and good grooming. For males, the demands are fewer. All that is needed is height and strength coupled with reasonably good grooming. One might speculate that, if the women in our society were independent and on an economic and political par with the male, they might have less need for glamour.

Perhaps a better view of love is as an interpersonal relationship in which two people contribute to the welfare and development of each other. Although love is

One of the most frequently used words in our vocabulary, the major theme of art in all its aspects, the principal industry of Hollywood and of countless magazines, the thing with which human beings are most concerned all their lives, the most important experience in the world, love is something about which most of us, at this late date, are still extremely vague. One has only to ask one's friends what they understood by "love" to discover how unclear the idea remains in the minds of many people (Montagu, 1962, p. 99).

The knowledge of love must issue from the early experience of love between mother and child. As Montagu (1962) notes, there is an old Talmudic proverb stating that, because God could not be everywhere, he created mothers; in the child's mother, the future image of the nature of love is formed. If the child grows without love, he is subject to extensive emotional deprivation and damage. A crucial part of the mother-child relationship is teaching the child to love himself—to accept himself and be reasonably content. If he learns how to love himself and others, he will be able to convey a feeling of deep involvement with and commitment to others. This kind of love is unconditional in the truest sense of "for better or for worse," and it is always supportive in that, come hell or high water, the lover can be counted on to help, not hinder.

Love is thus vital, it is inspiring, it is beautiful, and it is a happy circumstance in the eyes of most members of our society. The difficulty with love among young people is that it is seldom Platonic and seldom retains its sheerly romantic

" . . . lovers may suffer an emotional inflammation that may alter the soundness of their judgment."

form. Our fantasy of romantic love is as pure as the Prince Charming who awakened Sleeping Beauty with a pristine kiss and, as best we can tell, never went further. As the young soon learn, love also means sex, and sex constitutes a problem for young person and adult alike.

The socialization of sexuality is not an identical process for boys and girls. They must each achieve a different adult sex role, and they do so along different paths (Schoeppe, 1953). Becoming independent can be an evolutionary step for the girl but may require some minor revolutionary moves for the boy. Although the boy must display increased assertiveness and independence to appear masculine, the girl can continue to be submissive and emotionally dependent on others. She does not have to depart so radically from the role she has already learned, and she continues to remain under the wing of her parents for longer than the boy in the family does.

The easier access to freedom for the boy is consistent with the independence he is supposed to demonstrate as an adult male. However, this freedom exposes him to greater risks of suffering from inexperience and immature judgment. The girl is sheltered from this risk, but she is not always happy about such protection. Anxious to become independent, she may find herself engaged in a hot and heavy tug of war with parents reluctant to grant her freedom. Thus, conflict with parents over assuming the independent sexual role of an adult is more likely to be a problem for the girl than for the boy.

The Dating Game

The "date" is a distinctive institution designed by youths with the help of adults that performs a variety of functions for young people. First, the dating relationship is a training ground for self-assurance, broad social experience, and knowledge of manners, behavior, and dress. Second, dating provides an important link with a series of other institutions leading from the parental to the marital family. Dating initiates and perpetuates heterosexual relationships during a period when courtship is premature and marriage unattainable. The classic pattern of dating keeps youth from becoming overinvolved in an exclusive one-to-one relationship (going steady) that cannot be consummated. And third, the date sets its own norms for relationships that are relatively independent of, and may even be in conflict with, the adult culture. Dating, in contrast to courtship, is a period of dalliance and experimentation that may become ends in themselves. Thus, dating is not a serious step toward marriage and reproduction but a device for beginning sexual socialization by peers.

Perhaps the most significant sexual activity before the late teens is "petting" on dates. In general, petting is viewed by young people as a normal practice, but it is most often used as a sexual outlet by middle class high school and college students; Kinsey, Pomeroy, and Martin (1948) found that 92 percent of high school and college students engage in some form of petting. Among members of the lower class, social norms discourage petting but are less severe with regard to premarital relationships. According to one study (Newcomb, 1937), as many as 85 percent of lower class males with only a grade school level of education had premarital relations and seem, in general, to have skipped the petting stage and moved directly into overt sexual relationships.

The pattern of sexual socialization for lower class youths seems to be a series of sexual affairs that are eventually followed by marriage. Such love affairs approximate the steady date of the middle class except for the violation of the middle class sex taboo. Because lower class girls are more willing to acquiesce to premarital sexual activity, they become fair game for sexual exploitation by middle class boys. Consequently, the majority of college men have had their premarital experiences with lower class noncollege girls (Porterfield and Salley, 1946).

Although petting is an important sexual outlet before marriage, for engaged couples, there seems to be in contemporary America at least tacit approval of premarital intimacies. This weakening of the traditional norm of virginity may be a consequence of the cultural confrontation that we have set up between romantic sex attraction and taboos about sexual activity. It is as though our society has decided that the good intentions of the engagement period provide sufficient assurance to permit some relaxing of sexual rules. And, indeed, a generation ago, the rates of premarital experience with future spouses increased from 4.6 percent to 31.9 percent for men in a single generation and, in the same generation, from 8.7 percent to 45 percent for women (Derman, 1938). Recent estimates of sexual activity among the unmarried seem to confirm these observations. Love and sexuality are still linked for adolescents and young adults, but sexuality and marriage do not bear so strong a relationship to each other. In Burgess and Wallin's study (1953), 45 percent of the couples reported premarital intercourse. Karrin and Howard (1958) found a similar percentage in their sample. Despite the moral alarm that has been frequently sounded, there is no trustworthy evidence that this increase in premarital intercourse among engaged couples has adversely affected happiness in marriage.

Sex and the College Student

After Kinsey and his co-workers, probably Ehrmann (1959) has contributed most in the way of a detailed analysis of premarital sexual behavior among college students. Using questionnaire schedules and interviews, Ehrmann tried to tease out the patterns that characterize our culture. The questionnaires were designed to provide an overview and the interviews the depth in analysis. Over a seven year period, nearly 5,000 students took part in this research. The subjects were volunteers in one sense—they all agreed to participate in the study—but they were selected volunteers chosen to be asked in the first place. The students were white, generally from middle class families, and predominantly Protestant. This sample is hardly typical of our entire society, but Ehrmann's findings are an important commentary on modern middle class culture and are probably generalizable to most other samples of college students. Finally, the sample contained twice as many females as males, and that factor, too, should be taken into consideration when evaluating his conclusions.

In this sample, the dating pattern of the students differed by sex; females dated much more frequently than males. The female group of most frequent daters reported that they had had as many as 30 dates a month, or nearly one a day on the average. Indeed, 13 percent even reported a rate of 1.5 dates per day. At the other extreme, a few boys and girls reported not having had a date for a year or more, and some had never dated at all. Nevertheless, allowing for a certain amount of rounding out of figures here, the frequency of dating remains startling to those who have gotten along in years and would certainly be distressing to parents who sent their offspring to college for an education. Moreover, important deterrents to a high frequency of dating were not academic reasons but lack of money and lack of a car. In particular, a car carries with it the trimmings of status and seems in modern society to enhance one's attractiveness.

The pattern of sexual behavior on dates varied by sex in terms of both physical intimacy and moral judgment. The males were reported to be much more experienced sexually and more active sexually at the time of the study. Sexual activity for college males seemed to be a sporadic venture, while females tended to establish greater stability and continuity in their relations with others. For both sexes, kissing and hugging was the most frequent sexual behavior. Most dating behavior of a sexual sort involved substitutes for full genital sexual gratification; these most often assumed the form of light and heavy petting.

Males, as one might expect, were the initiators of sexual activity. The forces that kept sexual activity from "going all the way" were rated in order of importance by both males and females. The most important reason for limiting sexual activity to its preliminary stages was that neither boy nor girl tried to go farther. The next most frequent reason was the refusal of the girl to extend the sexual exploration. Lack of opportunity for sexual fulfillment came next, and inhibitory behavior on the part of the boy was the last reason for limitation of sexual advances. In general, then, the female limited premarital sexual activity on dates. The category "neither tried to go farther" was most often a disguise for the male's judging the female as unwilling to venture beyond certain prescribed limits.

These patterns of dating and sexual behavior are in part determined by the social class factor. Dating is most often carefully limited to activity within one's own social class. Males do tend to cross class lines with greater frequency than do females and, as a consequence, indulge in sexual experiences that go further than those that they would undergo in dating middle class girls. Females cross class lines less often if they are from middle class families; girls from the lower socioeconomic classes have affairs with middle class boys. However, these affairs are usually transitory and gauged to satisfy the sexual needs of the boys rather than the romantic interests of the girls.

Love and going steady are the prime movers for middle class sexual experience. This correlation is a profound one that seems to underscore the difference between male and female sexuality. The connection between sexual intimacy and the romantic notions vital to the female is clearly less important to the male in his pursuit of sexual gratification. This finding squares with the work of Kinsey and with the casual observations of every commentator on the sexual mores of every culture. For females, love implies permission; for males, love is a secondary consideration.

This view of love and sex is rooted in the peer culture. However, peer codes of proper moral behavior are much more flexible and free than are the actual individual codes of behavior; that is, what is sanctioned by the peer group is far from being a guideline to actual behavior among young people. For example, males tend to be less consistent than females in their personal sexual codes. Males talk a better game than they play; they insist that they are ethically free to do a great variety of things sexually, but their behavior gives the lie to their words. Females, on the other hand, seem to set an ethical code and then stick by it in their behavior.

These differences between males and females suggest that, in order to understand the ethical code of the youth culture, it is necessary to subdivide that culture into male and female subsections. Sex and love differ in their meaning for the young males and females in our culture; for males, eroticism is the primary issue, while for females, it is romanticism.

As an expanded proportion of the youthful population finds it necessary to prolong the educational process, college becomes the "place to go" for social rather than educational reasons. Social reasons for the female include not only the pleasure of participating in the dating and mating rituals of our civilization but also the deadly serious business of husband hunting.

One of the most interesting accounts of how the systems of marriage making and higher education mesh smoothly together is an article entitled "Sororities and the Husband Game," by Scott (1965). As Scott notes, the means of managing courtship in other, simpler cultures might seem obvious and perhaps a little vulgar to us today. He reports that the Bantok people of the Philippines, for example, keep their girls in a special house, called the *olag*, where lovers call, sex play is free, and marriage is supposed to result. Scott, with tongue only partly in cheek, states that this and other exotic examples of marriage preparation are a standard topic in anthropology lectures in most universities because it acts to keep the sorority girls in the audience alert and interested. Scott maintains that the sorority house of the modern campus is in many ways no more than a streamlined version of the *olag*.

The Sorority House

Parents in every society have always had a vital interest in getting their daughters married. The problem for the parents is to establish the proper conditions to assure that their daughters are available for marriage to the right kind of man and that they are protected from romantic contact with the wrong kind of man. Parents have, of course, tried to solve this problem in different ways in different eras and in different cultures. As an example of one solution, Scott describes the *shtetl* society of Jewish villages in eastern Europe, in which marriages were arranged by a *shatchen* (professional matchmaker). Because this society was strictly *endogamous*—that is, allowed marriage only within its group—the worth of a *shatchen* was defined by his ability to match girls and boys with a fine eye for relative family status within the subsociety as well as for the personal compatibility of the prospective couple.

With the disappearance of the old country customs of the *shatchen* and related devices for guiding marriage into the proper channels, a new solution was needed—one adapted to the delay in marriage occasioned by continuing education. For the members of the American middle classes, the shift in the technique for making sure that offspring marry at an equal, if not a superior, social level was far less drastic than that confronting the immigrant family from the *shtetl*. Shortly after college education for girls became an entrenched part of the American social structure, the parents established the interlocking sorority and fraternity systems as a means of protecting their own social position.

The fraternity system, which existed for many years before sororities were invented, became the model for the female version of fellowship. However, because the needs and problems of the females in our society differ substantially from those of the males, the fraternity model was transformed into something more comfortable and useful for women—home base in the husband hunt. Thus, sororities, according to Scott, became a kind of university convent in which the skills and mysteries of life are learned.

With the practical wisdom born of experience, parents realize that love will happen at this age however excellent the child rearing methods employed. The solution to the problem of love is simple, however: Let it happen but control the object most likely to receive that affection. The sorority system does exactly that. It regulates and refines the flow of men who will have close contact with marriageable daughters. To some degree, every sorority jealously manages the social life of its members and acts as a shield between the impulsive girl and a commitment to an improper path in life. This improper path is most often defined as marriage beneath her class and outside her ethnic, racial, or religious group.

The ritual of the sorority encourages a steady progression from casual dating to eventual marriage. Typically, the ritual involves a required and stylized participation in the public declaration of the girl's readiness for marriage and her willingness to continue along the socially dictated path.

" . . . *the fraternity model was transformed into something more comfortable and useful for women—home base in the husband hunt.*"

Thus, with fraternity boys serenading outside the sorority house after dinner, the pinning ritual is performed in full view of the social and cultural group in which the girl has invested her most important personal interest.

Nevertheless, the sorority house as a major agent in the sexual socialization of the college girl may be becoming less important. Every major campus is undergoing a shift in its conception of responsibility for the social life of its students. Consequently, although freshman girls are still viewed as requiring the *in loco parentis* treatment, women who have survived that first year are being granted the freedom to live life as their conscience dictates. It seems that the high rise apartment populated by three or four girls sharing the expenses of living is to be the new fashion of the times. And a pattern of conduct that is fitted to this living condition will evolve accordingly.

SEX AND DEVIATION

The dimensions of heterosexual adjustment are made most clear by contrasting it with the fate of those who fail to become fully masculine or feminine as defined by society, lead lives of desperate anxiety, and raise their young in their own image. When the socialization of sexuality fails, its impact reaches through a number of generations and affects the lives of many different people.

Sex thus poses a great many problems for this and every other organized society. Among young children, sexual problems (from the adult point of view) focus on too much, too early. Sexual language used by young children suggests that they know more than they ought to at such a tender age. Young children are essentially limited to sexual play (the inspection of the genitalia of one another while playing "doctor" games), early heterosexual experience among unsupervised children, and individual and group-organized masturbation among boys. We expect children to be asexual in the early years and then to reverse these

attitudes, interests, and feelings when society finds it comfortable for them to "become" sexual. The severe discontinuity between the before and after roles that we demand the growing child learn confronts us with one of the most delicate challenges of socialization.

Deviation in sexual practices or choice of object for sexual expression, the time in life at which one becomes a sexual person, and the kind of sexual self that others take one to be all become focal points for personal and social difficulty. At the extremes of sexual deviation, the problem is obvious to everyone as well as to the individual. However, it is perhaps in the invisible distortion of the average person's sexual expression that the greatest toll of sexuality is taken. Failures in socialization that result in homosexuality, lesbianism, sexual perversion, and the like probably ought to be of less concern to us than the uncounted number of adults in our society who lead moderately distorted, anxiety laden lives through overemphasizing sexual behavior as a crucial test of a successful life.

The socialization practices that produce deviation in sexual life are not exactly the same kind that result in sexual anxiety in otherwise acceptably adjusted adults. If the members of our society rely too heavily and dramatically on sexual success as a measure of the worth of the person, it can only be that socialization has reached beyond the intended goals to produce unintended side effects. The form of socialization practices must be unique to the direction that deviation takes; it is not merely a function of the intensity of the practices or the degree to which they are learned. However, the degree of overt, consistent deviation may differ in accordance with the intensity of the dynamic parent-child relationship.

Several steps are needed to socialize the child to a deviant sexual life. First, the developing child must learn that sexual feelings, attitudes, and functions are a vital theme in life—a theme that can encompass a host of lesser themes and culminate in a total focus of existence. In this way, he learns that sex can be used as a weapon to hurt others, as a means of providing missing self-assurance, as a way to validate role fulfillment, or as the basis for evaluating his developing self-image.

Moreover, deviation in sexual activity, at least for lower class adolescents, can be traced to socialization practices that involve a failure to encourage identification with like-sexed parents and an emphasis on sexual expression coupled with severe and harsh punishment. Punished harshly and hurt in a variety of ways, the young person may find in sexual activity a means of self-expression, reassurance, revenge, and assertion of power (McCord, McCord, and Verden, 1962).

Thus, studies of the early sex life of sex delinquents and sex criminals reveal that an extremely high percentage of them had been "frequently or severely" beaten between two and 17 years of age by one or both parents. Punished severely and violently, they sought such compensatory outlets as were available, and sex proved to be perfectly appropriate to their needs (Hartogs, 1951). When urges to heterosexuality are overlaid with pain and punishment, when the like-sexed parent is weak and ineffective and the opposite-sexed parent dominant and commanding, we have fertile ground for identification with and imitation of the parent of the wrong sex. Indeed, whether through identification with a poor model, inconsistently applied reward and punishment, or absence of supervision and control, an immature, self-indulgent, uncontrolled adult can be fashioned (Ellis, 1951). For this adult, heterosexuality is an impossible achievement.

For the male, sexual deviation most frequently assumes the form of homosexuality, although the outcome of sexual socialization may be fetishism (the use of some object other than a member of the opposite sex for sexual satisfaction) or exhibitionism (the compulsive display of genital organs). In both fetishism and exhibitionism, the socialization process has produced an infantile, fearful, immature person unable to identify with the adult sexual role and capable only of making abortive, symbolic imitations of full sexuality.

Estimates of homosexual experience among adolescents range from 11 to 50 percent (Kinsey, Pomeroy, and Martin, 1948; Landis, 1956), but there is a rough consensus that, following this period of experimentation, most males adjust to the heterosexual role. The fundamental basis for homosexuality is the failure to learn the social lesson on the object of sexual choice. This deviant socialization has been attributed to a lack of heterosexual companionship while growing up, inhibition of normal heterosexual drives, the gap between physical and social readiness for sexual experience, identification with the opposite-sexed parent, or pain and discomfort with first sexual adventuring.

The homosexual and the lesbian are similar in many respects. Both are "tense, restless, immature, bewildered, and fearful" (Bender and Pastor, 1941). The like-sexed sexual relationship is one dominated less by sex than by infantile interpersonal relationships that can never, because of their immaturity, be long-lasting or satisfying to those involved.

However, the different social views of these deviations produce different effects on males and females. The male seeks solace with members of his own sex only at substantial cost to his self-esteem, for our society violently rejects such unions and makes them illicit and anxiety laden events. Although lesbianism reflects a similar inability to accept the psychological and social role that society dictates as appropriate to one's biology, less social criticism is traditionally leveled against those females who choose not to become heterosexual.

In addition, the female socialized to a state of antagonism to males may engage in frequent heterosexual behavior (promiscuity or prostitution) in order to reaffirm a deep-lying belief in the essential worthlessness of the male. Thus, sexual promiscuity in girls can be a fundamental means of finding immediate social acceptance to compensate for deep-seated feelings of inferiority stemming from inadequate socialization in the early years. And promiscuity can be an expression of anger and resentment written large in retaliation against an unjust world. In this sense, too, promiscuity is another form of protest at an inadequacy accumulated in the process of growing up.

INSTITUTIONS, EMOTIONAL DISTURBANCE, AND SEX [1]

In emotionally disturbed children, sexual behavior is a delicate psychological problem that requires sensitive management by responsible adults. However, there are few clear and detailed accounts of the nature of sexual behavior among institutionalized children and of methods for dealing with it. Moreover, it is doubtful whether these reports reflect practices *typical* of most institutions.

Probably the most extreme statement of theory is A. S. Neill's description (1960) of Summerhill. He maintains, for example, that "sex is the basis of all negative attitudes toward life" (p. 206), "that heterosexual play in childhood is the royal road . . . to a healthy, balanced adult sex life" (p. 206), and that "at Summerhill, nothing is unmentionable and no one is shockable" (p. 233). However, he does not carry out his theory in practice; he notes, "if in Summerhill I approved of my adolescent pupils sleeping together, my school would be suppressed by the authorities" (p. 209). It is difficult to find a modern, systematic, and detailed representation of the more conservative point of view that probably characterizes the average institution.

Several factors are responsible for this scarcity of careful delineation of the principles of the institutional management of sex in emotionally disturbed children. One reason is that institutional life is a highly artificial subsociety that has unique needs. Another is that professional views of children's sexual attitudes and behavior are probably more "radical" and "permissive" than

[1] The material in this section is adapted with permission from E. B. McNeil and W. C. Morse, "The Institutional Management of Sex in Emotionally Disturbed Children." *Amer. J. Orthopsychiat.*, 1964, 34, 115–124.

those held by the average member of society. However, even professionally "liberated" child care workers do not respond to sexual behavior in children with as much psychological comfort as to other forms of behavior. Thus, the notion that extensive agreement exists on a psychologically healthy approach to sex education for children is an illusion that retains its apparent substance by avoiding close scrutiny.

The Fusion of Sex, Aggression, and Guilt

The problems of controlling sexual behavior and its attendant anxiety and guilt are primarily the consequence of the fusion of sex and aggression. Among disturbed boys, both sexual behavior and its concomitants are soon tinged with aggressive overtones. The male sexual role is normally one of enterprise and domination, and its regulation requires a high degree of sensitivity to the more passive female partner. The blunted sensibility of damaged children blurs the distinction between self-assertion and hostility; sex and aggression become almost indistinguishable.

Thus, whether the boy's sexual excursions are homosexual, heterosexual, or exhibitionistic, they have an assaultive quality about them. Sex language and gesture become desexualized as they are used to offend adults and peers. The child who hates adults, who have always been viewed as punishing, finds sexual acting out a natural weapon (McNeil, 1959). Moreover, sorting out sex and aggression is difficult for both the therapist and the child because sex is physically pleasurable. The child maintains that the excitement and gratification is a sufficient end in itself, so that any attempt to outline the aggressive components of his pleasure meets a wall of resistance.

A source of equal difficulty is the regularity with which sexual expression induces guilt that can be assuaged only by concrete punishment. Confession and discussion may not seem to be adequate atonement for what the child may see as the enormity of his transgression. In the magical thinking of the unconscious, the violation of a powerful taboo can be cleansed only by an antidote of equal power. In such instances, the offending child may embark on a program of violence and provocation calculated to force punishment and thus "even" his psychic score. The almost compulsive nature of the child's relentless search for freedom from guilt and anxiety can continue until his goal is reached and the adult finally disciplines the child (perhaps days later) for (in the child's mind) his sexual infraction.

By this time in the child's sequence of behavior, he may have provoked so much anger and resentment among peers and adults that the whole issue circles back on itself in a prolonged series of retaliations and counter-retaliations—all of which can be traced to the original sexual transgression. In much the same fashion, children who commit sexual acts that produce substantial feelings of guilt may redouble sexual as well as aggressive activity in an attempt to relieve guilt by sharing it with many others. The psychic isolation of being the lone offender is intolerable to most children, and they feel less guilt ridden if others share their plight.

Adult Responses to Sexual Behavior

The most common method used by child care workers in institutions is suppression of sexual behavior in the child. Although the motives for this action may be credible, its effect is seldom therapeutic. First, suppression ignores the meaning of the sexual act and, therefore, draws much too thin a line between "you shouldn't" and "it's wrong." Moreover, suppression is self-defeating because it attempts to cover up symptoms rather than deal with causes. Action of this sort sets the stage for a much greater outburst at some later time.

It is axiomatic that there is no neutral zone for dealing with the sexual expressions of children. Adults who lean too heavily on ignoring low-level expressions of sex soon find the child

taking advantage of this tacit permission to engage in a more advanced form of sexual misbehavior. One of the reasons for this common attempt to remain neutral is that adults react to sex as though legal rules of evidence were necessary for it to be discussed. Although adults can comfortably query a child about the possibility that he stole from or aggressed against another child, they seem to require incontrovertible evidence before initiating an inquiry about sexual misbehavior.

The child capitalizes on the adult's reluctance to probe the area of sexual behavior and uses it as a lever against the adult. Exploration of possible sexual incidents is, of course, an extremely tortuous task. The child obfuscates and lies to maintain a wall of silence toward the controlling adult. The tentativeness of the adult's approach to the task is often a sufficient cue for the child, and he reacts accordingly—that is, he launches his most powerful weapons at what he detects to be a flaw in the adult's psychological structure. Adult neutrality is most often a defensive avoidance of sex.

A similar approach is to "therapeutically" permit erotic arousal with an unclear view of what is therapeutic about the passive acceptance of overt sexual expression. The distinction between acceptance and permission is an indistinct one, and, although an adult is willing to sanction moderate sexual expression, he may not always be willing to sanction the excess to which it may shortly lead. The subtle encouragement provided by remaining passive at the first stages of such expression is always to the child an extreme contrast to the later restrictiveness that appears when the bounds of "propriety" have been crossed.

Ignorance of sexuality is just as dangerous as over-reacting to it. Evidences of sexual activity that would set off an alarm in the consciousness of an experienced worker are usually overlooked by novices. And it often seems that those closest to the child are unaware of sexual material that would seem blatant to an outside observer.

In any institutional setting, a certain amount of sexual by-play exists between the adults, which is subject to misinterpretation by the children.

Moreover, again and again, female child-care workers make friendly overtures to male children in a manner that may be indistinguishable from the seductiveness that is more appropriately expended on adult male courting partners. In much the same fashion, the male child-care worker can easily fall into a relationship with his charges that closely resembles that of a peer member of the "gang." Swapping tales of early sexual experiences and using a "one of the boys" approach has its dangers if it is not lodged in properly mature workers. Adults need to distinguish between personal and clinical sex attitudes and come to some understanding of the congruence between them.

SUMMARY

The socialization of sexuality is a continuous process, but it becomes urgent when the developing child reaches puberty. At that time, most of the early learning about sexual modesty and taboo areas of exploration is tested in the acquisition of new sexual roles. The transition from asexual young person to fully sexual adult (as this is defined in our culture at this time) is formalized by a social pattern of dating and mating calculated to control the approach to marriage and keep it within appropriate social, racial, ethnic, and religious circles.

The socialization of sexuality was always a trying task for parents, and it has now become even more difficult. The sexual revolution has made the process of socializing children's attitudes, values, ideals, beliefs, and motives a tenuous and anxiety laden affair and has become a source of increased intergenerational conflict. Patterns of boy-girl relationships have changed, and the female is being accorded greater choice in the execution of her sexual role now that she has attained greater social and economic freedom. The additional freedom from unwanted pregnancy has forced the proper male-female relationship both before and after marriage to be re-examined.

The socialization of sexuality takes a deviant form for a small proportion of the members of our society. Homosexuality, lesbianism, fetishism, and exhibitionism reflect a socialization that has produced an anxious, immature, inadequate adult incapable of performing the sexual role required by society. Clear-cut, overt deviation is a dramatic instance of the failure of socialization, but less than full and vigorous fulfillment of the adult heterosexual role may be more common and represent the greatest failure in our attempts to socialize sexuality.

Part six

Socialization in
the adult years

As every adolescent one day learns, becoming an adult is not a sudden and highly visible change in status. For most people, the change to adulthood is so gradual that it is usually apparent only after it has taken place. However, entrance into adulthood does not signal the end of change, for there is no period in life that is free of developmental tasks.

THE DEVELOPMENTAL TASKS OF EARLY ADULTHOOD

In the first years of adulthood, a great deal of exploration and testing of possibilities for the future take place. The young adult is for the first time free to try his wings in a variety of life circumstances without parental interference. The newness of this phase of life means that most situations must be encountered without the advantage of previous experience. At this time, many of the individual's occupational, marital, and social patterns of life may be formulated. The vocational and marital adjustments typical of this period account for the final weaning of the young person from financial and emotional support by his parents.

16

The socialization of the young adult

These adjustments thus constitute the major developmental tasks of early adulthood, which include mating, learning married life, rearing children, establishing a home, beginning an occupation, finding an appropriate social group, and accepting the responsibility of citizenship (Vincent and Martin, 1961). The male must become a husband, father, and wage earner, while the female must become a wife, mother, and homemaker. Each of these central roles involves a host of subroles, so that early adulthood is as complex a social, personal, and psychological event as any other in life. The individual must have great deftness and flexibility if he is to succeed equally in all his roles. Many of the roles are compatible, while others are in substantial conflict. Merging these roles into a comfortable whole becomes a particularly trying task for some adults.

Although the roles of the male do conflict, they are probably more stable than those of the female. The overall role of the female in our culture has been shifting and expanding for a number of years and continues to do so. Thus, it is particularly difficult for the female to learn a role pattern that she can use throughout her life. In many ways, much of the comfort with which either the male or the female will fulfill his or her role is a function of the condition of the society at the time that each enters early adulthood. Depression, violent cultural shift, war, and so forth are all potent factors in setting the limits of role playing, although the social class in which the individual struggles, his race, and a host of additional factors influence role adjustment.

It has been estimated that the time of greatest stability in the individual's life is when he is between the ages of about 30 and the early forties. At this time, he has reached the apex of his skills and abilities and normally experiences increasing security based on accomplishment. Further, in many respects, the direction that the future is likely to take becomes more visible to him, so that some continuity in life becomes increasingly apparent. Marriage and friendship patterns are also stabilized, and there is comfort in the successful transition through this age. At this age, many of the previous problems of adjustment become barely remembered remnants of the distant past.

When early adulthood brings with it success and social reward, this period can be one of the most satisfying times of life. The resultant sense of confidence is particularly valuable as a preparation for the tasks of life yet to come, but not all individuals find confidence and comfort in early adulthood. The problems of personal and social adjustment that occur at this time are more serious in some respects than those taking place earlier in life if for no other reason than that with age the chances of repair are considerably diminished. And, consequently, these problems bring with them a sense of finality and ultimate failure. This is not an easy stage of life to negotiate.

Most older people look back on young adulthood as the time of their greatest happiness. This period for men is one of a heavy investment of interest in work. Although a happy family life is important to them, it is less pre-eminent than work. For women, the satisfactions of housekeeping and raising children are usually most important (Morgan, 1937; Landis, 1942). Thus, cardinal features of young adulthood and important aspects of the socialization process at this time are work and marriage.

MARRIAGE, THE SOCIALIZER

In most if not all societies, marriage is a particularly important indication of transition from one social category to another. Society makes this transition formal and public through the use of ritual. For example, in one society, after the bride price has been paid, the girl's father organizes a feast for which the groom pays. At the feast, the couple eat in a separate room that only very close relatives can enter. At nighttime, the girl friends of the bride spirit her away and hide her in the village, so that the young man must sometimes search all night for her. Once he has found her, he enters a special room where the

"The rituals of modern American marriage are probably no less bizarre than those of ancient tribes."

guests have gathered. When he enters this room, he must break a red thread held across the threshold. If he fails to see the thread, he falls down and everyone makes fun of him. After he sits down, the guests depart one by one. When he is alone, the bride is brought to him by her girl friends. The bride removes his boots, he gives her a silver coin, and she is transported the next morning to the home of her in-laws, where she must not come face-to-face with her father-in-law for over a year (Van Gennep, 1960).

The rituals of modern American marriage are probably no less bizarre than those of ancient tribes. "Something old, something new, something borrowed, and something blue" sounds very much like the mystical incantation of tribesmen of the past bent on circumventing the multitude of taboos surrounding marriage. Yet somehow our marriage rituals seem to have become a sterile reflection of the more earthy rituals of the past. Our rituals have little current meaning and are no more than symbolic tokens connecting us with our past.

In our society, married life is considered to be the normal, desired condition that brings the

greatest personal happiness and fulfillment and permits the proper exercise of sex for procreation and individual satisfaction. The single adult life, by contrast, is viewed as empty and barren. Consequently, women are under considerable social pressure to marry, as are men—although the greater courting and sexual initiative assumed by men has obscured the comparable pressure on them. Adult males who postpone marriage into their thirties become objects of distress and conspiracy among friends and relatives.

Partly as a result of social pressure and partly as a result of individual decision making, most Americans marry in their twenties. The average age at first marriage for men is just under 23 and for females is about 21.5. Thus, among the 25–29 year olds, 81 percent of the males are married, as are 91 percent of the females.

According to our society, marriage should be based on affection and choice; arranged marriages are considered to be a musty relic of ancient times. In the same way, the criterion of a successful marriage is the personal happiness of the husband and wife. It is also generally agreed that some people are likely to attain more happiness in marriage than others (Terman, 1938; Burgess and Cottrell, 1939; Kelly, 1939; Burgess and Wallin, 1953). Because personality factors and the complementarity of the couple's needs are particularly important, the characteristics most predictive of happiness in marriage originate in early childhood experiences and reflect the happiness and lack of conflict of the parental marriage. Thus, a happy childhood seems essential for a happy marriage (Katz, Cohen, and Castiglione, 1963; Pond, Ryle, and Hamilton, 1963).

Finally, in our society, the family roles of husband and wife are supposed to be based on a sexual division of labor with the male status being superior. The husband is to be the head of his family, its main economic support, and its representative in the larger community. Women, consigned to domesticity, are to be mothers and homemakers.

This description of the values of the American family may seem like a severe and highly restricted portrait of how family life is to be led. It is apparent that this description fits some families better than others and is a total misfit for a number of families. Minority groups in our culture, for example, regularly reverse or alter certain of these prescriptions. Yet, because this is the model held to be ideal by the controlling middle class society, this one is the yardstick for measuring the success or failure of a family.

Further, this theoretical description is not completely accurate, for the relationships in every family are constantly changing, even though they may remain within the realm of what society considers desirable. Thus, for example, although there are broad prescriptions about how each role should be played, the fine details must be hammered out in the ability of each partner to influence the other's personality and behavior. Each spouse becomes the socializer of the other and attempts to shape the response of the partner by using the familiar devices of acceptance and rejection, reward and punishment. Vices, pastimes, hobbies, habits, and even old friends are abandoned or relationships to them modified in order to maintain the security and satisfaction of a happy marriage, for each partner was not socialized along exactly the same social, emotional, behavioral, and expressive lines that his mate was.

Consequently, in marriage, the previous socialization of each of the partners is modified. Engaged couples rarely make a systematic exploration of each other's attitudes, values, needs, habits, or motives, so that marriage becomes a prolonged learning of what courtship neglected. If one partner differs from the other on each of a host of dimensions, some compromise must be made. It is in the compromising process that continued alteration of one's pattern of socialization takes place. Moreover, work, children, and new social responsibilities and roles to fulfill in marriage mean the learning of new patterns of response. A new public role as a married couple must be established and practiced and a new private accommodation to intimacy achieved. The need to live harmoniously with a loved one, to succeed at marriage, and maintain a public image

as a happily married person are all important to the individual's self-esteem. Thus, for his own reasons, for the reasons of his mate, and to satisfy public pressure, the individual is modified along emotional, social, behavioral, and expressive dimensions.

OCCUPATION, THE SOCIALIZER

At the beginning of young adulthood, the individual must make the vitally important choice of an occupation, which will in large part determine the direction and tenor of the rest of his life. Making this decision may not be easy, for, to begin with, there are at least 20,000 different occupations from which to choose. Moreover, the individual may have to make up his mind by late adolescence because many occupations require several years of training in the educational system. Thus, early in his life, the individual must be able to recognize the abilities, interests, and needs that will characterize him for most of the rest of his life and then match them with an occupation.

Another factor complicating the decision on an occupation is our society's continuing technological advances. Many of the tasks previously dealt with by human beings are now being handled in a superior fashion by machines. And this trend toward replacing men with machines will doubtless continue. Consequently, the young person is confronted for the first time in history with the grave possibility that the career he chooses may become obsolete long before he retires—or even before he has finished training himself for it.

Nonetheless, how to find satisfying work is an important issue in our complex and industrialized culture, for if the young person cannot find work that will continue to satisfy him, he will have no self-respect and no peace of mind. The necessity of higher education is, of course, an important part of this issue. A greater number of occupations are open to the college graduate, so that it should be easier for him to find work congenial with his interests. However, many college graduates are not satisfied with their occupations. According to one survey of 9,000 college graduates (Havemann and West, 1952), 25 percent of the subjects wished that they had studied a different field. For example, 14 percent of the home economics majors thought that the humanities would have offered more promise, 18 percent of the predental students believed that some other profession would have been more rewarding, and 19 percent of the engineering students felt that some branch of engineering different from the one that they had studied would have been more rewarding. In fine arts and music, 22 percent of the graduates were convinced that the social sciences would have offered greater promise, 24 percent of those who had studied philosophy and religion also felt the social sciences would have been more appealing, and 24 percent of those who had studied either science or mathematics felt that a different branch of science would have been more compatible. On the other hand, only 9 percent of those in premedical studies wished that they had studied something else.

Medicine, besides being satisfying to most of those studying it, regularly has a high attraction for students in other fields. Thus, 25 percent of the agriculture and forestry students believed that medicine would have been more rewarding, 14 percent of the prelaw students felt that they would have been better off in medicine, and 33 percent of the students of history, literature, and language would have preferred medical practice as an occupation. A major reason for this preference is the social status attributed to certain occupations; it is easy to become dissatisfied with one's work if its image is less socially acceptable than another's. The highest social status has always been accorded to the physician. Next in rank, socially, are bankers, stock brokers, superintendents of state institutions, officers in the Army or the Navy, managers of businesses, hotel keepers, grade school teachers, real estate and insurance agents, retail traders, and, finally, commercial travelers. At the lowest end of the scale are laundry workers, unskilled factory workers, farm laborers, casual laborers, and coal miners.

Nonetheless, work assignments ranging from the low status psychiatric attendant (Simpson and Simpson, 1959) to the high prestige of medical practice (Becker *et al.*, 1961) all require the individual to learn the work role. The skills and knowledge needed for each role must usually be practiced on the job. And the successful mastery of that job means learning a new set of values, attitudes, motives, habits, and often interests (Corwin, 1961; Taylor and Pellegrin, 1960; Hughes, 1958). An example of this learning process is socialization in the armed services. Here the occupational socialization methods are consciously designed and carefully executed (Bidwell, 1961). Uniforms, regulations, fixed punishments, total control over the person to be socialized, peer pressure to conform, and models of success are all brought to bear on the civilian in order to make him value the military role quickly and to alienate him from his previous values, habits, attitudes, and motives. Military socialization re-establishes the child-parent kind of dependent and controlling relationship in order to achieve its goal, and it succeeds surprisingly well.

Civilian employers have a much less easy time in socializing employees. Without complete control over the individual, the socializers must rely more heavily on security needs, intrinsic motivation, incentives, and rewards. The married worker is easier to socialize into the proper work role because his failure to become properly socialized has economic consequences for others as well as himself. These methods work, however, with any individual because so much of his self-esteem is derived from his labor and from the prestige that he and others ascribe to his job. The secondary contributors to his self-esteem (material possessions, work satisfaction, and so forth) are an important part of his ability to be socialized for work. Finally, this ability must be a continuing one, for, from novice to retiree, the worker experiences a series of changes in his role. He must learn these new patterns and modify his internal experience to make them into familiar and accepted parts of the self.

HIGHER EDUCATION, THE SOCIALIZER

Advanced education is another agent of socialization for many middle class young people and for an increasing number of lower class youths. The decision to attend college is, for these young people, a function of their definition of their adult role. The transition from high school to the freshman year in college is a model of the transition from adolescence into early adulthood. The adolescent must separate himself from his parents, siblings, and close friends if he is to go to college. He must exercise greater autonomy in making decisions, assume increasing responsibility for regulating his own behavior, establish new friendships, face new internal and external pressures toward adult sexuality, and deal with new intellectual challenges.

The adolescent can prepare himself to face these tasks in a variety of ways, as a study by Silber *et al.* (1961) indicates. These researchers conducted individual interviews with a small group of students preparing for college who displayed *competence*. The criteria used to determine competence were the ability to achieve academically, the ability to maintain interpersonal closeness with a peer, and the ability to participate in social groups. The group studied lived in a suburb of Washington, D.C. that was composed primarily of middle class professional people.

The majority of the students interviewed expressed a positive attitude toward the newness of the experience that they were about to undergo. Newness in itself did not produce anxiety. Instead, the newness was seen as something desirable, exciting, and rewarding—something to look forward to rather than retreat from. These students looked forward to making new friends, being on their own, being separated from their families, and accomplishing the new tasks involved in attending college. The urge for new friendships and new bonds was coupled with a readiness to sever relationships of the past. Thus,

"Advanced education is another agent of socialization for many middle class young people and for an increasing number of lower class youths."

the avoidance of high school friends or acquaintances was a part of choosing roommates.

The preparations that these students made for college reflected a great deal of self-reliance. They managed correspondence with their colleges, prepared their clothes, worked out financial arrangements, and the like. In an example given by Silber, one student shopped for clothes, corresponded with his future roommate, attended a dinner for freshmen going to his college, arranged for medical examinations, and made financial arrangements with his parents. This student also corresponded with one of his advisers at college in order to develop early plans for getting a part-time job. He reviewed courses offered in the catalogue in order to get some idea of what he would like to study during his first year.

These competent students anticipated that the shift from high school to college would resemble the kind of adjustment they found necessary to make in moving from junior high to senior high school. They felt that the gap between themselves viewed as high school students and as college students would be less serious than most of us would expect; they felt competent and ready for the new experience. Many of the students prepared themselves by gaining information about the new situation in order to make it less threatening and less difficult.

In addition, many of the students rehearsed the kind of behavior that they thought would be associated with college students and thus underwent *anticipatory socialization*. These students discussed the grades that they might receive in college and prepared themselves for the possibility that they would not be as superior in college as they were in high school. Finally, there was a great deal of fantasy rehearsal of future behavior. A young person anticipating taking a job would undergo very much the same sort of experience and find it useful.

Education and Psychological Change

The college experience produces psychological as well as intellectual changes. One important psychological change that seems to occur is an increase in *world-mindedness* (Garrison, 1961). In their four-year stay in college, students modify their local, parochial grasp of domestic and international affairs in the direction of greater awareness of and concern for the population of the planet as a whole. The graduating senior has more awareness of events far removed from him and responds with greater involvement than does his freshman brother. Thus, attendance at college seems to alter the attitudes of students in a direction highly desirable for an enlightened democracy.

A related psychological change that occurs in college is a decrease in *dogmatism*. All dogma is belief accepted because of authority rather than belief based on evidence. Students become less dogmatic through exposure to the varied opinions, attitudes, and beliefs of their professors and fellow students (Rokeach, 1960). The process of socialization of the young adult in college is thus

in many respects a continuation of his prior experience with his peer group. Now, however, the composition of the available peer group has suddenly changed; it consists of persons whose views have been shaped by environments and people quite alien to the average student's experience. The student's frame of reference shifts imperceptibly as even his most firmly held convictions are eroded by the need to be accepted by his peers and not to deviate too far from the values to which they subscribe.

This modification of values, beliefs, and opinions could not occur in a young adult in whom the need for acceptance by others was absent. Such a student would enter a university with fixed ideas and emerge four years later with his convictions deepened and confirmed by all his experiences. The freshman student uncertain of his ideas and needful of acceptance by his peers is open to sudden and radical alteration of his view of life. The same freshman may find that these ideational changes are superficial and easily discarded when he is exposed to continued socialization in business and industry following graduation. As his peer group and frame of reference are changed in the business world, his attitudes and his behavior may change accordingly.

The belief systems of college students seem to become less opinionated and rigid no matter what kind of college they attend; Catholic universities, Protestant colleges, public and private universities, and junior colleges all report very much the same changes in their students. However, it may be that these findings are only evidence of the changes that usually occur in brighter than average young people whether they attend college or not, for, at this age, all such young people tend to become less dogmatic, less authoritarian, and less ethnocentric (Plant, 1962).

These psychological changes in the young adult alter, of course, his social and political views. Consequently, a small percentage of young people become picketing, placard carrying objectors to the current of social life. And, for others, exposure to college life moves them further to the right and its pronational values.

The Protest Generation

The protest generation is so colorful and so visible that young people of a conservative bent have been almost ignored. The history of the conservative position has always been one of non-participation in the activism of picket lines, protest marches, and so on, for the traditional conservative is a person who is satisfied with the existing social arrangement and content that he will achieve his goals within it. However, a new generation of conservative activists oriented toward the extreme right has arisen on many college campuses in the second half of the 1960s. For example, in 1965 and 1966, the Young Americans for Freedom recruited young people in the universities and high schools across the land who have begun to express openly a minority view about what is good and necessary for America.

The conservatism of today is hardly a movement to maintain the status quo. It is, rather, a massive attempt to alter both the present state of affairs and the direction that conservatives think America is taking. Conservatives seek, whether on the level of national politics, local government, or the college campus, a new and sometimes radical alteration of the American way of life. In some ways, the alteration is as radical as that sought by their archenemies, the radical left. This movement from inertia to activism seems to conservatives to be dictated by the visible successes of the left and the continuing struggle between communism and democracy.

This conversion of the college age conservative into a political activist is a concomitant of the socialization process. *Conversion* is in its essence a normal adolescent phenomenon, "incidental to the passage from the child's small universe to the wider intellectual and spiritual life of maturity" (James, 1902, p. 199). As the adolescent leaves home and secondary school for college, he faces the need to define for himself the ethical, moral, and social position that he will occupy—he needs to form an image of himself as an adult. While making this transition from dependent young per-

"*The protest generation is so colorful and so visible that young people of a conservative bent have been almost ignored.*"

son to independent adult, he makes "shocking" discoveries about the condition of the world that he is about to enter, and the seeds are sown for the conversion from passive to activist conservative (Schiff, 1964). In college and in contact with a wider range of opinions about morality, the adolescent becomes aware of his fundamentally conservative view of life at the same time that he reacts with shock and repulsion to the opinions and behavior of this new set of peers. For some college students, the threat of the strangeness of what they encounter and the challenge to their views of life act to solidify and reinforce their conservative outlook. The radical outlook is no doubt consolidated in much the same fashion as that of the conservative.

The college activist, whether of the right or of the left, must decide if he is to match his actions to his words. One way to do so—while keeping the missionary spirit intact—is to join a social movement that is apolitical but dedicated to helping one's fellow man see the light. A perfect outlet for this missionary zeal is the Peace Corps, which is filled with the dedicated from both political extremes.

Critics at first suggested that the Peace Corps would become a form of institutionalized escape from normal responsibility. This suggestion was based on the fear that our culture had failed to provide an adequate emotional outlet for its youth and that service outside the United States would only underscore our social inadequacy. Certainly university life was proving to be an inadequate model of involvement with the community, and, in fact, fostered a kind of isolation from the mainstream of life. If anything, our intellectually able young people were using universities as a refuge from the confrontation with maturity and responsibility.

However, the experience of successful Peace Corps volunteers working in other countries has proved to be almost a model of what every culture should provide for its youths. These volunteers seem to develop through their two years of hard work a sensitivity to others, patience with the world condition, and a set of humane and ethical values uniquely combined with the qualities of courage and independence. The image of a Peace Corps volunteer has become one of a mature, sensitive yet tough young person—an ideal to be envied in any society. This maturity issues from performing a vitally important task—one that is real and not just a game—and from testing oneself in isolation against a difficult and trying experience that has about it the quality of trial by combat and is almost the moral equivalent of war.

Thus, the Peace Corps has been a cultural solution to the pressing needs of a certain segment of our youth. The Poverty Program was invented to meet the needs of an additional and quite distinct part of the young members of our population. However, the important observation here is not whether these programs will meet the total needs of the culture but whether they are a reflection of more vigorous efforts by social planners to shorten the cultural lag that has usually existed between the needs of our young people and the readiness of our society to devise mechanisms to meet them.

ESCAPE FROM SOCIALIZATION

Neither the university, the world of work, nor other social institutions have provided a meaningful outlet for the energies of all our young people. For a few, the pressures of adult life prove to be too weighty and too all-pervasive to be met with actions that are directed outward in an attempt to change the shape of the world. Some of these young people seek meaning in inner experience rather than outer encounter. For them, drugs provide the way to self-experience and, in some respects, establish an underground means of withdrawing from the hubbub of life. One of the most controversial of these drugs is LSD.

The LSD Consumers

LSD (L.S.D.-25, lysergic acid) belongs to a class of drugs called the utopiates, or mind altering drugs, which include silocybin, peyote, and a number of kinds of mushrooms (Blum, 1964). Those who try these drugs regularly report changes in their sensory experiences, emotions, attitudes about themselves, and feelings toward other people. The drug takers seem to be gratifying some very basic impulses and to be kicking over the traces of our usually conformist society and, as a consequence, seem threatening to those who brave the world without benefit of chemical stimulation. It has been estimated that there are about 40,000 drug addicts in America.

Typically, LSD users come from the social strata least expected to display chemical dependence. Some young people depend on LSD for the "kicks" that are produced, but these people are no more than a few of the many users of LSD. LSD users are to be found among our intellectuals, professionals, and scientists—people not normally a source of threat to the standards and values that society holds dear. If taking LSD represents a revolt against the current form of society, then it is indeed a very quiet one because users of LSD are primarily people who are successful and socially favored. There are, of course, as many opponents to drug use among our intellectuals as there are users. The opponents of the drug experience raise the issue of ethics and suggest that users, in one way or another, are drawn from the more fallible and problem laden group of citizens in our society and thus do not reflect the norm.

Although a person taking LSD can detect the difference between it and a drug such as heroin, the users of LSD or heroin are marked by a number of social similarities. The way in which LSD users interact with one another, the special language that they use to refer to the drug, the methods that they use to get other people to try it, and the psychological dependence that the drug produces are strikingly similar to the way of life of the heroin user (Killam, 1965). However, for LSD users, the setting and purposes connected with taking the drug are vital to its effects. If LSD takers gather together secretly to have an outlawed experience, then the drug produces experiences that correspond with those intentions. On the other hand, if taking LSD is designed to accomplish scientific and experimental purposes, the behavioral effect of the drug appears to be substantially different.

With the realization that the response to LSD is determined as much by the personality of the user as by the chemical properties of the drug itself, a series of moral issues have become important. We have begun to ask whether it is proper for an individual to turn inward via drugs and dwell on inner experience while rejecting outward or object-oriented kinds of transactions. A related issue is the question of whether people should be allowed to seek voluntary pleasure without restraint. There is, further, a question of individual rights—that is, does each of us have the right to decide how he will treat himself medically? For those with a religious orientation, the question has become whether the use of LSD in some way violates the natural order or God's will. Others ask whether LSD produces merely a glorious deception or reveals something of truth, something of a new path to man's salvation.

Thus, the survival of our culture in its present form has become an issue. What would happen if 80 percent of our citizens, for example, turned to LSD and its intensely personal, internal experience and abandoned contact with the outside world? We do not yet know whether using LSD represents a new social movement or merely the deviant behavior of a small group of people who are alienated from the current form of our culture. If taking LSD is indeed a new social movement, in order to be successful, it must, of course, be more than a negative attack on things as they are. It must offer new values that are more appropriate for the future. But as yet, LSD users seem to suggest only that they have found the problems of living so exasperating or meaningless that they have turned to drugs producing psychological experiences that promise a means of escaping from real life.

Drugs and Society

Our culture is by no means the only one with drug taking citizens. The Navaho Indian becomes absorbed in prayer and contemplation while eating peyote buttons, as may the Winnebago. For them, taking these consciousness expanding substances is part of a religious attempt to commune with the Great Spirit in order to understand more of life. And in our society today, no one should be very much surprised at the extensiveness of the use of mind altering drugs.

We develop a variety of drugs, we advertise them widely, we have the professionals to dispense them, and we have the markets in which to sell them. Hundreds of tons of drugs are produced

"Hundreds of tons of drugs are produced each year to be consumed by tens of millions of Americans."

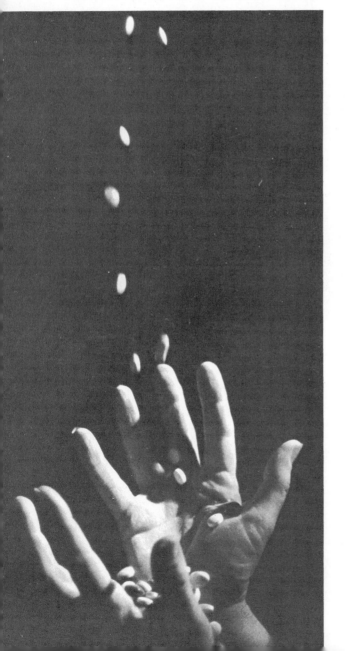

each year to be consumed by tens of millions of Americans. That seems to be a commentary on the nature of our society. It seems to provide both the misery from which drugs offer relief and the drugs designed to soothe them (Blum, 1964).

We are a society of sedatives, tranquilizers, energizers, stimulants, analgesics, and intoxicants. Alcohol is the most used and abused pleasure giving drug in our society. We have at least 40,000 liquor stores and thousands of other grocery and drug stores in which liquor is sold. In the United States, 800 million gallons of wine and distilled spirits and 100 million barrels of beer are produced each year. Considering that the alcoholic beverage industry spends about $200 million a year for advertising alone, the social reinforcement for drinking is enormous.

There are perhaps 6 million people in America who are psychologically dependent on alcohol. Moreover, the long-term physical effects of alcohol are more dangerous than those of almost any other pleasure giving drug. Alcohol, coupled with a disregard for health, can produce serious physical difficulties, including brain and liver damage. The total destructive reach of alcohol is, in fact, impossible to calculate. According to some estimates, about 15,000 deaths and 200,000 injuries are associated with drunken driving in the United States each year. Absenteeism, job loss, and accidents together produce an estimated annual loss of about $500 million in our economy.

Another class of drugs widely used in the United States is sedatives and tranquilizers. There are now more than 50 types of sedatives, or barbiturates, marketed under a variety of trade names. Most of them are easily available at moderate expense from drug stores by prescription or from the black market. It is calculated that in the United States nearly a million people are using these drugs extensively and perhaps in an abusive manner in the self-treatment of insomnia, anxiety, tension, and emotional disturbance. In each of the past 10 years, more than 700,000 pounds of barbiturates have been marketed in the United States; that is enough for more than 30 doses a year for every adult and child in the country

"Alcohol is the most used and abused pleasure giving drug in our society."

(Fort, 1965). Further, it is estimated that between 15 and 20 percent of all medical prescriptions are for these sedatives. Finally, there are more than 150 "non-habit forming" sleeping aids available without prescription.

The American population regularly uses a number of stimulants. Caffeine, which is contained in most coffee, tea, and cola drinks, is the most popular, and there are no legal or social controls exercised over it. The nicotine contained in tobacco might be classified as another stimulant. Among other stimulant drugs, the most prominent is a group called the amphetamines. Drugs such as dexedrine and benzedrine have been used since the early 1930s. They are not considered truly addictive although they may produce some toxic effects and dependence or habituation.

The drug marijuana (cannabis) is legally forbidden in the United States even though other cultures have used it freely for over 5,000 years. Marijuana comes from the dried leaves or tops of the female hemp plant. Medically, marijuana does not produce true addiction or nonreversible damage to the body but may produce some toxic effects and habituation. It has been suggested that marijuana might be medically less dangerous than alcohol. However, the social view of the danger of smoking marijuana outweighs any medical considerations—even though Fort (1965) maintains. that the use of marijuana does not lead to addiction, does not lead to the use of other narcotics, and is not responsible for juvenile delinquency or crime. Thus, the publicity about the catastrophic effects of marijuana may be more emotional myth than objective truth. Nonetheless, in our society, the use of this drug is viewed as dangerous in itself and symptomatic of social decay on the part of the user.

Opiates (narcotics), in the form of opium, have been in use in other societies for thousands of years. The active ingredients of the opium poppy—morphine and heroin—were refined at the turn of the century. Narcotics, like many other drugs, produce a sense of euphoria and relaxation in their users. This psychological state shortly results in addiction.

Other cultures besides ours have relied on drugs as a means of relieving their social misery. The Brahmin, for example, accepts the use of hashish at the same time that he rejects alcohol. The Western World accepts alcohol and rejects hashish or other opiates. The effect of drugs seems to differ by culture; in some cultures, drugs produce peace and quiet, while for others, they produce agitated emotional states. If it is reasonable to describe whole cultures in terms of inward or outward directions of orientation, then we might predict that a passive, contemplative citizenry would respond to the drug experience in a manner quite distinct from the inhabitants of an aggressive, warlike society (Slotkin, 1956; Finestone, 1960).

In any culture, the dependence on drugs may be a way of life for the rebel alienated from his fellow man. Drugs permit a kind of quiet revolution on the part of those who have reaped the harvest of material success but have found the crop strangely without intellectual nutrition or emotional satisfaction (Blum, 1964). In a society

oriented toward control of its citizenry, perhaps drugs offer the only escape for some of these men. The inner life is a region free of the clamor of the outside world—a region into which one can escape without fear of recrimination.

Perhaps there are pressures, tensions, and anxieties in our culture that force the middle class, upwardly mobile, aggressive, hard driving male to seek escape in chemistry. For example, it is the male in our culture who most often seeks out the LSD experience, and it is he who becomes the repeated user. Men, more than women, must contend with the push and shove of the Protestant ethic and the need to compete. Moreover, there are probably biological and social reasons that women are less likely to seek escape in this form. Women rely heavily for their social status and personal well-being on the kind of interpersonal relationship that they are capable of establishing with males. Thus, a husband's LSD experience must be threatening to his wife in a very fundamental way because it is an experience that must exclude all relationships with others; the drug experience is an intensely personal and private event that can be interpreted by the woman as a withdrawal from contact with her. LSD, then, is a way out of adulthood. Early adulthood makes demands on all of us, and drugs offer a way out for a few.

SUMMARY

The socialization process for the young adult occurs in settings in which there is less restriction than that usually provided by parents. As responsibility for learning the early adult role is passed to the person to be socialized, he is offered more freedom and simultaneously less protection. The agents of his continued socialization now assume the form of a wife, an employer, a professor, or a peer.

The attitudes, values, motives, beliefs, goals, and interests that the young adult acquired as a youth must now be tested against a real world in which the payoff of early socialization is in quite concrete and sometimes painful form. He must learn what the world is really like and accommodate to it by acquiring proficiency in those skills and patterns of behavior that will allow him to play a productive and satisfying adult role.

Socialization to these adult ends may be too painful, frightening, or unrewarding for some people. Thus, the destruction of the personality through emotional breakdown is the fate of some. Others choose not to be socialized. These young adults may attempt to escape from socialization through alcohol, stimulants, narcotics, tranquilizers, sedatives, or LSD.

Socialization during middle and later adulthood is fundamentally a process of resocialization that is stretched out over a long period of time. This process is concerned less with the taming of drives and the teaching of attitudes, habits, and beliefs than with the reformulation of values, interests, interpersonal relations, self-image, and patterns of response. Thus, in one sense, the aging person must retrace some of the steps in the process of socialization outlined in Chapter 1 (see Figure 1, p. 5).

The agents of this resocialization are usually those in the generations behind him. The older the person becomes, the more frequently he experiences a *role reversal*, in which he seeks advice and guidance from those younger than himself (Payne, 1960) and models some of his activities after them. This role reversal can be almost total in advanced years, with the children responsible for resocializing the parent. Consequently, over a period of years, any individual may progress through the stages of socializing his own children, resocializing his aged parents, and being resocialized himself by the younger generation. If the older person is institutionalized, his socializers may be a new and strange set of peers and authority figures.

During this time, the individual must adjust

17

The last stages of socialization

to a multitude of new roles and statuses. For example, he must adjust to the years when his children have grown up and left home and a new husband-wife relationship must be formulated. Soon afterward, he may have to adjust to the years of retirement and the years of widowhood. New patterns of response must be established with others, and their changing response to him must be integrated with a self-image that is also undergoing alteration. And the backdrop for the entire process is painted in the harsh colors of declining physical health and capacity.

Another way to view aging is as a prolonged process of disengagement from the social system (Cummings *et al.*, 1960; Cummings and Henry, 1961). This process of withdrawal from others can be initiated in middle age in anticipation of the years ahead, reinforced by fading hopes of success, and triggered by physical evidence of the coming decline. As we watch the process of aging through the middle and later years come to its culmination in death, it is important to keep in mind that the socialization process is continuous, that its components are ever alive and exerting steady pressures, and that as much socialization takes place in later life as in the brief span of the first few years.

THE PROCESS OF AGING

Aging is a dynamic process, for life and death are a continuous event for the billions of cells in the human body. In a way, the body dies and is reborn by a steady process of replacement of dead cellular tissue with new cells. However, the body is a self-renewing machine only up to a point. As Chief Justice Oliver Wendell Homes once said, "We must all be born again atom by atom from hour to hour, or perish all at once beyond repair." We continue to grow as long as new cells are produced faster than the old ones die. We feel the ravages of age when more die than are provided anew. And, of course, death can occur when any one system fails even though all other systems are still intact.

This process of aging generally begins soon after the individual has reached the age of 30. It is common knowledge that almost every test of physical strength and quickness favors people in their twenties and that these measures of physical capacity indicate a slow decline after that time (Fisher and Birren, 1947). With increasing age, a number of physiological changes become apparent: The ductless glands are less active, the heart beat rate increases inordinately with exercise, and even the body temperature adjusts more slowly to changes in the external temperature (Lansing, 1952). It is simply that the average person reaches his prime between 20 and 30 years of age and decreases in vigor and in health from then on, although people do age at different rates as a consequence of their own particular mixture of constitution, living patterns, diet, and health care (Tressey, 1952). In addition, there is always a rough correspondence between physical condition and mental accomplishment. Almost every study indicates that the best age for intellectual achievement in a variety of disciplines and creative endeavors is early in life rather than later (Lehman, 1953).

Although the individual's physical and mental decline begins so early, our society still wants to preserve his life for as long as possible. Thus, a current hope for beating the aging process is to replace worn or damaged parts—or strip the dead in order to reoutfit the living. There is some realistic expectation that advanced medical techniques will one day allow our civilization to establish organ banks of parts for tired humans. Failing this, it has been suggested that we ought to explore immortality by quick-freezing mortally ill people and keeping them in cold storage—tagged and identified by disease or difficulty—and awakening them when medical science has made the necessary strides to deal with the previously fatal problem.

Important as these physical changes are, however, the most vital changes for the individual are psychological ones. These changes are of at least two kinds: *senescence*, which is a steady but relatively balanced decline of all faculties, and

"Another way to view aging is as a prolonged process of disengagement from the social system."

senility, which is a rapid decline of mental abilities that is not always accompanied by physical decline. These physical changes do not bear a direct cause-and-effect relationship to the psychological well-being of the aging person. Although all senescent or senile individuals share a common burden of adjusting to a body that is not responding as it once did, how this loss is managed and how much of one's usual response to others is altered depends strikingly on the pattern of psychological response that has marked the individual throughout his life. In a very real sense, his psychological response to senescence and senility is determined throughout his life. Physical flaws in the brain present an adjustment problem; the practiced patterns of a lifetime of response determine how this problem will be solved.

As a result of these changes, the older person needs special encouragement in what he does; he lacks confidence, and he uses methods of approaching problems that differ from those used by younger people. Moreover, he may find learning new methods more difficult than when he was

younger, for new learnings interfere with and reorganize previous learnings—even though they may be inappropriate to a new day and age. Finally, he is, of course, slower in his work, though not necessarily less efficient than the younger worker who proceeds with greater speed at times when wisdom and caution, rather than dash and daring, are required (Clark, 1967; Kalish, 1967).

Another set of psychological changes that comes with age is related to motivation. A study by Kuhlen and Johnson (1952) found a clear-cut shift with age in the ambition of both male and female teachers. For example, 90 percent of the men teachers between the ages of 25 and 29 hoped for a promotion or a different job in education, but only half of the men between 45 and 49 had great expectations of a better position. After age 55, none were looking for a promotion, and over half of the male teachers were anticipating retirement. Interestingly, Kuhlen and Johnson report that, at about age 45, there was a sudden upsurge of ambition. It was as if the men realized that time was running out, and their appraisal of their prospects made them anxious in a "now or never" sort of way.

These findings underline the increasingly negative outlook of the aging toward life. Most people designate young adulthood (the ages between 25 and 45) as the best time of life and rate youth as next best. Only 5 percent of the people in one study (Landis, 1942) rated the best years of their lives as those occurring after the age of 60. As Tressey (1957) has noted, with increasing age may come mellowed, kindly wisdom and the finest flowering of personality. However, it is equally true that with organic deterioration, insecurity, ill health, and disappointment may come a substantial erosion of personality and character that perhaps eventuates in serious personal disorder.

Middle Adulthood

The problems of early adulthood forecast those to come in middle adulthood (the years between about 40 and about 65). Although this period of life is marked by the beginning of physical decline, the discovery of new drugs and medical techniques has safeguarded the health of many middle aged adults. Thus, this age range is tentative because it is determined less by biology than by the social view of chronological age. This social view of age dictates that middle adulthood is the time of greatest success and achievement— particularly in the professions. For all levels of work, the greatest earning capacity of the individual occurs when he is between 45 and 55 years of age.

However, at the same time, every individual is a complex bundle of hits and misses, of abilities and liabilities, of successes and failures in various parts of his life. Each middle aged adult must come to terms with his own combination of successes and failures and calculate whether his past performance is going to be predictive of his future

life. How each individual reacts to his assessment is not a random or unpredictable event; it is tied to the pattern of psychological strengths and weaknesses that has existed in all of his previous life.

Middle adulthood is also a time of psychological adjustment to the physiological events of middle age. The most obvious physical change is, of course, the inevitable alteration in appearance that takes place as we grow older. Even though a great many internal, invisible changes are happening with age, it is the appearance that the individual presents to himself and others that daily reminds him that he is not so young as he once was. Moreover, physical effort produces reminders of age that cannot be denied, ignored, or dismissed as a temporary condition of life; middle adulthood is a time of waning physical strength and capacity to rebound from illness. If the individual can compensate for these physical losses with rewarding social and psychological activities, he can adjust to the aging process with some grace. However, as Joyce Cary noted in A *House of Children*, the average man of 40 "is like a traveler who, when he has reached the most dangerous part of his journey among deep jungles and unknown savages, discovers all at once that his map is wrong, his compass broken, his ammunition damp, his rifle crooked, and his supplies running short. He must push on at high speed, blindly, or fail altogether and fail his companions" (Goldfarb, 1963).

A disabling disease will be the fate of the middle aged person—or at least the fate of his friends. The expectation of such illness becomes much more frequent and is greeted with greater resignation than would have been the case at an earlier age. Mental changes and mental well-being become especially important at this age in part as a result of the individual's increasing concern about death, the appearance that he presents to others, and his growing awareness of his physical deterioration. The consequence of this concern is that the individual's self-concept comes under scrutiny.

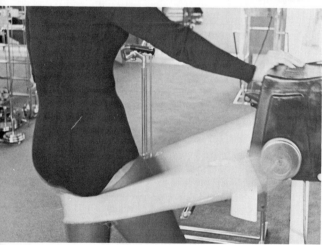

"Because our culture places such a premium on youth, women in their forties and fifties seek desperately for any and all means to keep the image of youth from fading."

The female in our society has particular problems with aging—problems perhaps more severe than those of the male. Because our culture places such a premium on youth, women in their forties and fifties seek desperately for any and all means to keep the image of youth from fading.

Our age of chemistry and synthetic production of hormones has become a handmaiden to this frantic search. And, like clockwork, new popular books and new articles in the women's magazines extend the promise of youth forever. Remaining vibrant, sexually desirable, and romantically attractive has been worth a severe price for some women, who undergo plastic surgery, diet strenuously, etch old skin from their faces with acid, and become the avid cultists of every new series of exercises and plans for renewed youth.

The particular problem for the female is the shift in her hormone economy with age. The woman's ovarian discharge of sex hormones decreases with fair regularity up to the time of menopause. When that happens, the disruption of her monthly cycle of ovulation and menstruation signals the end of her fertility as a woman. If the estrogenic hormones served only these functions, their loss would be a matter of little concern to anyone. These hormones, however, also act to keep the female's skin supple and free of wrinkles, her breasts firm, and her overall appearance feminine. Thus, the changes that come with age and the biological deficiency of hormonal output can be considered the same as any disease that leaves us short of what is necessary to maintain not life but appearance. The hormone world of estrogens, progestins, and androgens is now, however, more accessible to scientists, so that the future holds some hope for being able to retard the natural process of aging.

In addition to coping with the problem of psychological adjustment, the middle aged parent must adapt his socialization techniques and his relationships to his children to fit the needs of rapidly developing young people who are confronting challenges of their own. Consequently, while the adult works to assure his own security and self-esteem in middle age, he must invest a certain proportion of his energies in helping the young to manage the stages just before early adulthood. Having once lived through this stage, the parent has experience at his command, but he is also disadvantaged by having moved into a different phase of life, in which the problems of adolescence and early adulthood assume less importance than those with which he must grapple every day.

It is obvious that guiding the development of young people goes well or badly in part as a function of how well or badly the life of the parent is going in his attempt to adjust to middle adulthood. The temptation is great for the adult experiencing anxiety in dealing with his own life to see the emerging young person, consciously or unconsciously, as a way to relive his own life vicariously. It is unfortunate that those who must provide guidance for the next generation may be the very people least able to look at youth's problems through the eyes of youth.

Later Adulthood

By the time that someone in our society reaches 65 years of age (the arbitrary age of retirement), he has been made aware in a thousand ways that he is about to enter a new phase in life —whether he is willing to or not. The transition from middle to later adulthood in many ways recreates some of the stresses of being suddenly propelled from adolescence into early adulthood. At many junctures in life, a change in status is tied closely to chronological age, so that graduation from high school, eligibility for military service, the assumption of legal responsibility, and so forth occur for all with little regard for the matching of psychological readiness and status change. So it is with vocational retirement for the male. He is suddenly prevented from continuing the activity that has constituted his primary focus for nearly half a century. Our society has not designed for this phase of life a role that permits continuing growth, development, and achievement in the remaining years. Instead, later adulthood signals the end to much that has occupied the man's waking hours, and the focus of society swings back to the younger person entering early adulthood.

Few of those reaching 65 are prepared for the violence of the shift in how they are perceived. And they resent it. The newness of the problem of later adulthood suggests that our current treatment of older people is an unsatisfactory and transitional attempt to deal with the demands of our industrialized society. In fact, in recent years, the traditional age of 65 for retirement has been reduced to 60 (on a voluntary basis) in many companies. It is not that any alteration in life functions has taken place but that the need to eliminate older people to make room for the crush of younger ones has become more pressing in our society. At a reduced pension rate, it is even possible to leave the active, working life at 55 years of age.

Formal retirement is only one indication of the age at which a person is considered old. One's productive employment age is easily determined if the individual quits his job and seeks another. In most circumstances, he will find that he is too old to be considered employable by most industries in our society. Indeed, chronological age becomes a handicap rather than an asset as early as 45 years of age. Once unemployed after age 45, the chances are good that the individual will remain so if the economy is in recession and the labor supply exceeds the demand. After the age of 55, re-employment is particularly difficult. Thus, for some, the working life will end even sooner than the average for the working populace.

The conditions of old age are not particularly attractive to a society oriented toward youth. Of those people over 65, 23 percent are living on some form of charity, 27 percent are dependent on pensions, social security, and relatives, 31 percent are still working, and only 19 percent are retired and living on investments or savings. Physically, four-fifths of them have at least one chronic ailment, and the severity of that increases with age. After 65 and before 80 years of age, about half of these people have lost all their natural teeth. About one-fifth of those over 65 have heart disease, arthritis, or rheumatism, and these tend to be disabling chronic conditions. On the average, such acute or chronic conditions restrict the activities of older people about 38 days a year. Of these days, 14 require bed confinement.

"The conditions of old age are not particularly attractive to a society oriented toward youth."

People in middle adulthood, by contrast, per year average only 22 days of restricted activity and require only seven days of bed confinement.

When physical debilitation reaches a point where it limits psychological, physical, social, and economic activity, the individual's reaction is liable to be substantial. As others about him die, disturbance and depression may be a natural outcome. The correlation between physical illness and psychological impairment is very high, so that his ability to deal with somatic problems is reduced. The resultant disillusionment with life, coupled with feelings of abandonment and uselessness, may restrict the aged person's continued psychological development and speed up his withdrawal from life.

Society's lack of provision for meaning in the lives of these people is, in the stretch of history, a fairly recent development. When the economy was a rural one, the elders in a family could function as wise counselors who had accumulated invaluable skill, experience, and judgment over the years. In the early 1900s, our society changed little from year to year, so that the accumulated wisdom of the past was still applicable to new problems. In a technological society, it takes a desperate effort even to keep abreast of the changes that come with such bewildering speed. Consequently, obsolescence of skill and knowledge is almost continuous and is, in a way, unavoidable. Our treatment of the aged is, however, an unsuitable one that must be altered in the decades to come.

Society and the Aged

Despite our efforts to prolong life, we are a culture prejudiced against the aging and the aged. Nearly 12 million people in our society are over 65 years of age, and this number will soon be almost 25 million. Yet the aged are still a minority group in our society. Consequently, for all our concern with gerontology, the "twilight years," the "golden years," and "senior citizenship," we have done little to alter our social life to meet the needs of our older citizens.

Age is a slippery concept promoting traditional ways of thinking that reflect little of what is important in a man's relationship to his fellows. A person is as old as not only his physiology but also his attitude toward life and change. These measures of age are too difficult for the average citizen of our society to cope with, so chronological age has become the standard by which human capacity is typically judged. Perhaps a psychological age should be computed for each person—an age based on the personality and maturity of the individual with little regard for his physiological or chronological age (Montagu, 1962).

A change in the social perception of aging is needed for older people as well as for younger ones. This change is a prerequisite to the establishment of some dignified social position for the aged—which they must have if they are not to feel shunted aside as tired and unproductive members of society. But our society persists in establishing more and more communities populated solely by the old. And the way of life in these communities and its effect on their inhabitants serve to reinforce in both young and old the already existing social perceptions of the psychological nature of the aged.

Another increasingly popular institution for cultural dismissal of the problem of aging is "residences for the aged." Although the institutional settings we have devised for the aged vary in kind and quality (Veterans' Administration Domiciliaries, mental hospitals, homes for the aged, or supervised housing groups), they have certain important common features that must affect the inmates' sense of worth and dignity. In an institution of any sort, the inmates carry out their daily activities at one place in the company of others, all of whom are treated alike and required to do the same thing together. These activities are all tightly scheduled by an authority bent on the execution of some overall rational plan (Bennett and Nahemow, 1965). How well the aging person living under these conditions integrates his life patterns with the new demands and learns to conform to the changed rules of existence has a great deal to do with the pleasure or displeasure that he will find in the rest of his life.

It is clear that, whether an aged person lives in one of these institutions or not, adequate adjustment to old age involves continuing socialization and the learning of new rules of life. Our mythical cultural view of aging is a portrait of golden years filled with grace and satisfaction. But the harsh reality for many of our older citizens suggests that the preparation for the exit from life may be as demanding as early childhood was.

THE AMERICAN WAY OF DEATH

Death is the price of life. No fact of being is more inevitable than death, yet it has become a taboo topic in our society. We avoid facing the fact of death by concentrating on the careful rituals that we have constructed around it. Thus, dying in a civilized, socialized fashion is complicated. One increasingly important aspect of the complexity of dying is the role of the hospital. Today, over half of our population dies in hospitals. This number will probably increase, for death from chronic rather than acute disease will become more and more prevalent (Hinton, 1967).

Death and the Patient

The typical American's unwillingness to speak openly about the process of dying is shared by the professional in the hospital, who will be with most of us when we die. Medical students and nurses are trained to deal with the physical but not the psychological facts of dying, so that hospital workers must develop their own standards on and patterns of response to death. However, working with dying patients is emotionally upsetting. Therefore, most doctors prefer not to tell their patients that they are dying (Ferfel, 1963). These doctors justify their decision by believing in the notion that telling the patient would destroy him emotionally and that he really does not want to know anyway.

A widespread and comforting myth also helps doctors to come to this decision. According to that myth, doctors should make individual judgments with each patient and tell those who can "take it" and withhold the information from those who are less psychologically capable of handling the information. The problem is that few doctors have either the time or the proper training to make this judgment about their patients. Thus, few patients are informed of impending death because doctors are not often confident about their own ability to manage the emotional reaction of their patients.

Foreknowledge of impending doom is kept from the patient in a number of ways. He is not, of course, practiced in reading the signs of certain death. He may be aware that he is seriously and dangerously ill or injured, but that is not, for him, the certain equivalent of death. Nor can the patient discover much about his fatal condition from hospital records or personnel. These sources of information are carefully closed to him. Medical staff members may encourage the patient to believe his own optimistic but inaccurate self-diagnoses or mislead him to keep him from being aware of the seriousness of his situation. Thus, the staff of the hospital may even create a fic-tional set of explanations to account to the patient for unusual medical procedures or changes in his treatment. Hospital life "as usual" with no visible signs of undue anxiety on the part of the staff can be an effective way of convincing the patient that all is well.

Some patients come to suspect, despite the careful deception practiced by everyone around them, that they are about to die. Once a patient becomes suspicious, a kind of fencing match ensues between him and the staff. Part of this contest is the patient's attempt to find out "for sure" about his condition in order to confirm what he already suspects. The patient searching for the truth employs a series of tactics ranging from oblique questioning of the staff, to taking a peek, if possible, at his medical records, to encouraging others to make inquiries about his condition. The medical staff, of course, engages in countertactics once it becomes aware that the patient is suspicious. Carefully planned teamwork can present a formidable barrier to the patient's quest for infor-

"How well the aging person living under these conditions integrates his life patterns with the new demands and learns to conform to the changed rules of existence has a great deal to do with the pleasure or displeasure that he will find in the rest of his life."

mation. The strain on the staff of the hospital and on the family of the patient may be enormous. However, the real victim is the nurse, who must be in constant contact with the patient and must keep up the pretense the longest.

Once both the patient and the staff know that the patient is dying, one possibility is, as Glaser and Strauss (1965) indicate, that both parties will engage in a mutual pretense that the facts are otherwise. Because in this game both parties must participate willingly, each one must follow the rule of not initiating conversations about death. A kind of silent bargain is struck between the patient and those who take care of him, so that the masquerade can contribute to the psychological comfort of all. The doctor and the nurse will have had professional experience with this kind of game and so can, perhaps, act their part with greater skill than the patient can. In such instances, patient-doctor conversation focuses carefully on topics remote from death and pretends not to notice conversational slips that bring up the taboo subject of death.

This mutual pretense is difficult to maintain. If it breaks down, the outcome is most often open awareness or admission of impending death on the part of both patient and doctor. However, when both the patient and the staff members openly acknowledge the fact of certain death, the situation still remains psychologically complex. One reason for this complexity is that the patient is unable to know whether death will come suddenly and without warning or whether it will be a lingering affair marked by periods in which he will be comatose, in great pain, physically and psychologically deteriorated, or delusional and hallucinatory toward the end. Another reason is the presence of family and relatives, who often put additional strain on both staff and patient—whether or not he is aware of his impending death.

Death and the Family

Families and relatives play an integral part in the process of dying. Families interrupt the smooth routine of hospitals and present a full range of psychological problems to be met by medical personnel. If the family is kept unaware of the seriousness of the patient's condition, they become a source of constant pressure and closer questioning about why the patient is deteriorating rather than showing improvement. In keeping the family in the dark, the staff uses the same tactics employed in keeping the patient from knowing the seriousness of his illness.

If the doctor finds himself under sufficient pressure, he may resort to the tactic of telling only one member of the family that the illness is terminal and asking for a conspiracy of silence. This "strongest" member of the family is then responsible for deciding when the other members will be informed of the facts in the case. In general, however, unaware families may be expected—if the dying process is prolonged—to become suspicious, piece together observations and bits of information, and realize that the patient's condition is fatal.

Managing the family that becomes aware of the impending death adds a host of new dimensions. Restrictions on visiting the patient are usually relaxed, so that the staff must prepare itself to assist family members in maintaining their composure when facing death. The constant necessity of providing psychological help to relatives begins to force medical personnel to redefine their role. Finally, the need for additional and detailed information about the patient's condition becomes an added burden to the staff. These changes in hospital routine may arouse the suspicions of the patient, so that a fine balance must be maintained if the staff wishes him to remain ignorant of his condition.

The final stage in the process of dying in a hospital is "there is nothing more we can do for him." When this stage is reached, both the staff and the family begin to focus on providing the patient with comfort in the last moments of his life. For the medical staff, this orientation may mean a loss of interest in the patient because the ability to save patients carries with it greater reward and a greater sense of professional fulfillment. Thus, the staff's care of the patient may subtly shift as they turn their attention to ministering to those who still have a chance for recovery. The doctor stops visiting as often as he did in the past, the nurse does less in the way of personal care for the patient, and more of the responsibility for the patient is passed on to the immediate family. The patient may even be sent home because the hospital, according to medical personnel, ought to be devoted to those who can benefit from hospitalization.

The Final Farewell

Our culture has sanitized and denied death as a fact of life. One of the ways in which our society has done so is to rely on social institutions that make death a formal—and therefore remote —event. The most prominent of these is the funeral, which can be considered as a *rite de passage* or a rite of separation. Although the form of the funeral varies from culture to culture, era to era, and even within the same culture, the funeral always serves the same basic functions of declaring a person officially dead and thus separate from the living and of preparing him for what may follow his life on Earth.

Because our society emphasizes these functions so heavily, our burial rites have begun to resemble the most elaborate ones practiced in some primitive societies. When a member of one ancient society dies, his house is stripped of all its contents except for utensils. The corpse is dressed, placed in a dugout canoe, deposited on the ground where his clan is buried, and surrounded by all the things that he will need in the next world. The female relatives then make a doll in the image of the deceased and dress, wash, and feed it for two and a half years if the dead person is a man and for two years if a woman. Then the doll is placed in the tomb. Mourning for men lasts five months and for women four months.

In other societies, the face of the deceased is painted, a sacred headdress is placed on his head, and he is seated on the bier for from four to six days while magical songs are sung and all sorts of food, drink, and tobacco leaves are thrown on the "crying fire." In addition, the widow fasts for 10 days, uses a rock instead of a pillow, and bathes daily without washing her face.

These rituals have their modern, if symbolic, counterpart. The classic Irish wake held for the departed symbolically bears many of the features of the feasting and singing of ancient times. Modern Catholic rites are heavily laden with symbolic supplications to the All-Powerful and attention and comfort to the mourners. And, as we shall see, the materialistic orientation of our society is reflected in the conspicuous consumption of artifacts that accompany death and burial (caskets, flowers, crypts, luxury cars, and so forth) and with the lushness and comfort of the departure from this life.

Paying social and public homage to the dead takes the form of visiting the funeral parlor, viewing the body, and attending the burial ceremonies. In each instance, our death rituals are marked by religious ceremonies that retain the vestiges of exorcism of evil spirits plus assuagement of guilt among those who remain to continue life. The mysticism of modern times can be distinguished from that of primitive man primarily by the absence of an animistic investment of objects with spiritual significance and by the absence of belief in the living influence of the shades of long-departed ancestors.

Elaborateness or the lack of it in funeral rituals is in part a function of the society's religious beliefs because they determine the extent of the ritual involved in making the transition between this world and the next. Moreover, in special cases, religious beliefs may change the form of the ritual entirely. Present-day Catholics, for example, relegate children who die without baptism to a transitional zone, or Limbo, just as primitives bury the corpse of an unnamed, uncircumcised, or unritualized infant without the usual ceremonies. Finally, conducting funerals for suicides is a delicate social and psychological matter. In some societies, the suicide is considered normal, in others, he is thought to be rewarded or punished in the other world, and, in still others, he is thought to wander forever in the netherworld.

Anthropologists maintain that one of the best indicators of the nature of a society is its burial rituals. If the sanity and stability of our culture were to be judged solely on the basis of how we typically dispose of our dead, we would not look good in the pages of history. Our average funerary practices have become as strange as the quaintest death customs of the most primitive cultures. And, consequently, according to a definitive study of our mortuary manners, undertakers have been able "to perpetrate a huge, macabre, and expensive practical joke on the American public" (Mitford, 1963, p. 15).

The plain pine box for burial, the laying out of the dead by members of the family and close friends, and the hand carrying of the coffin to the grave were typical of the funeral in America until the end of the nineteenth century. In the twentieth century, the business of dying has become an expensive one in which the average total cost of a funeral is about $1,450. It has been estimated that in 1960 the American public spent at least $1.6 billion on funerals, but that is undoubtedly a grossly conservative figure. If the financial sacrifice of a funeral is severe enough, that monetary outlay can be a means of atoning for any real or fancied guilt that the survivors may feel. Grief therapy can be purchased by all, but the cost is extremely high. In addition, paying a dear price for a funeral bolsters family pride by displaying to all observers a symbol of the status that the family has in the society. Interestingly, there is a close correspondence between the cost of living and the cost of dying; as one rises, so does the other.

The artifacts of dying include all the visible indicators of the good life in our society. One can be buried in a hostess gown or a brunch coat and leave this vale of tears wearing the most stylish clothes possible. Caskets can be lined in luxury materials fit for a modern-day pharaoh and can contain a collection of burial artifacts that even reflect the dead person's personality and pattern

"Grief therapy can be purchased by all, but the cost is extremely high."

of previous life. For further posthumous beauty, the deceased can be laid to rest in an increasingly popular burial vault. These can be had in a variety of colors and designs and can be decorated to suit the tastes of the departed.

Perhaps the single clearest indicator of the degree to which modern society avoids the reality of death is the subtle alteration of the terminology that surrounds the fact of death. Undertakers have become "funeral directors," hearses have become "coaches" or "professional cars," the corpse has become "the loved one," and—even more Madison Avenue monstrous—cremated ashes are referred to as "cremains." The appearance of the "funeral home" has also been altered to deny the fact of death. It has now been displaced by the "chapel," complete with easily interchangeable artifacts suitable for every religion.

However, our culture is also addicted to viewing the dead, so we must take a number of steps to present a corpse that looks as "normal" as a dead person can look. We beautify our dead and erase any evidence of the ravages of disease, age, or discomfort that the deceased may have undergone. Thus, we pretty up death so that it seems to be an almost inviting state. As Mitford (1963) notes, we convert our dead into something resembling living dolls; the undertaker "has done everything in his power to make the funeral a real pleasure for everyone concerned. He and his team have given their all to score an upset victory over death" (p. 77). The rituals of death in our society are, therefore, directed· to the survivors rather than the deceased. Yet their grief and mourning are the inevitable consequences of living as a human being. *Grief* occurs when something has been lost that is essential to one's emotional life. This loss can be compared to a wound and *mourning* to the healing of that wound (Engel, 1962).

The usual first response to death is shock and disbelief. This disbelief may block out all evidence of the reality of the death. The grieving person may carry on his ordinary activities in an automatic fashion, or he may sit paralyzed, dazed, and unable to move. In some instances, the griever initiates the proper activities—making arrangements for the funeral, helping other people, discussing it rationally, and so on—but he can do so only by not allowing the full emotional impact of the loss to become real to him. This primitive denial of reality, which is a means of self-protection, most often occurs when death is sudden and there has been little opportunity to prepare for it.

Before long, the fact of loss penetrates the individual's consciousness and produces the expected pain, anguish, and feeling of emptiness. Sadness, helplessness, anxiety, and hopelessness may all be felt, but the kind of emotional display that they produce is in part culturally determined. In some societies, loud public crying and breast beating is expected; others demand that the individual avoid a public display of grief. However, when either public or private crying occurs, it is both an open means of acknowledging loss and a regression to a helpless and child-like state in which the individual indulges in self-pity. The inability to cry when one feels a great loss is a serious symptom of personal maladjustment and most often occurs when the relationship with the dead person has been an ambivalent one—that is, one of mixed feelings that produce a sense of guilt and shame.

The mourning that takes place within the psychic life of the individual is a process of restitution and recovery. During the first part of this process, the individual is not yet ready, of course, to replace the lost object with a new one, but he may become more dependent on nearby people and objects. And it is reasonable to expect that during this time the mourner will be preoccupied with thinking and talking about the lost person. This discussion of the dead makes the deceased seem almost perfect and free of negative qualities, which are gradually eliminated from the mourner's consciousness. The deceased, once ennobled by this portrait of perfection, becomes more and more distant from reality. Thus, the first steps have been taken in detaching oneself from the memory of loss.

With death, burial, and grieving completed, those who remain are once again free to turn their attention to the continuous succession of young people rushing into life to fill the void left by those who have departed. In an important sense, the meaning of life may be found in this process of continuous renewal of our society by the steady addition of new and recently socialized members. The living do well to look to youth for the vigor of life and for purpose in existence.

SUMMARY

During the years of middle and later adulthood, the process of socialization amounts to a resocialization. Life-long patterns of response to the world must be reformulated to accommodate a new set of roles and statuses and a changing set of anxieties in accomplishing the tasks of the later years. The decline in physical health and ability is a new aspect of the socialization process. The biological fact of aging is made more complicated by our society's emphasis on youth and our essentially negative evaluation of the aged.

Middle adulthood is a time of evaluation of the discrepancy between one's youthful aspirations and the hard fact of accomplishment. During this period, the individual appraises his success and failure when it is too late to turn back, raises his young, abandons his parental role, and becomes aware of the inroads of time.

Near the end of life, the score of previous socialization experiences is tallied and determines in great part the adequacy with which age is managed. Later adulthood involves more drastic alterations of roles and statuses in the form of retirement, widowhood, or institutionalization. This period, therefore, can mark a disengagement from society and a turning inward of interests and relationships.

The process of dying has about it a ritual form in that each of us must learn certain patterns of reaction if we are properly to play the role of patient or relative of the dying. Thus, even death has its usefulness in socializing the survivors in the ways of proper exit from the world.

One of the most pervasive current convictions goes something like this: The world is mad or sick, and modern society promises to become a misshapen travesty of all that we believe to be right and proper. In combination, the atomic age, the nuclear age, and the cold war have fashioned a cornerstone for a museum of horrors that will be inhabited by our children—to our generation an unholy and totally repugnant way to live. The gloom sayers and doom sayers of this era have held sway for some time now because it seems so right and so fitting to indict change and to view the future with alarm.

The difficulty with this thesis can be outlined quite simply. First, our times are, of course, perilous and fraught with terrors. But they are magnified by the fact that we must anticipate a horror that mankind has never before known. Because the reach of fantasy is substantially greater than that of reality, our fear is multiplied accordingly. Second, as psychologists, we regularly underestimate the resiliency of the human psyche and so underestimate the capacity of the normal personality to absorb shock, devastation, turmoil, and deprivation. Third, we have failed to comprehend that our perception of the world is formed primarily by contrasting things as they *were* with things as they *might be* and therefore have failed

Epilogue

The children of 1984

to realize that, for our children, things as they *are* more closely approximate *things as they will be*.

Signs exist in abundance telling us that this is an age of anxiety and tension. They include tranquilizers, consciousness expanding drugs, the beatnik era, the bomb shelter scare, the rightist movement, the moon shot fascination, long-haired men, mod dress, freedom marches, the "hot line," the pill, and Hiroshima and Nagasaki. Our descendants will understand that, in the face of a nameless horror, we over-reacted and contemplated the future with great misgivings. Probably at few other times in history has man looked with less favor on his prospects. The future is alien primarily because it threatens to change at a rate incomprehensible to those of us adapted to a slower movement of the course of history.

We are without an adequate notion of the effect of drastic alteration of one's social and psychological position in this world. Our studies of civilian catastrophe have been studies of isolated instances of deprivation when the rest of the world remained intact. We have never, except in novels, examined human response to total catastrophe in which man is suddenly and completely cut off from the normal supports of his society. We have no paradigm for total chaos, so we have yet to measure the degree to which developing human beings can live with psychic torment and a sense of psychological loss. Because we have been so preoccupied with psychic catastrophe, we have failed to note that most of the human race is capable of withstanding an incredible amount of trauma and that sometimes this trauma gives birth to new invention, new determination, and a more realistic appraisal of the fundamental values of existence. As psychologists, we have been guilty of selling the human race short.

We have also failed to be aware of the inevitable hardening of our perceptions as we age. We all suffer from awareness of our own past and from imprisonment in the perceptions of our childhood. In this sense, the future is regularly a threat to the past because the future acts to undo the past by changing it into an unrecognizable form. The future is without the comfort of recognizable objects placed in a familiar order. That is always frightening.

With all the talk of doomsday machines to destroy planetary life, of neutron bombs from which people will perish while buildings remain intact, and of outer space converted to a battlefield while we strangle on strange chemicals in our water supply, we forget that our children are maturing in this kind of LSD world, which is bizarre to us but commonplace to them because it is familiar. For example, an era of secrecy wedded to science is not alien to them. That man can for the first time not only kill his fellow man but also invisibly change his genetic structure into a misshapen future form does not startle our children, for they have already begun the process of absorbing a culture that we find necessary to adjust to and compensate for. Our children will become *less like us than we can comprehend*, and they will soon show the unmistakable signs of psychological evolution to a shape that will seem strange and alien to our generation. Like the conservative Neanderthal who could not comprehend the advances of the Cro-Magnon, the new generation promises to become a species suited to a social climate that seems chilling to the older generation.

The penalty of age is twofold: the memory of life as it once was and anxiety about the way life might be in the days to come. It is for this reason that the future is always reserved exclusively for the young, who are free of the fears of the past and who have the courage and eternal optimism to face the future without flinching. The expanding dark foundation of human culture is certain to alter the psychological nature of our children. Children raised under continuous tension, children raised in the kibbutz and the commune, and children raised in the shadow of world destruction need a psychological toughness that exceeds our own by a considerable amount. They will acquire it, and they will survive. For those of us bred in the sunlight, the darkness appears Stygian; for those who grow to maturity in the shadow, there seems to be light enough.

It is tempting to look to the future and recoil

in horror at what seems to be its dehumanizing directions, but this reaction can occur only if we suffer from a very short memory. If we recall the horrors of our own and past eras—the concentration camps, the extermination ovens, the Depression, the Inquisition, the Children's Crusades, the Roman arena, wars, plagues, and starvation—we can only marvel at the capacity of the human species to survive against seemingly impossible odds.

Referring to the nightmare of the world of 1984 has become so frequent that it almost seems as if familiarity has bred a kind of numb resignation in the face of an inevitable fate. What we fail to realize is that 1984 will not emerge suddenly, full-grown in a cataclysm of political thunder and lightning. The roots of 1984 are being nurtured now in the fertile soil of our children's minds. What looks misshapen to the elders of a society appears natural to their young, for whom the shape has long been familiar. Without this psychological phenomenon of perception, each generation would be held a prisoner of the past and would never survive the future.

Children perceive the real world, not the polite facade that we often try to present to them. For our children, 1984 will not seem noticeably different from 1983 because year by year they will have moved imperceptibly to wholehearted acceptance of the new state of things as they are. No era welcomes its death, nor is it much consoled by the vigor of its offspring when they seem fated for a world that seems to retain so little of traditional standards and values. But for our children, 1984 will hold fewer terrors and will seem less alien.

Abel, Theodora M. Resistances and difficulties in psychotherapy of mental retardates. *J. clin. Psychol.*, 1953, *10*, 107–109.

Abt, L. E., and Weissman, S. L. *Acting Out*. New York: Grune & Stratton, 1965.

Ackerly, S. Spafford, *et al*. Extension of a child guidance clinic's services to the schools. In M. Krugman (ed.), *Orthopsychiatry and the School*. New York: American Orthopsychiatric Association, 1958. Pp. 204–212.

Adlerblum, Evelyn D. Beginning school guidance early. *Ment. Hyg.*, 1950, *34*, 600–610.

Aichorn, A. *Wayward Youth*. New York: Viking, 1935.

Allen, G. B., and Masling, J. M. An evaluation of the effects of nursery school training on children in the kindergarten, first, and second grades. *J. educ. Res.*, 1957, *51*, 285–296.

Allinsmith, W., and Goethals, G. *The Role of Schools in Mental Health*. New York: Basic Books, 1961.

Allport, G. W. *Pattern and Growth in Personality*. New York: Holt, 1961.

Alt, H. *Residential Treatment for the Disturbed Child*. New York: International Universities Press, 1960.

Anastasi, Anne. Psychological research and educational desegregation. In J. E. O'Neill (ed.), *A Catholic Case against Segregation*. New York: Macmillan, 1961. Pp. 116–145.

Anastasiow, N. J. Success in school and boys' sex role patterns. *Child Developm.*, 1965, *36*, 1053–1066.

Bibliography

Anderson, J. E. *The Young Child in the Home.* New York: Appleton-Century-Crofts, 1936.

Andrus, R., and Horowitz, E. L. The effect of nursery school training: Insecurity feeling. *Child Developm.,* 1938, 9, 169–174.

Antes, J. To open the door. *Oberlin Alumni Magazine,* 1964, 60, No. 6.

Aronfreed, J. Conscience and conduct: A natural history of the internalization of values. In M. L. Hoffman (ed.), *Character Development.* New York: Social Science Research Council.

Asher, E. J. The inadequacy of current intelligence tests for testing Kentucky mountain children. *J. genet. Psychol.,* 1935, 46, 480–486.

Azrin, N. H., Hutchinson, R. R., and McLaughlin, R. The opportunity for aggression as an operant reinforcer during aversive stimulation. *J. exp. anal. Behav.,* 1965, 8, 171–180.

Bach, G. R. Father-fantasies and father-typing in father-separated children. *Child Developm.,* 1946, 17, 63–80.

Bacon, H. K., Child, I. L., and Barry, H. A. A cross-cultural study of correlates of crime. *J. abnorm. soc. Psychol.,* 1963, 66, 291–300.

Bahn, Anita, and Norman, Vivian. First national report on patients of mental health clinics. *Public Health Reports,* 1959, 74, 943–956.

Bakke, E. W. *Citizen without Work.* New Haven, Conn.: Yale Univ. Press, 1940.

Baldwin, A. L. Socialization and the parent-child relationship. *Child Developm.,* 1948, 19, 127–136.

Baldwin, A. L. The study of child behavior and development. In P. H. Mussen (ed.), *Handbook of Research Methods in Child Development.* New York: Wiley, 1960. Pp. 3–35.

Baldwin, A. L. *Theories of Child Development.* New York: Wiley, 1967.

Baldwin, A. L., Kalhorn, Joan, and Breese, Fay H. Patterns of parent behavior. *Psychol. Monogr.,* 1945, 58, No. 268.

Bandura, A. Influence of model's reinforcement contingencies on the acquisition of imitative responses. *J. pers. soc. Psychol.,* 1965, 1, 589–595.

Bandura, A. Vicarious processes: A case of no-trial learning. In L. Berkowitz (ed.), *Advances in Experimental Social Psychology.* Vol. II. New York: Academic Press, 1966. Pp. 1–55.

Bandura, A., and Huston, Aletha C. Identification as a process of incidental learning. *J. abnorm. soc. Psychol.,* 1961, 63, 311–318.

Bandura, A., and Kupers, Carol J. Transmission of patterns of self-reinforcement through modeling. *J. abnorm. soc. Psychol.,* 1964, 69, 1–9.

Bandura, A., and McDonald, F. J. The influence of social reinforcement and the behavior of models in shaping children's moral judgments. *J. abnorm. soc. Psychol.,* 1963, 67, 274–281.

Bandura, A., and Mischel, W. Modification of self-imposed delay of reward through exposure to live and symbolic models. *J. pers. soc. Psychol.,* 1965, 2, 698–705.

Bandura, A., Ross, Dorothea, and Ross, Shelia A. A comparative test of the status envy, social power, and secondary reinforcement theories of identification learning. *J. abnorm. soc. Psychol.,* 1963, 67 527–534.

Bandura, A., Ross, Dorothea, and Ross, Shelia A. Transmission of aggression through imitation of aggressive models. *J. abnorm. soc. Psychol.,* 1961, 63, 575–582.

Bandura, A., and Walters, R. H. *Social Learning and Personality Development.* New York: Holt, 1963.

Bandura, A., and Whalen, Carol K. The influence of antecedent reinforcement and divergent modeling cues on patterns of self-reward. *J. pers. soc. Psychol.,* 1966, 3, 373–382.

Barker, R. G., Dembo, Tamara, and Lewin, K. Frustration and regression: An experiment with young children. *Univ. Iowa Stud. Child Welf.,* 1941, 18, No. 1.

Barker, R. G., *et al. Adjustment to Physical Handicap and Illness: A Survey of the Social Psychology of Physique and Disability.* New York: Social Science Research Council, 1953.

Barker, R. G., and Wright, H. F. *One Boy's Day.* New York: Harper, 1951.

Barron, F. *Creativity and Psychological Health.* Princeton, N.J.: Van Nostrand, 1963.

Barry, H., Bacon, Margaret K., and Child, I. L. A cross-cultural survey of some sex differences in socialization. *J. abnorm. soc. Psychol.,* 1957, 55, 327–332.

Battle, Esther S., and Rotter, J. B. Children's feelings: A personal control as related to social class and ethnic group. *J. Pers.,* 1963, 31, 482–490.

Baumrind, Diana, and Black, A. E. Socialization practices associated with dimensions of compe-

tence in preschool boys and girls. *Child Devel‐
opm.*, 1967, 38, 291–327.

Baylor, E. M., and Monachesi, E. D. *The Reha‐
bilitation of Children.* New York: Harper,
1939.

Becker, H. S. The teacher in the authority system
of the public school. *J. educ. Sociol.*, 1953, 27,
128–141.

Becker, H. S., *et al. Boys in White: Student
Culture in Medical School.* Chicago: Univ.
Chicago Press, 1961.

Bell, E. H. *Social Foundations of Human Behav‐
ior.* New York: Harper, 1961.

Bell, N. W., and Vogel, E. F. Toward a frame‐
work for functional analysis of family behavior.
In N. W. Bell and E. F. Vogel (eds.), *The
Family.* New York: Free Press, 1960. Pp. 1–33.

Bender, L., and Poster, S. Homosexual trends in
children. *Amer. J. Orthopsychiat.*, 1941, 11,
730–744.

Benedict, Ruth. Continuities and discontinuities
in cultural conditioning. *Psychiat.*, 1938, 1,
161–167.

Bennett, R., and Nahemow, L. Institutional total‐
ity and criteria of social adjustment in resi‐
dences for the aged. *J. soc. Issues*, 1965, 21, 44–
75.

Berkowitz, L. *Aggression: A Social Psychological
Analysis.* New York: McGraw-Hill, 1962.

Berman, L. The mental health of the educator.
Ment. Hyg., 1954, 38, 422–429.

Bernard, H. W. *Human Development in Western
Culture.* Boston: Allyn & Bacon, 1962.

Bernard, Jessie. The adjustments of married
mates. In H. T. Christensen (ed.), *Handbook
of Marriage and the Family.* Chicago: Rand
McNally, 1964. Pp. 675–739.

Bernard, N. W. *Mental Hygiene for Classroom
Teachers.* 2nd Ed. New York: McGraw-Hill,
1961.

Berrill, N. J. Aging and everyman. *Atlantic*, 1966,
217, 86–90.

Bettelheim, B. Does communal education work?
The case of the kibbutz. In E. Shur (ed.), *The
Family and the Sexual Revolution.* Blooming‐
ton, Ind.: Indiana Univ. Press, 1964. Pp.
293–307.

Bettelheim, B. *Love Is Not Enough.* New York:
Free Press, 1950.

Bettelheim, B. The problem of generations. In
E. H. Erikson (ed.), *Youth: Change and Chal‐*
lenge. New York: Basic Books, 1963. Pp.
64–92.

Beverly, B. I. The effect of illness on emotional
development. *J. Pediat.*, 1936, 8, 533–544.

Biber, Barbara. Integration of mental health prin‐
ciples in the school setting. In G. Caplan (ed.),
Prevention of Mental Disorders in Children.
New York: Basic Books, 1961. Pp. 323–352.

Biber, Barbara. Teacher education in mental
health—From the point of view of the psy‐
chiatrist. In M. Krugman (ed.), *Orthopsychia‐
try and the School.* New York: American Or‐
thopsychiatric Association, 1958. Pp. 169–183.

Bidwell, C. E. The young professional in the
Army: A study of occupational identity. *Amer.
sociol. Rev.*, 1961, 26, 360–372.

Bindman, A. J. Mental health consultation: The‐
ory and practice. *J. consult. Psychol.*, 1959, 23,
473–482.

Birch, D., and Veroff, J. *Motivation: A Study of
Action.* Belmont, Calif.: Brooks/Cole, 1966.

Birch, J. M. Special classes in schools for malad‐
justed children. *Except. Child.*, 1956, 222,
332–337.

Bird, G. E. Effect of nursery school attendance
upon mental growth of children. *Yearbk. Nat.
Soc. Study Educ.*, 1940, 39, Part II, 81–94.

Bishop, B. M. Mother-child interaction and the
social behavior of children. *Psychol. Monogr.*,
1951, 65, 11.

Blair, F. B. Relations between the average amount
of insurance per policy and the height and
weight of the insured. *The Record* (American
Institute of Actuaries), 1940, 29, 211–223.

Blair, G. N., *et al. Educational Psychology.* New
York: Macmillan, 1954.

Bloom, B. S. *Stability and Change in Human
Characteristics.* New York: Wiley, 1964.

Blum, R., *et al. Utopiates.* New York: Atherton
Press, 1964.

Boboroff, A. Economic adjustment of 121 adults,
formerly students in classes for mental retar‐
dates. *Amer. J. ment. Def.*, 1956, 60, 525–535.

Bonney, M. E., and Nicholson, E. L. Compara‐
tive social adjustments of elementary school
pupils with and without preschool training.
Child Developm., 1958, 29, 125–133.

Bossard, J. H. S., and Boll, Eleanor S. *The Sociol‐
ogy of Child Development.* New York: Harper,
1966.

Bottrill, J. H. Effects of preschool experience on the school readiness level of privileged and underprivileged children. *Except. Child.*, 1967, 34, 275.

Bower, E. M. *The Education of Emotionally Handicapped Children*. Sacramento, Calif.: California State Department of Education, 1961.

Bower, E. M. The modification, mediation, and utilization of stress during the school years. *Amer. J. Orthopsychiat.*, 1964, 34, 667–674.

Bowlby, J. Forty-four juvenile thieves. *Int. J. Psychoanal.*, 1944, 25, 1–57.

Bowlby, J. *Maternal Care and Mental Health*. Monogr. No. 2. Geneva: World Health Organization, 1951.

Bowman, C. C. Cultural ideology and heterosexual reality: A preface to sociological research. *Amer. sociol. Rev.*, 1949, 14, 623–633.

Brim, O. G., Jr. *Education for Child Rearing*. New York: Russell Sage Foundation, 1959.

Brim, O. G., Jr., and Wheeler, S. *Socialization after Childhood*. New York: Wiley, 1966.

Broderick, C. B., and Fowler, S. E. New patterns of relationships between the sexes among preadolescents. *Marriage and Family Living*, 1961, 23, 27–30.

Bronfenbrenner, U. Freudian theories of identification and their derivatives. *Child Developm.*, 1960, 31, 15–40.

Bronfenbrenner, U. Socialization and social class through time and space. In E. E. Maccoby, T. M. Newcomb, and E. L. Hartley (eds.), *Readings in Social Psychology*. New York: Holt, 1958. Pp. 400–425.

Bronfenbrenner, U. Soviet methods of character education: Some implications for research. *Amer. Psychologist*, 1962, 17, 550–564.

Brown, A. W., and Hunt, R. Relations between nursery attendance and teachers' ratings of some aspects of children's adjustment in kindergarten. *Child Developm.*, 1961, 32, 585–596.

Brown, D. G. Sex-role development in a changing culture. *Psychol. Bull.*, 1958, 55, 232–242.

Brown, R. W., and Bellugi, U. Three processes in the child's acquisition of syntax. *Harv. educ. Rev.*, 1964, 34, 133–151.

Brownell, W. A. Readiness for subject-matter learning. *Nat. Educ. Assn. J.* 1951, 40, 445–446.

Burchinal, L. G., Hawkes, G. R., and Gardner, B. Marriage adjustment, personality characteristics of parents, and the personality adjustment of their children. *Marriage and Family Living*, 1957, 19, 366–373.

Burgess, E. W., and Cottress, L. S. *Predicting Success or Failure in Marriage*. Englewood Cliffs, N.J.: Prentice-Hall, 1939.

Burgess, E. W., and Wallin, P. *Engagement and Marriage*. Philadelphia: Lippincott, 1953.

Burkes, B. S. The relative influence of nature and nurture upon mental development: A comparative study of the foster parent–foster child resemblance and true parent–true child resemblance. *Nature and Nurture*. National Society for the Study of Education. 27th Yearbook. Part I. Bloomington, Ill.: Public School Publishing Co., 1928. Pp. 219–316.

Burkhart, R. C. *Spontaneous and Deliberate Ways of Learning*. Scranton, Pa.: International Textbook, 1962.

Burks, H. F. Research on pseudo-mental retardation. In J. H. Rothstein (ed.), *Mental Retardation*. New York: Holt, 1961. Pp. 64–68.

Burt, C. The factorial study of physical types. *Man*, 1944, 72, 82–86.

Burt, C. The inheritance of mental ability. *Amer. Psychologist*, 1958, 13, 1–15.

Burton, A. Psychotherapy with the mentally retarded. *Amer. J. ment. Defic.*, 1954, 58, 486–489.

Byrne, D., and Blaylock, Barbara. Similarity and assumed similarity of attitudes between husbands and wives. *J. abnorm. soc. Psychol.*, 1963, 67, 636–640.

Cameron, W. J., and Kenkel, W. F. High school dating: Study and variation. *Marriage and Family Living*, 1960, 22, 74–76.

Campbell, Eloise H. The social-sex development of children. *Genet. Psychol. Monogr.*, 1939, 21, 461–552.

Caplan, G. *Concepts of Mental Health and Consultation*. U.S. Department of Health, Education, and Welfare, Social Security Administration, Children's Bureau. Pub. No. 373. Washington, D.C.: Government Printing Office, 1959.

Caplan, G. (ed.). *Prevention of Mental Disorders in Children*. New York: Basic Books, 1961.

Carroll, J. B. *Language and Thought*. Englewood Cliffs, N.J.: Prentice-Hall, 1964.

Carter, R. S. How invalid are marks assigned by teachers? *J. educ. Psychol.*, 1952, 43, 218–228.

Cattell, J. McK. A statistical study of eminent men. *Popular Science Monthly*, 1903, 62, 359–377.

Cavan, Ruth S. *Juvenile Delinquency*. Philadelphia: Lippincott, 1960.

Charles, D. C. Ability and accomplishment of persons earlier judged mentally deficient. *Genet. Psychol. Monogr.*, 1953, 47, 3–71.

Charters, W. W. Social class and intelligence tests. In W. W. Charters and N. L. Gage (eds.), *Readings in the Social Psychology of Education*. Boston: Allyn & Bacon, 1963. Pp. 12–21.

Child, I. L. Socialization. In G. Lindzey (ed.), *Handbook of Social Psychology*. Reading, Mass.: Addison-Wesley, 1954. Pp. 655–692.

Child, I. L., and Waterhouse, I. K. Frustration and the quality of performance. I. A critique of the Barker, Dembo, and Lewin experiment. *Psychol. Rev.*, 1952, 59, 315–362.

Church, J. *Language and the Discovery of Reality*. New York: Random House, 1961.

Church, R. M. The varied effects of punishment on behavior. *Psychol. Rev.*, 1963, 70, 369–402.

Clark, E. J. Teachers' reactions towards objectionable pupil behavior. *Elem. Sch. J.*, 1951, 51, 446–449.

Clark, Margaret. The anthropology of aging, a new era for studies of culture and personality. *Gerontologist*, 1967, 7, 55–64.

Clarke, H. H., and Clarke, D. H. Social status and mental health of boys as related to their maturity, structural, and strength characteristics. *Res. Quart. Amer. Assn. Hlth., Phys. Educ., & Recrn.*, 1961, 32, 326–334.

Clarke, M., and Clarke, A. D. B. *Mental Deficiency: The Changing Outlook*. London: Methuen, 1958.

Clausen, J. A. Family structure, socialization, and personality. In M. L. Hoffman and Lois W. Hoffman (eds.), *Review of Child Development Research*. New York: Russell Sage Foundation, 1966.

Cloward, R. A., and Ohlin, L. E. *Delinquency and Opportunity*. New York: Free Press, 1960.

Cohen, A. K. *Delinquent Boys: The Culture of the Gang*. New York: Free Press, 1955.

Cohen, F. J. *Children in Trouble: An Experiment in Institutional Child Care*. New York: Norton, 1952.

Cohen, S. Lysergic acid diethylamide: Side effects and complications. *J. nerv. & ment. Diseases*, 1960, 130, 131.

Cole, C. C. Current loss of talents in high school. *Higher Educ.*, 1955, 12, 35–38.

Coleman, J. S. *The Adolescent Society*. New York: Free Press, 1961.

Coleman, J. S. Social climates in high schools. *Cooperative Research Monograph No. 4*. Washington, D.C.: U.S. Department of Health, Education, and Welfare. Pp. 9–29.

Conner, Ruth, Johannis, T. B., and Walters, J. Parent-adolescent conflicts: Current and in retrospect. *J. Home Econ.*, 1954, 46, 183–186.

Corwin, R. G. Role conceptions and career aspiration: A study of identity in nursing. *Sociol. Quart.*, April, 1961, 11, 69–86.

Cowles, J. T. Food tokens as incentives for learning by chimpanzees. *Comp. Psychol. Monogr.*, 1937, 14, No. 5.

Crandall, V. J. Achievement. In H. W. Stevenson (ed.), *Child Psychology. Yearbk. Nat. Soc. Study Educ.*, 1963, Part 1. Pp. 415–459.

Crandall, V. J., and Preston, Anne. Patterns and levels of maternal behavior. *Child Developm.*, 1955, 26, 267–277.

Crandall, V. J., Preston, Anne, and Rabson, Alice. Maternal reactions and the development of achievement behavior in young children. *Child Developm.*, 1960, 31, 242–251.

Crawford, P. R., Malamud, D. I., and Dumpson, J. R. *Working with Teen-Age Groups: A Report on the Central Highland Street-Clubs Project*. New York: New York Welfare Council of New York City, 1950.

Cronbach, L. J. *Educational Psychology*. New York: Harcourt, 1954.

Cuber, J. F., and Kunkel, W. F. *Social Stratification in the United States*. New York: Appleton-Century-Crofts, 1954.

Cummings, Elaine, *et al.* Disengagement—A tentative theory of aging. *Sociometry*, 1960, 23, 15–21.

Cummings, Elaine, and Henry, W. E. *Growing Old: The Process of Disengagement*. New York: Basic Books, 1961.

Cutler, R. L., and McNeil, E. B. *Mental Health Consultation in Schools: A Research Analysis*. Ann Arbor, Michigan, 1962.

Dager, E. Z. Socialization and personality development in the child. In H. T. Christensen (ed.), *Handbook of Marriage and the Family.* Chicago: Rand McNally, 1964. Pp. 740–781.

Darwin, C. A biographical sketch of an infant. *Mind,* 1877, 2, 285–294.

Davenport, C. B., and Danielson, Florence H. *The Hill Folk.* New York: Cold Spring Harbor, 1912.

Davie, J. S. Social class factors and school attendance. *Harv. educ. Rev.,* 1953, 23, 178.

Davis, A. *Social-Class Influences upon Learning.* Cambridge, Mass.: Harvard Univ. Press, 1948.

Davis, A. Socio-economic influences upon children's learning. *Understanding the Child,* 1951, 20, 10–16.

Davis, A., and Dollard, J. *Children of Bondage.* Washington, D.C.: American Council on Education, 1940.

Davis, A., and Gardner, J. *Deep South.* Chicago: Univ. Chicago Press, 1941.

Davis, A., and Havighurst, R. J. Social class and color differences in child rearing. *Amer. sociol. Rev.,* 1946, 11, 698–710.

Davis, E. A. The form and function of children's questions. *Child Developm.,* 1932, 3, 57–74.

Davis, K. *Human Society.* New York: Macmillan, 1949.

Dawe, H. C. An analysis of two hundred quarrels of preschool children. *Child Developm.,* 1934, 5, 139–157.

Delp, H. A., and Lorenz, Marcella. Follow-up of eighty-four public school special class pupils with I.Q.'s below fifty. *Amer. J. ment. Def.,* 1953, 58, 175–182.

Dennis, W. Variations in productivity among creative workers. *Sci. Mont.,* 1955, 80, 277–278.

Dennis, W., and Najarian, T. Infant development under environmental handicap. *Psychol. Monogr.,* 1957, 71, 1–13.

Dennis, W., and Sayegh, Yvonne. The effect of supplementary experiences upon the behavioral development of infants in institutions. *Child Developm.,* 1965, 36, 81–90.

Denny, R. American youth today: A bigger cast, a wider screen. In E. H. Erikson (ed.), *Youth: Change and Challenge.* New York: Basic Books, 1963. Pp. 131–151.

Derman, L. M. *Psychological Factors in Marital Happiness.* New York: McGraw-Hill, 1938.

Deutsch, M. Minority group and class status as related to social and personality factors in scholastic achievement. In M. Grossack (ed.), *Mental Health and Segregation.* New York: Springer, 1963.

D'Evelyn, Kathrine. *Meeting Children's Emotional Needs: A Guide for Teachers.* Englewood Cliffs, N.J.: Prentice-Hall, 1957.

Devereaux, G. *Therapeutic Education.* New York: Harper, 1956.

Dewey, R., and Humber, W. J. *An Introduction to Social Psychology.* New York: Macmillan, 1966.

Dinger, J. Postschool adjustment of former educable retarded children. *Except. Child.,* 1961, 27, 353–360.

Ditman, K. S., Hayman, N., and Whittlesey, J. R. B. Nature and frequency of claims following LSD. *J. nerv. & ment. Diseases,* 1962, 134, 346–352.

Dollard, J. *Caste and Class in a Southern Town.* New Haven, Conn.: Yale Univ. Press, 1937.

Douglas, J. W. B. *The Home and the School: A Study of Ability and Attainment in the Primary School.* London: MacGibbon & Kee, 1964.

Dreikurs, R. Coping with the child's problems in the classroom. In G. Monroe and Gloria B. Gottsegen (eds.), *Professional School Psychology.* New York: Grune & Stratton, 1960. Pp. 162–176.

Dunn, L. M. Educable mentally retarded children. In L. M. Dunn (ed.), *Exceptional Children in the Schools.* New York: Holt, 1963. Pp. 53–128.

Dunn, L. M. A historical review of the treatment of the retarded. In J. H. Rothstein (ed.), *Mental Retardation.* New York: Holt, 1961. Pp. 13–17.

Dunn, L. M. Mentally retarded children. *Encyclopedia of Educational Research,* 3rd Ed. 1960. Pp. 835–848.

Duvall, Evelyn M. *Family Development.* Philadelphia: Lippincott, 1962.

Duvall, Evelyn M. *In-Laws—Pro and Con.* New York: Association Press, 1954.

Eaton, J. W., and Weil, R. J. *Culture and Mental Disorders.* New York: Free Press, 1955.

Edwards, A. S., and Jones, L. An experimental and field study of North Georgia mountaineers. *J. soc. Psychol.,* 1938, 9, 317–333.

Eells, K. Some implications for school practice of the Chicago studies of cultural bias in intelligence tests. *Harv. educ. Rev.*, 1953, *23*, 289–290.

Ehrmann, W. *Premarital Dating Behavior*. New York: Holt, 1959.

Eisenberg, L. The autistic child in adolescence. *Amer. J. Psychiat.*, 1956, *112*, 607–612.

Elder, G. H., and Bowerman, C. E. Family structure and child rearing patterns: The effect of family size and sex corporation. *Amer. sociol. Rev.*, 1963, *28*, 891–905.

Elkin, H. Aggressive and erotic tendencies in army life. *Amer. J. Sociol.*, 1946, *51*, 408–413.

Ellis, A. *The Folklore of Sex*. New York: Grove Press, 1961.

Ellis, A. A study of 300 sex offenders. *Int. J. Sexol.*, 1951, *4*, 127–134.

Elser, R. The social position of rearing handicapped children in the regular grades. *Except. Child.*, 1959, *25*, 190–192.

Engel, G. L. *Psychological Development in Health and Disease*. Philadelphia: Saunders, 1962.

English, H. B., and English, Ava C. *A Comprehensive Dictionary of Psychological and Psychoanalytical Terms*. New York: McKay, 1958.

Ericson, Martha C. Child rearing and social status. *Amer. J. Sociol.*, 1946, *53*, 190–192.

Erikson, E. H. *Childhood and Society*. New York: Norton, 1950.

Ervin-Tripp, Susan. Language development. In M. L. Hoffman and Lois W. Hoffman (eds.), *Review of Child Development Research*. New York: Russell Sage Foundation, 1966. Pp. 55–105.

Estabrook, A. H. *The Jukes in 1915*. Washington, 1916.

Estabrook, A. H., and Davenport, C. B. *The Nam Family*. New York: Cold Spring Harbor, 1912.

Feinberg, M. R., Smith, M., and Schmidt, R. An analysis of expressions used by adolescents at varying economic levels to describe accepted and rejected peers. *J. genet. Psychol.*, 1958, *93*, 133–148.

Fichter, J. *Sociology*. Chicago: Univ. Chicago Press, 1957.

Finch, S. M. *Fundamentals of Child Psychiatry*. New York: Norton, 1960.

Findley, J. D., and Brady, J. V. Facilitation of large ratio performance by use of conditioned reinforcement. *J. exp. anal. Behav.*, 1965, *8*, 125–129.

Finestone, H. Cats, kicks, and color. In M. Stein, A. Vidich, and D. White (eds.), *Identity and Anxiety: Survival of the Person in Mass Society*. New York: Free Press, 1960. Pp. 435–448.

Fisher, L. C., and Wolfson, I. N. Group therapy of mental defectives. *Amer. J. ment. Def.*, 1953, *57*, 463–476.

Fisher, M. D., and Birren, J. E. Age and strength. *J. appl. Psychol.*, 1947, *31*, 490–497.

Fiske, D. W. A study of relationships to somatotype. *J. appl. Psychol.*, 1944, *28*, 504–519.

Flinner, I. A. Rating students on the basis of natural capacity and accomplishment. *Ed. Adm. Sup.*, 1923, *9*, 87–98.

Folsom, J. K. *The Family and Democratic Society*. New York: Wiley, 1943.

Fort, J. Social and legal response to pleasure giving drugs. In R. Blum *et al.* (eds.), *Utopiates*. New York: Atherton Press, 1965. Pp. 205–223.

Fosdick, H. E. *On Being a Real Person*. New York: Harper, 1943.

Fraiberg, Selma H. *The Magic Years*. New York: Scribner's, 1959.

Francis, R. J., and Rarick, G. L. *Motor Characteristics of the Mentally Retarded*. Cooperative Research Bulletin No. 1, U.S. Office of Education 35005. Washington, D.C.: Government Printing Office, 1960.

Frazier, E. F. *Black Bourgeoisie*. New York: Collier Books, 1962.

Frazier, E. F. *Negro Youth at Crossways*. Washington, D.C.: American Council on Education, 1940.

Fretsch, J. L. (ed.). *Educating the Gifted*. New York: Holt, 1959.

Freud, A. The role of bodily illness in the mental life of children. *Psychoanal. study Child.*, 1952, *7*, 70.

Freud, S. *New Introductory Lectures on Psychoanalysis*. New York: Norton, 1933.

Freud, S. *An Outline of Psychoanalysis*. New York: Norton, 1949.

Friedman, R., *et al. Principles of Sociology*. New York: Holt, 1956.

Furfey, P. H. *The Growing Boy*. New York: Macmillan, 1930.

Gaier, E. L., and Jones, S. Do teachers understand classroom behavior? *Understanding the Child*, 1951, 20, 104–109.

Gaines, B. LSD: Hollywood's status symbol drug. *Cosmopolitan*, November 1963.

Gallagher, J. J. *Teaching the Gifted Child*. Boston: Allyn & Bacon, 1964.

Gardner, L. Pearl. An analysis of children's attitudes towards fathers. *J. genet. Psychol.*, 1947, 70, 3–28.

Garrison, K. C. World minded attitudes of college students in a Southern university. *J. soc. Psychol.*, 1961, 54, 147–153.

Geiss, G. L., Steffins, W. C., and Lundin, R. W. *Reflex and Operant Conditioning: The Study of Behavior*. Vol. I. New York: Appleton-Century-Crofts, 1965.

Geleerd, Elizabeth R. The beginnings of aggressiveness in children. *Child Study*, 1957, 34, 3–7.

Gibson, Eleanor J., and Olum, Vivian. Experimental methods of studying perception in children. In P. H. Mussen (ed.), *Handbook of Research Methods in Child Development*. New York: Wiley, 1960. Pp. 311–373.

Gibson, Eleanor J., and Walk, R. D. The "visual cliff." *Sci. Amer.*, 1960, 202, 64–71.

Gilbert, G. N. A survey of "referral problems" in metropolitan child guidance centers. *J. clin. Psychol.*, 1957, 13, 37–42.

Glaser, B. G., and Strauss, A. L. *Awareness of Dying*. Chicago: Aldine, 1965.

Glazer, N. Introduction. In S. M. Elkins, *Slavery*. New York: Grosset & Dunlap, 1963.

Glueck, S., and Glueck, Eleanor, *Unravelling Juvenile Delinquency*. New York: Commonwealth Fund, 1950.

Goddard, H. H. *The Kallikak Family: A Study in the Heredity of Feeble-Mindedness*. New York: Macmillan, 1912.

Goldaimond, I. Justified and unjustified alarm over behavioral control. In O. Milton (ed.), *Behavior Disorders: Perspectives and Trends*. Philadelphia: Lippincott, 1965. Pp. 237–262.

Goldberg, I. I., and Cruickshank, W. N. The trainable but non-educable: Whose responsibility? *Nat. Educ. Assn. J.*, 1958, 47, 662–663.

Goldfarb, A. I. Age and illness. In H. I. Lief, V. F. Lief, and Nina R. Lief (eds.), *The Psychological Basis of Medical Practice*. New York: Harper, 1965. Pp. 203–218.

Goldfarb, W. Effects of early institutional care on adolescent personality (graphic Rorschach data). *Child Developm.*, 1943, 14, 213–223.

Goldfarb, W. Effects of early institutional care on adolescent personality: Rorschach data. *Amer. J. Orthopsychiat.*, 1944, 14, 441–447.

Goode, W. J. *After Divorce*. New York: Free Press, 1956.

Goode, W. J. Family disorganization. In R. K. Merton and R. A. Nisbet (eds.), *Contemporary Social Problems*. New York: Harcourt, 1961.

Goode, W. J. A theory of role strain. *Amer. sociol. Rev.*, 1960, 25, 483–496.

Goodenough, Florence L. *Exceptional Children*. New York: Appleton-Century-Crofts, 1956.

Goodenough, Florence L., and Mauer, K. M. The mental development of nursery school children compared with that of non-nursery school children. *Yearbk. Nat. Soc. Study Educ.*, 1940, 39, Part II, 161–178.

Goodenough, Florence L., and Tyler, Leona E. *Developmental Psychology*. New York: Appleton-Century-Crofts, 1959.

Gordon, N. The hallucinogenic drug cult. *The Reporter*, 1963, 29, 35–43.

Gordon, W. C. *The Social System of the High School*. New York: Free Press, 1957.

Gorer, G. *The American People: A Study of National Character*. New York: Norton, 1948.

Gottlieb, D., and Reeves, J. *Adolescent Behavior in Urban Areas*. New York: Macmillan, 1963.

Gowin, E. D. *The Executive and His Control of Men*. New York: Macmillan, 1927.

Greene, W. A. Role of a vicarious object in the adaption to loss. I. Use of a vicarious object as a means of adjustment to separation from a significant person. *Psychosom. Med.*, 1958, 20, 344.

Gregory, I. Anterospective data following childhood loss of a parent: Delinquency and high school dropout. *Arch. gen. Psychiat.*, 1965, 13, 99–109.

Gross, E., and Stone, G. P. Embarrassment and the analysis of role requirements. *Amer. J. Sociol.*, 1964, 70, 1–15.

Grünbaum, A. Causality and the science of human behavior. *Amer. Sci.*, 1952, 40, 665–676.

Guilford, J. P. Structure of intellect. *Psychol. Bull.*, 1956, 53, 267–293.

Habe, D. F., and Azim, N. H. Conditioned punishment. *J. exp. anal. Behav.*, 1965, 8, 279–293.

Hadley, S. T. School marks—Fact or fancy? *Ed. Adm. Sup.*, 1954, 40, 305–312.

Hall, G. S. *Adolescence.* 2 Vols. New York: Appleton-Century-Crofts, 1904.

Hall, G. S. The contents of children's minds on entering school. *Pedological Sem.*, 1891, 1, 139–173.

Harlow, H. F. Love in infant monkeys. *Sci. Amer.*, 1959, 200, 68–74.

Harlow, H. F. The nature of love. *Amer. Psychologist*, 1958, 13, 673–685.

Harlow, H. F., and Harlow, Margaret K. The effect of rearing conditions on behavior. *Bull. Menninger Clinic*, 1962, 26, 213–224.

Harlow, H. F., and Harlow, Margaret K. A study of animal affection. *Nat. Hist.*, 1961, 70, 48–55.

Hartogs, R. Discipline in the early life of sex delinquents and sex criminals. *Nerv. Child*, 1951, 9, 167–173.

Hatfield, J. S., Ferguson, Lucy R., and Alpert, R. Mother-child interaction and the socialization process. *Child Developm.*, 1967, 38, 365–414.

Havemann, E., and West, Patricia S. *They Went to College: The College Graduate in America Today.* New York: Harcourt, 1952.

Havighurst, R. J. *Human Development and Education.* New York: McKay, 1953.

Havighurst, R. J. What are the cultural differences which may affect performance on intelligence tests? In K. Eells *et al.* (eds.), *Intelligence and Cultural Differences.* Chicago: Univ. Chicago Press, 1951. P. 20.

Healy, W., and Bronner, A. F. *New Light on Delinquency and Its Treatment.* New Haven, Conn.: Yale Univ. Press, 1936.

Heath, C. W. *What People Are: A Study of Normal Young Men.* Cambridge, Mass.: Harvard Univ. Press, 1945.

Heath, D. H. *Explorations of Maturity.* New York: Appleton-Century-Crofts, 1965.

Heinicke, C. L., and Whiting, Beatrice B. *Bibliographies on Personality and Social Development of the Child.* New York: Social Science Research Council, 1953.

Heiser, K. Psychotherapy in a residential school for mentally retarded children. *Training Sch. Bull.*, 1954, 50, 211–218.

Henning, Carol J. Discipline: Are school practices changing? *Clearing House*, 1949, 23, 267–273.

Heron, J. S. How teachers rate their pupils. *Dept. Elem. Sch. Prin.*, 1929, 8, 235–239.

Herrick, V. E. What is already known about the relation of the I.Q. to cultural background? In K. Eells *et al.* (eds.), *Intelligence and Cultural Differences.* Chicago: Univ. Chicago Press, 1951. P. 12.

Hertzman, J., and Mueller, Margaret L. The adolescent in the school group. In M. Krugman (ed.), *Orthopsychiatry and the School.* New York: American Orthopsychiatric Association, 1958. Pp. 225–234.

Heyns, R. W. *The Psychology of Personal Adjustment.* New York: Dryden Press, 1958.

Hilgard, E. R. *Introduction to Psychology.* 3rd Ed. New York: Harcourt, 1962.

Hill, R., and Rodgers, R. H. The developmental approach. In H. H. Christensen (ed.), *Handbook of Marriage and the Family.* Chicago: Rand McNally, 1964. Pp. 171–211.

Hinton, J. *Dying.* Baltimore: Penguin Books, 1967.

Hoch, O. Improving the present status of the creative student. *High Sch. J.*, 1962, 46, 14–22.

Hoffman, M. L. Child rearing practices and moral development: Generalizations from empirical research. *Child Developm.*, 1963, 34, 295–318.

Holland, J. G., and Skinner, B. F. *The Analysis of Behavior.* New York: McGraw-Hill, 1961.

Hollingshead, A. B. *Elmstown's Youth.* New York: Wiley, 1949.

Horowitz, E. L., and Smith, R. B. Social relations and personality patterning in pre-school children. *J. genet. Psychol.*, 1939, 54, 337–352.

Horrocks, J. E. Adolescent attitudes and goals. In M. Sherif and C. Sherif (eds.), *Problems of Youth: Transition to Adulthood in a Changing World.* Chicago: Aldine, 1965. Pp. 15–27.

Horrocks, J. E. *The Psychology of Adolescence.* Boston: Houghton Mifflin, 1962.

Hsia, J. C. A *Study of Sociability of Elementary School Children.* New York: Teachers College, Columbia Univ., 1928.

Hughes, E. C. *Men and Their Work.* New York: Free Press, 1958.

Hunt, J. M. The psychological basis for using pre-school enrichment as an antidote for cultural deprivation. *Merrill-Palmer Quart.*, 1964, 10, 209–248.

Hunter, E. C. Attitudes and professional relationships of teachers: A study of teacher morale. *J. exp. Educ.*, 1955, 23, 345–352.

Hurlock, Elizabeth B. *Adolescent Development.* New York: McGraw-Hill, 1955.

Hutchinson, W. L. Creative and productive thinking in the classroom. Doctoral dissertation. Salt Lake City: Univ. Utah, 1961.

Inlow, G. M. Job satisfaction of liberal arts graduates. *J. appl. Psychol.*, 1951, 35, 175–181.

Jahoda, Marie. Toward a social psychology of mental health. In M. J. E. Senn (ed.), *Symposium on the Healthy Personality.* Supplement II. New York: Josiah Macy, Jr., Foundation, 1950.

James, W. *Varieties of Religious Experience.* New York: McKay, 1902.

Jersild, A. T. *Child Psychology.* Englewood Cliffs, N.J.: Prentice-Hall, 1960.

Jersild, A. T. *When Teachers Face Themselves.* New York: Bureau of Publications, Teachers College, Columbia Univ., 1955.

Jersild, A. T., and Fite, Mary D. The influence of nursery school experience on children's social adjustments. *Monogr. soc. res. child Developm.*, 1939, No. 25, 1–112.

Joel, W. The influence of nursery school education upon behavior maturity. *J. exp. Educ.*, 1939, 8, 164–165.

Johnson, C. S. *Growing Up in the Black Belt.* Washington, D.C.: American Council on Education, 1941.

Johnson, G. O. A study of social adequacy and of social failure of mentally retarded youth in Wayne County, Michigan. *Except. Child.*, 1957, 24, 136–138.

Johnson, G. O., and Kirk, S. A. Are mentally handicapped children segregated in the regular grades? *Except. Child.*, 1950, 17, 65–67.

Johnson, H. *Sociology.* New York: Harcourt, 1960.

Johnson, O. A study of social position in mentally handicapped children in the regular grades. *Amer. J. ment. Def.*, 1950, 55, 60–89.

Johnson, R. C., and Medinnus, R. G. *Child Psychology: Behavior and Development.* New York: Wiley, 1965.

Jones, H. E. Adolescence in our society. In *The Family in a Democratic Society: Anniversary Papers of the Community Service Society of New York.* New York: Columbia Univ. Press, 1949. Pp. 70–82.

Jones, H. E., and Jorgensen, A. P. Mental growth as related to nursery school attendance. *Yearbk. Nat. Soc. Study Educ.*, 1940, 39, Part II, 207–222.

Jones, L. W. The new world view of Negro youth. In M. Sherif and C. Sherif (eds.), *Problems of Youth.* Chicago: Aldine, 1965. Pp. 65–68.

Jones, Mary C. The later careers of boys who were early- or late-maturing. *Child Developm.*, 1957, 28, 113–128.

Jones, Mary C., and Bayley, Nancy. Physical maturing among boys as related to behavior. *J. educ. Psychol.*, 1950, 41, 129–148.

Jones, Mary C., and Burks, Barbara S. Personality development in childhood. *Monogr. soc. res. child Developm.*, 1936, 1, 205.

Jones, Mary C., and Mussen, P. H. Self-conceptions, motivations, and inter-personal attitudes of early-late maturing girls. *Child Developm.*, 1958, 29, 491–501.

Jordan, A. M. Parental occupations and children's intelligence scores. *J. appl. Psychol.*, 1933, 17, 103–119.

Jordan, T. E., and DeCharmes, R. The achievement motive in normal and mentally retarded children. *Amer. J. ment. Def.*, 1950, 55, 60–89.

Josselyn, Irene. Acting out in adolescence. In L. E. Abt and S. L. Weissman (eds.), *Acting Out.* New York: Grune & Stratton, 1965. Pp. 68–75.

Kahn, R. L., et al. *Organizational Stress: Studies in Role Conflict and Ambiguity.* New York: Wiley, 1964.

Kalish, R. A. Of children and grandfathers: A speculative essay on dependency. *Gerontologist*, 1967, 7, 65–69.

Kamii, Constance K. Socioeconomic Class Differences in the Preschool Socialization Practices of Negro Mothers. Unpublished doctoral dissertation. Univ. Michigan, 1965.

Kanner, L. Autistic disturbances of affective contact. *Nerv. Child*, 1943, 2, 217–250.

Kanner, L., and Lesser, L. I. Early infantile autism. *Pediatrics Clinic of North America*, 1958, 5, 711–730.

Kaplan, L. The annoyances of elementary school teachers. *J. educ. Res.*, 1952, *45*, 649–665.

Kardiner, A. *The Individual and His Society*. New York: Columbia Univ. Press, 1939.

Kardiner, A. *The Psychological Frontiers of Society*. New York: Columbia Univ. Press, 1945.

Karrin, E. J., and Howard, D. H. Post-marital consequences of pre-marital sex adjustments. *Amer. sociol. Rev.*, 1958, 23, 556–562.

Katz, I., Cohen, M., and Castiglione, C. Effect of one type of need complementarity on marriage partners' conformity to one another's judgments. *J. abnorm. soc. Psychol.*, 1963, *67*, 8–14.

Kawi, A. A., and Pasamanick, B. Prenatal and paranatal factors in the development of childhood reading disorders. *Monogr. soc. res. child Developm.*, 1959, 24, No. 4.

Kay, P. The acting out child. In L. E. Abt and S. L. Weissman (eds.), *Acting Out*. New York: Grune & Stratton, 1965. Pp. 48–67.

Kelly, E. L. Concerning the validity of Terman's ways for predicting marital happiness. *Psychol. Bull.*, 1939, 306, 202–203.

Kennedy, W. A., Van De Reit, W., and White, J. C., Jr. A normative sample of intelligence and achievement of Negro elementary school children in the southeastern United States. *Monogr. soc. res. child Developm.*, 1963, 28, 1–112.

Kenniston, K. Social change and youth in America. In E. H. Erikson (ed.), *Youth: Change and Challenge*. New York: Basic Books, 1963. Pp. 161–187.

Killam, K. Psychopharmacological considerations. In R. Blum *et al.* (eds.), *Utopiates*. New York: Atherton Press, 1965. Pp. 118–123.

Kinsey, A. C. *Sexual Behavior in the Human Female*. Philadelphia: Saunders, 1953.

Kinsey, A. C., Pomeroy, W. B., and Martin, C. E. *Sexual Behavior in the Human Male*. Philadelphia: Saunders, 1948.

Kirk, S. *Early Education of the Mentally Retarded*. Urbana, Ill.: Univ. Illinois Press, 1958.

Kite, Elizabeth A. *The Pineys*. New York, 1913.

Kitto, H. D. F. *The Greeks*. Harmsworth, England: Penguin Books, 1951.

Klineberg, O. Negro-white differences in intelligence test performance: A new look at an old problem. *Amer. Psychologist*, 1963, *18*, 198–203.

Kluckholn, C. *Mirror for Man*. New York: McGraw-Hill, 1949.

Kluckhohn, C. Variations in the human family. In N. W. Bell and E. F. Vogel (eds.), *The Family*. New York: Free Press, 1960. Pp. 45–51.

Kobler, J. The dangerous magic of LSD. *The Saturday Evening Post*, November 5, 1963.

Kogan, J. The concept of identification. *Psychol. Rev.*, 1958, *65*, 296–305.

Kohn, M. L. Social class and parent-child relationships: An interpretation. *Amer. J. Sociol.*, 1963, *68*, 471–480.

Kolstoe, O. An examination of some characteristics which discriminate between employed and non-employed mentally retarded males. *Amer. J. ment. Def.*, 1961, *60*, 472–478.

Konopka, G. *Group Work in the Institution: A Modern Challenge*. New York: Morrow, 1954.

Kostir, Mary S. *The Family of Sam Sixty*. New York, 1916.

Kough, J., and DeHaan, R. F. *Identifying Children with Special Needs*. Vol. I. Chicago: Science Research Associates, 1955.

Krasner, L. The behavioral scientist and social responsibility: No place to hide. *J. soc. Issues*, 1965, *21*, 9–30.

Krech, D., Crutchfield, R. S., and Ballachy, E. L. *Individual and Society*. New York: McGraw-Hill, 1963.

Kuhlen, R. G., and Johnson, G. H. Change and goals with increasing adult age. *J. consult. Psychol.*, 1952, *16*, 1–14.

Kvaraceus, W. C. *Anxious Youth: Dynamics of Delinquency*. Columbus, Ohio: Merrill, 1966.

Kvaraceus, W. C. *The Community and the Delinquent*. New York: Harcourt, 1954.

Lafore, G. G. *Practices of Parents in Dealing with Preschool Children*. New York: Columbia Univ. Press, 1945.

Lamson, E. E. A follow-up study of a group of nursery school children. *Yearbk. Nat. Soc. Study Educ.*, 1940, 39, Part II, 231–236.

Landis, J. T. Experiences of 500 children with adult sexual deviation. *Psychiat. quart. Suppl.*, 1956, 30, 91–109.

Landis, J. T. The trauma of children when parents divorce. *Marriage and Family Living,* 1960, 22, 7–13.

Landis, J. T. What is the happiest period of life? *Sch. & Soc.,* 1942, 55, 643–645.

Langford, W. S. Physical illness and convalescence: Their meaning to the child. *J. Pediat.,* 1948, 33, 242.

Lansing, A. I. (ed.). *Problems of Aging.* Baltimore: Williams & Wilkins, 1952.

Larrich, Nancy. The all-white world of children's books. *Saturday Review,* 1965, 48, 63–65.

Lawson, P. *Frustration.* New York: Macmillan, 1965.

Laycock, F., and Caylor, J. S. Physiques of gifted children and their less gifted siblings. *Child Developm.,* 1964, 35, 63–74.

Lazarus, R. S. *Psychological Stress and the Coping Process.* New York: McGraw-Hill, 1966.

Leahy, A. N. Nature, nurture, and intelligence. *Genet. Psychol. Monogr.,* 1935, 17, 236–308.

Leahy, A. N. A study of certain selective factors influencing prediction of the mental status of adopted children. *J. genet. Psychol.,* 1932, 41, 294–329.

Leary, T., Metzner, R., and Alpert, R. *The Psychedelic Experience: A Manual Based on the Tibetan Book of the Dead.* New York: University Books, 1964.

Lee, J. J., Hegge, T. G., and Voelker, P. H. *A Study of Social Adequacy and Social Failure of Mentally Retarded Youth in Wayne County, Michigan.* Detroit: Wayne State University, 1959.

Lehman, H. C. *Age and Achievement.* Princeton, N.J.: Princeton Univ. Press, 1953.

Lehman, H. C. The age decrement in outstanding scientific creativity. *Amer. Psychologist,* 1960, 15, 128–134.

Lehman, H. C. The most proficient years at sports and games. *Res. Quart. Amer. Assn. Hlth., Phys. Educ., & Recrn.,* 1938, 9, 319.

Levine, S. Stimulation in infancy. *Sci. Amer.,* 1960, 202, 80–86.

Levinger, G., and Breedlove, J. Interpersonal attraction and agreement: A study of marriage partners. *J. pers. soc. Psychol.,* 1966, 3, 367–372.

Levy, D. M. *Maternal Overprotection.* New York: Columbia Univ. Press, 1943.

Lewin, K. *A Dynamic Theory of Personality.* New York: McGraw-Hill, 1935.

Lewin, K. *Field Theory in Social Science.* New York: Harper, 1951.

Lewis, Claudia. *Children of the Cumberlands.* New York: Columbia Univ. Press, 1946.

Lewis, Gertrude M. *Educating Children in Grades Four, Five, and Six.* Washington, D.C.: U.S. Office of Education, U.S. Department of Health, Education, and Welfare, 1958.

Lewis, M. M. *Language, Thought, and Personality in Infancy and Childhood.* New York: Basic Books, 1963.

Lewis, O. *The Children of Sanchez.* New York: Random House, 1961.

Liss, E. The ego ideal role in learning. In M. Krugman (ed.), *Orthopsychiatry and the School.* New York: American Orthopsychiatric Association, 1958. Pp. 102–104.

Loeb, Janice, and Price, J. R. Mother and child personality characteristics related to parental marital status in child guidance cases. *J. consult. Psychol.,* 1966, 30, 112–117.

Loeb, M. M. Implications of status differentiation for personal and social development. *Harv. educ. Rev.,* 1953, 23, 168–169.

Loevinger, Jane. Patterns of parenthood as theories of learning. *J. abnorm. soc. Psychol.,* 1959, 59, 148–150.

Lowe, C. M. Value orientations: An ethical dilemma. *Amer. Psychologist,* 1959, 14, 687–693.

Lowrie, S. H. The factors involved in the frequency of dating. *Marriage and Family Living,* 1956, 18, 46–51.

Lucito, L. J. Gifted children. In L. M. Dunn (ed.), *Exceptional Children in the Schools.* New York: Holt, 1963. Pp. 179–238.

Luria, A. R. *The Role of Speech in the Regulation of Normal and Abnormal Behavior.* New York: Liveright, 1961.

McClelland, D. C. *The Achieving Society.* Princeton, N.J.: Van Nostrand, 1961.

McCord, W., McCord, J., and Verden, P. Family relationships and sexual deviance in·lower class adolescents. *Int. J. soc. Psychiat.,* 1962, 8, 165–179.

Mackie, R. P., and Dunn, L. M. *College and University Programs for the Preparation of Teachers of Exceptional Children.* Washington, D.C.: U.S. Office of Education, 1962.

McNeil, E. B. *The Concept of Human Development*. Belmont, Calif.: Wadsworth, 1966.

McNeil, E. B. *The Nature of Human Conflict*. Englewood Cliffs, N. J.: Prentice-Hall, 1965.

McNeil, E. B. The paradox of education for the gifted. *Improving College and University Teaching*, 1960, 8, 111–115.

McNeil, E. B. Psychology and aggression. *J. Conflict Resolut.*, 1959, 3, No. 3, 195–293.

McNeil, E. B. Two styles of expression: Motoric and conceptual. In D. R. Miller and G. E. Swanson (eds.), *Inner Conflict and Defense*. New York: Holt, 1960. Pp. 337–356.

McNeil, E. B., and Morse, W. C. The institutional management of sex in emotionally disturbed children. *Amer. J. Orthopsychiat.*, 1964, 34, 115–124.

McNeill, D. Developmental psycholinguistics. In F. Smith and G. A. Miller (eds.), *The Genesis of Language: A Psycholinguistic Approach*. Cambridge, Mass.: M.I.T. Press, 1966.

Maier, H. W. *Three Theories of Child Development*. New York: Harper, 1965.

Maier, N. R. F. *Frustration*. New York: McGraw-Hill, 1949.

Maier, N. R. F. Frustration theory: Restatement and extension. *Psychol. Rev.*, 1956, 63, 370–388.

Maier, N. R. F., and Ellen, P. Can the anxiety reduction theory explain abnormal fixation? *Psychol. Rev.*, 1951, 58, 435–445.

Malinowski, B. Parenthood—The basis of social structure. In V. F. Calverton and S. D. Schmalhausen (eds.), *The New Generation*. New York: Macaulay, 1930. Pp. 113–168.

Mandler, G., Mussen, P., Kogan, N., and Wallach, M. A. *New Directions in Psychology III*. New York: Holt, 1967.

Marquis, D. G. Scientific methodology in human relations. *Proc. Amer. Phil. Soc.*, 1948, 92, 411–416.

Marshall, Hermine H. Behavior problems of normal children: A comparison between the lay literature and developmental research. *Child Developm.*, 1964, 35, 467–478.

Marshall, H. R. Relations between home experiences and children's use of language in play interactions with peers. *Psychol. Monogr.*, 1961, 75, 1–76.

Martin, B. Reward and punishment associated with the same good response: A factor in the learning of motives. *Psychol. Bull.*, 1963, 60, 441–451.

Martin, J. M., and Fitzpatrick, J. P. *Delinquent Behavior*. New York: Random House, 1964.

Masland, R. L. *Mental Subnormality*. New York: Basic Books, 1958.

Maslow, A. H. Self-actualizing people: A study of psychological health. *Personality*. Symposium 1, 1950, 11–34.

Mayer, A. J., and Hauser, P. Class differentials in life expectation at birth. In R. Bendix and S. N. Lipset (eds.), *Class, Status, and Power*. New York: Free Press, 1953.

Mayer, M. F. *A Guide for Child-Care Workers*. New York: The Child Welfare League of America, 1958.

Mead, Margaret. *Male and Female*. New York: Morrow, 1949.

Mead, Margaret. *Sex and Temperament in Three Primitive Societies*. New York: Morrow, 1935.

Medinnus, G. R. The relation between interparent agreement and several child measures. *J. genet. Psychol.*, 1963, 102, 139–144.

Mednick, S. A. *Learning*. Englewood Cliffs, N.J.: Prentice-Hall, 1964.

Merrill, B. A measurement of mother-child interaction. *J. abnorm. soc. Psychol.*, 1946, 41, 37–49.

Merrill, F. E. *Courtship and Marriage: A Study in Social Relationships*. New York: Sloane, 1949.

Meyerowitz, J. H. Self-derogation in young retardates and special class placement. *Child Developm.*, 1962, 33, 443–451.

Meyerson, L. Somatopsychology of physical disability. In W. M. Cruickshank (ed.), *Psychology of Exceptional Children and Youth*. Englewood Cliffs, N.J.: Prentice-Hall, 1963. Pp. 1–52.

Miller, D. R., and Swanson, G. E. *The Changing American Parent*. New York: Wiley, 1958.

Miller, W. D. Lower class culture as a generating milieu of gang delinquency. *J. soc. Issues*, 1958, 14, 5–19.

Mitford, Jessica. *The American Way of Death*. New York: Simon and Schuster, 1963.

Mogey, J. Family and community in urban-industrial societies. In H. T. Christensen (ed.), *Handbook of Marriage and the Family*. Chicago: Rand McNally, 1964. Pp. 501–534.

Monahan, T. P. One hundred years of marriages in Massachusetts. *Amer. J. Sociol.*, 1951, 56, 534–545.

Montagu, A. *The Humanization of Man.* New York: Grove Press, 1962.

Morgan, C. N. *The Attitudes and Adjustments of Recipients of Old Age Assistance in Upstate and Metropolitan New York.* New York: Archives of Psychology, 1937, 30, No. 214.

Morris, C. W. *Varieties of Human Values.* Chicago: Univ. Chicago Press, 1956.

Morris, M. *Cognitive Processes.* Belmont, Calif.: Wadsworth, 1966.

Morse, W. C. The mental hygiene dilemma in public education. *Amer. J. Orthopsychiat.*, 1961, 31, 324–331.

Morse, W. C., and Cutler, R. L. *Public School Classes for the Emotionally Handicapped: A Research Analysis.* Ann Arbor, Michigan, 1964.

Murdock, G. P. Comparative data on the division of labor by sex. *Soc. Forces*, 1937, 15, 551–553.

Murphy, G., Murphy, Lois B., and Newcomb, T. M. *Experimental Social Psychology.* New York: Harper, 1937.

Murphy, Lois B., *et al. The Widening World of Childhood: Paths toward Mastery.* New York: Basic Books, 1962.

Murray, E. J. *Motivation and Emotion.* Englewood Cliffs, N.J.: Prentice-Hall, 1964.

Mussen, P. H. Early socialization: Learning and identification. In G. Mandler *et al., New Directions in Psychology III.* New York: Holt, 1967. Pp. 53–110.

Mussen, P. H., and Jones, Mary C. Self-conceptions, motivations, and interpersonal attitudes of late-early maturing boys. *Child Developm.*, 1957, 28, 243–256.

Nash, J. The father in contemporary culture and current psychological literature. *Child Developm.*, 1965, 6, 262–297.

National Education Association. Teacher opinions on pupil behavior, 1955–1956. *Res. Bull.*, 1956, 34.

National Education Association, Research Division. The status of the American public school teacher. *Res. Bull.*, 1957, 35, 5–63.

Neill, A. S. *Summerhill.* New York: Hart, 1960.

Newcomb, T. Recent changes in attitudes toward sex and marriage. *Amer. sociol. Rev.*, 1937, 2, 659–667.

Newman, J. Psychological problems of children and youth with chronic medical disorders. In W. M. Cruickshank (ed.), *Psychology of Exceptional Children and Youth.* 2nd Ed. Englewood Cliffs, N.J.: Prentice-Hall, 1963. Pp. 394–447.

Northway, M. L. Outsiders: A study of the personality patterns of children least acceptable to their age mates. *Sociometry*, 1944, 7, 10–25.

Ojeman, R. H. Basic approaches to mental health. *Personnel and Guidance Journal*, 1958, 37, 377–397.

Ostrovsky, E. S. *Father to the Child.* New York: Putnam's, 1959.

Otlo, H. A. Criteria for assessing strength. *Fam. Process*, 1963, 2, 329–338.

Parsons, T. Certain sources and patterns of aggression in the social structure of the Western World. *Psychiat.*, 1947, 10, 172.

Pasamanick, B., Constantinou, F. K., and Lilienfeld, A. M. Pregnancy experience and the development of childhood speech disorders. *Amer. J. dis. Child*, 1956, 91, 113–118.

Pasamanick, B., and Kawi, A. A study of the association of prenatal and paranatal factors with the development of tics in children. *J. Pediat.*, 1956, 48, 596–601.

Pasamanick, B., Knobloch, Hilda, and Lilienfeld, A. M. Socioeconomic status and some precursors of neuropsychiatric disorder. *Amer. J. Orthopsychiat.*, 1956, 26, 594–601.

Pasamanick, B., and Lilienfeld, A. M. Association of maternal and fetal factors with development of mental deficiency. I. Abnormalities in the prenatal and paranatal periods. *J. Amer. Med. Assn.*, 1955, 159, 155–160.

Pasamanick, B., and Lilienfeld, A. M. Maternal and fetal factors in the development of epilepsy. II. Relationship to some clinical features of epilepsy. *Neurology*, 1955, 5, 77–83.

Pasamanick, B., Rogers, M. E., and Lilienfeld, A. M. Pregnancy experience and the development of behavior disorder in children. *Amer. J. Psychiat.*, 1956, 112, 613–618.

Pate, J. E. Emotionally disturbed and socially maladjusted children. In L. M. Dunn (ed.), *Exceptional Children in the Schools*. New York: Holt, 1963. Pp. 239–283.

Paterson, D. G. *Physique and Intellect*. New York: Appleton-Century-Crofts, 1930.

Payne, R. Attitudes toward the working wife. *Marriage and Family Living*, 1956, *18*, 345–348.

Payne, R. Some theoretical approaches to the sociology of aging. *Soc. Forces*, 1960, *38*, 359–362.

Pearl, A. Youth in lower class settings. In M. Sherif and C. Sherif (eds.), *Problems of Youth*. Chicago: Aldine, 1965. Pp. 89–109.

Pearson, G. J. H. *Adolescence and the Conflict of Generations*. New York: Norton, 1958.

Peck, R. F., and Havighurst, R. J. *The Psychology of Character Development*. New York: Wiley, 1960.

Peckham, R. Problems in job adjustment of the mentally retarded. *Amer. J. ment. Def.*, 1951, *56*, 448–453.

Pettigrew, T. F. *A Profile of the Negro American*. Princeton, N.J.: Van Nostrand, 1964.

Phelps, H. Postschool adjustment of mentally retarded children in selected Ohio cities. *Except. Child.*, 1956, *23*, 58–62.

Piaget, J. *The Child's Conception of Physical Causality*. London: Kegan Paul, 1930.

Piaget, J. *The Child's Conception of the World*. New York: Harcourt, 1929.

Piaget, J. *Judgment and Reasoning in the Child*. New York: Harcourt, 1928.

Piaget, J. *The Language and Thought of the Child*. New York: Harcourt, 1926.

Piaget, J. *The Moral Judgment of the Child*. New York: Harcourt, 1932.

Piaget, J. *The Origins of Intelligence in Children*. New York: International Universities Press, 1952.

Piaget, J. *The Psychology of Intelligence*. New York: Harcourt, 1950.

Pine, G. J. Social class, social mobility, and delinquent behavior. *Personnel and Guidance Journal*, 1965, *43*, 770–772.

Plant, W. T. *Personality Changes Associated with a College Education*. U.S. Department of Health, Education, and Welfare, Office of Education, Cooperative Research Project No. 348 (S.A.E. 766). San Jose, Calif.: San Jose State College, 1962.

Plutarch. The education of children. In Plutarch (M. Hadas, Translator), *Selected Essays on Love, the Family, and the Good Life*. New York: Metro-Books, 1957.

Podolsky, E. The emotional problems of the stepchild. *Ment. Hyg.*, 1955, *39*, 49–53.

Pond, D. A., Ryle, A., and Hamilton, Madge. Social factors and neurosis in a working-class population. *British J. Psychiat.*, 1963, *109*, 587–591.

Porterfield, A. L., and Salley, H. E. Current folk ways of sex behavior. *Amer. J. Sociol.*, 1946, *52*, 209–216.

Powdermaker, Hortense. *After Freedom*. New York: Viking, 1939.

Powdermaker, Hortense. The channeling of Negro aggression by the cultural process. *Amer. J. Sociol.*, 1943, *48*, 750–758.

Prescott, D. A. *The Child in the Educative Process*. New York: McGraw-Hill, 1957.

Pressey, S. L., and Kuhlen, R. G. *Psychological Development through the Life Span*. New York: Harper, 1957.

Rabin, A. I. Some psychosexual differences between kibbutz and nonkibbutz Israeli boys. *J. proj. Tech.*, 1958, *22*, 328–332.

Radke, Marian J. The relation of parental authority to children's behavior and attitudes. *Univ. Minn. Inst. Child Welf. Monogr.*, 1946, No. 22.

Rapaport, D. Psychoanalysis as a developmental psychology. In B. Kapland and S. Wapner (eds.), *Perspectives in Psychological Theory*. New York: International Universities Press, 1960. Pp. 209–255.

Reckless, W. C. *The Crime Problem*. New York: Appleton-Century-Crofts, 1960.

Redl, F. The concept of ego disturbance and ego support. *Amer. J. Orthopsychiat.*, 1951, *21*, 273–284.

Redl, F. The strategy and techniques of the life space interview. *Amer. J. Orthopsychiat.*, 1959, *29*, 1–18.

Redl, F., and Wineman, D. *Children Who Hate*. Glencoe, Ill.: Allen & Unwin, 1951.

Redl, F., and Wineman, D. *Controls from Within*. New York: Free Press, 1952.

Reese, Ellen. *The Analysis of Human Operant Behavior*. Dubuque, Iowa: Brown, 1966.

Reeves, F. W., and Bell, H. M. *American Youth Faces the Future*. Washington, D.C.: National Council for the Social Studies, National Education Association, 1942.

Rheingold, Harriet L., Gewirtz, J. L., and Ross, Helen W. Social conditioning of vocalizations in the infant. *J. comp. physiol. Psychol.*, 1959, 52, 68–73.

Rich, J. M. How social class values affect teacher-pupil relations. *J. educ. Sociol.*, 1960, 33, 355–359.

Riese, Hertha. *Heal the Hurt Child*. Chicago: Univ. Chicago Press, 1962.

Riesman, D., Denney, R., and Glazer, N. *The Lonely Crowd: A Study of the Changing American Character*. New Haven, Conn.: Yale Univ. Press, 1950.

Riessman, F. *The Culturally Deprived Child*. New York: Harper, 1962.

Riessman, R. Teaching the culturally deprived. *Nat. Educ. Assn. J.*, 1963a, 52, No. 4.

Robertson, J. *Young Children in Hospitals*. New York: Basic Books, 1959.

Rogers, C. R. *On Becoming a Person*. Boston: Houghton Mifflin, 1961.

Rokeach, M. *The Open and Closed Mind: Investigations into the Nature of Belief Systems and Personality Systems*. New York: Basic Books, 1960.

Rosenblatt, B. Some contributions of the psychoanalytic concept of development to personality research. *Monogr. Soc. Res. Child Developm.*, 1966, 31, 18–35.

Rosenblum, S., and Keller, J. E. Davis-Eells (culture fair) test performance of lower class retarded children. *J. consult. Psychol.*, 1955, 19, 51–54.

Rosenthal, D. Changes in some moral values following psychotherapy. *J. consult. Psychol.*, 1955, 19, 431–436.

Rousseau, J. J. *Emile*. New York: Appleton-Century-Crofts, 1895.

Rugg, H. O. Teachers' marks and marking systems. *Ed. Adm. Sup.*, 1915, 1, 117–142.

Sampson, E. E. The study of ordinal position: Antecedents and outcomes. In B. Maher (ed.), *Progress in Experimental-Personality Research*. Vol. II. New York: Academic Press, 1965. Pp. 175–228.

Sanford, R. N., *et al.* Physique, personality, and scholarship. *Monogr. Soc. Res. Child Developm.*, 1943, 8, 1–105.

Sarason, S. B. *Psychological Problems in Mental Deficiency*. 3rd Ed. New York: Harper, 1959.

Saul, L. J. *Emotional Maturity*. Philadelphia: Lippincott, 1960.

Savage, C., *et al.* LSD: Therapeutic effects of the psychedelic experience. *Psychol. Rep.*, 1964, 14, 111–120.

Sawrey, J. M., and Telford, C. W. *Educational Psychology*. Boston: Allyn & Bacon, 1958.

Schaefer, E. S., and Bell, R. Q. Patterns of attitudes toward child rearing and the family. *J. abnorm. soc. Psychol.*, 1957, 54, 391–395.

Schalock, H. D. Observation of Mother-Child Interaction in the Laboratory and in the Home. Unpublished doctoral dissertation. Univ. Nebraska, 1956.

Schiff, L. A. The obedient rebels: A study of college conversions to conservatism. *J. soc. Issues*, 1964, 20, 74–95.

Schmideberg, Melitta. Psychotherapy of juvenile delinquents. *International Research Newsletter in Mental Health*, 1959, 1, 1–2.

Schoeppe, A. Sex differences in adolescent socialization. *J. soc. Psychol.*, 1953, 38, 175–185.

Schofield, W., and Balian, Lucy. A comparative study of the personal histories of schizophrenic and nonpsychiatric patients. *J. abnorm. soc. Psychol.*, 1959, 58, 59.

Schrupp, M. A., and Gjerde, C. N. Teacher growth and attitudes toward behavior problems of children. *J. educ. Psychol.*, 1953, 44, 203–214.

Schullian, Dorothy M. College slang. *Sch. & Soc.*, 1943, 58, 169–170.

Schur, E. M. Social science and the sexual revolution. In E. M. Schur (ed.), *The Family and the Sexual Revolution*. Bloomington, Ind.: Indiana Univ. Press, 1964. Pp. 3–15.

Scott, J. F. Sororities and the husband game. *Transaction*, 1965, 2, 10–14.

Seagoe, May V. Factors influencing the selection of associates. *J. educ. Res.*, 1933, 27, 32–40.

Sears, R. R. Development of gender role. In F. A. Beach (ed.), *Sex and Behavior*. New York: Wiley, 1966. Pp. 133–164.

Sears, R. R. Ordinal position in the family as a psychological variable. *Amer. sociol. Rev.*, 1950, 15, 397–401.

Sears, R. R., Maccoby, E. E., and Levin, H. *Patterns of Child Rearing*. New York: Harper, 1957.

Sears, R. R., Pintler, N. H., and Sears, Pauline S. The effect of father-separation on pre-school children's free-play aggression. *Child Developm.*, 1946, *17*, 219–243.

Sechrest, L., and Wallace, J. *Psychology and Human Problems*. Columbus, Ohio: Merrill, 1967.

Selye, H. *The Stress of Life*. New York: McGraw-Hill, 1956.

Seward, Georgene H. *Sex and the Social Order*. New York: McGraw-Hill, 1946.

Sewell, W. H. Some recent developments in socialization theory and research. *Ann. Amer. Acad. Pol. Soc. Sci.*, 1963, *349*, 163–181.

Sexton, Patricia. Negro career expectations. *Merrill-Palmer Quart.*, 1963, *9*, 303–316.

Shapiro, A. Social class theory. *Clearing House*, 1960, *34*, 521–525.

Shaw, C. R., and McKay, H. D. *Juvenile Delinquency in Urban Areas*. Chicago: Univ. Chicago Press, 1942.

Sheldon, W. H. Constitutional factors in personality. In J. McV. Hunt (ed.), *Personality and the Behavior Disorders*. New York: Ronald, 1944.

Sheldon, W. H., Hartl, E. M., and McDermott, E. *Varieties of Delinquent Youth*. New York: Harper, 1949.

Sheldon, W. H., and Stevens, S. S. *The Varieties of Temperament*. New York: Harper, 1942.

Sheldon, W. H., Stevens, S. S., and Tucker, W. B. *The Varieties of Human Physique*. New York: Harper, 1940.

Shields, J. *Monozygotic Twins*. London: Oxford Univ. Press, 1962.

Siegman, A. W. Father absence during early childhood and antisocial behavior. *J. abnorm. Psychol.*, 1966, *71*, 71–74.

Silber, E., *et al.*, Adaptive behavior in competent adolescents: Coping with the anticipation of college. *Arch. gen. Psychiat.*, 1961, *5*, 354–365.

Silverman, Sylvia S. *Clothing and Appearances: Their Psychological Implications for Teen-Age Girls*. New York: Bureau of Publications, Teachers College, Columbia Univ., 1945.

Simpson, R. L., and Simpson, Ida H. The psychiatric attendant: Development of an occupational self-image in a low status occupation. *Amer. sociol. Rev.*, 1959, *24*, 389–392.

Skeels, H. M. Mental development of children in foster homes. *J. consult. Psychol.*, 1938, *2*, 33–43.

Skeels, H. M., and Fillmore, E. A. Mental development of children from under-privileged homes. *J. genet. Psychol.*, 1940, *57*, 49–56.

Skodak, Marie. *Children in Foster Homes: A Study of Mental Development*. University of Iowa Studies of Child Welfare, *16*, No. 1. Iowa City, Iowa: Univ. Iowa Press, 1939.

Skodak, Marie. Mental growth of adopted children in the same family. *J. genet. Psychol.*, 1950, *77*, 3–9.

Sloan, W. Motor proficiency and intelligence. *Amer. J. ment. Def.*, 1951, *55*, 394–405.

Slotkin, J. S. *The Peyote Religion: A Study in Indian-White Relations*. New York: Free Press, 1956.

Smith, G. H. Sociometric study of best-liked and least-liked children. *Elem. Sch. J.*, 1950, *51*, 77–85.

Smith, W. M., Jr. Rating and dating: A re-study. *Marriage and Family Living*, 1952, *14*, 312–317.

Solomon, R. L. Punishment. *Amer. Psychologist*, 1964, *19*, 239–253.

Spaulding, C. D. Cliques, gangs, and networks. *Sociology and Social Research*, 1948, *32*, 928–937.

Spearman, G. *The Abilities of Man*. New York: Macmillan, 1927.

Speigel, L. A. The child's concept of beauty. *J. genet. Psychol.*, 1950, *77*, 11–23.

Spitz, R. A. Hospitalism. *Psychoanal. Stud. Child*, 1945, *1*, 54–74.

Spitz, R. A. Hospitalism: A follow-up report. *Psychoanal. Stud. Child*, 1946, *2*, 113–117.

Sprague, H., and Dunn, L. Special education for the best. *Except. Child.*, 1961, *27*, 415–421.

Starch, D. *Educational Measurement*. New York: Macmillan, 1916.

Stendler, Celia B. Critical periods in socialization and overdependency. *Child Developm.*, 1952, *23*, 3–12.

Stendler, Celia B. Social class differences in parental attitudes toward school at grade one level. *Child Developm.*, 1951, *22*, 36–46.

Stendler, Celia B., and Young, N. The impact of beginning first grade upon socialization as reported by mothers. *Child Developm.*, 1950, *21*, 241–260.

Stendler, Celia B., and Young, N. Impact of first grade entrance upon the socialization of the child: Changes after eight months of school. *Child Developm.*, 1951, 22, 113–122.

Stolz, L. M., *et al. Father Relations of War-Born Children.* Stanford, Calif.: Stanford Univ. Press, 1954.

Stone, J. L., and Church, J. *Childhood and Adolescence.* New York: Random House, 1957.

Stouffer, G. A. W., Jr., and Owens, Jennie. Behavior problems of children as identified by today's teachers and compared with those reported by E. K. Wickman. *J. educ. Res.*, 1955, 48, 321–331.

Stouffer, S. A., and Shea, P. D. *Higher Educational Plans.* Chicago: Science Research Associates, 1959.

Strause, A. A., and Lehtinen, Laura E. *Psychopathology and Education of the Brain Injured Child.* Vol. 1. New York: Grune & Stratton, 1947.

Stroup, A. L. Marital adjustment of the mother and the personality of the child. *Marriage and Family Living*, 1956, 18, 109–113.

Stuart, I. R. Intergroup relations and acceptance of Puerto Ricans and Negroes in an immigrants' industry. *J. soc. Psychol.*, 1962, 56, 89–96.

Sunley, R. Early nineteenth century American literature on child rearing. In Margaret Mead and Martha Wolfenstein (eds.), *Childhood and Contemporary Cultures.* Chicago: Univ. Chicago Press, 1955.

Sutherland, F. H., and Cressey, D. R. *Principles of Criminology.* 5th Ed. Philadelphia: Lippincott, 1955.

Sutton-Smith, B., and Rosenberg, B. G. Age changes on the effects of ordinal position on sex-role identification. *J. genet. Psychol.*, 1965, 107, 61–73.

Swanson, G. E. Determinants of the individual's defenses against inner conflict: Review and reformulation. In J. Glidewell (ed.), *Parental Attitudes and Child Behavior.* Springfield, Ill.: Thomas, 1961.

Swift, Joan W. Effects of early group experiences: The nursery school and day nursery. In M. L. Hoffman and Lois W. Hoffman (eds.), *Review of Child Development Research.* New York: Russell Sage Foundation, 1964. Pp. 249–288.

Swift, J. *Gulliver's Travels.* 1726 Citation. Boston: Beacon Press, 1963.

Swift, J. *A Modest Proposal for Preventing the Children of Poor People from Being a Burden to Their Parents, or to the Country, and for Making Them Beneficial to the Public.* Dublin: Harding, 1729.

Symonds, P. M. *Measurement in Secondary Education.* New York: Macmillan, 1927.

Talbot, Mira. A bridge: Orthopsychiatry and education. In M. Krugman (ed.), *Orthopsychiatry and the School.* American Orthopsychiatric Association, 1958. Pp. 23–35.

Tasch, Ruth J. The role of the father in the family. *J. exp. Educ.*, 1952, 20, 319–361.

Tasdall, W. J. A follow-up study of trainable mentally handicapped children in Illinois. *Amer. J. ment. Def.*, 1960, 65, 11–16.

Taylor, C. W. *Creativity: Progress and Potential.* New York: McGraw-Hill, 1964.

Taylor, M. L., and Pellegrin, R. J. Professionalization: Its functions for the life insurance occupation. *Soc. Forces*, 1960, 38, 110–114.

Terman, L. M. Mental and physical traits of a thousand gifted children. In L. M. Terman (ed.), *Genetic Studies of Genius.* Vol. I. Stanford, Calif.: Stanford Univ. Press, 1925.

Terman, L. M., *et al. Psychological Factors in Marital Happiness.* New York: McGraw-Hill, 1938.

Terman, L. M., and Oden, M. H. The gifted child grows up. In L. M. Terman (ed.), *Genetic Studies of Genius.* Vol. IV. Stanford, Calif.: Stanford Univ. Press, 1947.

Terman, L. M., and Oden, M. H. The gifted group at mid-life. In L. M. Terman (ed.), *Genetic Studies of Genius.* Vol. V. Stanford, Calif.: Stanford Univ. Press, 1959.

Thorndike, E. L. *Educational Psychology: Briefer Course.* New York: Teachers College, Columbia Univ., 1914.

Thorndike, E. L., *et al. The Measurement of Intelligence.* New York: Bureau of Publications, Teachers College, Columbia Univ., 1927.

Thurstone, L. L., and Thurstone, T. G. *The Chicago Tests of Primary Mental Abilities: Manual of Instructions.* Chicago: Science Research Associates, 1943.

Toby, J. Some variables in role conflict analysis. *Soc. Forces*, 1952, 30, 323–327.

Torrance, P. *Gifted Children in the Classroom.* New York: Macmillan, 1965.

Tressey, S. L. Potentials of age: An exploratory study. *Genet. Psychol. Monogr.*, 1957, *56*, 159–205.

Ullmann, L. P., and Krasner, L. (eds.) *Case Studies in Behavior Modification.* New York: Holt, 1965.

Vaillant, G. E. John Haslam on early infantile autism. *Amer. J. Psychiat.*, 1962, *119*, 376.

Van Gennep, A. *The Rites of Passage.* Chicago: Univ. Chicago Press, 1960.

Vargas, E. The jet-age malady. *Saturday Review*, May 29, 1965, *48*, 18–19.

Vassar, Rena L. *Social History of American Education. Vol. I: Colonial Times to 1860.* Chicago: Rand McNally, 1965.

Verhave, T. *The Experimental Analysis of Behavior: Selected Readings.* New York: Appleton-Century-Crofts, 1966.

Vincent, Elizabeth L., and Martin, Phyllis C. *Human Psychological Development.* New York: Ronald, 1961.

Vitz, P. C. Some changes in behavior of nursery school children over a period of seven weeks. *J. nursery Educ.*, 1961, *16*, 62–65.

Wall, B. D. Education's mental hygiene dilemma. *Ment. Hyg.*, 1960, *44*, 569–576.

Wallin, J. E. W. *The Education of Handicapped Children.* Boston: Houghton Mifflin, 1924. Pp. 275–283.

Walters, J., Connor, Ruth, and Zunich, M. Inter-action of mothers and children from lower-class families. *Child Developm.*, 1964, *35*, 433–440.

Walters, R. H., and Demkow, Lillian F. Timing of punishment as a determinant of response inhibition. *Child Developm.*, 1963, *34*, 207–214.

Walters, R. H., and Parke, R. D. Influence of the response consequences to a social model on resistance to deviation. *J. exp. child Psychol.*, 1964, *1*, 269–280.

Walters, R. H., Parke, R. D., and Cane, Valerie A. Timing of punishment and the observation of consequences to others as determinants of response inhibition. *J. exp. child Psychol.*, 1965, *2*, 10–30.

Warner, W. L., Junker, B. H., and Adams, W. A. *Color and Human Nature.* Washington, D.C.: American Council on Education, 1941.

Watson, G. *Social Psychology.* Philadelphia: Lippincott, 1966.

Weatherley, D. Self-perceived rate of physical maturation and personality in late adolescence. *Child Developm.*, 1964, *35*, 1197–1210.

Weaver, A. *They Steal for Love.* New York: International Universities Press, 1959.

Webster, H., Freedman, H., and Heist, P. Personality changes in college students. In N. Sanford (ed.), *The American College: A Psychological and Social Interpretation of Higher Learning.* New York: Wiley, 1962. Pp. 811–846.

Wechsler, D. *The Measurement and Appraisal of Adult Intelligence.* 4th Ed. Baltimore: Williams & Wilkins, 1958.

Wellman, B. L. The effects of preschool attendance. In R. G. Barker, J. S. Kounin, and H. R. Wright (eds.), *Child Behavior and Development.* New York: McGraw-Hill, 1943. Pp. 229–243.

White, R. W. *Lives in Progress.* New York: Dryden Press, 1952.

Whiting, J. W. M. Resource mediation and learning by identification. In I. Iscoe and H. W. Stevenson (eds.), *Personality Development in Children.* Austin, Tex.: Univ. Texas Press, 1960. Pp. 112–126.

Wickman, E. K. *Children's Behavior and Teachers' Attitudes.* New York: Commonwealth Fund, 1928.

Williamson, E. G. Value orientation in counseling. *Personnel and Guidance Journal*, 1958, *36*, 520–528.

Winterbottom, Marian R. The relation of need for achievement to learning experiences in independence and mastery. In J. W. Atkinson (ed.), *Motives in Fantasy, Action, and Society.* Princeton, N.J.: Van Nostrand, 1958. Pp. 453–478.

Wittenborn, J. R. A study of adoptive children. *Psychol. Monogr.*, 1956, *70*, 1–115.

Witty, P. One hundred gifted children. *University of Kansas Bulletin of Education*, 1930.

Witty, P. A. *The Gifted Child.* Boston: Heath, 1951.

Witty, T. P. Who are the gifted? In N. D. Henry (ed.), *Education for the Gifted. Yearbk. Nat. Soc. Stud. Educ.*, 1958, 57, Part II.

Wolfe, D. Diversity of talent. *Amer. Psychologist*, 1960, 15, 535–545.

Wolfe, J. B. Effectiveness of token rewards for chimpanzees. *Comp. Psychol. Monogr.*, 1936, 12, No. 60.

Woods, Sister Frances Jerome, and Carrow, Sister Mary Arthur. The choice-rejection status of speech-defective children. *Except. Child.*, 1959, 25, 279–283.

Wooley, H. T. The validity of standards of mental measurement in young children. *Sch. & Soc.*, 1925, 21, 476–482.

Wrenn, R. L. *Basic Contributions to Psychology: Readings.* Belmont, Calif.: Wadsworth, 1966.

Wrinkle, W. L. *Improving Marking and Reporting Practices in Elementary and Secondary Schools.* New York: Rinehart, 1947.

Yarrow, L. J. Separation from parents during early childhood. In M. L. Hoffman and Lois W. Hoffman (eds.), *Review of Child Development Research.* New York: Russell Sage Foundation, 1964.

Zelditch, M. Cross-cultural analyses of family structure. In H. T. Christensen (ed.), *Handbook of Marriage and the Family.* Chicago: Rand McNally, 1964. Pp. 462–500.

Zimmerman, K. A. Mental hygiene implications of policies leading to change of social practices. In K. Soddy (ed.), *Mental Health and Infant Development.* Vol. 1. New York: Basic Books, 1956.

Zunich, M. Study of relationships between child-rearing attitudes and maternal behavior. *J. exp. Educ.*, 1961, 30, 231–241.

Index